ALTERNATIVE AMERICA

ALTERNATIVE AMERICA

Henry George, Edward Bellamy,
Henry Demarest Lloyd
and the Adversary Tradition

John L. Thomas

The Belknap Press of
Harvard University Press
Cambridge, Massachusetts, and
London, England   1983

LIBRARY OF CONGRESS CATALOGING IN PUBLICATION DATA

Thomas, John L.
Alternative America.

Includes bibliographical references and index.
1. Social reformers—United States.
2. Utopias.
3.   United States—Social conditions—1865–1918.
4. George, Henry, 1839–1897. Progress and poverty.
5. Bellamy, Edward, 1850–1898. Looking backward.
6. Lloyd, Henry Demarest, 1847–1903. Wealth against commonwealth.
I. Title.
HN57.T48   1983   303.4′84   82-15448
ISBN 0-674-01676-9

For Pat

PREFACE

If, as John Dewey has taught us, ideas have consequences, so do books for their authors. Henry George, Edward Bellamy, and Henry Demarest Lloyd wrote three of late-nineteenth-century America's best-sellers. *Progress and Poverty, Looking Backward,* and *Wealth Against Commonwealth* spoke to the condition and influenced the thinking of countless readers here and abroad who were increasingly apprehensive about the costs of rapid modernization and in need of assurance, not only of the reality of progress, but also of the meaning of providential history. This assurance the three authors provided. At the same time, their books solved for each of them the problem of a vocation by defining a set of alternative social arrangements, propelling all three toward a redemptive politics, and assigning them the task of building the sacred society. It is this connection between writing and acting, between the text and the program, that these three interlocking portraits seek to illuminate.

In the course of writing this book I have acquired several intellectual debts. In particular I would like to thank Donald H. Fleming, Paul A. Glad, Barry D. Karl, William G. McLoughlin, James T. Patterson, and Robert H. Wiebe. Thanks are also due the Charles Warren Center at Harvard University and the John Simon Guggenheim Foundation for their generous support. Finally, I would like to thank the State Historical Society of Wisconsin for permission to quote from the microfilm edition of the Henry Demarest Lloyd Papers; the Houghton Library of Harvard University for permission to quote from the Edward Bellamy Papers; and the New York Public Library for permission to quote from the Henry George Papers.

CONTENTS

ILLUSTRATIONS

ALTERNATIVE AMERICA

1

THE FATE OF EMPIRE

In 1872, the year that marked the grand opening of the Gilded Age, three young American newspapermen surveyed the republic from geographically distinct but historically similar vantage points. From his crowded boxlike office at the Springfield *Union* Edward Bellamy looked out across a grimy, sprawling New England mill city. From another newly acquired editorial desk, this one at the Chicago *Tribune*, Henry Demarest Lloyd examined a fire-ravaged but frantically rebuilding midwestern metropolis. And in San Francisco that same year Henry George, peering over the compositor's stand at his own *Evening Post*, watched the waning promotional frenzies of the biggest boomtown in American history. All three were alarmed by the materialism and the ugliness they saw around them, and to each there came the same reminder of the tragic fate of Rome.

To a generation of Americans returned from the Civil War and now standing uneasily on the threshold of industrial prosperity, the specter of Rome in decline from republican splendor to imperial decadence appeared with disturbing clarity. The image of a once-mighty civilization wasted by decay and prostrate at the feet of invading barbarians was not a new one for Americans but had long

been received as one of the legacies of the Enlightenment. Ever since
Gibbon it had threatened in recurring moments of crisis to turn the
American dream to nightmare, and by the middle of the nineteenth
century had fixed disquieting notions of mortality firmly in the
American consciousness. While artisans and mechanics kept green
the memory of Tom Paine in rites and ceremonies filled with images
of Republican Rome, clergymen railed against immigrant "barbarians" and politicians denounced slavery expansion by holding aloft
the fearful example of the late empire sunk in sloth and depravity.
From the days of John Adams to those of his great-grandsons the
theme of decline and fall served Americans as standard rhetorical
fare.

Until the coming of the Civil War, however, these portents of
death and decay lay buried beneath the accumulated facts of national abundance. Their country, most Jacksonian Americans
agreed, stood majestically among the nations of the earth, yielding
up its riches to an energetic and deserving people whose numbers
doubled with each successive generation and whose achievements
promised endless republican progress.

Yet the Civil War, viewed in the light of its aftermath, appeared
to many of these same observers to have marked a turning in the
national road. The Union had been saved and its citizens rescued
from the sin of slavery. But to those young men like Bellamy, Lloyd,
and George coming to maturity in the postwar world and given to
noting historical parallels, the defeat of the South also signaled the
end of an agrarian civilization and the arrival of an urban industrial
order marked by increasing inequality of wealth and power. Seen
against the backdrop of classical history, the various meanings of the
Civil War were all sufficiently ominous: an imminent decline of
public virtue presaging a new age of luxury and licentiousness; the
seizure of power by a new breed of oligarchs; military dictators
trampling underfoot the rights of the people; and—most disturbing
of all—a class war between the new money power with its myrmidons and a declassed and desperate yeomanry. Once again as in the
days of their Revolution a century earlier the ghost of Rome returned
to haunt the American people.

Edward Bellamy, at twenty-one the youngest and least experienced of the editorial trio, was a disillusioned apprentice who had
just come home to Springfield following one of his recurring "min-

istries of disappointment," as he wryly called them, this one served briefly under William Cullen Bryant on the New York *Post*. In full flight from the impersonality and loneliness of the city and recently awarded a place on the staff of the proadministration Springfield *Union*, young Bellamy took stock of his impressions of the new age in the fall of 1872 and concluded that political preferment and material ambition had already undermined inherited American values. Progress came at too high a price when all religion and morality were forced to plead before the bar of wealth and pretension. Lacking the wholesome checks of deference and self-restraint, all the great civilizations of antiquity had ultimately perished. "The grandest instance of this terrible truth," he mused, "was seen in the awful sinking of Rome, sinking down with itself into the depths, that splendid civilization which gave place to the barbarous polity of the Gothic tribes."[1] A similar fate surely awaited any modern nation whose citizens were obsessed with moneymaking and forgetful of their mutual obligations.

Across the continent that same autumn Henry George also singled out the fraud and greed that had destroyed Rome and now threatened the future of the American republic. Thirty-three years old, George was the oldest and most experienced of the three journalists, having served a dozen years of his apprenticeship drifting from one assignment to another before joining the partnership on the *Post*. Where Bellamy discerned somewhat dimly the urge for profits as the cause of an imminent decline, Henry George, with a sense of reality sharpened by years of poverty, pointed to huge cities and the hostility of urban classes as the dominant features of the new age. The key to these dangerous developments, George was convinced, lay in the monopoly of land, which was driving the Jeffersonian yeomen off their homesteads and herding them into great cities where they were quickly reduced to penury while a speculative mania wasted the body politic. Unchecked, land monopoly and urban growth were already dividing, not simply California, but the whole country into warring classes preparing for battle.

Here George paused in his analysis, and with the aid of Macaulay's gloss on Gibbon pondered the meaning of Rome, another great empire, "so powerful in arms, so advanced in the arts," that nevertheless had succumbed to forces of dissolution. "How did this once incredible thing happen?" The answer was clear. "In the land policy of Rome may be traced the secret of her rise, the cause of her fall." In the beginning a nation of freeholders, Rome had become the private preserve of a patrician class bent on engrossing all of her arable lands. "The Senate granted away the public domain in large tracts, just as our Senate is doing now; and the fusion of the little farms into large estates by purchase, by force, and by fraud, went on, until whole provinces were owned by two or three proprietors, and chained slaves had taken the place of the sturdy peasantry of Italy." Stripped of their livelihoods and driven into the cities where they joined the ranks of the proletarians, Rome's yeoman farmers simply disappeared. "There came to be but two classes—the enormously rich and their dependents and slaves; society thus constituted bred its own destroying monsters; the old virtues vanished, population declined, art sank, the old conquering race died out, and Rome perished . . . from the very failure of the crop of *men.*" Lest readers miss the force of his comparison, George drove it home: the United States presently confronted precisely the same crisis, its weakest point "the heart of our great cities," where "poverty and ignorance might produce a race of Huns fiercer than any who followed Attila, and of Vandals more destructive than those led by Genseric."[2]

Chicago in 1872 hardly seemed the proper setting for dire predictions like these, and Henry Demarest Lloyd, fresh from reform campaigns in the East, scarcely the jaded young man to contemplate the destiny of empires. Three years older than Bellamy and eight younger than George, he had just arrived in Chicago to accept a junior editorial post on Horace White's *Tribune,* court the daughter of one of the paper's richest stockholders, and lend a hand to local businessmen in rebuilding their city. Nevertheless, in one of his first editorials in the *Tribune's* new Sunday literary page, Lloyd lashed out at the railroad managers of the country whose disregard of the "commercial code of civility" and whose "callous brutality" suggested nothing so clearly as the rapaciousness of Roman patricians. The railroad barons, like their classical counterparts, were carving up the public domain into their own private provinces, which they ruled with supreme contempt for the rest of the nation. In the next few years this classical allusion would occur to Lloyd again and again until, during the Great Railroad Strike of 1877, he would equate the wage cuts and pooling devices of the railroad magnates with the exploitation of Roman farmers by greedy patricians. And by then a figure of speech had become a prediction—just as the plundering of Rome's independent farmers had ended in civil war, so now in the late nineteenth century the "stealing of land grants" by a new breed of robber barons threatened to destroy free government in the United States.[3]

The common appropriation of the image of Rome in decline by three reform journalists was not simply a rhetorical flourish or an exercise in jeremiad. At the center of their collective historical consciousness lay the concept of "democratic republicanism," a term that defined a world of remembered experience already receding into an antebellum past. What made the thermidorean habits of Gilded Age businessmen and politicians so unpalatable to George, Lloyd, and Bellamy was their recognition that the world of their fathers had suddenly grown too complicated to be governed by the precepts they had once taken for granted. For them, as for most Americans in the years before the Civil War, these democratic-republican precepts had clustered around the twin truths of natural law and Christian faith. Americans, it was agreed, were indeed a Chosen People selected by Divine Providence and charged with an Anglo-Saxon mission to redeem the world. The directives for their redemptive enterprise had been provided by the Declaration of Independence and the Bible, matching texts that assigned the rights and prescribed the duties of a Christian democratic people. The American creed could thus be reduced to a set of self-evident propositions: the genius of a democratic people for self-government; the spiritual mission of a Christian nation; the moral primacy of the individual; equality of opportunity; and laissez-faire as the surest guide to progress. Attached to this body of doctrine were several useful myths—simple government, the virtues of life lived close to the soil, and the power of democratic education to diffuse happiness and virtue across the land.

If these articles of the American faith had tended to lose some of their clarity under close inspection, they nevertheless described an ideal prewar society of imposing symmetry. Whether, like George, you were born in Philadelphia in 1839, or, like Lloyd, in New York City eight years later, or, like Bellamy, in Chicopee Falls at mid-century—whether your family was Low-Church Episcopalian, Dutch Reformed, or New England Baptist—whether your father voted for Old Hickory or Tippecanoe—these common assumptions shaped a mode of discourse that had released social and class tensions by fostering myths of localism, popular sovereignty, and natural nobility. Such truths might be received as the intuitive wisdom of an Andrew Jackson or the transcendental musings of a Ralph Waldo Emerson, both of whom offered their audiences the same democratic-republican hope. From Jackson and his followers came assurances of the omnicompetence of the average man, the blessings of minimal government, disdain for privilege, and faith in an infinitely expandable area of freedom. To those of his countrymen attuned to a higher sphere Emerson spoke in terms of the sufficiency of the private man, distrust of the "little shops" of formal organization, and the power of the self in communion with nature to turn the world toward good.

These articles of the antebellum faith represented the fruits of an Enlightenment tradition that had been Christianized by the powerful forces unleashed by an evangelical movement after 1800. They did not always furnish agreed-upon policy directives, they held a different appeal for Whigs and Democrats, and they conspicuously failed to prevent a civil war. But in spite of party differences, sectarian strife, and the growing tensions over slavery, families like the Bellamys, the Lloyds, and the Georges held fast to these tenets and raised their sons to follow their example. It was their common remembrance of this lost world of their childhoods that so perplexed the three would-be reformers and shaped their image of the fall of Rome.

When the official propagandist of Jacksonian Democracy, John L. O'Sullivan, once pictured for his readers "the democratic principle walking hand in hand with the sister spirit of Christianity," it was to the likes of Henry George's father that he appealed. Richard Samuel Henry George was a loyal Democrat and an ardent churchman in whom politics and piety combined to feed hopes for respectability as a member of lower-middle-class Philadelphia society. In 1837, two years before Henry George's birth, his father, a widower in his late thirties, had taken a second wife and a substantial brick house near the center of the city, where in a home already crowded with the children and relatives of two marriages Henry George was born on September 2, 1839. A few years earlier Richard George had quit his job at the Philadelphia Customs House and embarked on a risky venture in religious publishing. By the time of Henry's birth Richard's partner had resigned, leaving him the sole proprietor of a tiny bookshop on the corner of Fifth and Chestnut Streets that served as the depository for the General Episcopal Sunday School Union. Within a few years straitened circumstances drove Richard George back to the Customs House and an annual salary of $800. Neither the slim harvests of Philadelphia's evangelical plantings nor Jacksonian spoils ever furnished the parents of Henry George with more than a narrow margin of gentility.

When hard times and a growing family dictated a move to larger and less expensive quarters in the mid-forties, the Georges settled in South Third Street, a workingman's quarter removed from Market Street and the center of respectability. The Southwark District had been the scene of labor riots during the Panic of 1837 and still retained its Locofoco loyalties. Southwark represented the outlook and values of the original community of artisans and mechanics that had rallied to the side of Tom Paine during the Revolution and championed his "moral economy" of the "producing classes," with their hatred of entrenched privilege, a legacy of eighteenth-century popular politics and egalitarianism. Henry George inherited this artisanal tradition which he would nurture carefully for the rest of his life.

The George household on South Third Street was also filled with Christian solicitude for young souls easily tempted by the attractions of the waterfront, but it echoed too with Jacksonian debates, talk of Lewis Cass and the "Little Giant," Stephen A. Douglas, the Compromise of 1850, and the Kansas-Nebraska Act. The spirit of Christian rectitude fostered by family Bible-reading and churchgoing was intended to steer entrepreneurial energies and political ambitions into the proper channels. To be a Democrat in the 1850s was, first of all, to cherish the memory of Andrew Jackson and his fight for the little man, to distrust "aristocracy" and fear "monopoly," and to hold fast to the principles of self-help and equal opportunity. The Democracy of Polk and Pierce also symbolized Young America and Manifest Destiny—the opening of the entire continent to the "people," freely distributed in local communities and practicing popular sovereignty unmolested by a distant federal government with its antislavery notions. Richard George met all of these tests, deploring the rise of abolitionist fanatics and regularly voting for Doughface

candidates in the hope of redressing the party balance in favor of the
northern workingman. There was little talk of the evils of slavery in
the George home, and none at all of racial equality.

Henry George learned to practice the ideals of individualism and
self-culture prescribed by Jacksonian Democracy and evangelicalism, and quickly exhausted the options they afforded a lively but
undirected intelligence. Henry, according to his family and friends,
was an amiable if occasionally trying youngster, quick, articulate,
strong-willed, and refractory. As the father of nine children and the
conductor of a failed religious enterprise, Richard George found sol-
ace at nearby St. Paul's, which formed the center of his son's early
intellectual life. For a time the elder George hoped that Henry would
one day join the benevolent network of the church, and he duly enrolled him in the new Episcopal Academy on scholarship. Here the
boy remained less than a year, and at the public high school, which
he entered at fourteen, he lasted just five months before deciding
with impeccable Jacksonian logic and no doubt parental approval
that training in a trade offered the shortest route to success, a bit of
misplaced confidence to which he held all his life.

Inevitably the boy's intellectual horizons narrowed to an occasional lecture at the Franklin Institute, books borrowed at random
from the Appentices' Library, diaries dutifully stuffed with statistics
on the area and population of European countries, and weekly
meetings of a juvenile literary society devoted to readings of Byron
and other Romantic worthies—altogether just such a haphazard experiment in self-culture as an age of the common man prescribed.
There were also menial jobs, one at two dollars a week as stock boy
in a china and glass firm, another as handyman in a marine insurance
adjuster's office near the waterfront, where the boy found his means
of escape from the restrictions of pietistic Philadelphia.

At sixteen Henry George was a short, wiry, athletic boy with
piercing blue eyes and a hard mouth, a full head of reddish hair, and
a disposition to match—sensitive, ambitious, willful, and restless. As
a seaport, Philadelphia, though entered upon declining days, still
stood at the edge of America's first frontier and held out the promise
of adventure to a youngster who had grown up watching the big
clipper ships unload their cargoes at nearby docks. Hearing of an
opening as cabin boy aboard the *Hindoo,* an ancient brig captained
by a friend of the family, the boy applied and was accepted. On

April 2, 1855, carrying a Bible, the gift of St. Paul's, and his mother's copy of *James's Anxious Enquirer*, Henry George set out for New York to join the crew of the merchantman bound for Australia. His real education was about to begin, and in a sense he would never come home.

If a voyage to the ends of the earth seemed to promise adventure, the reality as recorded in the boy's sea log spelled monotony and hard work aboard an old hulk manned by an ill-treated and surly crew. Henry George saw his first strike broken in Melbourne when the crew refused to unload the cargo and the captain had them thrown into jail. Making the slow passage up the Hooghly River to Calcutta, he caught a chilling glimpse of opulence and human misery scarcely dreamed of in Philadelphia.

> As we approached the city, the banks on both sides were lined with handsome country residences of the wealthy English ... On the right hand or Calcutta side, are the East India Company's works, for repairing their steamers, numbers of which, principally of iron, were undergoing repairs. On the other side was an immense palace-like structure (the residence, I believe, of some wealthy Englishman) surrounded by beautiful lawns and groves. The river was covered with boats and presented a bustling scene. One feature which is peculiar to Calcutta was the number of dead bodies floating down in all stages of decomposition, covered by crows who were actively engaged in picking them to pieces. The first one I saw filled me with horror and disgust, but like the natives, you soon cease to pay any attention to them.[4]

Such scenes crowded out assurances from Third Street that the same God who watched over the family at home "is about you and sees what you do."[5] The benign deity presiding over Philadelphia seemed very far away.

The *Hindoo* dropped anchor in New York harbor in June 1857 after a fourteen-month voyage—"an eventful year," the boy wrote self-consciously, "one that will have a great influence in determining my position in life."[6] On the credit side of his ledger was a measure of independence gained, a wider look at the world, and, most important, a new habit of recording his observations in lean, muscular prose. Still to be resolved was the question of what to do with his life. Back in Philadelphia under his father's uneasy eye once more, he was set to work as an apprentice typesetter in a printing firm. He began to take an interest in politics and to ask questions about the slavery crisis that his parents found disconcerting. By 1857 as the struggle over slavery entered its final phase, the debate in the George household was argued along generational lines. Both father and mother took their places behind Jacksonian property rights and refused to listen to the moral indictment of the abolitionists. To his parents' insistence that slaveholders were doubtless "humanely disposed people," Henry replied that slavery was a matter of principle—not just a question of what southern planters were inclined to do but what they were legally empowered to do. Here was the first sign of revolt, but one stemming from an adolescent distaste for authority rather than a hatred of slavery.

In other respects young George remained safely within the confines of Jacksonianism, searching for the key to instant success and blaming himself when he failed to find it. His greatest enemy was a short-fused temper that exploded regularly. He quit one job after quarreling with the foreman, whose "impositions and domineering insolence" he resented. Then he worked as a strike-breaker, setting type for a local newspaper until the union made terms and he was let go. His moods were mercurial, plummeting from self-satisfaction to deep despair and vows to reform. "I have taken your advice and am trying to improve myself all I can," he would report. "I shall shortly commence to study book-keeping. After I get through that I shall be Jack of three different trades, and, I am afraid, master of none."[7] Prospects in Philadelphia appeared bleak following the Panic of 1857, and an impatience driving him toward each "lucky windfall" made them seem no brighter. By this time he was proving more than his parents could handle—engaging but without direction, boisterous, opinionated, with a taste for liquor, cigars, and boon companions.

It was through neighbors that Henry George first learned of Oregon as a promising place for adventurous young bucks, and by the summer of 1857 he had determined to go. "The times here are hard and are getting worse every day," he explained in an attempt to collect a five-dollar loan, "factory after factory suspending and discharging its hands."[8] In December, one "hard-fisted mechanic," as he now styled himself, took a berth on a lighthouse tender headed around the Horn for San Francisco, and after a stormy five-month passage he arrived there in May 1858.

Richard George, mindful of the difficulties of governing his eighteen-year-old son, professed to see the hand of Providence in his decision to follow his Jacksonian star westward. In so doing he would escape the "nigger question," although, he confided to Henry, he did not fear for the Union. "They may bluster North, East, South and West as much as they please. Our nation is in the hands and under the guidance of a higher Power, who created this republic for a higher and holier destiny, which is not revealed, and will not be until I am long gathered to my fathers."[9] Less than three years later Richard George's prophecy crumbled under the Confederate batteries at Fort Sumter, but by then Henry was far removed from the national scene and engaged in his own desperate struggle with poverty.

"I am now setting out for myself in the world," George reported to his family, "and though young in years, I have every confidence in my ability to go through whatever may be before me."[10] With the wild scrambling days of the Gold Rush a recent memory, California in 1858 represented a journey backwards in time to an earlier stage of development, a frontier environment still raw and unshaped, seemingly the perfect setting for a young man on the make. San Francisco, still a jumble of half-finished mansions, wooden storefronts, cheap hotels, gambling houses, and outlying shanties, appeared a "dashing piece" to the new arrival, who was immediately caught between the lure of a wide-open city and the promise of steady wages in Oregon. "My mind is not fully made up as to what I shall do," he admitted. "I do not think I shall remain where I am at present, as I wish to settle down as soon as possible; and the old Oregon fever has not entirely died . . . I have worked hard and long to get here and have at last succeeded, and I feel convinced that the same spirit will carry me through."[11]

It was not Oregon and a steady job that first attracted George but rumors of a gold strike on the Frazer River in British Columbia that sent him rushing off along with thousands of other prospectors in search of a quick fortune. He went no farther than Victoria, however, and a cousin's store, where he worked round the clock assembling the outfits of those who had arrived before him—hardly the stroke of luck he had hoped for. After a quarrel with his cousin he tried tenting in the mud for a while and then returned to San Francisco, disconsolate and dead broke.

Reluctantly he admitted that he had only one skill to offer, and in December 1858 he was setting type in a local printing firm for sixteen dollars a week, still sure that he would "soon strike something better." Yet even the Poloniuslike advice from his father to "nurse your means, lay up all you can, and *owe no man anything*" could not keep him at the compositor's desk for long.[12] Two months later he was working as a weigher in a rice mill—"until I am sure I can make a change for the better"—still hopeful that times would improve. Instead they got worse, as the first shock waves of the Panic of 1857 rolled toward the Pacific slopes, and George succumbed to still another attack of gold fever. In the spring of 1859, convinced that he could still strike it rich, he set out for the gold fields across the state. But for the second time he stopped short of his destination, tramping the countryside instead, doing odd jobs and sleeping in barns until, worn out, he came back to San Francisco once again, out-of-pocket and in low spirits. Then just as suddenly another typesetting job mended his mood. His principal object from now on, he promised, would be to master his trade. "So anxious am I now to get ahead and make up for lost time that I never feel happier than when at work, and that, so far from being irksome, is a pleasure. My heart just now is really in my work. In another year I'll be twenty-one and I must be up and doing."[13]

George's early years in California provided him with a moratorium, one well suited, in its distance from the national scene, to selfexamination and a variety of experiments with formulas for success. Events in the East—the Lincoln-Douglas debates, John Brown's raid at Harpers Ferry, and the bitter fight for the Presidency—made surface impressions on his mind, but at a deeper level he was preparing for what was to become his "calling." There were still occasional bouts of gold fever, but for sustained promotional activity he lacked both the talent and the funds. Slowly he began to turn to journalism. He was working now on the *California Home Journal*, one of a number of struggling weeklies in the new state, and earning an apprentice's wage of twelve dollars a week. His routine as he approached his twenty-first year consisted of hard work and little leisure. "I don't read much now," he admitted in a letter to his sister Jennie, "except the newspapers." It took all his free time simply keeping up with news from the East. "What a time we live in, when great events follow one another so quickly that we have not space for wonder. We are driving at a killing pace somewhere—Emerson says to heaven, and Carlyle says to the other place; but however much they differ, go we surely do."[14]

In September 1860 Henry George turned twenty-one. He had recently joined the Methodist church, more for social purposes than from any profound spiritual need. In fact, he was already something of a freethinker, no longer able on faith alone to accept the Christian doctrines of his childhood. In this sense he, like Lloyd and Bellamy after him, was carrying forward the "come-outer" tradition of the antebellum moral reformers who had sought to universalize the religious instinct by removing it from the churches. A devout Christian upbringing, however, had left permanent marks on his mind. He knew the Bible by heart and took from it a set of religious precepts that reinforced his democratic beliefs. This mutually sustaining set of political rights and Christian duties seemed to George, as it did to Bellamy and Lloyd, demonstrable from both the Declaration of Independence and the New Testament. The product of these two forces was a Christian capitalism that combined equal opportunity with Christian benevolence. A key to George's thinking from then on was his use of the word "natural," by which he meant self-evident universal truths demonstrable from scriptural and secular texts alike.

A second and even stronger effect of his evangelical upbringing was a deeply rooted faith in the Protestant ethic and the fierce hunger for success that it justified. All his life George would crave success and constantly blame himself when he failed to achieve it. Always hovering just over the horizon lay opportunity, security, independence, and fame—elusive shapes drawing him into one risky venture after another. Now, in the spring of 1861 as the country went to war, George abandoned the ailing *Home Journal*, and, investing his total savings of $100, joined five other young adventurers in launching the San Francisco *Daily Evening Journal*—yet another experiment in personal journalism which, with an optimism now habitual, he pronounced "a certainty (comparatively speaking)." When this venture collapsed like the others, bringing down with it his hopes for an "independence for a lifetime," George was once more out of pocket and out of a job.[15]

It was while nursing the nearly moribund *Evening Journal*, having given up his rooms and set up a cot in his office, hungry and growing shabbier by the day, that George first entertained the possibilities of utopia. In a forlorn letter to his sister, he told of a recent dream in which he scooped up great handfuls of treasure from the ground only to awake next morning and find his pockets as empty as ever. Was the dream a portent? "Or do dreams always go by contraries, and instead of finding, am I to lose?" He supposed most people dreamed of things lost or denied them, and he now professed to understand for the first time the "lust for gold" that drove them to cast aside the "purest and holiest desires" for the false security that money offered.

> What a pity we can't be contented! Is it? Who knows? Sometimes I feel sick of the fierce struggle of our high civilized life, and think I would like to get away from cities and business, with their jostlings and strainings and cares altogether, and find some place on one of the hillsides, which look so dim and blue in the distance where I could gather those I love, and live content with what Nature and our own resources would furnish; but, alas, money is wanted even for that.[16]

Here briefly revealed in a moment of doubt was the pastoral vision that would form the core of *Progress and Poverty*, a dream, derived from Jefferson, of recovered innocence in a natural order where self-sufficient yeomen, free from the compulsions of money-making, could find peace and rest. "How I long for the Golden Age," George continued, "for the promised Millennium, when each will be free to follow his best and noblest impulses, unfettered by the restrictions and necessities which our present state of society imposes upon him—when the poorest and meanest will have a chance to use all his God-given faculties, and not be forced to drudge away the best part of his time in order to supply wants but little above those of the animal."

In the literary convention of the Golden Age, so congenial to the utopian imagination, the religious and secular halves of Henry

George's heritage were momentarily fused in fantasy. The language of release—"free," "God-given," "unfettered"—described the values and defined the goals he would one day develop in detail. But for the present, these pictures of a harmonious natural order faded as marriage and family responsibilities drew him into a struggle for survival that nearly broke him.

In 1861 George married Annie Corsina Fox, after a tempestuous courtship that ended in elopement when Annie's guardian objected to her threadbare suitor who appeared to have no prospects whatever. In the years that followed, both of them recalled with obvious delight the night when he suddenly took a single coin from his pocket and, holding it up to her, declared: "Annie, that is all the money I have in the world. Will you marry me?"[17] He was twenty-one, out of work, and deep in debt; she, eighteen, wholly sanguine and very much in love with her truculent suitor. By all accounts theirs was a supremely happy marriage. George needed his wife's good sense and domestic efficiency, while she was seemingly content to be a housewife and mother, leaving to him the problems of the world. These, during the first years of their marriage, proved formidable as the couple followed the path of California's downward economic spiral into destitution.

The Georges settled first in Sacramento, where Henry took a job as substitute printer on a local paper. A regular paycheck helped him pay his debts and even save a little, but this windfall was wiped out by a speculative plunge in worthless mining stock. Then came another wrangle with his employer, which cost him his job and sent him back to San Francisco where he tramped the streets selling newspaper subscriptions and clothes-wringers. By this time Annie was expecting their first child, a boy born on November 3, 1862, and named for his father. Grandiose plans for acquiring his own newspaper were quickly dispelled by the acquisition of a small job-printing plant for which there was no business. San Francisco during the Civil War remained caught in the grip of depression, and for thousands of able-bodied young men like George there was simply no work. Soon he was reduced to swapping the advertising cards he printed for food, which consisted chiefly of corn meal, milk, bread, and potatoes. He recorded his downhill slide into despair in a diary which he began to keep in the hope that good intentions and a strong will would mend his fortunes.

December 25 [1864]. Determined to keep a regular journal, and to cultivate habits of determination, energy and industry. Feel that I am in a bad situation, and must use my utmost effort to keep afloat and go ahead. Will try to follow the following rules for one week.

1st. In every case to determine rationally what is best to be done.

2nd. To do everything determined on immediately, or as soon as an opportunity presents.

3rd. To write down what I shall determine upon doing for the succeeding day.[18]

With his press at a standstill and no prospects of work, George grew desperate as the birth of his second son approached. Rather than pile up bills her husband could never pay, Annie took in sewing and then pawned her jewelry in an act of Victorian sacrifice on which Dickens could scarcely have improved. One evening just before the birth of his second son, Richard, George left home determined to accost the first man he met and demand money. "He asked what I wanted it for. I told him that my wife was confined and that I had nothing to give her to eat. He gave me money. If he had not, I think I was desperate enough to have killed him."[19] Soon he sold his share of the printing works on promise of payment when times improved and joined the ranks of the city's unemployed.

Given the standards of the Protestant ethic by which George had been taught to judge himself, there seemed only one explanation for his persistent failure—a want of character—and to this judgment of himself he returned with vows to reform. He, not society, must be at fault—he with his improvident ways and foolish pride. "I have been unsuccessful in everything. I wish to profit by my experience and to cultivate those qualities necessary to success in which I have been lacking." There followed the inevitable resolutions: "1st. To make every cent I can. 2nd. To spend nothing unnecessarily. 3rd. To put something by each week, if it is only a five cent piece. 4th. Not to run into debt for one cent if it can be avoided."[20]

Self-reproach, however, was beside the point. It was true enough that he was a spendthrift, constitutionally incapable of staying clear of debt. All his life George was plagued by a positive genius for mismanaging money. Yet, as he now told himself, he could work hard enough if only given the chance. His father's ethic had taught that poverty was either temporary and enobling or permanent and well deserved, but now he knew better. But still only vaguely did he sense that there was something radically wrong with an economic system in which the will to work counted for nothing. Then suddenly with the end of the war the grip of the depression in California was broken, and as if responding to his will to succeed, George's fortunes took a turn for the better. By April 1865 he was working fairly regularly and the crisis had been weathered.

Fifteen years later, when Henry George came to define the problem of poverty in modern industrial society, he recalled his own fears and frustration during the war years. The riddle of the Sphinx—"which not to answer is to be destroyed"—of deepening want in the midst of growing abundance, was in large measure a personal symbol distilled from intense suffering. Then he described poverty as Nemesis stalking the unwary and the weak, just as it had once pursued him.

> The poverty to which in advancing civilizations great masses of men are condemned is not the freedom from distraction and temptation which sages have sought and philosophers have praised; it is a degrading and embruting slavery that cramps the higher nature, and dulls the finer feelings, and drives men by its pain to acts which the brutes would refuse ... Poverty is not merely deprivation; it means shame, degradation; the searing of the most sensitive parts of our moral and mental nature as with hot irons; the denial of the strongest impulses and the sweetest affections; the wrenching of the most vital nerves.[21]

In this indictment George summarized his own struggle with his adversary, but by 1879 he would be sure that he had found the answer to the riddle of the Sphinx, whereas now he only knew that his father's Jacksonian faith in the main chance had somehow failed him.

The Panic of 1857, which sent young Henry George to California as an advertisement for the safety-valve theory he was soon to champion, also brought the family of Henry Demarest Lloyd in re-treat from a rural parish in downstate Illinois to the relative security of mercantile New York City. Though he served faithfully as pastor in the arch-conservative Dutch Reformed church, Aaron Lloyd, like Richard George, was also a loyal son of the Democracy, whose own father had risen under party tutelage to postmaster and judge of the county court in Belleville, New Jersey. Local tradition held that dur-ing the dark days of John Quincy Adams's ascendancy Henry Dem-arest Lloyd's grandfather had kept the faith by nailing placards on village elms denouncing the fiend of executive privilege and the lo-custs of monopoly who devoured the bread of honest workingmen. Less hostile to tradition and privilege, Aaron Lloyd worked his way through Rutgers Theological Seminary, accepted a small parish, and courted and won the daughter of one of New York's well-to-do merchants, Maria Christie Demarest, whom he married in the bosom of her family home just off Washington Square. There Henry Dem-arest Lloyd, the eldest of three sons, was born on May Day 1847.

If the Lloyds represented a rural nonconformist tradition running back to seventeenth-century English regicides, the Demarests stood solidly for the Huguenot wing of the Reformation, whose radical politics had been softened by two centuries of mercantile prosperity but whose rigorous Calvinism had not. As an interloper Aaron Lloyd had no success in breaking the monopoly of Dutch dominies on the best New York pastorates and was quickly rusticated to a series of backcountry churches until the Board of Domestic Missions found him a small living in Pekin, Illinois, in the early fifties. Sandwiched in between proslavery "Egypt" to the south and upstate Yankee strongholds, Pekin in Tazewell County was part of Stephen A. Douglas's territory, where the senator's campaigns for squatter sov-ereignty and a transcontinental railroad flourished like the corn and wheat grown by his constituents. By the time Henry was old enough to attend the local academy, however, the railroad boom had col-lapsed and with it the high staple prices that paid his father's salary. Early in 1860, when it became clear that his stern sectarian Calvinism could not compete with a lively evangelical revival in the Old Northwest, Aaron Lloyd packed up his wife and four children and returned to his father-in-law's substantial home in New York City wearing the appearance of failure.

In the brownstone formality of Washington Square the young Henry Demarest Lloyd grew up in an atmosphere even thicker with patriarchal piety than that which had enveloped Henry George's Philadelphia home. Although many of the city's original Knicker-bocker families had long since moved uptown, Grandfather Demarest still paid his pew rent at the Middle Dutch Church in Lafayette Square and each Sunday marched three generations of his family to sit it the gloom of the half-empty church to listen to sermons heavily accented with Dutch and doctrines of depravity. At home in the front parlor decorated with horsehair sofas and a display copy of Baxter's *Saints' Rest*, the youngster fidgeted through daily prayer meetings conducted under the censorious eye of John Knox, whose stern visage peered down from the mantel.

In all this austerity Aaron Lloyd remained the outsider he had always been. His tiny bookshop crammed with the works of long-forgotten Puritan divines brought in even less money than Richard George's similar venture had twenty years earlier. Even though he and his children were made welcome at 27 West Washington Place, he was expected to pay his family's way out of his slender earnings. Henry and his younger brother David were soon set to work at the Mercantile Library in Astor Place to help repair the family budget, but even so, a Sunday outing to Belleville required a forced sale of Aaron's religious tracts to pay for the tickets, and Henry's overshoes were bought with the proceeds of the family silver that his mother pawned. The Demarests may have enjoyed an inherited social prestige among the old families of lower Manhattan, but the Lloyds managed at best a shabby gentility.

The Civil War polarized New York City and sharply divided the members of Henry Demarest Lloyd's extended family, presenting the quick and impressionable youngster with a choice of loyalties. To the city, war brought unparalleled prosperity but also savage protest from the working classes together with widespread corruption. Aaron Lloyd remained unswervingly faithful to the Democratic party and its New York chieftain, Fernando Wood. The Demarests, like the rest of the city's old families, were equally fervent Unionists who helped organize the Sanitary and Christian Commissions, provided an upper-class constabulary during the draft riots of 1863, and subsidized hundreds of Loyal Publication Society pamphlets in which they identified the cause of the Union with the defeat of Tammany and the return to power of a gentlemen's government.

The adolescent Henry matured rapidly under the patrician tutelage of the Demarests. When he entered college at sixteen and began to follow the progress of the war in earnest, the boy unhesitatingly accepted the establishment's definition of the conflict and began to train himself to play his part in the civic counterrevolution envisioned by the city's better classes. If Henry George, who was locked in his own private battle against poverty, missed the conservative meaning of the Civil War, its lessons were not lost on the eager youngster from Washington Square who would launch his reform career as a convert of the "best man" seeking to overthrow the rule of the spoilsmen.

Yet in matters religious—the central preoccupation of all three generations in the Washington Square household—the boy grew openly defiant of his conservative elders. The grim Calvinism of the Demarests, with its insistence on innate depravity, Henry soon discarded in his search for a more useful faith. His revolt against patriarchalism carried him across the East River on Sundays to Henry Ward Beecher's Plymouth Church, where he listened to patriotic sermons unencumbered with excess theological niceties. Finally a family truce was struck when his mother decided upon the more stylish Church of the Strangers downtown where Commodore Vanderbilt was known to worship. It seemed a sensible compromise with an age of enterprise, and the boy agreed.

In 1863, as the Civil War approached a turning point and Henry George was feverishly hunting work in San Francisco, Henry Demarest Lloyd, another "poor boy" of good family, entered Columbia College with a windfall scholarship from the Drydock Savings Bank. At sixteen, Lloyd was a slender, small-boned young man with a shock of wavy brown hair rising high over a broad forehead, a prominent Roman nose, slightly receding chin, and—his most notable feature—large, heavy-lidded gray eyes that belied his outgoing and frequently combative nature. Voluble and seemingly self-assured, young Lloyd was also intense and very ambitious, an able and aggressive student who was already trying on styles with which to play the liberal man of letters.

Columbia proved an ideal laboratory for an aspiring intellectual whose disposition and family background directed him to the task of returning good government and Christian rectitude to the halls of state. In the sixties the college stood on 51st Street, an academic enclave in a spreading metropolis whose generally undistinguished faculty sought to apply polish to the sons of New York's patrician families. Its single luminary, Henry soon learned, was Francis Lieber, the ponderous German political theorist who five years earlier had abandoned the cause of the South for the more rewarding work of educating a rising generation in the North in the ideals of liberal nationalism. It was Lieber who gave Lloyd his first lessons in the principles of political economy.

While Columbia's curriculum may not have provided very hearty intellectual fare, it did manage to feed Lloyd's appetite for distinction as a leader of men. As a scholarship student who paid his way by shelving books in the Mercantile Library downtown, he was ignored by the exclusive Greek letter societies and instead joined the more democratic college literary society, whose members he regaled with calls for academic reform. The challenge of the age, he announced in one of his productions, came, not from the "cultivation of extinct languages," but from an engagement in politics, law, and political economy. "In this age of utility and progress the educational system has alone remained stationary. Is it right, is it natural?" In another outburst he proposed establishing a new Columbia as the "Oxford of America" by relocating it in a sylvan retreat up the Hudson.

As champion of the nonfraternity students Lloyd organized his fellow "plebeians," who in turn elected him class poet and listened appreciatively to endless couplets celebrating the victory of democratic talent over the monopoly of social prestige. His first triumph in the war against authority came with a sharp forensic encounter with President Frederick A. P. Barnard, who attempted to assess the class of '67 collectively for the willfull destruction of college property, to wit, one classroom door unceremoniously kicked in. Appointed counsel for the defense before a faculty court-martial—these were war years and Judge Advocate Barnard was a firm believer in military justice—Lloyd entered a special plea denying corporate responsibility, and, matching technicalities with his learned foe, argued successfully for vacating the charges, thus winning lasting fame with his classmates as "the man who threw Prex."[22]

By the time he graduated in 1867, Lloyd, like Henry George a few years earlier, was hard at work teaching himself to write. His literary heroes were Carlyle, in whom he discovered a mordant irony much to his liking, and Emerson, on whose granitic phrases he began to model his own style. Thus a Class Day oration entitled "Soda and Society" hymning the glories of soap and the gospel: "when Capital saw profit in African civilization, it invested largely in African missions," with the result that now "noble men . . . go forth and explore the country in the double character of missionaries and commercial agents, with a Bible in one hand and a contract for fat in the other."[23]

Six months after graduating in 1867, the twenty-year-old Lloyd, admitting ruefully that a diploma opened few doors to ready talent, returned to Columbia Law School, where he might at least reap the harvests of Francis Lieber's courses in jurisprudence. Enrolled the following year, he managed to complete the two-year course in a year and a half, and in 1869 was admitted to the New York bar. The question now confronting the fledgling lawyer with no very compelling urge to practice was how to fashion a career for himself in the business of reform.

It was Francis Lieber who first introduced Lloyd to the study of political economy and provided directions for exploring a Whig theory of politics. The veteran teacher took an immediate liking to his student who showed greater interest in questions of political behavior than in the technicalities of the law. Lieber discussed legal ethics with Lloyd, recommended a course of readings, and lent him the books that pointed directly to the principles of patrician reform. In the course of a long unsettled life, the celebrated German refugee had produced two major contributions to the literature of American politics: the massive *Manual of Political Ethics* in the 1830s, and the two-volume *On Civil Liberty and Self-Government* published in 1853. As commentaries on antebellum politics Lieber's works inclined toward Whiggery and the institutionalist views of Chancellor Kent and Justice Story rather than to Jacksonian beliefs in little government. But taken in broad outline as a system of liberal nationalism, Lieber's ideas could also be read as a variant of democratic republicanism and a modernized defense of the rights of the free individual.

The key to Lieber's thought and its chief appeal to an earnest young student of American politics was his updated version of natural rights which, while retaining many of Locke's original premises, dispensed with his notions of a state of nature and the social contract. In a sense Lieber was playing the American Burke, extricating natural law from its outworn fictions and adapting it to new concepts of history and evolution. In Lieber's thought natural rights, though neither absolute nor inalienable, nevertheless entered strong claims against the state in the name of an "individuality" which he defined as a "fundamental attribute of humanity." At the opposite pole from individual rights Lieber located the counterprinciple of "sociality," a collective force controlling private interests and giving all citizens a shared national purpose. Government, he argued, must tread warily within the boundaries marked by these two laws. Yet Lieber's ideas, as Lloyd first approached them, remained curiously abstract and bloodless. The old German liberal sought a strengthened national government but could envision no real assignments he wished it to undertake. Lieber feared unchecked legislative power above all, and much preferred an executive active but not prone to overexert its authority in the realm of economic regulation or social planning. Lloyd would learn little of the actual uses of government from his master.

Lieber's ideas on civic duty, on the other hand, made a close fit with young Lloyd's religious upbringing and reform ambitions. Lieber's ethics, though wholly secular, laid the foundation for an ideal of national citizenship that middle-class reformers like young Henry Demarest Lloyd found irresistible. His legacy to his pupil and a whole generation of young Gilded Age intellectuals was an idealized role as servant of the state, which they proceeded to rewrite for the American gentleman trained as a Christian steward, standing above partisan politics and seeking to reorder American democracy from the motives of purest altruism. It was Lieber who first steered his student toward the principle of free trade as the most promising cause for a young man ready to set out on a mission. In 1869, with recommendations from President Barnard as a thorough gentleman and the blessings of his aging mentor, Lloyd applied to the staff of the American Free-Trade Association and was immediately hired as an agent.

The new recruit joined the free traders in their hour of need. The American Free-Trade League had been formed in 1864 when New York City's merchant and shipping interests, hard hit by the war tariff, organized to win the West to their cause. The League's first president was the stately Jacksonian editor William Cullen Bryant, and by the time Lloyd joined the staff its roster included a sizable remnant of antislavery veterans and free-soil campaigners—William Lloyd Garrison, Wendell Phillips, O. B. Frothingham, Edward Atkinson, Carl Schurz—who wore the scars of their many battles against the peculiar institution. The program and the methods of the Free-Trade League, in fact, were reminiscent of the great days of antebellum reform: it aimed its message directly at the public conscience by distributing pamphlets, holding mass meetings, dispatching agents into the hinterland, and once a year gathering in New York for a rousing convention. By 1869, however, the League had split into two distinct groups, the first a collection of businessmen less concerned with international harmony than with lowering the tariff. The other wing of the League consisted of veteran moral reformers from New England and New York for whom the victory against the slave power and present battles for free trade were merely successive acts in an unfolding moral drama. For such men as these free trade was less an interest than a faith. Their hopes, it soon became clear, were precisely those of their new agent.

Lloyd threw himself into his new cause with all the zeal of a religious convert. As traveling agent for the Free-Trade Association he spent the summer of 1869 canvassing four states and thirty-eight towns and cities, by his own count making over a thousand personal calls and distributing 50,000 pieces of propaganda. His employers were duly impressed with Lloyd's promotional energy but also with the editorial talent of their new agent, whose articles in behalf of free trade began to appear regularly in the New York *Post*. Soon he was promoted to assistant secretary and placed in charge of the League's monthly magazine, *The Free Trader*.

The novice editor announced a set of laissez-faire principles and a program of reform stemming in part from a Jacksonian tradition of antimonopoly but also from the patrician liberalism taught by Francis Lieber. Lloyd read avidly in the literature of free trade—Adam Smith, Bastiat, Brougham, Cobden—and copied long passages into his journal. Study of *The Wealth of Nations* convinced him that Adam Smith's declaration of economic independence had done even more for mankind than Jefferson's. And from Wendell Phillips's collected speeches he drew the lessons that "civilization dwarfs political machinery" and that "free trade is the international law of the almighty."[24] A true political economy would teach Americans to avoid the violations of economic law that bred corruption. The reformer's first task, as Lloyd envisioned it, was to broadcast the truths of classical economics and spur the nation's thinking classes on with the work of restoring republican simplicity, fiscal responsibility, and clean government.

For his models in the great reform adventure Lloyd took the moral agitators of his boyhood—William Lloyd Garrison and Wendell Phillips—those noble giants who had first uncovered American violations of the moral law and labored thirty years to correct them. But the victory of the abolitionist pioneers had been incomplete, and their principles needed to be invoked once more, this time against monopoly and political corruption. With the end of the Civil War, Lloyd reasoned, his own generation, fresh from college or the army, could now finish the job of moral cleansing. For such an assignment there were already thousands of young recruits like himself, educated in civic virtue or steeled in recent combat, who could make their power for good felt with a force that the lonely giants of antebellum reform had never been able to muster. Where the Garrisons and the Thoreaus had been driven outside the political arena to stand in lonely splendor, his own army of reformers would carry their banners into the cities of the nation—those citadels of political corruption—and proceed to seize command posts, demolish the bastions of the bosses, and set free the beleaguered inhabitants. In the glowing colors of high moral combat Lloyd painted the scenes of struggle between the knight-errants of free trade and good government against the dark forces of corruption, which in New York City in 1870 meant that "tremendous engine for political burglary," Tammany Hall.

By the time Lloyd joined the fight against bossism Tammany Hall had long since fallen on evil days, as disclosure of its monumental misdeeds finally aroused the voters and filled reform associations with New York City's "best people" bent on throwing the rascals out. Quickly a reform coalition sprang up that included the prestigious Union League but also eager and footloose young gentlemen like Lloyd himself, organized into the Young Man's Municipal Reform Association and dedicated to the defeat of Tammany in the upcoming municipal elections. Lloyd's major contribution to the cause was a hastily compiled broadside, *Every Man His Own Voter*, which he and his cohorts distributed all over the city. Heading his list of proposals for cleaning up New York City politics were de-

mands for cadres of "ballot guards" supplied with police vans to
haul repeaters off to jail; a massive publicity campaign; and revival
meetings of the right-minded to consolidate the various "crude and
inexperienced" nonpartisan reform groups into a single "compact
and practical organization."[25] Armed with these honorable intentions and little else, Lloyd and his youthful reform band marched
down into the East Side to beard the Tiger in his lair and—so they
hoped—separate the newly arrived immigrant voter from his corrupt
provider.

Lloyd shared with his elders a set of patrician assumptions that
developments in the 1870s would steadily undermine. First there
was his conviction that American politics was at best a sordid business and in the case of Boss Tweed an orgy of plunder. An informed
citizenry, he was further convinced, had no need for complicated
and cumbersome political machinery. The challenge for reformers
like himself was to help organize a nonpartisan managerial elite to
take the country back into their own hands. Although at twenty-
three Lloyd could scarcely realize the nostalgic appeal of liberal reform as rule by the wise, the just, and the good, in fact the free traders and good government liberals were attempting to refurbish an
old and battered politics of notables dating from Federalist days, before the triumph of King Andrew and unlettered presumption. The
government that patrician liberals sought to restore was to be strictly
limited, austere, efficient, and above all economical. The heart of the
liberal reform dream, as Lloyd came to understand, was the wholly
fanciful notion that American voters would be willing to turn the
clock back to a time when the Founding Fathers, given a popular
mandate, presumably ran the country without the help of politicians.

For the moment, however, Lloyd accepted the charges lodged
against Tammany by its enemies and willingly identified himself
with the vanguard of gentlemen reformers who, he boasted, would
"do away with the corruption and ignorance which now disgrace the
nation." Led by sturdy young men like himself, the responsible
classes must turn and fight: "We must come to bay some time—now I
say!"[26] With the vision of an educated elite leading the American
people out of the sloughs of corruption, Lloyd eagerly awaited the
presidential election of 1872 and the chance to replace Grant and his
minions with a champion of free trade and good government. Events
in the next year would teach the headstrong young reformer that it

was one thing to capitalize on a moment of civic chagrin in unseating a city boss and quite another to organize the whole country for a general moral cleanup. Lloyd's education in the realities of the Gilded Age, like that of Henry George 3,000 miles away, was about to begin.

Edward Bellamy was a boy of fifteen when the Civil War ended, the frail, precocious son of a Baptist minister in Chicopee Falls, Massachusetts. To an adolescent imagination already stuffed with accounts of martial exploits and dreams of derring-do, the war figured less as a contest over slavery than as a setting for splendid modern heroes whose lineage extended back through the pages of his history books to Philip and Alexander. In an autobiographical fragment written in the third person years later, Bellamy vividly recalled boyhood evenings spent sprawled on the floor of his father's study in company with "Plutarchian demigods" or "charging over the bridge of Lodi with the Corsican." The inner world of his books, self-contained and satisfying, seemed more real to the boy than the bustling family life around him. "The tales," Bellamy remembered, "were . . . in reality mere projections of himself in imagination . . . The intense luxury of this ecstasy of sympathy with noble deeds he felt a thing almost sacred, not to be indulged for the pleasure of it like a common thing."[27]

The heightened world of romance contrasted sharply with the placid surface of his father's parish routine. Rufus Bellamy was an amiable if indolent New England country parson, rotund, sanguine, indifferent to the challenge of unraveling the knots of a snarled Calvinist skein, and wholly content with his role as village patriarch. The Bellamy heritage nevertheless embraced the First Great Awakening and that formidable Calvinist divine Dr. Joseph Bellamy, friend and disciple of the great Jonathan Edwards, who in his time had prophesied the "last general battle" for the Lord to be fought by "veteran troops, noble heroes, brave followers of the Lamb." After more than a century Joseph Bellamy's vision lived on, not in his easygoing great-grandson, but in the fierce spiritual hunger of Rufus Bellamy's wife. Maria Bellamy presented to her family and the world at large the face of unsmiling Christian zeal. Spare, angular, strong-willed, and with an inherited tendency to tuberculosis which she bequeathed to her son, she managed husband, children, and parish-ioners with a righteousness that only accented her wintry personal-ity. If the Puritan promise of a regenerate America had dimmed for Rufus Bellamy, it still burned brightly in the eyes of his wife, who frankly admitted to young Edward her determination to make of him a living sacrifice to her God. With her constant anxiety concerning his spiritual welfare, Maria Bellamy nurtured a religious obsession in her son that combined with an inherited illness to produce in the man a profoundly dislocated sensibility.

The clash between eighteenth and nineteenth centuries marked Bellamy's boyhood in other ways as well. The Civil War accelerated the transformation of Chicopee Falls from pastoral village to an ugly industrial city packed with factories, tenements, and French Cana-dian millhands struggling to make a living. The Bellamys lived in the city's social middle-ground, in an unpretentious frame house sur-rounded by a picket fence—symbol of a beleaguered gentry—at a distance from the imposing mansions of the town's new industrial elite but also from the smokestacks and grimy lives of the working-class. In one direction lay the industrial plains hard by the Connecti-cut River; in the other, rocky fields sloping up to woods and hills—a countryside not so different from Thoreau's at Walden twenty years earlier, a pastoral garden awaiting invasion by the machine.

Bellamy grew up a painfully shy and introspective boy in what he recalled as "entire conformity to the rules of propriety," encased in his world of books and seemingly amenable to the Christian man-agement of his parents. His mother, a remarkably well-educated woman for her day, held strong ideas about the kind of education proper for a minister's son, and when she admonished Edward to "get a book," she meant an improving text designed to strengthen Christian habit. She stood over her twelve-year-old son approvingly as he transcribed resolutions "not in any way to equivocate or try to convey the wrong impression," "not to speak before I think," and "never to stand by silently and hear others cheat and lie."[28] Maria Bellamy willingly indulged Edward's appetite for the heroic as he listed for her approval the qualities of the good soldier—self-control, obedience, determination—in which she recognized the virtues of the saint.

Both public and private evidences of the true Christian spirit were in demand in the Bellamy household. Edward and his brothers,

Frederick and Charles (an older brother, William, died of tuberculosis in 1868), were expected to prepare themselves for a life of service by undergoing the rigors of conversion and joining their father's church. To this trial the fourteen-year-old Edward dutifully subjected himself but with an intensity that set it apart from more conventional adolescent experiences. Looking back on the incident from young manhood, Bellamy saw it as a severing of self from the egocentric world of childhood in a religious trauma brought on by powerful convictions of guilt.

> In this desire to escape self he became greatly captivated by the idea of service. He would be the servant of God, of humanity. He would in fine, shuffle off the responsibility of being selfish upon somebody else, either God or humanity, by devoting himself to them ... But he had been taught to believe that he was a grievous sinner, accursed from God with whom he must make peace or suffer the most terrible consequences. He had never thought at all upon such subjects but had accepted this state of the case as an undoubted reality. Accordingly, he submitted to the emotional experience of a religious conversion. He came to feel a sense of intimacy and enjoy an indescribably close and tender communion with what seemed to him a very real and sublime being. The mental and moral revolutions of later years never blotted from his mind the strange and touching experiences of this epoch. In prayer he took a deep and awful pleasure; it was to him a sensation at once of the most sensuous happiness as of an ineffable sublimity when at such times his heart seemed to throb with that of deity and his soul seemed fused and melted in perfect union with the divine. A love more tender and passionate than any with which human charms ever moved him seemed then to bind him to the infinite. From school he hastened home to pray, not that he wanted anything, save only to be with God ... He saw the world with new eyes, no other reward save communion with Him ... His earlier ambitions he did not renounce but they were in suspense.[29]

The moment of mystical apprehension concealed in this piece of conventional religious rhetoric furnished the materials for the central drama in Bellamy's life, one in which his antagonist was Nemesis—not the specter of poverty that stalked Henry George or the fear of failure that came to haunt Henry Demarest Lloyd, but a pure metaphysical dread from which Bellamy constantly struggled to free himself. By the mid-1870s, having broken, like George and Lloyd, with the Calvinist world of his parents, the young agnostic discarded the specifically Christian content of the conversion experience. But the act itself, the sudden miraculous escape from Nemesis, Bellamy kept as the core of his new philosophy. When he abandoned his father's church in 1874, he complained that religion feminized the believer and that conversion consummated a kind of spiritual rape. "It is better adapted to women than men," he insisted, "on whose minds it has the effect to degenerate the masculine virtues of self-reliance and valor." Nevertheless, the release from guilt in the instant of transcendence that one day would provide the psychological foundations for Bellamy's utopian faith he first experienced as a fourteen-year-old boy.

Outwardly young Bellamy's life from his adolescent religious experience to his decision at twenty-two to settle in Chicopee Falls was uncomplicated and uneventful. In 1867 he applied to West Point and was rejected because of his health, the first of a series of setbacks which he came to accept wryly as his lot. Then, after sampling the limited offerings of the local schools, he joined his brother for a year at Union College, where as a special student he audited courses in literature and began to contemplate a career as a man of letters. A year later he was packed off to Europe and spent a lonely winter in Dresden before coming home with plans to study law. In Springfield he joined a local law firm just as Henry Demarest Lloyd was finishing his course at Columbia, and was admitted to the bar with the highest recommendations.

Yet law held little appeal for Bellamy. Legend has it that his first case—an action for the dispossession of a widow—so disgusted him with his work as "public blood-hound" that he marched straight home and took down his shingle. In the fall of 1871, as Henry George's fortunes in San Francisco began to mend and Henry Demarest Lloyd launched his invasion of New York's lower East Side, Bellamy learned of an opening as a contributor to William Cullen Bryant's New York *Post*. Reluctantly he decided to try free-lancing in New York. For six months he sat in his room in Stuyvesant Square, not far from the Demarest home, churning out stories and editorial comment. Although he published a couple of pieces in Theodore Tilton's *The Golden Age* and may have made a few anonymous contributions to the *Post*, the precarious state of his finances and, above all, the intense loneliness of life in the city soon sent him home to the family circle. In the spring of 1872 he heard of another opening, this one on the recently established Springfield *Union*, whose editors had bolted the more liberal Springfield *Republican* and set up shop as a Grant administration sheet. For a young man with literary ambitions but few prospects, determined "to be something greater than other men," but diffident and a bit frightened of the world, a junior position as literary editor offered clear advantages. In June 1872 he accepted the job and came home to Chicopee Falls where, except for a voyage to Hawaii in 1878 and later editorial excursions to Boston, he would remain for the rest of his life.

Bellamy's inner life, however, clashed with the predictability of a small-town journalistic routine. As he readily confessed, he was not naturally socially inclined, and, if not a recluse, he was nevertheless an extremely reserved and abstracted young man for whom collision with other personalities was always disturbing and sometimes painful. A deeply rooted sense of place and need for domestic security made any kind of change uninviting. All his life he was happiest among familiar people and things, content to accept a narrowed intellectual horizon as the price of serenity. Henry George and Henry Demarest Lloyd, ebullient, energetic, extroverted, turned outward to the Gilded Age in an effort to understand and challenge it. Bellamy appeared to reject an uncongenial world at the outset and to turn inward to observe the workings of his own mind which, he admitted, was badly out-of-joint with modernity.

Bellamy's small world was ruled by his subconscious, which expressed itself in fantasy. "Might-have-been-land," he wrote in one of his frequent attempts at self-appraisal. "Let me reach it by a stair between my real and potential self which produces a parting. Having fully calculated upon and expected a thing, I am so justly disappointed by its failure to come to pass that the balance of my nature goes over to the potential world, and I go to Might-have-been-land."[30] Bellamy's fantasy world contained both lurking fears of death and the magical contrivances for defeating them. His notebooks provide a running commentary on his struggle with a wasting

disease. The entries are readings of a psychic barometer of a mind
"quite out of conceit" with his infirmity. "I think I have got my
death," he noted dispassionately during one of his recurring bouts of
illness:

> I had always supposed the hour when this conviction im-
> pressed itself on my mind would be marked by strange expe-
> riences. But I do not find it so . . . I may recover from my pres-
> ent ailment but to me it somehow seems almost a foregone
> conclusion that I shall not. Nor should I much care but for the
> bitter blow my death would be to my parents. For their sake I
> shall obstinately fight a disease with which otherwise I should
> have no quarrel. The most common tragedy is the fight of a
> man against disease. Herein is Laocoön daily repeated all
> about us.

These were the moments when a sharp sense of his own mortality—the immediate presence of Nemesis—gave rise to hatred of his
"real" self for its failure to keep pace with his "potential" self. Then
followed "desperate mental states" when his mind was emptied like
a harbor at low tide, "a dreary expanse of mud banks and malarial
flats."[31] Such moods brought the shock of discovery that he was,
after all, only "a mediocre person." "I am unable to play the role I
had dreamed of and find it altogether not worth my while to learn
another." And just as suddenly these black moods gave way to the
urge for wild assertion when "a man's vagabond instincts, all his
longings for a wide free life rise in terrible insurrection."

As records of a confused search for self the early entries in Bellamy's notebooks center on the themes of terror and escape: meticulous analysis of a split personality; constant references to suicide as
the sole means of escape from the prison of self; a fascination with
relativity and the tricks of time; magical devices for obliterating
memory; and—the most sustained note of all—an obsession with the
problem of the passions as doorways either to total freedom or self-
destruction. In the notebooks fantasy replaces the outer world that
the young book reviewer explored in the pages of the *Union*. The
bustling world of Springfield and the Connecticut Valley, which furnished the materials for disapproving editorials in the next decade,

made a limited impression on Bellamy, for whom events and sur-roundings frequently served as occasions and settings for dramas of a mind intent on solving moral puzzles. Once, following the success of *Looking Backward*, he was asked whether it was in Bismarck's Ger-many that he first imbibed his socialist ideas. "Sir," he snapped, "the only thing I learned to imbibe in Germany was beer."[32]

He was more accurate than he knew! The principal evidence of the impact of a winter in Germany on his younger self was the sketch for a story that he wrote shortly after his return to New York. In this unfinished tale an American student, having fallen into "an unhealthful habit of introspection and self-engrossment," leaves Germany for a vacation on the Dutch coast where he hopes to re-cover his emotional balance. There in a windswept fishing village he spends an evening drinking in the local tavern, wanders out into the night in a distracted state, and falls asleep only to awaken alone on a desolate strand beside a raging sea. "Then foaming crests shone with phosphorescent light and as they came on scaling their huge black walls an awful sight met my eyes. On the faces of the waves came riding toward me scores of dead men's bodies shining with the glow of corruption . . . fettered with seaweed." For Henry George, the young cabin boy, the sight of decomposing bodies floating down the river in Calcutta was a reminder of the waste of human life. For Bel-lamy, with his adolescent taste for the gothic, death was personified in an adversary sea. "The North Sea had its coils about me and the monster was engulfing me in its powerful maw. Its foam-flecked teeth were all around me . . . With a great cry I rushed toward the shore and saved my life."[33]

Now safe, the narrator watches from his hiding place as a fierce band of seventeenth-century pirates—fictionalized followers of his distant ancestor—row ashore and proceed to bury a treasure chest which he instantly recognizes as the key to life and happiness. Se-cretly he returns in the dead of night to dig it up for himself, but his overwrought nerves play devilish tricks on him as he imagines the pirates peering over the edge of the pit and plotting to bury him alive. Once again he "swoons" and wakes to find himself the pos-sessor of the treasure but horribly altered by it—anguished and de-formed. Nothing is left to him now but the "peaceful haven" of an artist's garret in New York. "I have supported a precarious existence by writing tales and stories for the Press. But I have told all the stories I know and cannot manufacture any more tales. I am young yet, but my life is broken and I expect nothing more."

In the next fifteen years, as he turned from journalism to fiction as the vehicle for social criticism, Bellamy would write dozens of similar fantasies, all of them probing states of anguish and providing release from impotence in dreams. Julian West, the narrator of *Looking Backward*, transported to a Boston of the year 2000, emerges from a long line of literary antecedents, all cast from the same autobiographical mold.

Though a low-paying job as book editor hardly yielded the treasure uncovered by Bellamy's fantasy figure, it did provide the social middle-ground on which to confront his secret musings with the jarring realities of an American society on the make. Bellamy's choice of profession, made almost by default, had the advantage of supplying him with a critic's voice without for the moment requiring anything more of him. Yet as surely as Henry George and Henry Demarest Lloyd, though seemingly from a less promising direction, he was approaching the task of reforming an acquisitive society and reshaping its values.

George, Lloyd, and Bellamy were the children of an age of Christian nationalism and moral mission that reached a climax in the Civil War. The antebellum years of their childhoods were ones in which the search for an American identity had been guided by a religious vision. By mid-century an original Enlightenment faith in natural religion, the moral economy, and secular association had been engulfed by the tides of evangelicalism surging out of the Second Great Awakening. In a dramatic denial of Calvinism, a doctrine of Christian perfectionism rallied individual American consciences and enlisted them in a huge crusade against social sin—alcohol, prostitution, inhumane treatment of criminals and deviants, and ultimately slavery. Though collective by design and communal in intent, Christian perfectionism inevitably disrupted patterns of deference and removed restraints on individual entrepreneurial energies. By 1860 the American republic had been both Christianized and commercialized, and in place of an older mercantile order stood an expansive capitalism complete with a doctrine of stewardship, the moral certainties of competition, and a bright millennial promise.

Thus the sons possessed a double inheritance: an original faith in the virtuous republic drawn from the secular demonstrations of the Enlightenment; and a more recent commitment to the sacred that called Americans to their task of building the blessed community. All three came from devout Christian homes and had grown to manhood as communicants in a religion of Christian progress. If in none of their households was the hand of the divine seen as immediately controlling of human events, there was still little doubt in the minds of Richard George, Aaron Lloyd, and Rufus Bellamy that God had charted the course of the nation toward perfection. It was the fathers' faith in the millennial promise that formed the common element in their sons' several patrimonies.

Yet the contradictions inherent in this simple faith had emerged rapidly after mid-century and acquired an irreversible momentum with the coming of the Civil War. By 1872, when the three young men began to inspect the American scene closely, the gap between the old ideals of Christian nationalism and the new facts of Gilded Age materialism seemed to each too great to be bridged by outworn pieties. Each came to realize that he was heir to an intellectual tradition that had been shattered by the guns of war, and each in turn sought to reassemble the fragments and apply them to the needs of a modernizing society.

In this joint enterprise none of them was to derive much comfort or guidance from his father's example. If not precisely failures, Rufus Bellamy, Aaron Lloyd, and Richard George offered little in the way of vocational models or professional advancement. They were the spokesmen for a middling America that was already being threatened by economic concentration and new wealth. Their lives, domestically cluttered and intellectually muddled, appeared to reflect the declining influence of a religious outlook; their uncertain advice and example were too haphazard to help their sons find useful careers. Fittingly, perhaps, in a new age of feminized American culture, it was the mothers who ruled their sons' lives and shaped their ambitions, Maria Bellamy with her contempt for self-indulgence and her fierce faith in Christian sacrifice, Marie Lloyd and Catherine George with a softer piety and maternal solicitude. The

mismatching of parental forces left the three young men with powerful success drives but also with weakened religious sanctions and
limited intellectual resources for the work of perfecting America.

To the utopian task of preserving and at the same time adapting
their inherited liberal creeds to serviceable ends in an age of enterprise the three would-be reformers brought varying talents and quite
different personalities. George, by far the most sanguine and least
complicated of the three, looked behind Jacksonian Democracy and
the Great Revival to the certainties of an eighteenth-century moral
order. Younger, introspective, and wholly bewildered by the forces
of the new age, Bellamy sought his roots in the communal traditions
of a late Puritan New England. Lloyd carried forward yet a third
variation of an Enlightenment heritage in a politics of notables suitably refurbished for a democratic epoch. Common to all three, however, as they set out on careers as journalists, was an awareness of
the vast secularizing force set loose by modernism and the need for
new religious resources to counter and contain it.

2

UNDISCOVERED COUNTRY

1872 MARKED A TURNING POINT in American politics and the beginnings of an education in the meaning of reform for each of the three fledgling journalists. The triumphal reelection of Ulysses S. Grant, engineered by Republican regulars in spite of the frantic maneuverings of liberal malcontents in both parties, signaled the onset of a twenty-year period of political stability. Throughout the Gilded Age a smoothly functioning party system repaired the sectional damage of the Civil War and, in closely contested elections full of sound and fury but short on issues, maintained the balance and limited the options of a rapidly industrializing society. After the disruption of political parties in the 1850s and experiments with one-party rule during the Civil War, the American people had seemingly discovered the means of securing national unity and social peace.

The growing frustration of Bellamy, Lloyd, and George with this new politics of equilibrium was the result of their discovery of a whole range of problems that somehow escaped the attention of the professionals. Deep within each of them was a distrust of machine politics and its practitioners, a skepticism that grew stronger as they studied the behavior of the spoilsmen and witnessed their refusal to face what each of them sensed was a mounting social crisis.

If Edward Bellamy seemed least concerned with the foibles of politicians, this was because he discounted their importance from the beginning. The editors of the *Union* were bent on saving the Connecticut Valley for General Grant, and Bellamy was expected to manage the literary column and compose such editorial commentary as they might approve. By the time he joined them his senior colleagues were in full partisan cry, trumpeting the virtues of regular Republicans and denouncing the "abstraction and reaction" of their Democratic critics.

Bellamy spent most of his energy on the *Union's* literary patch, nurturing its thin crop as best he could. The novels of Thackeray, George Eliot, Turgenev, Howells, and Twain called forth appreciative reviews, but there were also the likes of Charles Reade, Edward Everett Hale, and M. T. R. Hamilton to be recommended to less discerning readers. The editorial columns of the paper, on the other hand, offered a broader scope for the talents of an eager but untested New England conservative and son of a local parson—reserved, formidably proper, judicious but as yet possessed of no very original ideas.

Although he had failed to fulfill his mother's hopes for a religious vocation, Bellamy had inherited her conviction that a life spent seeking creature comforts in a materialist society was a snare and a delusion. The old ways of a New England gentry seemed best. Chicopee Falls, though no longer a simple mill village, still stood on the fringes of America's industrial revolution, clinging to its social distinctions and prejudices even as the townsfolk apprehensively watched the changes that were transforming it. Traditions died hard in Chicopee Falls, and the habits of Bellamy's middle-class neighbors seemed reassuringly familiar to the young rural Tory. He encountered few challenges to settled opinion along the five-mile route from his father's house, where he composed his editorials, and the newspaper office, where he corrected the copy. His ideas settled into a predictable conservative mold, one editorial deploring the corrupt state of American morals, another pointing to the increase of crime in the nation's cities, and still another urging young men to stay home on the farm where a true independence might yet be enjoyed by those with a permanent stake in society.

The public conservative in Bellamy was responding to the need in the private man for harboring his energies carefully to combat what he recognized as "the feverish excitement of modern life" that threatened to "exhaust the vital powers with frightening rapidity."[1] His fear of the frenetic pace of American life was fed by a constant awareness of the precarious state of his health and of the incursions that tuberculosis were already making in his frail body. Bouts of fever leaving him prostrate alternated with days of slow recovery, measured by the pendulum swings of his mind from exultation in his fitness for the "great work" awaiting him to periods of despair when he contemplated suicide. These mercurial moods, he realized, needed to be controlled somehow: the wild veerings of his mind from affirmation to dreams of death needed to be checked by a set of limited expectations that would slow the pace of his life and moderate its intensity. If he were ever to live to finish the great work he envisioned, he needed a regimen imposed by a carefully contrived sense of limits.

Just such a routine he was already, as a young man of twenty-two, prescribing for the American body politic. Was the Republic screaming down the tracks like a runaway locomotive? Then put on the brakes! Did his own generation lack the personal qualities essential to civic virtue? Then educate American youth in self-discipline. Did excess of democracy breed luxury and licentiousness? Check these unhealthy tendencies by imposing public order. Strengthen appointive offices, and find the right men to fill them. Enforce the law and limit trial by jury. Above all, cultivate the habits of spartan self-denial. Justice, a concept Bellamy tended to identify with the patriotism of military heroes like George Washington and Andrew Jackson, seemed to him less a question of rules and procedures than of intent and will. New York's Boss Tweed—that rogue and swindler whom Henry Demarest Lloyd had helped run to ground—was a case in point. "Entrenched in the traverses and intricacies of the law," Tweed merely smiled at the "impotent efforts" of the citizenry to punish him.[2] Clearly laws were not enough. Social control must properly begin with self-control.

An even more fundamental source of Bellamy's conservatism was a deeply rooted love of place that made the neighborhood, with its unhurried pace and quiet routine, comforting and reassuring. Now, it seemed, all this was being lost to a people willing to give up the genuine satisfactions of small-town life for the empty promises of the city, where they joined all the other parasites of modern life, the "aggressive, ubiquitous, inevitable" drummers of a commercial civilization.[3] Bellamy's sense of limits was social and geographical as well as psychological.

Still, he conceded, there was something strident and ill-natured about would-be reformers, those despairing prophets who droned on about "these dreadful days" and whose lamentations over abounding wickedness resounded through American society like the crack of doom. These cranks, croakers, and one-idea men, whether Marxists or millennialists, offered little but placebos to ailing spirits. The evils of industrial America—sweatshops, subsistence wages, child labor, wretched housing—were all real enough and readily observable in the mill cities up and down the Connecticut Valley. But there was something repugnant to Bellamy in the very enthusiasms of reformers whose prophecies afforded so little light. Perhaps, instead, an all-wise providence was working mysteriously to prepare for a coming age of cooperation. In exactly what guise the new cooperative spirit might appear, the young conservative did not pretend to say.

There was a second self in Bellamy, however, an unbridled romantic and adversary pleader for the imagination, who flouted the rules enjoined by the outward conservative and ignored the limits he imposed. This interior person, entertaining strange notions and seeking release in fantasy, announced its presence secretly in the notebooks and journals he filled with musings and jottings, sketches and plot lines for his stories and romances. This interior world of Bellamy's second self, free from time and space, could be explored with various contrivances—telepathy, time machines, memory extirpation processes, and a complete stock of magic tricks. Here the imagination broke free from the restrictions imposed by the stern and inhibited censor. The oddities and grotesqueries that struck the outer man on trips to and from the office or intruded on editorial thought processes were filed away for inspection late at night when the conservative censor had retired.

Into these late-night notebooks went accounts of puzzling dreams, possibly to be unraveled in time but meanwhile to be recorded in exact detail. One such dream relaying messages from the libido remained for Bellamy the enigma it necessarily was for the pre-Freudian imagination. Its scene he recalled as a New York City theater and a performance of a burlesque of *Faust*—he seated beside an unknown young woman, not pretty, "a little thin and passé but still . . . not unattractive." Marvelously lifelike scenery—"several views representing mostly shores of the sea with numerous rivulets and creeks" on the banks of which the tenor sings an opening aria with "peculiar staccato effects." *Entre-acte* spent wandering the lobby with "a large lead pencil which stood point emerging in my vest pocket sending showers of sparks from its pointed black lead tip," an object of admiration for gentlemen who crowded around him demanding an explanation. "I told them it was very simple. Contrary to the unique idea on the subject all things burned from the center outward . . . With my nail I cracked open the pencil and showed them its core was a red hot coal which flashed and cracked as the air struck it." Following the opera escorted young lady, now "prettier as well as sweeter," home, asked to call on her, got address, and after leaving remembered no such street in the city. Tried to find house again but instead stumbled into a park guarded by "a truly ill-looking policeman."

> The grass of the park was cumbered with dying dogs which had been shot but not killed, so that I had to pick my steps to avoid being snapped at by them . . . I saw all the dogs get up on their hind legs and begin to dance in front of the policeman, wagging their bloody heads and shaking their paws derisively at him. This surely reproached him for being such a poor marksman in that he had not put them out of their misery, and contemptuously contrasted him with his predecessor in office who had always shot straight and made a good ending of each dog with one bullet. And then I understood that the policeman was one whose business it was to shoot the mad dogs of the city which were brought to him for that purpose. Presently a number of acquaintances of mine came into the park and the dogs also turned to them and all talked together of a certain trial in the police court which they had attended and in which all but myself seemed interested. I was greatly bored with this conversation and declared I would

take my departure. The others urged me to stay and among them appeared my lady friend of the theater and she got my coat from me and hid it so I could not go away. I now perceived that she was much prettier than I had before thought. She had smiling roguish brown eyes and delightful brown hair, curving low over her forehead. When I took her to task for hiding my coat, she cut short my impertinence by throwing her arms about my neck, at which I embraced her on the neck, and that is all or nearly all that I remember.[4]

The sexual content of such dreams Bellamy was never able to fathom. Nor was his treatment of the passions in the short stories he continued to write ever more than oblique, subject as they always were to the keen eye of the conservative censor who insisted on chaste desire, lust purified by love, and the fallen woman's redemption. Bellamy's confusion of waking and dream states and the compulsion to mark the passageway between them; his fear of Nemesis which he identified with the city; his dread of losing his way in a hostile world—all these were the work of the censor, who resented the inner freedom of the author and sought to impose on him the regimen of the journalist-observer of the real world.

The discoveries of his second self, however, seemed to Bellamy at once richer and more real than the elaborate hoax of Gilded Age politics. Here was a "citadel of self" to whom the universe and even the Creator were outsiders. Between the exterior world of Chicopee Falls and the inner life, he realized, lay a nearly impassable gulf. "That is to say, I suppose, the feeling of utterly isolated and necessarily self-dependent personality is previously developed in my mental constitution," he admitted. "I feel that I have an inexpungable fortress of self-existence where I may retire when my outposts advanced here in the world among men or among Gods in the realm of thought are driven in."[5]

For much of the time Bellamy's interior castle needed no elaborate defense but stood stoutly against the forces of a commercialized civilization with its shallowness and sham. For the next fifteen years the secret rebel would contend quietly with the conservative social commentator content to point out the excesses of an unregulated capitalist society. As yet the alienated second self could offer the social critic little guidance beyond describing vaguely an alternative state of mind—Nirvana, "the ideal state on which I pin my faith." Occasionally, however, there came to him a vision of the good society which linked the isolated sensibility to the common life.

One such moment of clarity came to him in 1872 in the midst of his political editorializing when he agreed to address the Chicopee Falls Lyceum on the subject of socialism. He opened his lecture by flatly denouncing the American capitalist system as a "barbarism" that subjected the poor to the rich. Then he asked two questions. First, "Why is the prejudice so deeply rooted in the popular mind that the integrity of our civilization is so intimately bound up with the maintenance of the grossest perversions of the principle of property?" The answer to this question he left to his listeners. But the second question he asked of himself. "Is it then . . . absurd to dream of the reign of justice on earth, chimerical to anticipate an era when, by equality in the distribution of the fruits of labor, every man at the price of moderate exertion shall be as secure of abundance and comfort, of the means to education and recreation, as he is today secure in his political rights and independence?" He disclaimed any knowledge of such a society. "It is an undiscovered country, no community of men ever essayed its Elysian climes, no human foot ever trod its shores. But I know that it exists—the faith of humanity points to its existence—and we must find it."[6] But in what direction lay the route to utopia? How could a mere dropout from an age of exploitation find it? Did his undiscovered country lie all around him—was he in fact already at its frontiers?—or did it exist only as an image in the inner mind's eye?

What remained undiscovered country for Bellamy was already known territory to Henry Demarest Lloyd, the golden land of the classical economists who long ago had mapped and plotted its theoretical terrain for true believers like himself. In fact, Lloyd boasted, he himself had walked its boundaries—free trade on one side, civil service along the other, minority representation and laissez faire, making a fence of stout iron laws that enclosed his ideal society. All he had to do now was to lead the American people into his utopia and settle there. This was the task he hoped to accomplish at the convention of the Liberal Republicans in Cincinnati in 1872, called in the hope of defeating Grant and cleaning up the country.

A keen observer of American politics, with few doubts and a vaulting ambition, Lloyd had watched the leisurely stirrings of liberal reform in New York and New England with keen interest. As presiding genius of the *Pictorial Tax-Payer* he was charged with spreading the gospel of free trade across the country and uniting patrician free traders in the East with western low-tariff interests, or as he put it in his editorials, combining eastern money with western votes. He tackled his assignment with confidence. He had secured his father's mild approval of his crusade, and, more important, the support of his mother, who endorsed his fight against evil and wickedness in a crooked world. The Demarest name, a respected one in the city's mercantile circles, opened doors for him, and so did the patronage of Francis Lieber. Lloyd was excited by the thought that together with his brother David Demarest he was part of "the life and soul of the reform party" of his generation, marching at the head of a powerful citizen army preparing to descend on the nation's capital. "I do not know what day I may be ordered to Washington," he wrote to his brother who was clerking for Chief Justice Chase. "The times are ripening." First of all, there must be a banding together of dispossessed Republicans and worthy Democrats, the "largest and best men in the country," among whom he now numbered himself. "The League may send me to Washington," he joked with his brother David, "and then we will run, between us, the politics and the law of this Great Republic."[7]

Lloyd's new model reform engine, however, was fueled by a highly volatile mixture of principle and expediency, and the motor had been hastily assembled from a handful of ill-fitting parts: patrician fears, mercantile hopes, antimonopoly ambitions, and simple desire for office. Lloyd, as became a seasoned veteran of the Tweed wars, stood for strict principles—equal rights and free trade, sound currency and honest government. When the call came for a new party, he was ready with his proposal for "thorough reform" and wholesale political reorganization that would strike "at the root of the whole monopoly system." Above all, he sought a presidential candidate for his reform party who would be neither "a good shopkeeper" nor a Tammany type bent on the "reckless subversion" of good government, but a gentleman of seasoned talents, the likes, he thought, of Charles Francis Adams. The route to power, he reasoned, lay through a third party, precedents for which abounded in the history of Conscience Whigs, Free Soilers, and prewar Republicans. His new party would consist of all those whole-souled patriots whom Grant had driven off, together with the Independents whom "fear of Tammany and remembrance of Repudiation and Copperheadism have cut away from the Democratic party." His skirmish with Tammany the previous year had taught him the importance of "militant and efficient concentration of . . . disunited elements into a compact and practical organization," and this lesson he in turn meant to teach the assembly of liberal reformers at Cincinnati.[8]

It was a supremely confident young ideologue who carried his free trade banner to the Liberal Republican convention. By his own lights "very deeply a student and superficially a teacher of Political Science," Lloyd commanded the full battery of free trade arguments, from appeals to self-interest to praise for the self-regulating market. Around the propositions of his *Pictorial Tax-Payer* he foresaw his counterparts from all over the nation gathering in the spirit of restoration and applying the rules of classical economy. These rules dictated a strict hands-off policy in obedience to the laws of trade, absolute fiscal integrity, and very little more. Here were the slim rations with which he proposed to feed the lean and hungry politicians seeking larger loaves and fishes in Cincinnati.

At the convention Lloyd looked on first with dismay and then with outrage as his elaborate plans for reform were reduced to rubble by the professionals who quickly set aside the free trade issue and improvised a platform on which they set, not the sterling figure of Charles Francis Adams, but the chipped and homely form of Horace Greeley. Lloyd was forced to stand aside and watch the stampede. His own choice, he realized with chagrin, had never stood a chance. Furious but powerless, he made a futile protest before the convention and walked out.

In New York, once again, thoroughly beaten but unrepentant, Lloyd made a final half-hearted attempt to rally the free traders in a rump convention, hoping to nominate Adams or some other suitably principled candidate, but was once more thwarted by the professionals. In a letter to his new friend and fellow enthusiast Henry Keenan he explained the painful lesson administered him in Cincinnati, "the last lesson of its kind I trust that will be necessary." And this was the "physiological fact" that "though a Free Trade ass and a Protectionist stallion might have copulated at Cincinnati and produced a hybrid party, that hybrid could not propagate anything, any more than a mule can." A reform party without Greeley at its head would have been smaller but more principled, and he had no one but himself to blame. He had put his trust in the politicians and had been "led to slaughter." "No more of the false guides for me," he announced to Keenan, "no more thimble-rigging in politics—I am going in (if at all) for a straight persistent fight, with homogeneous elements and in utter disregard of political compromise. I will make success come to me—I will not run after it."[9]

At twenty-four Lloyd was the temperamental opposite of Edward Bellamy, at once energetic, high-strung, impetuous, and seemingly resilient. Bellamy conversed with a secret self, listening as his double made a shambles of the real world. Lloyd confessed himself openly to others—to his brother Demarest, to his new friend Henry Keenan—in conversations and letters in which he played to the hilt the various roles assigned him by a lively fancy. There was the inside dopester with a mastery of the mechanics of wire-pulling; the jaded and slightly cynical newspaperman wise to the ways of the world; and when these palled, the sensitive suitor and rival for the affections of sundry young ladies. Lloyd openly shared his moments of "icy melancholy" and his "distrust of earthly enjoyment," and could yearn quite publicly for "some pure, unqualified joy, some certain love, some release from the ceaseless grind of commonplace existence."[10] In half-serious moods tinged with bombast he declared himself driven by a high ambition that made "the whole of life a fraud." "The meanness of men," he declaimed to no one in particular, "the fickleness of fortune, the inevitable quota of disaster, subjection to some irresistible power that deludes us with the apparition of our wills through our appetites, the temperature, the circumstances of others and ourselves, it winds us helpless in the meshes of fate." What, then, would be his own fate? What was the particular challenge in store for him?

Lloyd's bewilderment in selecting a profession, for all his posturing, was as real as that of Edward Bellamy or Henry George. All three were part of a generation responding to the apparent lack of direction in post-Civil War America, a vocational crisis most sharply felt by young intellectuals who envied their elders the great moral causes that formerly had shaped the nation. Before the Civil War young men of talent and social conscience had solved their own problems in finding suitable careers by turning to transcendentalism, joining a Brook Farm or an Oneida, or launching a crusade for prison reform, public education, better hospitals and asylums. Common to all these benevolent enterprises was an awareness of individual suffering and a vision of perfectibility that by mid-century had come to center on the institution of slavery, the great denial of moral progress. This was the generation that had fought the Civil War, saved the Union, freed the slave, and in so doing, found useful careers.

From the political dimness of the seventies, the heroes of that earlier age, in spite of their failure to reconstruct the South, still loomed large in the eyes of Lloyd, Bellamy, and George. The abolitionist pioneers William Lloyd Garrison and Wendell Phillips, the humanitarian reformers Samuel Gridley Howe and Horace Mann, the prophets Emerson and Theodore Parker had all enjoyed the luxury of a compelling purpose to which to give themselves. But what remained of their vision to ennoble the Great Barbecue of the spoilsmen?

Some of Lloyd's contemporaries whose lives, like his, spanned the Civil War, were already exploring avenues of escape from a business civilization. Oliver Wendell Holmes, Jr., returned from the war scarred in body and mind, was building a new science of the law on the ruins of self-reliance and discovering in skeptical inquiry and scaled-down expectations serviceable alternatives to Emersonian certainties. Henry Adams was attempting to found an intellectual establishment on the fringes of government in Washington in the hope of educating benighted politicians. For a few men of the postwar generation a revived professionalism of their war years was still to be found in those government bureaus hospitable to training and expertise. Soon, for the many more deserters from the ranks of commercialism, graduate training, at first in Germany and then at home in the new universities they helped to staff, offered opportunities in medicine, law, the social sciences, and policymaking in what was to become Progressivism.

In the immediate aftermath of the Civil War, however, these alternatives to a business career seemed to men of very moderate means like the three journalists privileged sanctuaries involving a retreat to the private sphere, lengthy apprenticeship, training in new disciplines, and, more important, wholly new perceptions of reality that were alien if not actually hostile to the old formalism of their fathers. To give oneself to science of whatever sort and agree to a rigorous discipline imposed by one's colleagues required a shift in values for which nothing in the individualist heritage of the three men had prepared them. All of them had considered a career in law—Bellamy in an aimless way in Springfield, Lloyd with scarcely more enthusiasm, and George briefly during his enforced idleness in San Francisco. And all had as quickly rejected it as a confidence man's game. Instinctively they turned to journalism and the examples of William Lloyd Garrison and William Cullen Bryant, whose personal imprint on their age they hoped to match.

Lloyd was reluctant to abandon the Free Trade League, although he admitted that it could never convert American businessmen with their innate distrust of the "purest philanthropy of the Privileged." But what about a big city newspaper like the Chicago *Tribune*? Lloyd had acquired a bit of experience, knew how to write an editorial, and was fortunate enough to have made the acquaintance of the *Tribune*'s editor, Horace White, who had commended the *Pictorial Tax-Payer* and promised Lloyd consideration should an opening develop. In the summer of 1872 he elected to try Chicago and the crusty White.

It was disconcerting to realize that perhaps he had chosen journalism only because he was unfitted for anything else. Law he dismissed as too technical. He despised all forms of moneymaking. He was "too unconventionally and unaffectedly pious" for the ministry. Political office, the last refuge of the scoundrel, appealed only to "a subservient, crawling, chronic candidate." Suddenly he understood the real force propelling him toward journalism:

> I want power, I must have power, I could not live if I did not
> think that I was in some way to be lifted above the insensate
> masses who flood the stage of life in their passage to oblivion,
> but I want power unpoisoned by the presence of obligation.[11]

In the late summer came "Horace's offer" which, though "paltry," held the promise of advancement. By October he was writing copy for the financial page of the Chicago *Tribune*.

Henry Demarest Lloyd in the early 1870s.

Henry George in the early 1880s.

Henry George's interest in reform politics at the opening of the seventies stemmed from frustration as he watched the growth of monopoly and the increase of land speculation in California. "Capital is piled on capital," he complained, "to the exclusion of men of lesser means and the utter prostration of personal independence and enterprise on the part of the less successful masses."[12] The new forces of exploitation, he was convinced, now threatened to destroy the state unless its people moved quickly to counter them. No longer was it a question of "old wealth" checking the ambitions of aspiring Jacksonian entrepreneurs like his father. Now it was "new money" itself, in corporate form and backed by federal subsidies. In the October 1868 issue of Bret Harte's *Overland Monthly*, he published an article, for which he received the welcome sum of forty dollars, entitled "What the Railroad Will Bring Us." This brief study in alternating nostalgia and apprehension was the lineal ancestor of *Progress and Poverty*, built like the major work on the paradox of increasing misery in the midst of growing affluence.

He began his article with an estimate of the benefits that the railroad would bring. Over its tracks, it was obvious, would come an army of men-on-the-make equipped with "the sharpest sense of Americans—the sense of gain." The transcontinental line would mean a vast population, the mushroom growth of cities, huge fortunes, and the steady increase in the price of land. In short, "the new era will be one of great material prosperity if material prosperity means more people, more houses, more farms and mines, more factories and ships."[13]

Yet progress, George was sure, would have its hidden costs. For every apparent gain a universal law of compensation would ensure a corresponding loss. As California grew richer, it would cease to be a land of opportunity. "She will have more luxury and refinement and culture; but will she have such general comfort, so little squalor and misery; so little of the grinding hopeless poverty that chills and cramps the souls of men and converts them into brutes?" Why was the unchecked growth of population universally considered a blessing? Why was there more vice and suffering in New York City than in San Francisco? Seen in the light of questions like these, the prospects opened by the railroad—increased pressure on land, political corruption, class antagonism, low wages, and sweated labor—appeared uninviting if not downright hazardous.

George's ideal society, which was the same as Lloyd's and Bellamy's, was the antithesis of the speculative sprawl he saw out of his windows in San Francisco: a remembered arcadia, pastoral, resting on "diffused proprietorship" and peopled with farmers, mechanics, artisans, and small tradesmen, all living and producing harmoniously within a network of local loyalties and natural limits. Central to the thinking of all three men as they began to examine American society in the last quarter of the nineteenth century was the concept of a balanced and diversified economy resting on immutable laws and composed of relatively small economic units competing briskly for shares in gradually expanding regional markets. Bellamy derived his vision from the truly socialized New England small town; Lloyd his version as the product of the unhampered workings of free trade. George's picture of the idyllic society was a copy of the community of his Millennial Letter, a collection of homesteads where each man might sit under his own vine and fig tree with none to vex him or make him afraid.

The American determination to sustain the socialized community was at least as old as Federalism, and by the third quarter of the nineteenth century it had become the distinguishing mark everywhere of conservative institutionalists and local notables who agreed in deploring the rise of national democracy and in cherishing inherited ways. To the three journalists, however, the harmonious society appeared a naturally progressive one in which the pursuit of self-interest could be guided by a clear sense of religious obligation. Their ideal society was a sacred but at the same time a developing one, and they felt no need for the strictures of a Fisher Ames or an appeal to the wise, the just, and the good.

Now George measured in secular terms the loss of an old California that once had fostered "large-heartedness" and "open-handedness."

In a country where all had started from the same level— where the banker had been a year or two before a journeyman carpenter; the merchant a foremast hand; the restaurant waiter had perhaps been educated for the bar or the church, and the labourer once counted his "pile," and where the wheel of fortune had been constantly revolving with a rapidity in other places unknown, social lines could not be sharply drawn, nor a reverse dispirit. There was something in the great possibilities of the country; in the feeling that it was one of immense latent wealth; which furnished a background of which a better filled and more thoroughly developed country is destitute, and which contributed not a little to the active, generous, independent social tone.

These frontier habits George even now romantically identified with mining, a way of life that promised quick fortunes and still held a terrible fascination for him. In the glory days of the Gold Rush, he believed, life had lain close to an elemental reality; and the miner had worked for himself alone, taking his hard-won earnings directly out of the ground. Mining, as George mythopoetically conceived of it, had carried a full complement of social benefits. "If it could have been united with the ownership of land and the comforts of home, it would have given us a class of citizens of the utmost value to a republican state." But now, in the seventies, the miners had retreated into history before the advance of the syndicates with their gigantic rock-crushers. With them had come the interlopers—"the Chinaman, the mill-owner and his laborers, the mine superintendent and his gang," advanced agents of a "giant centralizer" that "kills little businesses and builds great ones."

Yet progress, George could see, created the possibilities of a genuine culture. During the pioneer stage of California's economic growth its people had been too busy getting ahead to concern themselves with creating a civilization, but now the growth of cities and the clustering of people had created the conditions for a splendid public life. "We shall have our noble charities, great museums, libraries and universities; a class of men who have leisure for thought and culture; magnificent theatres and opera houses; parks and pleasure gardens." But at what price? Here George reached the paradox he would spend the next ten years unraveling: "One millionaire involves the existence of just so many proletarians." Hard by the Nob Hill mansion stood the drifter's shack. Tagging along behind liveried carriages came their "corollaries," ragged barefoot children begging for food. While urban splendor might have tamed the "masculine energies" of the few original buccaneers by fostering "home feeling" and a "deeper religious sentiment," the impersonality of the city had also bred a parasitical and predatory behavior among the many more inhabitants, a "low, brutal, cowardly rowdyism."

Here, then, was the unmistakable tendency of the new age: "to the great power of the few." The question of the future was whether Americans could enjoy progress without accompanying poverty. George's tentative answer: "We might, perhaps." On this hunch he set to work on solving the problem, assembling the evidence that went to prove the ominous pressures of population growth, increasing inequality, and the threat of monopoly. Missing still was the flash of insight that would connect these several developments and explain their meaning. This revelation came to him now in what he later called "one of those experiences that make those who have them feel thereafter that they can appreciate what mystics and poets have called the 'ecstatic vision.' " His own vision came in the form of a commonplace answer to a practical question in a moment that "crystallized, as by lightning-flash, my brooding thoughts into coherency, and I there and then recognized the natural order." One day in early spring, absorbed in his own musings, he had taken a long horseback ride into the hills behind Oakland and the line of settlement.

> I had driven the horse into the hills until he panted. Stopping for breath, I asked a passing teamster, for want of something better to say, what land was worth there. He pointed to some cows grazing off so far that they looked like mice and said: "I don't know exactly, but there is a man over there who will sell some land for a thousand dollars an acre." Like a flash it came upon me that there was the reason for advancing poverty with advancing wealth. With the growth of population land grows in value, and the men who work it must pay more for the privilege. I turned back, amidst quiet thought, to the perception that then came to me and has been with me ever since.[14]

As George grew older there would be other moments of insight when "every nerve quivered," in particular a chilling experience in the streets of New York, much like the fictional one Bellamy would give to Julian West in Boston's South End, when he saw the contrast between "monstrous wealth" and "debasing want" savagely dramatized. But at a deeper level of his mind the adventure in the Oakland hills remained his central perception—a religious experience that gave sudden coherence to a series of partial intuitions. In years to come he would learn that his private vision was simply a moment in the history of modern political thought—a tradition running from the French Physiocrats through the English radicals William Godwin and Thomas Spence to Tom Paine and *Agrarian Justice*—in which the equitable distribution of land, the even dispersal of population, and steady economic growth were seen as linked within a natural system of justice. Then he would consider the insights of his predecessors as dim foreshadowings of his own discovery.

Equipped with his new insight and carrying the credentials of a local sage that his occasional writings had earned him, George turned to the Democratic party in California to advance the cause of antimonopoly and not incidentally his own career. His connections with the Democracy dated from a meeting of a branch of Henry Demarest Lloyd's American Free Trade League in 1868 and a chance conversation with Governor Henry H. Haight, who found him a post on the Sacramento *Reporter*, a party organ. Under George's brief management the *Reporter* served faithfully the cause of resurgent Democracy in the state, as its editor called for an end to federal interference in the South and recognition that "this government was instituted by and for white men and their posterity forever"; free trade, and strict antimonopoly. George, who was already casting covetous eyes on a seat in the state legislature, also attacked Republican "aggrandizement" and the "tainted" political atmosphere in Washington, and warned his working-class readers of the "colossal fortunes" to be made by "mammoth" corporations should the Republicans succeed in electing Grant. From Philadelphia, appropriately, came a letter from his father congratulating him on his loyalty to "the good old Democratic principles."

Out of these partisan concerns came two pamphlets in time for the state elections of 1871, the first a sixteen-page polemic for the party faithful, *The Subsidy Question and the Democratic Party*, calling for a halt in public land grants. "The only method of preventing the abuse of subsidies is prohibiting them altogether," George announced. The Democrats' alternative of free homesteads and hands-off would stimulate needed railroad construction more effectively than all of the Republican giveaways combined.

More important in advancing his own ideas if not his immediate prospects was a second pamphlet, *Our Land and Land Policy,* his first major exploratory tract. In the spring of 1871 he began to jot down in his diary the details of various large land transactions with which to illustrate his text, but the actual writing proceeded slowly. Annie, though proud of her husband's literary accomplishments, hardly understood his growing obsession with developmental theory; and his political cronies, always good for long-winded debates on the party's chances at the polls, were unable to keep up with an original mind already preoccupied with making a grand synthesis of his ideas. George labored alone and worked slowly and hesitantly. "Not much progress in pamphlet," he noted in his diary. "Got to 18th page through reasoning about property in land; but resolved to leave it out."[15] He was tempted to include a section denying the right of individual property in land but realized the danger of pushing his moral theories too far beyond conventional Democratic party wisdom. Yet already his ideas were running ahead of received doctrine.

Nevertheless, the pamphlet was a morality play with the yeoman farmer cast as protagonist and the corporation and the greedy speculators as his enemies. Misconception and mismanagement, George insisted, had combined to produce a monstrous land policy at just the time when "no child born this year or last year, or even three years before that, can possibly get himself a homestead out of Uncle Sam's farm, unless he is willing to take a mountain-top or an alkili patch, or emigrate to Alaska."[16] Meanwhile both federal and state governments continued to grant land to the railroads with an abandon hard to credit. "Landgrabbers have had it pretty much their own way in California—they have moulded the General Government; have dictated the legislation of the State; have run the land offices and used the Courts." Now it was time for the Democrats to ring down the curtain on this sordid tale of double-dealing, floating grants, blackmail, and fraud.

Capitalizing on his sudden prominence as an editorial spokesman for the California Democratic party, George accepted a place on the ballot for state assemblyman, a post he had been eyeing hungrily for some time. He spent the weeks before the November 1871 election in a campaign sweat, addressing every ward caucus in San Francisco, buttonholing voters, and feeding his misplaced hopes for office. On election night he strode into dinner to announce to the startled Annie that the Democrats were sweeping all before them and that without question she saw before her State Assemblyman Henry George. His political predictions unfortunately proved no more accurate than his financial forecasts. When his prophecy collapsed under a hail of Republican votes, he came home again to admit with chagrin: "Why Annie, we haven't even elected a constable."

His dream of office smashed and his bank balance in need of repair, George was again at loose ends and even considered returning to Philadelphia. Then on a hunch he decided to pool his slender capital with that of two friends and form a partnership in the San Francisco *Daily Evening Post*, the state's first penny newspaper. The first edition of the *Post* appeared in December 1871, and for the next four years it served its editor as a forum for discussing national affairs and a standard for the Democratic party, with which George continued to identify his prospects. When it became clear that the slim hopes of the Democrats in the election of 1872 rested with "Uncle Horace" Greeley, the new editor of the *Post* dutifully described the remarkable qualities of that "benignant old man" even though his heart was not in it. For now his interest in land and land policy had become a preoccupation that was leading him far beyond the politics of equilibrium.

Although it is probable that none of the three men knew of the others' existence in 1872, in fact all of them were engaged in a common enterprise: the fashioning of a language of social criticism with which to found a national community of discourse.[17] Such a community, each instinctively knew, would be bound together by shared values and aspirations but also by a similar style of inquiry and mode of analysis.

When, for example, Henry George described his discovery of the key to the land question in terms of religious conversion, he reached out to a wide range of people whose Protestant evangelical backgrounds, like his own, had prepared them for a way of thinking about the world—a system of conceptualizing problems—with which they felt familiar and comfortable. Inherent in the image of conversion were assumptions about the human personality, the nature of change, and the role of the individual. George's metaphor supplied the linguistic currency for a community whose conceptions of the social process, like his own, were essentially religious rather than secular.

Similarly, when Edward Bellamy addressed his neighbors on the subject of socialism, he too was resorting to a mode of analysis that was drawn primarily from the sacred rather than the secular. His exploration of socialism was a moral inquiry proceeding from certain assumptions that he knew his listeners shared, assumptions about causation, the apprehension of reality, and the power of ethical persuasion. His discussion thus had less to do with programs and platforms than moral attitudes and the informed conscience.

All of these assumptions and attitudes had been embodied in Henry Demarest Lloyd's boyhood heroes, the antebellum giants of reform—William Lloyd Garrison and Wendell Phillips, Theodore Weld and Theodore Parker—whose personal force, he knew, derived from the stark terms of their social inquiry based on Christian universals. In consciously casting himself in the same heroic mold Lloyd, along with Bellamy and George, was calling for a community of moral discourse with a reform agenda based on the conviction that the fundamental questions of the age concerned the good community, how to achieve and, more important, how to preserve it.

In framing the problem of their age as that of building the just society, the three reformers were reaching back through memory to the constituency of the Free Soil community in the North before the Civil War, a regional coalition of farmers, merchants, small-town businessmen, professionals, and upwardly mobile artisans and mechanics. Speaking the same language of Protestant pietism, using the same moral categories for interpreting the slavery crisis, this was the community that shaped the meaning of the Civil War.

By the time Bellamy, George, and Lloyd arrived on the postwar scene the old reform alliances of the antebellum years were breaking up, and their several parts were being assembled in a new coalition that sought to combine abolitionist moral concerns with Jacksonian working-class values. As yet merely a persuasion undergoing redefinition and still searching for a political voice, this evangelical political culture was beginning to connect the old antislavery notions of moral accountability and material progress with Jacksonian working-class preferences for shopfloor solidarity, natural cooperation, and grassroots politics. As the panic and depression of the 1870s hastened the consolidation of the American economy by concentrating increased power in the hands of organized businessmen, a saving remnant of Lincoln Republicans and aging agrarian Democrats, hard-pressed farmers, veteran labor organizers, and new ethnics were banding together in a defensive alliance and preparing to fight a rearguard action against the revolutionary forces of big business.

Throughout the seventies these groups continued to experiment with educational politics and third parties in Greenback and Farmer-Labor endeavors, dreaming all the while of a new age of co-operation among the true producers of the world who lived by the sweat of their brows. Here was the community that the lonely reform journalists were attempting to contact. What was needed to sharpen their own concepts and to recruit followers was a sense of crisis that would transform the original community of discourse into a broad social movement and adversary culture seeking to defend itself from the forces of an unchecked capitalism. This crisis the Panic of 1873 and a four-year depression furnished in abundance.

3

THE MAKING OF A REFORMER

THE INDUSTRIAL CRISIS of the seventies—financial panic followed by deepening depression that saw prices collapse, the work force halved, and wages pared to the bone—sharpened the social outlook of Henry George and Henry Demarest Lloyd. In the ruins of the Great Railroad Strike of 1877, the most violent labor upheaval in memory, they recognized the bankruptcy of American social theory. After the violent summer of 1877 they centered their investigations on the paradox, illuminated by burning railroad yards, of abundance for the few and increasing misery for the many. Islands of privilege in a sea of poverty. The waste of human resources hailed by penny-ante politicians as a cheap price for progress, while men went jobless and their families starved.

Their moral response to economic crisis, however, was partial and incoherent. For each of them the seventies were diagnostic years, a preparatory stage out of which emerged at the end of the decade the alternatives to unchecked development they had been seeking. Meanwhile they fought back against the social disorder of the seventies with their feelings—shock, pity, outrage—and only

gradually honed them into concepts with which to launch a coun-
terattack.

Henry George's compassion for the underdog frequently appeared as a mammoth truculence, comic but formidable. The dimin-
utive figure of the editor of the San Francisco *Evening Post*, compact
and erect, topped by a broad, high-colored face framed with a sandy
beard, became a familiar sight among the city's journalistic fraternity, perched atop his shaggy pony as it loped through the streets, its
rider staring off into the distance deep in thought. Or with feet
planted in front of the bar in Mint's saloon heatedly arguing the fine
points of his indictment of monopoly. Or, again, weaving his way
around the mounds of books and papers in his office as he dictated
last-minute editorials at a furious pace, always ready to break off for
a chat with any chance visitor. The *Post*, it was understood by friends
and foes alike, was a reform paper and its editor a born fighter.

The paper, launched with $1800, which represented the com-
bined life savings of its partners, first appeared as a four-page sheet,
eleven by fourteen inches, crowded with microscopic print, and selling for a penny. In the next four years, under George's combative
management, the paper acquired standard size, a healthy circulation,
and widespread notoriety as a defender of justice. There was the
case of the ship *Sunrise* and its tyrannical captain, whose arrival in
port was accompanied by dark rumors of three members of the crew
driven overboard and drowned in mid-passage. George promptly
ran the story down, demanded prosecution, and when the captain
disappeared, posted a reward and gained the satisfaction of seeing
him apprehended and convicted. Then there was his investigation of
charges of brutality at the City House of Correction, when he
brushed aside an irate warden barring the door with gun in hand,
proceeded to collect the evidence he needed, and returned to the office to write a series of blistering editorials. When a Monterey land
baron murdered a woman in a quarrel over boundaries and was
lynched by his neighbors, the editor of the *Post* expressed satisfaction
at justice done, however crudely, an opinion he saw no reason to
change when an outraged relative of the lynch victim stormed into
his office demanding a retraction and receiving instead a punch on
the jaw.

Nor were city officials exempt from George's civic wrath. The chief of police, annoyed at reading in the *Post* of his failure to clean up Chinatown, despatched one of his lieutenants to Mint's, where he accosted George and suggested that he hold his editorial tongue— another request that did not recommend itself to the volatile editor who had to be restrained from defending freedom of press with his fists. In his first editorial George informed his readers in the spirit of William Lloyd Garrison that the *Post* would be "the organ of no faction, clique or party," and it was quickly clear that he meant what he said.[1]

Retired to his den at home, the lion of San Francisco journalism grew tame if not quite toothless. By the mid-seventies George was the affectionate if exacting father of two boys and a girl, whose training he supervised with a firm benevolence. On weekends he would take the boys sightseeing, swimming, or rowing along the waterfront, where he pointed out the ancient hulk of the lighthouse tender that had carried him around the Horn. In the evenings he liked to stretch full-length on the family couch and, while Annie sewed and the children sprawled on the floor around him, read aloud—unearthing the fantasy treasures of the *Arabian Nights* or recounting the adventures of Robinson Crusoe, whose desert isle would figure so prominently in *Progress and Poverty*.

In a succession of rented cottages, the George household was the scene of frequent invasions of guests come to enjoy Annie's bountiful cooking and their host's conversation that ran far into the night. When their slender means permitted, there was the theater, in which both of them delighted, but as often as not George's resources were strained by one of his speculative plunges that paid off only in sharp warnings from his wife.

These occasional relapses of gambling fever represented the sole aberration in George's otherwise exemplary middle-class lifestyle. Unorthodox as his views on land monopoly came to seem to a younger generation of trained economists, they rested squarely on a triad of eternal verities—religious, moral, and aesthetic—which he never stopped to question. He believed in the sanctity of marriage, the need for chastity, and the enduring beauty of the moral life. "Marriage," he once wrote to Annie on one of his periodic trips, "is not only the foundation of society; it is the divinely appointed state which confers the highest and purest happiness." His own contentment he never doubted.

> How much fresh delight there is in our love [he told Annie].
> From the time I first saw you and was captivated by that
> something in face and voice and manner, which I never could
> explain in words, it has gone on increasing and increasing.
> Husband and father, I am still more lover than when I used to
> stop in my work to take out your picture and steal a glance at
> it. Satisfaction only crowns desire, and the love of the mature
> man is not only deeper, but more passionate than that of the
> boy. And this is the great thing with me. All outside ups and
> downs are trivial compared to that.[2]

No longer a churchgoer or even a conventional Christian, George was still a deeply religious man with an unswerving faith in a benevolent God and the immortality of the soul. His personal deity, he explained in language that would soon be called the social gospel, was an immanent one—"not a God who is confined to the far-off beginning or the vague future, who is over and above and beyond men, but a God who in His inexorable law is here and now; a God of the living as well as the dead; a God of the market place as well as of the temple; a God whose judgments wait not another world for execution, but whose immutable decrees will, in this life, give happiness to the people that heed them and bring misery upon the people who forget them."[3] This simple creed George taught to his children, together with a commonsense morality that he considered the hinge of the universe. In direct and powerful language *Progress and Poverty* would call for a repair of that moral order which he believed had been so badly dented and tarnished by an age of materialism.

If such Victorian truisms reassured George with their promise of harmony and moral progress, they also restricted his search for the good society with their emphasis on Anglo-Saxon, Protestant absolutes that excluded those outsiders who, for whatever reason, did not share them. This was the case, he was convinced, with the Chinese on the West Coast, whose growing numbers and alien habits appeared to threaten the very foundations of his natural religion. All of Richard George's prejudices against blacks—slave or free—re-emerged in his son's fear of a yellow peril. If his view of the virtuous republic encompassed the rural cottage complete with garden and family hearth, then hell on earth was Chinatown with its fetid alleys and filthy tenements brimming with yellow devils. It was as though his boyhood glimpse of decomposing bodies floating down the Hooghly River, obscured by the intervening years, had now reappeared as a chilling reminder of the anonymity and randomness of death. What chance had faith in individual worth and innate goodness have in a world flung open to barbarian hordes from the East?

This dark side of George's intellectual background deepened into an ethnocentric exclusivism which he modified as he grew older but never completely relinquished. As he watched the flood of Chinese coolies pour into California, uprooting the native-born working force, he wrote an article, "The Chinese on the Pacific Coast," for the New York *Herald*. Ostensibly his argument for total exclusion was economic, an adaptation of the wage-fund theory borrowed from John Stuart Mill. Since a universal law of wages allotted a fixed sum for labor, it followed that an influx of unskilled Chinese coolies could only depress wages and cause tension as more and more workingmen of all colors and creeds were forced to accept smaller and smaller shares of the wage-fund.

With this analysis Mill, to whom George sent a copy of his article, had no quarrel, but he sensed correctly that the author's chief objection to the Chinese was not economic but cultural and, at bottom, racist. Driven to defend himself, George could only agree. Until recently, he explained, the United States had been peopled chiefly by members of the same race—excepting, of course, the Negro slaves whose chidlike docility and lack of culture contrasted sharply with the heathen and hostile Chinese. "The negro when brought to this country was a simple barbarian," he added with all the smugness of his age, "the Chinese have a civilization and history of their own, a vanity which causes them to look down on all other races, habits of thought rendered permanent by being stamped upon countless generations." These character traits marked them as "sensual, cowardly and cruel." To support his case George invoked all of the lurid fantasies of his boyhood: the Chinese practiced infanticide, the arts of assassination, and other "unnameable vices of the East." They were hopelessly filthy in their personal habits. Most sinister of all, they possessed an evil genius for secret combinations that made

them a state within a state. In short, they were wholly unassimil-
able—"incapable of understanding our religion . . . still less are they
capable of understanding our political institutions." The only answer was to deny the vote to those already arrived and shut the gates
on the rest as soon as possible.[4]

Except for a handful of abolitionists the antebellum habit of defining American social problems in the language of Christian duty
had proved wholly compatible with a set of racial prejudices that
only intensified the need to lift up the lowly and despised peoples of
the world. Both of these impulses—the urge to spread light among
the benighted and the accompanying conviction of white superiority—survived the Civil War, the first weakened and the second
strengthened by a new evolutionary science that provided the rationale for the concept of a hierarchy of races rising from inferior black
and yellow peoples to a properly dominant white race. The two
halves of this argument were combined in the postwar years in the
image of the White Man's Burden, which George and the postwar
evangelicals understood as a distinctly national task assigned to
white Americans.

George's hostility to the Chinese, rooted in fears of cultural declension, never really abated. Twenty years later, when William
Lloyd Garrison, Jr., like his father a strict racial egalitarian, up-
braided him for his illiberal views of other races, George restated his
opinion that the Chinese were an inferior people and hence undesir-
able citizens. He rejected Jefferson's geographical pursuit of happiness in favor of the exclusionary right of the natural community. "Is
there no such thing as family, nation, race?"[5] Was not a corollary of
the right of association the right of exclusion? George's antipathy toward alien cultures was strongest in the seventies when the Yellow
Peril rocked California, but his belief that the Chinese threatened to
subvert American values never really wavered.

To the land question, on the other hand, George brought ingenuity and imagination. The signs of an agricultural revolution were already clear in California's new squatter class working for landlords
who treated land as a source of speculative profit. "The farm houses,
as a class," he noted, "are unpainted frame shanties, without garden
or flower or tree." The farmer raised only wheat and bought his
flour, eggs, butter, and vegetables at the nearest store. "He hires
labor for his planting and his reaping, and his hands shift for them-

selves at other seasons of the year. His plow he leaves standing in the furrow, when the year's plowing is done; his mustangs he turns upon the hills, to be lassoed again when needed."[6] He bought on credit and was usually in debt. Lording it over this tenant stood the absentee landowner, who, like the cotton snobs in the South before him, boarded in fancy city hotels and spent the social season in fashionable watering spots while his lands were being systematically exhausted. "His land is rented for one-third or one-fourth the crop, or is covered with scraggy cattle, which need to look after them only a few half-civilized vaqueros; or his wheat fields, of from ten to twenty thousand acres, are plowed and reaped by contract." In his flight the absentee landlord left a huge desolate landscape crisscrossed with "ill-kept, shadeless, dusty roads," down which plodded armies of tramps with blankets on their backs looking for a day's work.

George's initial survey of the land problem in California rested on two crucial assumptions. The first was in reality a model of growth and development. He was convinced that it was land itself, and not simply the mode of cultivating it, that held the key to social development. In the early pamphlet, *Our Land and Land Policy*, and in frequent editorials in the *Post* he began to make explicit the model of growth which his masterpiece would one day develop in detail: gradual and controlled colonization of new lands by small farmers and independent townsmen producing and freely exchanging their goods in local markets clustered within regional economies. In George's idealized world both the yeomen farmers and the small entrepreneurs are "true producers" who neither speculate nor monopolize. Neither do they pioneer in unseemly haste beyond the line of settlement but instead arrange themselves "naturally" in towns and villages, consolidate neighborhoods, instinctively seek means of cooperation, and proceed to develop the country resolutely and sensibly.

Caught and held in this temporal frame, the good society envisioned by George results from the arrest of community growth *after* the pioneer stage of individual hardship and isolation but *before* the arrival of massive engrossment of land, absentee ownership, and forced urbanization.

Under such a policy as this settlement would go on regularly and thoroughly. Population would not in the same time

spread over as much ground as under present policy; but
what it did spread over would be well settled and well cultivated. There would be no necessity for building costly railroads to connect settlers with a market. The market would
accompany settlement. No one would go out into the wilderness to brave all the hardships and discomforts of the solitary
frontier life; but with the foremost line of settlement would go
the church and school-house and lecture room. The ill-paid
mechanic of the city could find a home on the soil, where he
would not have to abandon the comforts of civilization, but
where there would be society enough to make life attractive,
and where the wants of his neighbors would give a product
for his surplus labor until his land began to produce.

In his concern with the problem of an economically retrogressive
dispersal of people across an empty continent—a concern for which
there were as yet few American precedents—George was restating
the views of an earlier English observer, Edward Gibbon Wakefield,
a chief architect of the second British Empire, whose annotated edition of Adam Smith (1830–1843) he may already have read. Forty
years earlier Gibbon Wakefield had analyzed the problem of colonization in a comparative study, *England and America* (1833), and concluded that the key to the successful planting of colonies was a "sufficient price" set on undeveloped land, a figure high enough to
discourage random settlement and the engrossment of large tracts,
maintain an adequate supply of labor concentrated in towns, and
ensure the growth of functional urban settlements. Like George after
him, Gibbon Wakefield feared both the sprawling metropolis and
the seductive wilderness, and he too stressed the importance of balanced regional development along the lines of provincial English
towns. In its larger social aims Gibbon Wakefield's "sufficient price"
on undeveloped land was calculated to prevent just such chaotic development as George now found flourishing in California.

George also objected to a speculative land policy because it arti-
ficially quickened the pace of economic growth by removing natural
obstacles. In a wholly capricious manner speculation disrupted nature's schedule for opening and developing new lands in the West.
No one could argue that without huge land grants the railroads
would never have been built, only that without these giveaways they

would not have been built so soon or so badly. In their obsession with saving time and cutting corners Americans had been victimized by the very *idea* of the railroad, an abstraction for which they had renounced their patrimony. Unplanned railroad building, he was convinced, retarded rather than hastened actual settlement and the productive use of the land because the railroad companies charged excessive rates in order to finance further construction of naturally unprofitable roads. Worse still, land grants accelerated the unequal distribution of wealth all along their lines by excluding the real farmer from the best lands and forcing him to pioneer wastefully and hazardously on inferior land far from the nearest market. Progress of this sort, whether measured in population density, taxable property, new millionaires, or railroad mileage, was a very Sodom's apple to the poor settler.

George's indictment also derived from another premise, one that served him less as an analytical tool than as an article of faith. This was his mystical sense of the land as prescribing with Old Testament rigor the conditions of human life. As he would preach again and again—"On the land we are born, from it we live, to it we return again—children of the soil as truly as is the blade of grass or the flower of the field." Land as the gift of nature George thought of in two common but seemingly contradictory images—materially as a huge mine with rich lore buried deep in its recesses, a figure all too appealing to a nineteenth-century extractive mentality. But at another level—spiritually—George conceived of land as God's storehouse furnishing men's psychic needs for a home, family, possessions, and a sense of place. In this fundamental sense land signified a coming home, a return to primal wholeness, that same feeling he himself frequently experienced and which he attributed to the original California settler, "coming over sage brush plains from the still frost-bound East," descending the spring slopes of the Sierras through bristling ranks of evergreen giants and endless meadows of wildflowers, and glimpsing for the first time but with a strange sense of recognition "the vast fertile valleys stretching out to the dark blue Coast Range in the distance."

This deeper meaning of land in America, George sensed, could never be encompassed by describing it simply as wealth but demanded an intuitive response of the individual to the "general possibilities" of nature offered as a free gift. And if land was not properly wealth but only the means to it, then an increase in its value did not mean additional wealth but only a shift in its distribution. In fact, George could now see, high land values actually decreased the wealth of a community by siphoning it off as luxury on the one hand and low wages on the other.

Here in stark relief stood revealed the root fact of all social analysis: the value of land and the value of labor are inversely related. "And thus we see it," George wrote with sudden insight, "all over the world, in countries where land is high, wages are low, and where land is low, wages are high." Twenty years earlier in California the value of labor had reached its natural maximum while land in untold quantities was there for the taking, a sign of social health now fatally reversed. For the higher the price of land and the lower the prevailing wages, George could now predict with confidence, "the stronger the tendency towards still lower wages, until this tendency is met by the very necessities of existence."

George's discovery of the paradox of economic growth posed many questions and afforded few answers. First, if land was indeed a storehouse open by right of nature to all men, how came the right of ownership to be vested in particular individuals? He had no answer. Much as he wished to believe in land as a common bounty, George had inherited a strong Jacksonian preference for private property and the God-given right of the yeoman "to the use of so much of the free gifts of nature as may be necessary" so long as he did not interfere with the rights of others to do the same. The progress of civilization, it seemed to George, depended on the right of private property. "When the millennium comes and the old savage instincts have died out, land may perhaps be held in common; but not till then."

But how then prevent monopoly? How reverse the steady drift of the nation toward concentration of wealth and power? Finally, how to answer the question that pressed insistently on him as the depression following the Panic of 1873 continued to deepen:

> Why is it that, with all our labor-saving machinery, all the new methods of increasing production which our fertile genius is constantly discovering . . . that the general condition of the working class is becoming worse instead of better; and the

employment of women and children at hard labor is extending; that though wealth is accumulating, and luxury increasing, it is becoming harder and harder for the poor man to live?

Then in 1875 the *Post* itself became a victim of the depression as
George and his partners were besieged by a hungry creditor. "I felt
like fighting," George recalled, "and a short article in the 'Post'
would have ended all hopes of his getting anything from it, but my
partner, Mr. Hinton, pleaded the duty of our providing for the employees who were friends, and tired out with the fight, I finally succumbed, and without a cent of compensation . . . almost four years to
the day after we started it, gave over the paper."[7] On the street once
again and now with a sizable family to support, George decided to
cash in his overdue claim on the state Democratic party and approach
Governor William S. Irwin, whose candidacy the *Post* had championed. Irwin promptly obliged by appointing him State Inspector of
Gas Meters, a sinecure that provided him with the leisure to write.

Patronage from the state machine drove George back into the
temporary embraces of the party. He took to the stump for Tilden in
the campaign of 1876 and loudly denounced Republican misrule as
the heyday of the tax-gatherer and the coupon-clipper. In taking to
the hustings, he explained, he was proving that he could make a
name for himself even without a newspaper. "I have always felt that
I possessed the requisites for a first-class speaker, and that I could
make one if I could get practice; and I started this campaign with the
deliberate purpose of breaking myself in." His early oratorical hopes
were misplaced. With an uneven, reedy voice that chattered with
machinegun rapidity, he lacked at first a feeling for his audience,
whom he was apt to bombard, until he found that with a prepared
text he could marshal his arguments rather than waste them in spo-
radic fusillades. But even so he needed a reminder of the virtue of
brevity like the one accorded his centennial Fourth of July Address,
"The American Republic," which he delivered to a sweltering throng
in San Francisco's California Theater. "The gas measurer," sneered
the opposition press, "kindly spoke for several hours on the God-
dess of Liberty and other school-reader topics."

Yet George was determined to improve, for he suddenly realized
the power of the spoken word for the would-be reformer. "From not
being known as a speaker I have come to the front," he boasted to

his mother, who had expressed misgivings concerning a political career. "I wanted to do this, not as a matter of vanity or for the mere pleasure of the thing; but to increase my power and usefulness." Here was the same ambition that drove Lloyd and broke the surface of Bellamy's placid routine—the appeal of power without obligation. "I do not propose to mix in lower politics," George assured his mother, "nor do I propose to chase after nominations." He could afford to wait until the politicians came to him, and in the meantime he intended to "write some things which will extend my reputation and perhaps deliver some lectures with the same view."[8]

George's political ambitions were checked by an even stronger resolve to attempt a grand synthesis of political economy that would unravel the paradox of increasing wealth and growing want. If he could only clear away the accumulated rubble of false premises and nonsequiturs, this would be a challenge worthy of his talents. The book he now contemplated would have to be a model of close reasoning and foolproof analysis, and it must also provide a call to action. Then and only then would the workaday chores of the professional politicians be worth his time.

There were signals of his new intention in a speech he gave in the spring of 1877 across the bay at the recently established University of California at Berkeley. President John LeConte's school still lacked a professor of political science, and rumors were already circulating that George was a prime candidate. If so, he quickly scotched them with a harangue which, to the dismay of the faculty and the delight of the students, rebuked academia for its limited vision and lack of courage.

In carrying his private war into the camp of the enemy, George was cutting himself off, not simply from financial support, but from the intellectual sustenance that American institutions of higher learning were just beginning to provide. As a self-made man in the artisanal tradition of practical learning, George displayed a deep distrust of the aims and purposes of the new universities that were being established to exploit the intellectual resources of the country in more systematic ways. His misgivings were mixed: part fear of an ethical relativism implied in the ideal of disinterested scholarship; part distaste for privilege and the occasional snobbery of higher learning; and part apprehension at the thought of confronting minds more sophisticated than his own. His instinctive response pointed him away from the future and the challenge of new social science methods and back toward the past, where modernity had presumably taken a wrong turning. It would be an increasingly lonely road.

In the century since Adam Smith's *Wealth of Nations*, George told the Berkeley students, political science had failed to make a single advance. Why was that? Because the economic interests that stood to lose by its development had not permitted it. Accordingly, the science of political economy had become a fair field for the "pretentious quackery" of the professors who indulged in hairsplitting and other forms of trivia. "Thus has been given to a simple and attractive science an air of repellent abstruseness and uncertainty" which befuddled the average man and convinced him that there was nothing he could do to better his lot. Political economy as currently practiced by a kept intellectual class was doomed unless it could be restored to its original state of simplicity. And for that great work of restoration, George announced to his startled audience, neither library nor laboratory was needed, neither textbooks nor teachers.

> All that you need is care in reducing complex phenomena to their elements, in distinguishing the essential from the accidental, and in applying the simple laws of human action with which you are familiar . . . All this array of professors, all this paraphernalia of learning, cannot educate a man. They can but help him to educate himself . . . A monkey with a microscope, a mule packing a library, are fit emblems of the men—and unfortunately, they are plenty—who pass through the whole educational machinery, and come out but learned fools, crammed with knowledge which they cannot use.[9]

If, instead, his youthful audience, those "favoured few" enjoying the "happy accidents" of a life of learning that fell only to the fortunate, would lift their eyes from their books and look beyond the university walls, they would find, not only suffering, but the means for curing it. Their freshened eyes would help them see that "the true law of social life is the law of love, the law of liberty . . . that the golden rule of morals is also the golden rule of the science of wealth." With this plea George stopped, and so did talk—if there had ever been any—of his filling a university chair.

If his public addresses had opened up new moral vistas, they had not advanced the hard analytical work of building a political science of his own. Declarations of intent, they offered few clues to his method. For these the American public would have to wait two years. In an entry in his diary for September 18, 1877, George noted briefly: "Commenced Progress and Poverty."[10]

Unlike Henry George's prolonged vigil in San Francisco, Henry Demarest Lloyd's assault on the journalistic citadel of Chicago proceeded according to plan. Lloyd's rapid ascent of the editorial ladder at the *Tribune* seemed the rewards of pluck and luck, proof of Horatio Alger's maxim that with diligence and deference any bright young man could make his way in the world. Having taken bachelor's quarters on Wabash Avenue where, he reported to his family, "everything is quiet, neat," he spent all of his waking hours in his office writing sample paragraphs for the scrutiny of his seniors and adapting himself to the frenzied routine of a big city daily. Presently editor White assigned him to the night city desk, a choice he immediately regretted when the exuberant newcomer, without orders, fired off an editorial salvo at his favorite target, protectionism. "Horace White stepped up to me to-night," the crestfallen Lloyd reported, "and said in a voice which gave my marrow-bones a premonitory chill—'Mr. Lloyd, I have decided that you have not sufficient experience to fill the position you now occupy . . . You have commendable zeal and application, but need further practice.' "[11] He was transferred forthwith to the literary desk.

Zeal Lloyd certainly had, for he desperately wanted to succeed. White's icy reserve and baleful eye, he admitted, left him "skittish as an untamed steed" but more than ever determined to "show H.W. how to write and run a newspaper." He was beginning to develop a style of his own, and soon he was boasting of working "like a horse." "Horace White told me yesterday I had done very well so far . . . He seemed appalled when I told him that I did not get to bed till four."

Lloyd's path to the upper reaches of Chicago society had been smoothed by his friend Henry Keenan, who introduced him to Jessie Bross, the spirited daughter of William Bross, president of the Tribune Publishing Company and one of the paper's chief stockholders. "Deacon" Bross had been one of the founders of the

Republican party before the war and a member of original Division Street Society. A former lieutenant governor of Illinois whose extensive real estate holdings and *Tribune* stock attested publicly to his worth, he was also a doting father who took pains to investigate Lloyd's background until he could pronounce his "entire confidence" in the young man's integrity. Though Lloyd had no difficulty passing muster, he would have need in the future of all the probity credited him by a loving but possessive father-in-law whose estimate of men and events so frequently clashed with his own.

At twenty-seven, Jessie Bross was fast approaching a fashionable spinsterhood as nurse to an ailing mother and her father's hostess and companion. Soft-featured, sprightly, intelligent, and heiress to a considerable fortune, she was something of a catch, at least for Lloyd, who fell head over heels in love with her. As befitted a well-read junior editor and a bookish young woman, theirs was a literary courtship with quotations from George Eliot serving as the medium of exchange. Perusing Jessie's copy of *Adam Bede*, which she lent him, he came across a passage that *"she herself had marked"* in which Adam tells his brother not to lose heart in his suit for the hand of Dinah Morris. He countered with a lengthy review of *Middlemarch* in which he quoted Lydgate's extravagant praise of Dorothea as a creature with the heart of the Virgin Mary: "A man can make a friend of her. Her love might help a man more than her money." Jessie was swept up in a whirlwind courtship and quickly surrendered to the odd combination of wit and earnestness in her suitor. Lloyd confessed himself tossed on "a wild sea of hopes and fears." Ecstatic letters to his now outdistanced rival Keenan marked the rapid progress of his suit. "I am drowned in love for Jessie." "I shall never be the same . . . I am and ever shall be a new man." How could drudgery ever again lie in his path, "which is lit by the hope that is now my life"? All roads "of pleasure, work, memory and hope" led to Jessie's door. Jessie, after a brief demur at the difference in their ages, consented, the Deacon gave his heartiest blessing, and they were married on Christmas Day, 1873, in the new Bross home on Calumet before a gathering of "very excellent people."

"Felicity Flat," the Lloyd's small apartment in Eldridge Court, served as a base of operations for forays into the genteel world of Chicago's Gilded Age—symphony concerts, evenings at the Beethoven Club singing "the grand old chorales," Sunday services at Robert Collyer's stylishly liberal Unity Church, and meetings of the Library Club which Lloyd helped found shortly after his marriage. Lloyd happily indulged his enthusiasm for worthy causes. Part of him—the social man always available to friends and colleagues—was open, genial, gregarious, sympathetic, a gifted conversationalist, and a good listener who liked nothing better than swapping opinions with a range of acquaintances that widened every year. He tried reviving Liberal Republicanism in Chicago by founding the Illinois Free Trade League and inviting Charles Francis Adams, Jr., David Wells, and other liberal luminaries as guests. The Deacon's patronage made a slim salary seem more substantial, and Bross connections provided entry for the young couple everywhere. Two years after their marriage they enjoyed a vacation in the White Mountains paid for by Bross, and then made plans for a European tour he promised them. It was the Deacon who supplied the lot on Michigan Avenue where John Root built them a house after the birth of their first son, whom they named for his grandfather. And again it was Bross's gift of one hundred shares of *Tribune* stock that made Lloyd's financial position secure. The price of his security Lloyd would learn when he decided to quit the *Tribune* and strike out on his own.

The literary column of the daily and Sunday editions of the *Tribune* was filled with the junior editor's unexamined liberalism, in particular his concern with reconciling traditional Christianity with the new science. He wrote reviews of Darwin, Tyndal, Huxley, and David Friedrich Strauss, and accounts of the reform work of Ruskin and Charles Kingsley, along with notices of the new histories of Buckle, Froude, and Lecky. By this time Lloyd, like Bellamy and George, had acquired a strong distaste for religious fundamentalists with their scriptural legalism and sectarian quarrels. One of his first editorials, entitled "The Coming Christian," called for a new religion of altruism which he would spend the rest of his life clarifying and explaining. Only a universally accepted public faith, he predicted, one that ignored the "incomprehensible polemics of the Christian metaphysicians," could ultimately reconcile private virtue and public duty. Only a widely accepted faith, preached by ministers who practiced marital fidelity (a pointed barb at Henry Ward Beecher, whose peccadilloes had sorely embarrassed Chicago's

hard-shells), enjoining temperance in all things, and encouraging benevolence could finally turn mankind from silly disputes over the
age of the world to the work of making it better.

Lloyd's editorials on religious liberalism were minor skirmishes
in a running war between Horace White's *Tribune* and Chicago's
conservative clergy intent on rooting out "heresy" in the city. The
war of the clerics and Lloyd's small part in it came to a sudden end in
1874 when Joseph Medill returned to Chicago, resumed control of
the paper, ousted Bross as president of the company, and transferred
Lloyd to the financial desk, a post he would hold for the next six
years.

The shakeup at the *Tribune* roused Lloyd's interest in acquiring a
paper of his own. A month after Medill took the helm Lloyd was exploring the chances of buying the nearly defunct Chicago *Post and
Mail*, a hidebound Republican sheet which he intended to convert to
Tilden and Free Trade. Convinced that Medill would steer a straight
Republican course, he tried bargaining for the paper over which he
must have "complete control or nothing." He would have to be
practical, he reminded himself: "Running a newspaper is like any
other enterprise—it is your business."[12] He even compiled a list of
the issues he intended to pursue: "The pacification of the country, &
decentralization, specie payments, *administrative reform*, anti-Repub-
licanism"—altogether a platform on which Henry George would
have been proud to stand. His friends advised quick purchase, and
even Medill was enthusiastic. All he lacked was the $65,000 and his
father-in-law's blessing—two insuperable obstacles.

In a second bid for editorial control a few months later Lloyd
went further and this time succeeded in raising the implacable opposition of the Deacon. The Chicago *Daily News*, another penny
paper on the verge of collapse, offered a glittering opportunity for a
would-be independent. Lloyd assumed the operating deficit out of
his own pocket and acquired the right of purchase. He summoned
his younger brother John from New York to serve as business man-
ager, and in an exhausting stint of moonlighting continued to bring
out the *Daily News*. Meanwhile he completed his plans for a genuinely liberal sheet, "absolutely fearless and independent, guided by
what is right and true," resolutely opposed to "Class legislation" and
all attempts to "rob the people." Increasing the circulation, however,
meant increasing the advertising budget, and that involved a major

outlay of funds. Lloyd approached Bross, who flatly refused to advance the money and reprimanded his son-in-law for his disloyalty to the family firm. Worn out by weeks of double duty, overborne by the Deacon's refusal, Lloyd pulled out of the scheme, sent his brother packing, and took to his bed with a "severe neuralgia of the head."

In this, the first of a series of personal crises, Lloyd disclosed a side of himself that had not been apparent to Jessie and her father, who had seen in him only the energetic man of good sense. Now twenty-six, with deep-set gray eyes hooded by a prominent brow, his wispy moustache draped about the corners of his mouth, he looked the very model of imperturbability and ease. The portrait was deceptive, for he was also frail and what his friends called "high-strung," his delicate constitution prey to various ailments connected with his intense nature. Moody and restless, he suffered from insomnia and, in times of stress, from nervous collapse. His closest friends learned to watch his moods with care as they plunged from high humor and antic glee to dark periods of introspection when his self-confidence seemed eaten away by doubt. By all accounts he was a kindly and courtly man, sympathetic and keenly sensitive to the views of others, self-possessed and supportive. Yet beneath the surface of an almost professional kindliness, he remained torn by a powerful yearning for independence and fame and an equally strong need for security, both financial and personal. He was at least partly aware of this conflict and of the need for devising a strategy to cope with it. "There are always unpleasant things about being a hired man," he confessed to his father, who might have been expected to understand. "I suppose I have a minimum of them."

> I never receive blame or praise, I am never directed what to do—I come and go and work absolutely at my own discretion—but there is no growth in my work in any direction I specially care to grow in, and I can foresee—feel already— that before many years I shall need more money and more liberty than I can have on a salary. I don't care to be rich, and I have no idea of ever being famous. I would like to be independent and I would like to feel that I was doing some good in the world. Perhaps my day will come—perhaps it never will. Either way, I hope to behave philosophically.[13]

The collapse of his bid for independence, however, was no time for equanimity. When the *Daily News* began to flourish under new management, he wondered why he had not taken the chance. Was it, at least in part, a failure of nerve? Then as if to put aside a painful question, he refused to discuss the matter further. Twenty-five years later he still could not bear to have the subject mentioned.

His nerves shattered, his self-confidence gone, unable to work, Lloyd retreated to Winnetka on the North Shore for "country peace" and spent weeks trying to regain his health. On a tree-shaded village street within sight of the lake, he and Jessie discovered an old deserted inn, the Wayside, which they bought and restored. In 1878 they left the city for good, and Lloyd took up the life of a suburban commuter, finding in these new domestic arrangements and the beauty of the surrounding woods the restoratives he needed. In the homely furnishings of his study following long excursions into the nearby woods, and with Jessie's efficient management of the household, he began to mend his spirits so badly dented by defeat. Gradually he recovered the energy for a return to work and a different try at independence.

Back at his desk at the *Tribune*, he began writing a series of commentaries on the American economic policy calculated to appeal to moderate midwestern Republicans. Medill's return, capped by the marriage of his daughter to Robert Patterson of the staff, effectively blocked Lloyd's path to the chief editorship of the paper, but promotion to the financial desk gave him all the intellectual freedom he sought. In the beginning his "Money and Commerce" column reflected conventional opinion and faith in the good intentions of honest men. He called for reform of the Board of Trade and an end to corners in grain. He demanded stricter business ethics and pointed to the mismanagement of New York insurance companies and collusion between the big mining syndicates and San Francisco banks as examples of financial skulduggery. These and other suspect firms he included in his "National Black List," where he denounced them as "an appalling exhibition of social dishonor and moral corruption." Beyond finger-pointing and demands for voluntary self-policing, however, he was not yet ready to venture.

It was the railroad question—the explosive issue of the seventies—that first disclosed to Lloyd the weakness of his classical liberal ideas. American railroads, he realized, were just entering a phase of consolidation that had already ended in England and on the continent, a process in which the entire country was being "partitioned out among some half-dozen great corporations." Attempts by the states to regulate these giants were bound to fail. Recent German legislation suggested the utility of national instrumentalities. "Now that we've got the nation," Lloyd remarked, "let us use the nation." It was time "to face the sad truth that in allowing Free Trade in R.R." the American people had made "a great though not irreparable blunder."

Then in the summer of 1877 came the Great Railroad Strike, a spontaneous outbreak of labor violence in response to wage cuts imposed by the suddenly overextended railroads. The upheaval, which quickly paralyzed American business and struck terror into the hearts of businessmen, began in the small railhead town of Martinsburg, West Virginia, where workers learned of the wage cuts ordered by the Baltimore and Ohio, and in retaliation stopped all trains and shut down the yards. When the local police failed to get the trains rolling again, troops were called in. Then a switchman attempting to derail a cattle train was shot and killed by the militia, and a crowd that had gathered to protest was dispersed with force.

The incident at Martinsburg was the beginning of a week of violence spreading rapidly from one major city to another, as wage cuts were met by angry workers and rioters bent on sabotage and looting. In Baltimore, a regiment dispatched to protect B & O property retreated before a hail of rocks, while a second contingent of militia, taking refuge in a local armory, finally broke out and panicked, firing at random into the crowd and killing ten onlookers. In Pittsburgh, militia units proved completely unreliable until reinforcements from Philadelphia succeeded in clearing a railroad crossing and killing twenty strikers in the process. Fighting back, workers burned the railroad yards, overturned cars, looted storehouses, and penned up the soldiers in a roundhouse into which they continued to pour rifle fire until they were finally driven off. In Buffalo, another mob, infuriated by the wanton killing of eleven of their members, tore up track and broke into an arsenal for the guns with which to defend themselves.

Chicago experienced its share of violence that July. Here too the strike began in the railroad yards when 500 switchmen protested against wage cuts by roaming through the shops and calling out their

comrades. The next day the strikers, their numbers growing by the
hour, moved on to the stockyards and packinghouses along Canal
Street and Blue Island Avenue, and the city suddenly came to a
standstill. Streetcars stood idle, business shut its doors, and heavy
industry, without coke or coal, closed its gates. For the first time the
citizens of Chicago, like millions of middle-class Americans, became
aware of the power of labor to disrupt their routines.

The Great Railroad Strike brought the shock of recognition to
Lloyd, jarring him out of his preoccupation with self. As he followed
the day-by-day accounts of violence and made hurried notes for his
Tribune stories, he found the evidence that called into question all of
his classical liberal assumptions.

> Tuesday, July 17. Martinsburgh, Va. strikers *turned* a freight
> train back, damaging engine & some cars, injuring firemen &
> brakeman.

> Armory plundered. President U.S. ordered out local militia
> [on] appeal of Gov. of W. Va. for protection.

> Momentous strike at Pittsburgh. Gov. of Ohio called upon
> gov. troops for Newark.

> Middle-aged man standing in the drizzling rain . . . said "I
> might as well be shot as to die by slow starvation, for it will
> amount to this in the end."

> The miners of Piedmont joined the strike because their wages
> would not get their families the necessaries of life.

> no longer a private enterprise, Citizens sympathize with strik-
> ers. Car men join . . . Insurgent camp fires blazing around
> freight houses of Pittsburgh.

> Carnage in Pullman—five soldiers wounded. 10 citizens killed
> in Baltimore.

> B & O workmen 90¢ a day & men at Newark . . . desperate.
> Bullet or starvation. By Friday strike had extended along B &
> O & Pa. from Pittsburgh to Balt.

> 21 Tuesday—Pittsburgh 14 killed, mostly women and chil-
> dren.

These telegraph jottings nervously traced what Lloyd and millions of Americans believed was the beginning of a class war presaging the "final disintegration of society." "Present laws and present tendencies," Lloyd noted, "will make an end of free government
in this country. Our gov[ernment] must be changed *in the right way.* It
is only the people who can do that." What made the strike so alarm-
ing was not only the national scale of the violence, but also the new
alignment of forces: workers against railroad managers, artisans and
mechanics defending their moral economy against new businessmen, the deserving poor against the filthy rich. "The grandest
political mission to which any man or boss can be committed is to
organize this struggle."[14] But how? For the second time Lloyd saw
the task of educating the American people as falling to publicists like
himself, but now he wondered what the lesson was he ought to
teach.

One meaning of the Great Railroad Strike was clear to Lloyd: the
example of Rome. "Either the attention of the people must be arrested & turned into resolution & resolution into action or else the
country will drift into a convulsion as much greater than the convulsion that wrecked the Roman Empire as the Americans are more numerous than the Romans." From his reading of Froude's *Caesar* the
parallels emerged with inflexible logic: "the dissatisfaction of the
poor . . . the armies . . . of the rich—the Senate . . . the great causes of
the Roman catastrophe."

> As long as there are slaves there is a chance to raise a Spar-
> tacus for the Slaves, and Cataline for himself the cry of
> Emancipation . . . We have already had warnings of the final
> struggle between the rich and poor—just as Rome saw the
> phantoms of the Goths and Vandals at its gates more than
> once before it was overwhelmed by the flood.

How did the lessons of fifth-century Rome apply to nineteenth-
century America? Change a few terms, modify certain social relationships, adapt them to industrial society, and the similarity was
striking. The masters of the modern world were not Caesars but
Vanderbilts and Rothschilds. "They do not care to be Presidents or
Consuls. They want modern power—money—and the control of
corporations." In the Gilded Age political power had become com-

mon, and the plutocrats held the real dominion. "They can buy governors and laws, and laugh at the people going through the forms of government."

Yet political forms without the animating spirit of a civic religion were only dead letters. Acquiring a new public philosophy, in turn, meant jettisoning classical political economy. Adam Smith's original ideas, he could see now, had been pushed by his followers in the intervening century to the point of absurdity. The Manchester school viewed the workingman as a machine to tend machines, and had eliminated people from their equations, substituting aphorisms about the flow of labor and the behavior of the market. Lloyd was now prepared to discard the whole tradition as a pseudoscience. "Economics is not a science," he reminded himself in noting the "unscientific rejection" of the family, education, and the "personal equation" as forces operating on economic man. Following a whole new generation of economists on both sides of the Atlantic whom he began to study, Lloyd aimed his attack at the formalism of the Manchester school. Reading the work of Sir Henry Maine and the American anthropologist Henry Lewis Morgan helped him to question the whole concept of economic man. Henry George found in Adam Smith the principle of the self-regulating market. Lloyd rejected the principle as abstract, unhistorical, and thus false. The mistakes of the classical political economists could be enumerated with precision: "that Gov. has nothing to do with industry except let it alone"; "that reduction of price [occurs] unless demand and rise checks it"; and "that excessive profits are corrected by competition." None of these axioms, he concluded, accounted for the presence of monopoly or the huge profits of unregulated business.

Lloyd was driven to explore the idea of the state as a regulatory agency by his reading in the new English and German social sciences. "Whole theory of state false," he noted in his diary. "State is an enormous force." It was necessary to recognize peoples, races, and nationalities as agents of human betterment. "The States of the world are . . . human forces of the world and whether they move right or wrong, when they do move the consequences will be felt in markets as well as politics." How strange, then, that a Malthusian doctrine still had its adherents. Malthus postulated a world of "don'ts": don't waste human energy; don't tinker with the social order; don't attempt impossible improvements. Lloyd could see that the

Manchester school had proceeded to turn a divine dispensation discovered by Malthus into the rules of an economic game which the
business classes played with a stacked deck. "Dominant Pol. Ec.
written by professors," he complained, echoing Henry George's
sneer at the academicians, "sitting in chairs endowed by the wealthy
merchants and manufacturers of Eng[land] . . . by their enchaining
laws of nature utterly unable to free themselves from their environment . . . in the strictest scientific sense the results of their causes."
Their contribution? "A second hand Pol[itical] Ec[onomy] . . . that by
its complexities and its inefficiencies . . . puts justice out of reach of
any but the wealthiest & most powerful."[15] It was time for a replacement.

Lloyd saw that the new political economy he envisioned would
have to be fashioned from materials furnished by the concept of the
state. Despite his training under Francis Lieber, at first he did not like
the word "state" and continued to use it as signifying a moral collectivity synonymous with the "people" and the "community." Nevertheless, the idea of the state, which he continued to examine, supplied him with two insights. The first was an identification of ethics
with the state as an instrument of the popular will. The second, and
even more important, was a new historical view of alternative social
and legal forms—property arrangements, family patterns, communal groups—that lay far outside the American experience. Seen suddenly from this new historical perspective, the whole human past
seemed to open before him at once richer and deeper than he had
ever imagined. Now a society consisting of atomistic individuals—of
pell-mell, get-ahead, and devil-take-the-hindmost—appeared lacking because it was spiritually impoverished.

What Lloyd, like Bellamy and George, was searching for was a
civic religion. First he determined to explore the possibilities of an
appeal to all Americans, "not to the individuals who are runners in
the race for success—but to the masses who can only succeed in the
right." The people must be taught to love the right and hate the
wrong. By this Lloyd meant something more than the reasoned
identification of self-interest with the public good, something more
akin to the instinctive loyalty of citizens that could be called a "collective conscience." This was the phrase he used in demanding a new
politics. "The basis of political principle for the people must be the
collective conscience—that rule of conduct which has to perceptibly

develop from the Stoicism of the Greeks through the morality of the Romans into the Christianity of modern days itself now crystallizing into new forms."

Lloyd's collective conscience could be implanted in a variety of citizens, one of whom was the liberal independent like himself. Political watchdogs, the independents nevertheless tended to consider themselves conservators of tradition, and alone would never be adventurous enough to challenge the reign of privatism. Their ranks needed reinforcements from the solid yeomanry and workingmen of the nation who could provide the muscles and sinews for building the new republic according to the dictates of the collective conscience. The average citizen, however, confused, misled, or otherwise engaged, required an education in a new science of society. Lloyd then would teach him.

Meanwhile an atmosphere of repression hanging heavily over Chicago following the Great Railroad Strike dampened Lloyd's spirits. As Henry George plunged ahead with the writing of *Progress and Poverty*, Lloyd looked back over the route he had traveled to his present point of intellectual isolation and succumbed to melancholy. "The events of my life—my life has no events—" he complained to Keenan, "a few new books read, 365 columns a year written of financial slush, a *very few* cents saved against the old age that I may cheat Time out of, a new baby, no new friends—except the baby, the gradual extirpation of the—let us call them theories of my green days." Beneath the self-mockery his disappointment was real. Taking stock of his marriage and career after five years, he felt that the early promise of both had worn a bit thin, that even with an affectionate wife and an openhanded father-in-law he had not conspicuously succeeded in realizing his youthful dream of power without obligation. Yet he had managed to discard a number of his less useful ideas and now caught a glimpse of the outlines of a new social philosophy. Whatever the costs, he would continue.

4

THE RELIGION OF SOLIDARITY

FOR EDWARD BELLAMY the seventies were also years of preparation. In spite of his small salary and the limited forum provided by the *Union*, he was satisfied with his "competence" and the freedom to compose most of his editorial matter at home. For ten years he continued to live with his parents, an eligible but elusive bachelor whose odd silences and erratic habits, disregard of routine and impatience with trifling talk made his presence something of a challenge. He was apt to write his editorials and reviews in any room in the house that suited his muse and leave piles of manuscript and books everywhere. Far into the night after the family had retired he sat propped up in bed, scribbling plots for the short stories he had begun to write into one of several lined notebooks. In the morning, just as he might be needed for an errand or a household chore, he was nowhere to be found, having slipped out for a walk in the fields, returning unannounced to take up his work again.

His parents knew the torment his disease caused him. There were days when he lay on his bed feverish and drained of energy. But they also knew better than to sympathize lest they invite an outburst of cold rage. "You know if there is one thing above another which that

young man abhors it is anything in the shape of sympathy," his father warned Edward's brothers in counseling a discreet silence.[1]
Even his mother, to whom he was closest, reproached him for his
"extreme reticence," which, she complained, kept him far "out at
sea" in his dealings with people, and she urged him without success
to talk more freely about himself.[2]

Bellamy's only confidants were his notebooks into which he
poured his private thoughts. Sometimes he personified his journals
as grave companions and witnesses to his "decorous fancies, sober
imaginings, goodish sentiments, which will stand publication, which
the Philistines will approve," reserving for another diary the role of
fellow-rakehell and conspirator in dark doings: "God damn you, you
are the journal I can confide in . . . you, old boy, are confidant of
wicked moments of careless, reckless, drunken, blasphemous moods
when I have creation or creators for my contempt or laughter."[3]

Nemesis continued to stalk him in its many guises that demanded a variety of defenses. One of his strategems was borrowed
from his mother's Calvinist belief in life as a preparation for eternity.
What he called fore-knowledge—the awareness of the time and circumstances of one's death—might blunt the sword of Damocles, he
reasoned, and in his notebook explored an idea for a short story in
which a spokesman from Mars lectures earthlings on their misplaced
confidence in forgetfulness as a means of cheating death. "It seems
queer, unspeakably childish in you actually to imagine that such ignorance adds to your happiness," the Martian remarks. "The terror
of death consists greatly in its sudden breaking in upon all our hopes
and plans. With us there is gradual preparation for it and . . . no
shock." Such a race of supermen organize their lives around the
precise knowledge of their deaths and thus circumvent terror by cen-
tering both their lives and their communities on a pleateau of the
senses too arid for the "lofty dreams of youth" and all other "extravagant aspirations." With the coming of this perfect race everyone
could take the measure of his own future and cultivate a "settled
calm and restful balance of the faculties."[4]

Though he craved such certitude, Bellamy knew that it required a
more systematic organization of his beliefs than he had yet managed
to arrange. "There are times," he wrote as if by way of apology,
"when a man's vagabond instincts rise in terrible insurrection
against all the stable conservative habits and circumstances of his life

which [bear] him down." But these moments of rebellion were soon followed by an "acute realizing sense" of his own mortality. "What an unutterably funny spectacle we mortal men present," he wrote in another passage. "We stroll along side by side gaily disporting, gravely plodding in fine apparel and fine spun refinement of companionship. Yet we cannot see where we put down our feet. We know there will come a step—it may well be the very next—beyond which we shall take no other but of a sudden drop eternal fathoms deep."[5] Meditations like these, recalling Jonathan Edwards's arrows of death flying "unseen at noon," traced a closed circle as flight from Nemesis returned him to his point of origin.

When Bellamy left his father's church and abandoned his mother's faith, there began a period in his life which he later described as one of "profound anxiety and longing almost to sickness," as he, like the young William James in these same years, experienced the psychic shock of breaking parental bonds. He kept a record of his search for a substitute faith in his notebooks. The theme to which he returned obsessively was the dual nature of the self, its divisibility into what he termed the "personal" and the "impersonal" self. The personal self, he observed in sounding a theme he would repeat over and over again, was of "comparative infinitesimality . . . comprising merely personal conceptions." Each individual, however, housed a second self, an abiding personality, infinite, eternal, and in the final analysis the only true self. Thus people, if they were at all like himself, lived a "double life," one of pure sensation and absorption in the moment, and a second larger life of pure contemplation divorced from the personal. His Gilded Age contemporaries, squirming in the grip of powerful materialist forces, were prisoners of the partial and the selfish, getting and spending as though there were no tomorrow. "As the world now wags a man of no great mental or moral sensitiveness is happiest. I believe the time will come, through more perfect development of our universal sympathies for taking hold of infinite things, when the keenest minds and the most sensitive natures will find full compensation for their pains in mighty exhilarations."[6] But that time of millennial expectation was not yet. Americans had first to learn the limitations of individualism.

The human mind—again if his own experience was typical—becomes aware of the infinite side of its nature when the second self suddenly announces its presence and draws the lonely individual "into the realms of infinity and impersonality." The precise meaning of this state of dissociation Bellamy found difficult to describe. He tried changing the terminology by referring to the "self" and the "not self," and even wrote imaginary dialogues in which the questioner asks: "Is then, this conscious yet impersonal being whom you claim as the real essence of every man the one God and Sovereign of the Universe?" And receives this reply: "I can only guess at that. To my apprehension this, my true self, has the aspect of infinity and seems to be all." In these exalted moods he would urge himself to "seek a home, a center, a more ultimate ego in the universe." At such times all nature seemed to reflect the "double life"—"overcast skies, gloomy seas awake the same desire to lose the personal in the universal of nature, as do bright skies and glittering waters."[7] Then the mind approached another Copernican revolution that promised to free it for a leap to a new level of consciousness.

Gradually his scattered impressions gathered coherence in the years after 1874 when he left his father's church. He collected them in a rambling essay, "The Religion of Solidarity," which he refused to publish, taking a perverse pleasure instead in envisioning himself as an old man "holding in shrivelled hands these pages grown yellow with the lapse of many years." "The Religion of Solidarity" nevertheless marked the focal point, not simply of his immediate religious and psychological interests, but also of his concern with the larger life of the imagination from which all of his social criticism would be drawn.

The informing premise of "The Religion of Solidarity" is the human instinct for perfect communication with the infinite, the drive to break through the barriers of time and circumstance that prevent the individual from joining with the cosmic. This "restless and discontented element," uncomfortable in its narrow confinement in the personality, seeks an escape and snaps the slender ties attaching it to its twin. "It is homesick for a vaster mansion than the personality affords."[8] The yearning for the infinite, Bellamy argued, can be found in all people, sometimes taking the form of a "veritable orgasm" of desire, at other times assuming the shape of memory—"some ruined specimen of ancient handiwork, some dead city or deserted site"—offering release from the self shut up in today. Suddenly the individual grows "strange to terrestrial things and seeks refuge out of the body," until "with a start and a wrench" the personality with its

THE RELIGION OF SOLIDARITY

"pigmy standards" again asserts itself. The meaning of these strange double states was clear: people have more in common with the universal life toward which they are mysteriously drawn than with their own "isolated and incommodious" personalities.

How could the ephemeral experience of universal solidarity be caught and held? Bellamy pointed to several "doorways" to the mystical experience: the "sexual relation" with its resolution of mutual antagonisms; a more refined "sex of the intellect" or confluence of souls; and the embrace of the family in which the rough edges of personality are worn away by time and intimacy. Above all, he was persuaded, solidarity was a moral state to be compassed by purposeful endeavor. The life of solidarity could be planned and sustained by cultural habit. "It remains for us, drawing forth our partially latent universal instincts, to develop into a consciousness as coherent, definite, and indefeasible as that of our individual lives, the all-identical life of the universe within us." The new vistas thus opened to mankind would necessarily include action as well as contemplation. Neither the Indian mystic nor the American go-getter could serve as models of behavior in the society he imagined, but only the complete man who could view life both microscopically and telescopically. Not Alexanders or Caesars, Savonarolas or St. Teresas, but serene and selfless citizens moved by the instinct of cohesion which "manifested in men . . . takes the form of loyalty or patriotism, philanthropy or sympathy." If the American people could be directed toward such a state of spirituality, then for the first time in history utopia would become a distinct possibility.

In "The Religion of Solidarity" Bellamy's revolt against romantic egocentricity ended in a retreat into mysticism. He had come to suspect the romantic rebel with his "bundle of mental and psychical experiences." In Europe the romantic revolt had culminated in the "mad self-assertion" of a Byron or a Baudelaire. In America, where its range was narrowed by evangelical Protestantism, it had produced a politics and a morality of "inexpressible loneliness." The romantic idealists, convinced of their centrality in a benevolent universe, had turned outward for confirmation of their assessment of the cosmos. Such self-assurance seemed to Bellamy unwarranted and in any case pointless. The coincidence of the Civil War and the arrival of a mechanistic and morally neutral view of the universe had upset the balance which the transcendentalists had assumed permanent. The analytical mind—his own, for example—must now turn inward to itself, and with a strenuosity which the transcendentalists could never muster, explore its own recesses in the hope that newly discovered psychological techniques would disclose a true moral philosophy. This was Bellamy's method from then on: probing the depths of the inner life and attempting to assemble intuitions into a coherent ethical system. There would be no place for tragedy in his design, no room for the monomania of a Captain Ahab or the diabolism of a Roger Chillingworth. The life of solidarity as he first glimpsed it ten years before *Looking Backward* was to be pastoral comedy set in utopia, where harmony reigns and there is no guilt or sorrow, no deprivation, loneliness, or death. This is the "good place" that Julian West discovers in the year 2000.

It was easy to apply the Religion of Solidarity in dismissing the Gilded Age as an orgy of humbug, but the principles of the true republic were harder to find. Bellamy's sense of political impotence stemmed from his certainty that the moral absolutes of his childhood were no longer relevant to an age of industrial consolidation. The Civil War had damaged beyond repair the sanctity of the private conscience, and the man of exquisite moral sensibility, once a hero in the antebellum age, now appeared in a dimmer light. Encased in their invulnerable selves, the veterans of the moral reform wars seemed to have acted less as liberators of the spirit than as noble despots unwilling to sacrifice private certitude for the preservation of the Union. As he duly noted the failures of Reconstruction and tallied them in the arithmetic of the Religion of Solidarity, Bellamy also reexamined the assumptions of Emerson's generation, along with the absolutist temperament that had made them with such great confidence. His medium was the short story, which now furnished the vehicle for his philosophizing. In a story entitled "The Boy Orator," which he never published, he explored the moral dilemmas of action from principle.

Joseph Claiborne, the boy orator in the fable, is an eighteen-year-old Garrisonian abolitionist canvassing western Massachusetts on the eve of Lincoln's election. The son of an antislavery pioneer and the product of a lyceum culture, Joseph is nevertheless a naturally shy and inarticulate disciple who achieves eloquence only in a state of self-hypnosis induced by pondering accounts of the atrocities of southern slaveowners. Before each lecture he secludes himself and meditates on horror tales of mutilation and murder until, sympathizing abstractly with the slave victim, he is filled with a poetry of denunciation. About politics he knows and cares nothing. "I know slavery and that's all I know," he tells his host, a political abolitionist who has been questioning him closely on Lincoln's chances.[9] His sponsor pronounces him a fool, but Joseph, like his perfectionist teachers, thrives on antagonism. "His electricity required the opposition of a negative body to discharge itself." With the self-assurance of the morally innocent, Joseph retires to his room to prepare his performance, unaware that he is about to make a terrifying discovery that will change his life.

Joseph's favorite atrocity tale concerns a degenerate white boy his own age who brutally whipped his slave companion, pausing now and then to force his victim to his knees to beg forgiveness for an unnamed crime. This time, however, Joseph's experience is alarmingly different: instead of identifying with the black victim, he feels an almost sexual thrill of absolute power along with the white tormentor.

> The very intensity with which he sympathized with the slave heightened the sweet voluptuousness that thrilled through his shuddering nerves at fancying himself the master and tyrant. It was as if a devilish plant had sprung out of the very hotbed of his indignation and pity [and] by subtle chemistry had now transformed their bitter and fiery juices into sensuous intoxicating fumes. The brutal reveries held him by irresistible fascination till the new abhorrent lust had flowed through every vein.

Joseph rushes horrified to the mirror to confront the devil but sees only a pale frightened face staring back "as if he had been turned outside himself and saw demons looking out his windows." Gradually his terror subsides, and by a desperate act of will he rallies his principles which have been scattered "by this sudden appearance of a traitor in the center of the camp." That evening on the platform he surpasses all of his previous performances. To his listeners he appears to be wrestling with an invisible demon. "His antagonist was himself, out of whom with fiery invective, argument, illustrations, appeal, he was striving with frantic earnestness to cast out the lust of slavery." He finishes to tumultuous applause but aware, now that the circuit to the divine has been broken, that he is a fraud who all along has hungered for absolute power without knowing it. "Never so much as tonight had he given himself up to the pleasure of gratified vanity." Joseph has been betrayed by the discovery of evil in himself.

At this point the narrative thread is broken, and the story resumes ten years later—five years after Appomattox—in a shabby boardinghouse in Pittsfield where Joseph, now thoroughly corrupted by self-knowledge, is preparing to leave for Brazil, the last refuge of slavery in the Western Hemisphere. He is taking with him $3,500 with which to indulge his perverted taste for tyranny. To his friend, an ex-Confederate who has accepted defeat and emancipation, he explains that unfortunately southerners born into a slave system and inhibited by economic interest had never truly savored the pleasures of absolute ownership of a human being. "No sir, a man must be born and bred in a free land, in a turbulent angular democracy like this Massachusetts of ours, to enjoy with a keen palate the rich cloying sweetness of exercising pure despotism over his fellows." His conversion to satanism, Joseph continues, is simple. Abstract sympathy such as he felt for the slaves masks a potential tyranny. "There is only a very narrow margin between a morbid aversion for a thing and a morbid attraction to it. One is always in danger of passing from one extreme to the other. A man's feelings, you know, are subject to the law of the see-saw." The balance of Joseph's own nature has been permanently tipped toward the demonic, and he is off to Brazil to seek immolation for his former innocence by buying a slave.

In this unfinished sketch left buried in his notebooks Bellamy was reassessing the psychology of reform of the prewar generation, both the moment of revelation and the false premises on which it rested. In its transcendental and evangelical versions the mystical moment or conversion experience afforded insight into the beneficent order of the universe. The isolated sensibility experiences a brief but complete union with all being and in so doing discovers new capacities for good. Through communication with the divine the self is moved to moral action.

Bellamy rejected this proposition. What Joseph Claiborne sees staring back at him from the mirror is the evil side of his own nature, a presence too strong to be denied. The moment of revelation, which in transcendental and Christian doctrine discloses a benevolent universe, has been inverted by Bellamy in an insight closer to the dark imaginings of a Jonathan Edwards or a Nathaniel Hawthorne than to the optimism of an Emerson or Theodore Parker. Bellamy never finished the story, perhaps because he sensed in his melodramatic handling of the theme of initiation into evil a paralyzing dilemma of his own making. In a world where pure sympathy breeds pure tyranny no moral action is possible. Translated into political terms the Religion of Solidarity and the dozens of fantasies it spawned provided no solutions for an age suffering from moral declension. Bellamy might continue to denounce the corrupt practices of Gilded Age politicians and to call for "a new supply of some regal intellects and men of magnetic force," as Henry Demarest Lloyd was doing in Chicago. But if politics, as he insisted, was only a "monstrous game" played by seedy gamblers with "sharp practices," then what good did it do to demand a new set of players? The Religion of Solidarity, in fact, offered no very useful guides for would-be reformers. It had been designed for a society in which politics and programs had become superfluous.

Meanwhile prospects for meaningful reform of American society appeared to him bleak. "Reform," once the finest word in the English language, Bellamy lamented, had been cheapened beyond recognition. "The specimen self-styled 'reformer' of this day is everywhere recognized as a politician who relies upon slander and hypocrisy as his sole weapon."[10] The country, in fact, seemed to him one vast arena for "low principles," bribery, deceit, and the "traditions of dissimulation worthy of a Metternich." Mired in a deepening disenchantment, Bellamy, like Henry George across the continent, professed to find in an American yeomanry living close to the soil the last defense against encroaching materialism and selfishness. The agrarian migration to the metropolis, he predicted with all the passion of a Bolingbroke, presaged the end of the virtuous republic. Cities manufactured "shoddy" for a people ruled by an itch to buy and sell. The decline in American public health could be traced directly to "the substitution of the indoor life of the shop, store, mill, for the vigorous agricultural life of former generations."[11] Cities overstrained the nerves and weakened the muscles of any people who preferred "living by its wits to living by its hands." Cities were the scenes of "harassing ambitions" and "intensifying strife."

In the radical reactionary voice of a descendant of the Country party, Bellamy registered the same fear of sprawling cities that led Henry George to dream of a cottage in the California hills and Henry Demarest Lloyd to seek country peace in the woods and fields of Winnetka. Bellamy also joined them in deploring the loss of elbow-room in a still comparatively new country where land should have been plentiful. Gazing out of his windows in downtown Springfield, he could see ramshackle tenements of raw wood crammed into empty lots, "wedged in amongst other buildings in a way to shut out all pure circulation of air if not most of the light of heaven." In these "choked-up" huddles lived a new class of "city proletaires" in "ignorant and vicious intercourse," raw recruits for the coming revolution.

Bellamy reserved his sharpest barbs for the commercial classes, who measured all worth by the dollar sign. "Snobbery and shoddy, toadyism and venality, have made such public characters as Franklin and Washington and Lincoln almost an impossible conception so far have [the American people] drifted from their fast anchorage in unimpeachable integrity."[12] Incorruptible as the American yeoman might be, it seemed to Bellamy that left alone to contend with commercialism, he could never prevent the nation's slide into degeneracy. As the decade wore on, Bellamy found himself returning to the model of the Founding Fathers who had presumably managed the early republic with selflessness and good sense.

His editorials for the *Union* showed only a casual acquaintance with economics and, at first, little understanding of the plight of the unemployed. As the depression advanced on the centennial year and business in the Connecticut Valley shut its doors, he pronounced "dull times" a blessing in disguise, a needed check on the "feverish intensity" of American bsiness life, "compelling the busy workers to take life easy."[13] He urged workingmen to use their enforced leisure to read Cairnes's *Some Leading Principles of Political Economy* so that they might understand that trade unions could never succeed in enlarging a fixed wage-fund. Could government action help restore confidence in a shattered economy? "We have no hopes from legislation . . . Everything of this description is liable to excite new complaints."[14] In place of legislative interference he recommended the simple solution prescribed by the Religion of Solidarity—the elimination of selfishness which was "the curse of the whole matter." With this moral platitude as an organizing premise his clichés fell neatly into line: the need for more "self-government of a firmer tone"; cultivation of "a broader and every way better sense of responsibility to the community"; and the duty to aid the less fortunate that fell to those classes "where there is most intelligence, wealth and social influence."[15]

Like George and Lloyd in the depression years, Bellamy feared the "yawning" chasm between capital and labor which, in some measure at least, could be blamed on the "pernicious communist teachings" of demagogues. Less than ten years before the appearance of *Looking Backward* he wrote an editorial, "Communism Boiled Down," in which he raised all the historicist objections to collectivism that his millennialist lyceum lecture had ignored.

> The cure-all for our labor and capital frictions and smash-ups seems, then, to be this, to put into the hands of government all the carrying, transfer, exchange, productive industry of the country, its manufactures, agriculture, trade and its entire use of capital; permitting no private employment of this for personal profit . . . Now go to, ye dreamers, and find such material for a government equal to such an administration of this or any other country, in intelligence and honesty. Here we would have a civil service to stagger the immortals! No such material exists on the face of the globe. And if it did, how are we to get this machine on the track and set it running? Well may the answer come back—we don't know! You might as well fly from the haystack to the moon. For a man to neglect his business and his family to study up such a scheme as this, is lunacy or worse.[16]

As the country slid deeper into depression, however, Bellamy's sympathies shifted from management, whose social outlook appeared callous, to the operatives who, even in their "discontent and hostility," made a good case for higher wages and better working conditions. "They are made to suffer a reduction in wages and consequent discomforts," he exclaimed with the force of sudden discovery, "simply because they are in the power of their employers."[17] No

wonder the laboring classes showed signs of "feverish, moody irritation." Too many American families—"uncomplaining families in
the most critical condition"—stood on the verge of starvation. As the
number of strikes and walkouts rose dramatically in the centennial
year, Bellamy could not bring himself to denounce the motives of
the workers even though he disapproved their methods. Yet American workingmen, he was convinced, could never solve the problems
of a malfunctioning economy even though their justifiable anger
might well serve as a warning.

His working-class neighbors in nearby Chicopee, Bellamy might
have learned had he troubled to examine their lives, held values and
cherished hopes not so very different from his own. Many of them
were recent arrivals from Canada and Europe, and in coming to
America they broke ties to the land and the workplace as small
holders and artisans forced off their plots and out of their shops by
mechaniz₁ tion. Arrived here to recoup, they joined their native-born
counterp₁ rts in attempting to knit together again the strands of individual liberty, economic independence, and communal obligation
that had formed the texture of their fathers' lives. While middling-
rank Americans like young Bellamy generally ignored their efforts,
American workingmen, both foreign- and native-born, were responding to the depression of the 1870s by assuming an adversarial
posture with respect to corporate capitalism and turning to unions
for control of the workplace, to farmer-labor coalitions for a political
forum, and to a host of neighborhood organizations—credit unions,
night schools, mutual savings associations, and consumer cooperatives—for community solidarity.

Bellamy approached the "social question," as his generation was
beginning to call it, as a problem in restoring a harmony of interests
which fell to the sober and high-minded citizens drawn from the
middling ranks of American society and determined to reverse the
anarchical tendencies of finance capitalism. These true patriots were
the guardians of civic virtue without which a republic could not long
survive. Their numbers were few, and they were now in danger of
political dispossession. Hemmed in by a new wealthy class on one
side and the unreasoning poor on the other, they held the balance of
power in modern society. They alone possessed the impartiality
needed to save the nation: they were at once the centurions at the
gate of the republic and acolytes at the altar of the Religion of Soli-

darity. A century earlier they had fought for national independence; within memory they had fought again to preserve the Union. Would they stand idly by or could they rally once more to save the country?

By 1877 Bellamy's fragile health had broken completely, and he was forced to resign from the *Union* and agree to a restorative voyage to Hawaii prescribed by his parents. He continued to keep a journal and to fill it, not with accounts of his long trip around the Horn or the exotic Sandwich Islands, but with the same detached musings of a mind wholly engrossed in other matters. Travel, he decided, made a man an aristocrat by sharpening class distinctions. "At home our relations to people are so much habituated that we are not conscious of their causes and motives, but as we travel, we meet constantly new persons with whom our relations must be established." Without making any new friends himself and only slightly improved in health, he was back in Chicopee Falls within the year to pick up a project he had been considering for some time, a book on Shays's Rebellion, another critical point in the history of the nation that might conceivably shed light on the present industrial crisis. The events of Shays's Rebellion offered the double advantage of a century's distance in time and cultural proximity in location in the misfortunes of hardscrabble Berkshire farmers. He had already sketched out a story line that showed how sharp were his fears of class violence but at the same time his reluctance to join the reformers. "Story illustrating ideas of liberty, equality, fraternity and rights of labor," he had written. "Scene taken from the late riots. One of the characters man who is finishing great book and has fear of death before it is finished which makes him a coward though naturally brave."[18] *The Duke of Stockbridge* was not the "great book" he himself intended to write, nor did it deal with the "late riots" of 1877. The novel was nevertheless conceived as a commentary on the contemporary social scene and its hero as the prototype of the modern patriot with whom Bellamy's hopes now lay. In the "Romance of Shays Rebellion," as he subtitled his novel, he was canvassing at a historical distance the possibilities for effective action in his own day. His conclusions were not encouraging. On the surface the novel is a story of a revolution that failed, but in a deeper sense it is the story of the failure of politics.

The Duke of Stockbridge recounts the abortive revolution of the followers of Daniel Shays in western Massachusetts in 1786. There are three classes in Bellamy's Stockbridge: the gentry or court party, privileged and haughty; the yeomanry comprised of small farmers, mechanics, and artisans; and a nascent proletariat made up of local foundry workers and landless war veterans. The gentry rules Stockbridge through an alliance of leading families cemented by marriage. Like their counterparts a century later, they are nouveaux riches, gorged on war profits and suffering from the social myopia of their class. Squire Woodbridge summarizes their ambition in a simile that Bellamy would use again even more effectively in *Looking Backward.* "There had been a little runaway, and he had been pitched out on his head. Let him once get his grip on the lines again, and the whip in his hand, and there would be some fine dancing among the leaders, or his name was not Jahleel Woodbridge, Esquire, and the whipping post on the green was nothing but a rosebush."[19] Their recently acquired power has hardened the gentry into self-centered oligarchs who flaunt their unearned superiority and manage the affairs of the town with a contemptuous disregard of the common good. Like the robber barons of a later age, they are disposed to exploit the habit of deference but are unable to fulfill their roles as natural rulers.

Arrayed against the gentry in Stockbridge are the hard-pressed yeoman farmers and artisans who have watched the golden days of wartime prosperity darken into economic depression. Only a generation or two removed from the English peasant, they still cling to the "inherited instincts of servility." Uneducated and politically inarticulate, without leaders and wholly lacking in social vision, they seem at first poor revolutionary material. "They had thought little and vaguely, but had felt much and keenly, and it was evident the man who could voice their feelings, however partially, however perversely and for his own ends, would be the master of their actions." But without the leaders to set them the example of altruism the yeomanry is also blinded by self-interest. Nostalgically the farmers recall the Edenic war years when, as one of them explains, "rich folks and poor folks lived together kinder neighborly . . . an' 'cordin tew scripter," but they have neither the wit nor the inclination to discover the cause of their present plight. Patient, docile, long-suffering, they are also potentially surly, mean-spirited, and dangerous if driven too far into personal hardship. Honesty in the governed, Bellamy makes clear, is no substitute for honor among the governors.

Stockbridge also contains an embryonic proletariat in the iron foundry workers and landless veterans whose army service has served to "exasperate them against the pretensions of the superior class, without availing to eradicate their inbred instincts of servility in the presence of the very men they hated." Their leader is a dema- gogue named Hubbard, clearly intended as the forerunner of the modern labor agitator, who can teach them to destroy but not to cre- ate. Hubbard's philosophy is a crude Machiavellianism. "It's all in a nutshell," he tells the workers. "If we don't give them the devil, they'll give us the devil. Take your choice." No true community will be forthcoming from the likes of Hubbard and his myrmidons for all his efforts to mold them into "good insurrectionary" material.

Into a postrevolutionary society riddled with class antagonisms comes Bellamy's hero, Captain Perez Hamlin, the patriot who has fought the war, not in local skirmishes with the militia, but in great battles with Washington's army where he has learned the lessons of leadership. As he rides into Stockbridge after an absence of ten years, his buff uniform faded and threadbare but with the habit of authority written on his face, it is evident that here is a man apart. Army service, that "school of democratic ideas," has transformed the son of a poor farmer into a natural leader of men.

> It was not . . . alone any details of dress, but a certain distinc-
> tion in air and bearing about Perez, which had struck them.
> The discipline of military responsibility, and the officer's
> constant necessity of maintaining an aspect of authority and
> dignity, before his men, had left refining marks upon his face,
> which distinguished it as a different sort from the counte-
> nances about him with their expressions of pathetic stolidity,
> or boorish shrewdness.

Perez Hamlin is at once recognizable as the archetype of the Mugwump-Progressive hero, a figure particularly congenial to a dis- placed New England intellectual elite after the Civil War. He appears in various attitudes in the fictional portraits of Bellamy's contem- poraries and successors. In the novels of John W. DeForest, John Hay, Edward Everett Hale, and Thomas Wentworth Higginson, as in the later productions of Paul Leicester Ford and Winston Churchill, he is given the role of victor over the forces of corruption, a moral champion who triumphs through force of example. As the ex-Confederates Carrington in Henry Adams's *Democracy* and Basil Ransome in Henry James's *The Bostonians*, the hero's range of effective action is circumscribed and his high principles neutralized by political impotence. Whatever the scope assigned him, the Mugwump hero is an embodiment of the ideal of the natural aristocrat whose virtue and personal magnetism lift him above the reach of petty politicians. He is the leader who while wielding power remains uncontaminated by it and who stoops to play politics only to finally transcend it. Bellamy's version of the Mugwump hero is colored by a pessimistic appraisal of democratic politics similar to that of Adams and James. As a leader without a following Perez Hamlin is doomed to failure.

The course of the revolution traced by Bellamy follows an all but predetermined sequence from the collapse of the old regime through a rule of the moderates to a reign of terror, thermidorean reaction, and, finally, restoration. The reduced scope imposed by provincial rebellion does not significantly alter the pattern first discerned by the Romantic historians of the French Revolution. Berkshire County is peopled with Irreconcilables, native Girondins and *Enragés*, and even the inevitable Man on Horseback. The action rises from the first hesitant steps of the rebels, gains momentum with their early successes, falters as the revolutionary party splits, and is dramatically reversed with the resurgent counterrevolution and the return to power of a repressive legitimacy. The scale of *The Duke of Stockbridge* is miniature backcountry rebellion, but the informing design and dramatic point are those of Carlyle. Bellamy's diagnosis is likewise a moral rather than a purely historical one. There is little doubt that if the people are to be delivered from themselves, Perez Hamlin will be their savior.

After a premature attempt at counterrevolution falters, the nerve of the court party fails and Perez rules by force. Nominally a member of a triumvirate committee of correspondence, he is in fact the single figure of authority in the town, incorporating in himself executive, judicial, administrative, and police functions. Government is reduced to its simplest terms, and Perez, like the administrators of the utopian state in *Looking Backward*, works with directness, efficiency, and a rough-hewn justice. For the moment complex forms of law are unnecessary because the spirit of equity is embodied in Perez, a kind of provincial Patriot King. Soon, however, it becomes clear that Perez, or the "Duke," as he is now called, lacks a permanent power base. With the gentry temporarily subdued, the rebels divide into two factions, a smaller party of rural Girondins who are convinced that matters have gone far enough, and a larger group of Jacobins "without a stake in the community" who lack the initiative or the incentive to get out of debt. "As a fever awakes to virulent activity the germs of disease in the body, so revolution in the political system develops the latent elements of anarchy." The restless and discontented form a band of "regulators" who threaten to abolish property rights but spend most of their time lounging on the village green and consuming Squire Edwards's supply of rum. The Duke is trapped between the rabble and a resurgent gentry impatiently awaiting the arrival of Governor Bowdoin's troops and the opportunity of stringing him up. When the government in Boston offers conciliatory terms and dispatches the militia to secure their enforcement, the revolution stalls. The Duke is faced with imminent dethronement, if not at the hands of the gentry, then by the more dangerous forces of irresponsible radicalism.

The blame for Shays's Rebellion, Bellamy suggests with the industrial upheavals of the 1870s clearly in mind, lay with an atomistic society which by fostering greed in the ruling class inexorably drove the masses to revolt. For the Shaysites as for all revolutionaries, however, ultimate defeat is inescapable. The court party organizes an expeditionary force of local *jeunesse dorée*, drives the Duke into exile, and kills him. His death signals the onset of restoration: the tax collector makes his rounds as before, the red flag flies from the ridgepoles of farmhouses condemned for taxes, and the sound of the sheriff's whip is heard on the village green. The revolution is over.

The Duke of Stockbridge is Bellamy's statement on the impossibility of revolution and the insufficiency of history. The failure of the Shaysites is plainly intended as a lesson for a post-Civil War generation. The fictional anatomy of revolution discloses the futility of class politics and secular programs. When the natural leaders of society become so hardened by wealth and power that they ignore the sufferings of the people and turn to repressive measures, a revolution is inevitable. But the masses need leadership, a commodity not to be found in their ranks. The only hope for revolution rests on the command of an outsider—the independent classless man of virtue. Such a leader is able to win the temporary allegiance of the revolutionaries through superior personal force, but unless he can succeed in converting them to his own lofty standards of solidarity and impersonality, he cannot hold them. Once the destructive phase of revolution is over, they have no moral foundation on which to build a better society, no sacred devotion on which to unite. They too become corrupted, betray the revolution, and destroy their leader. Though not fully aware of his redemptive role in a moral drama that transcends profane history, the leader seeks to redeem the people by the power of his example and train them to the task of building the just society. He tries to lift them above class interest and political hatred, but they fail to understand him. In the end the leader is abandoned to his heroic but suicidal mission. Revolutions cannot succeed.

The Duke of Stockbridge is the last will and testament of a disillusioned observer of the Gilded Age scene. When Bellamy finished the novel, he closed a door on a phase of his intellectual development. He had tried politics and found it wanting. And in a larger sense he had written his novel as a rejection of the world of history and historical time, replacing them with the moral diagrams and the religious fables of "romance." His Religion of Solidarity had failed to furnish him with the guidelines for reform. With the decline of his hopes for a change in the moral climate of the Gilded Age, however, came a new sense of artistic freedom given now to his "other" self to explore the "double life" unhampered by social considerations and freed from fidelity to fact. From now on utopia as a private model in the mind rather than the editorial critique of policymakers would consume all his energies. In the next six years he would publish five more romances and some two dozen short stories in an extended campaign to outflank reality. A fantastic science-fiction machine for blotting out memory—flashes of extrasensory perception transfiguring loneliness into intimacy—a mysterious psychical alchemy for distilling hope from despair—all devices for effecting what he called "a sudden transformation of an otherwise hopeless situation." Nearly all of his work now came to center on the retrieval from imminent disaster or escape from Nemesis through magic. "Abracadabra, the conquering word," he wrote in explaining his method. "Let an apparently inevitable and highly tragical situation be carefully developed, to be happily solved by showing the supposed fatal fact, or element, all along supposed to be real, is imaginary."[20] The meaning for social reform as it emerged from Bellamy's fiction in the next few years was unmistakable—solidarity through thaumaturgy.

By 1879, as Henry George finished the final revisions on his gigantic manuscript and Henry Demarest Lloyd recovered from his melancholia and began to study the problem of industrial combination, Bellamy turned aside from political paths to explore his "Might-have-been-land." Nevertheless, his route would take him, as different courses were leading George and Lloyd, to the outskirts of utopia.

5

PROGRESS AND POVERTY

WHILE EDWARD BELLAMY was taking the measure of social crisis in *The Duke of Stockbridge*, across the continent in 1878 Henry George labored to complete the massive structure of *Progress and Poverty*. Events pressed him sharply, and he felt as though he were racing the clock. Hard times in California had been deepened by winter drought and declining industrial production. When the state's railroad managers, taking their cues from eastern lines, announced a series of wage cuts, workers in San Francisco responded with angry meetings and threats of violence. At first their protests stirred little more than the wrath of the propertied defenders of law-and-order, who formed a committee of public safety and armed it with rifles and pick handles with which to defend the railroads. At this, the city's workingmen began to organize in earnest. Their leader was Dennis Kearney, a talented rabble-rouser and turncoat who had carried a club for the railroad barons but now jumped sides to organize the Workingmen's party of California, an upstart third party that threw state politics into disorder. For the flamboyant Kearney and his harebrained third party George had scant respect, but he realized that if he were to find

an opening between Kearney's demagoguery and the calloused poli-
cies of the railroad managers, he would have to work quickly.

There were other distractions that slowed the completion of the
book. Annie was expecting another baby, and George willingly devoted much of his time to her, seldom leaving the house and spending long evenings reading *Middlemarch* to her after concentrated
bursts of writing. His working habits were as casual as ever. He
would lie flat on his couch in the study, cigar jutting straight up,
watching clouds of smoke trail upwards toward the ceiling, until he
found his idea. Then he would leap up and rush to the desk, scribble
furiously for an hour or so, and return to the couch to await further
instructions from his muse. Annie and the boys accepted with good
grace his growing self-absorption, and learned to tolerate the suddenly vacant stare and the lapse in conversation.

The writing proceeded slowly. George was a meticulous crafts-
man who polished his chiseled blocks of argument carefully before
arranging them on a solid foundation. Some evenings after a day at
the desk he would read portions of the manuscript to friends who
dropped in regularly to inspect the ascending structure while he
paced back and forth in the parlor, disheveled, cigar ashes spilling
down his shirtfront, his plump hands shuffling piles of papers and
waving in the air as he explained and elaborated. His study was lined
with over 800 volumes into which he frequently dipped for a fact or
a quotation. But he admitted openly that he read "at" his books instead of approaching them systematically, pulling out of them the
telling example or chance piece of information rather than the informing idea. The principles of his analysis he had already discovered.

The most immediate threat to his book was economic. His fees
from reading gas meters had been reduced to a trickle, and he was
$500 in debt, circumstances which tempted him to put aside work on
the manuscript and undertake a lecture series. His friends, the
handful of newspapermen and politicians who had been converted
to his views on land monopoly, now urged him to form a Land Reform League of California to help spread the word. George, habitually optimistic, saw in the prospect of a series of subscription lectures a means of replenishing the family till. He gave his first lecture
in March 1878 in the city's Metropolitan Temple before a slim audi-

ence who came to hear his explanation of "Why Work Is Scarce, Wages Low and Labour Restless." The proceeds barely covered the cost of the hall, and reluctantly he gave up hope of enlightening his fellow citizens from the podium for a fee.

Still, he hungered for an audience as he watched the class lines in California being pulled taut by working-class protests and the resistance of the comfortable classes. Already he saw himself as a mediator—a lone figure of altruism and good will akin to Bellamy's Duke of Stockbridge—standing between the contending parties and helping to settle their differences in the combined roles of teacher, counselor, and spiritual guide. This sudden discovery prompted him to lay aside the manuscript for a lecture to the Young Men's Hebrew Association on the figure of Moses.

The lecture "Moses," which George would deliver again and again in the course of his career, answered a deep personal need. It clarified for him the organizing scheme for *Progress and Poverty* and his own role as prophet leading a modern pilgrimage out of the land of oppression into the realm of abundance. In features strikingly similar to those given Bellamy's Perez Hamlin he delineated the new hero in history. It was the great achievement of Moses, George believed, to have founded the true commonwealth "whose ideal it was that every man should sit under his own vine and fig tree, with none to vex him or make him afraid." In a piece of historical projection George ascribed to the Jewish people precisely those agrarian virtues—communal sharing, cooperation, family affection—needed to bind a people together. Here the example of Moses could instruct the American people, for Moses had first recognized the wrongfulness of unrestricted private property and had fixed the community's claim to land once and for all. His plan, never carried to fruition in his own lifetime, contained the seed of a solution which a modern age must now plant, cultivate, and harvest.

In his contrasting picture of contemporary America George drew more heavily from the lamentations of Jeremiah than from the original Mosaic example. What had Americans done with their providential bequest? They boasted of freedom and denied it to the poor. They bragged of equality and tolerated inequality. Closer and closer, as he neared the end of his lecture, George brought his audience to the central paradox of the book he was writing: "Beside the glutted warehouse human beings grow faint with hunger and shiver with cold; under the shadow of churches festers the vice that is born of want."[1]

The paradox in the center of his lecture on Moses provided George with direct entry into *Progress and Poverty*. In the opening fable of the introduction, which carried the force of a confessional, he introduced the original average American as he might have been accosted leaving the world of the eighteenth century and asked to predict the nation's future. Surely that man would have described a clearly marked set of "necessary sequences" in the perfecting of the moral talents and material welfare of its citizens. The doctrine of progress bequeathed to the nineteenth century had once seemed common sense, and even after a century it still yielded "haunting visions of higher possibilities."[2] But now George's average man could see in the harsh realities of industrialization another pattern of depression, wasted capital, business distress, and human suffering. Not simply a dream gone smash but a whole system of thought in ruin, the wonderful eighteenth-century engine of progress a shambles, its gears stripped and parts strewn across the landscape. The universal breakdown of the idea of progress, George insisted, proved that there was a common cause of the paradox since it was in all the older and more developed countries of the world—in just those societies where material progress had advanced furthest—that the counter-tendency toward inequality and poverty was most evident.

> The "tramp" comes with the locomotive, and the almshouses and prisons are as surely the marks of "material progress" as are costly dwellings, rich warehouses, and magnificent churches. Upon streets lighted with gas and patrolled by uniformed policemen, beggars wait for the passer-by, and in the shadow of college and library and museum are gathering the more hideous Huns and fiercer Vandals of whom Macaulay prophesied.[3]

Nemesis for George assumed the collective form of the barbarians at the gates of the city, dim figures still, for most Americans, but real enough to one who knew the rootlessness and desperation of the urban poor. A century of American progress had acted as a gigantic wedge splitting society down the middle and leaving a fault line not so different from Karl Marx's division—"at a point intermediate between the top and the bottom, shoving up those above its pathway through the social fabric and crushing those who are below." Here in the unequal exactions of the law of progress lay revealed the "great enigma" of the modern age.

> It is the riddle which the Sphinx of Fate puts to our civilization and which not to answer is to be destroyed. So long as all the increased wealth which modern progress brings goes but to build up great fortunes, to increase luxury and make sharper the contrast between the House of Have and the House of Want, progress is not real and cannot be permanent. The reaction must come.[4]

"The promised land," George added, "flies before us like a mirage." With a final warning against retrogression and relapse he set out through the enemy territory of the classical economists in search of utopia.

The search for the true political economy, George warned his readers, would take them backwards in time and across difficult theoretical terrain, their route crossed by numberless byways and dead ends followed by his predecessors who had entered the domain of economic science only to become hopelessly lost. Some of the pioneer explorers had been charlatans, others mere adventurers and special pleaders who stumbled into an undergrowth of population theories and wage-fund nostrums. Retracing the history of political economy meant following the path back to Adam Smith in order to discover the wrong turning taken by the nineteenth century. All he asked of his readers was common sense and deductive logic as their compasses. Their goal would be a perfectly symmetrical economic theory. Thus at a time when marginalism and the hypotheses of the Austrian school were introducing psychology and an indeterminancy into economics in the attempt to understand the functionings of the market, George led the way back into the eighteenth century in search of a lost world.

He announced his point of departure in his subtitle: *An Inquiry into the Cause of Industrial Depressions and of Increase of Want with Increase of Wealth*. But in order to advance toward an explanation he had to demolish two roadblocks in his path: the wage-fund theory and the population theory of the Reverend Thomas Malthus. To the question of why, in spite of increasing powers of production, wages universally failed to keep pace, the proponents of the wage-fund theory replied that the amount of wages was fixed by the ratio between the number of laborers and the amount of capital available. Why, asked George, had the wage-fund theory come to be accepted? Because of the dominance of a capitalist class convinced against all reason that its own contribution to production was indispensable. Overimpressed with their own limited role in transforming English industrial life, investors and managers had failed to realize that the wages they paid out were not drawn from previously accumulated capital stocks but from current labor continuously expended. This first correction of classical economics, George knew, was crucial, for with the collapse of the foundation of the wage-fund theory the whole Malthusian superstructure would also come crashing down. Accordingly, his first task was to establish beyond any doubt the temporal and the ethical priority of labor by proving "that production precedes enjoyment, that wages are earnings—that is to say, the makings of labor—not the advances of capital," and that workers receive their wages as a "draft" upon the general stock of wealth they are helping to create.

After defining capital in its "common sense" meaning of "wealth devoted to procuring more wealth," George proceeded to give example after example of the priority of labor and its indispensable role in creating capital.[5] Take, first of all, the simplest case of self-employment, the primitive bushman who gathers berries and ground-nuts for his own consumption—his produce constitutes his wages. The same was true of the "lay" aboard whaling ships among sailors who have nothing to offer but their labor. Nor did the situation differ where some men worked for others or where the product remained unfinished or unsold. To clarify his essentially moral argument George turned to his favorite example—the building of a ship.

> It may take a year, or even years, to build a ship, but the creation of value of which the finished ship will be the sum goes on day by day, and hour by hour, from the time the keel is laid or even the ground is cleared. Nor by the payment of

wages before the ship is completed, does the master builder
lessen either his capital or the capital of the community, for
the value of the partially completed ship stands in place of the
value paid out in wages. There is no advance of capital in this
payment of wages.[6]

Capital, George agreed, performed many useful functions—providing plant investment and stimulating the development of laborsaving
machinery—but it was not the source of wages. These the laborer
created as he expended his labor.

This distinction made all the difference for George's theory, since
it allowed him to substitute for the static wage-fund concept his own
model of continuous production that sustained his utopia. Previous
production, he insisted, was *not* essential to present productivity. "It
is only necessary that there should be, somewhere within the circle
of exchange, a contemporary production of sufficient subsistence for
the laborers, and a willingness to exchange this subsistence on which
labor is being bestowed." George's naturally productive community
is constantly reproducing itself. The concept of continuous production pointed directly toward a society composed of men who, at least
in the beginning, combine labor and capital in their own persons and
who therefore work diligently and cooperatively creating the wealth
which justice assigns them with a rough equality. "Imagine such a
suspension of labor in any community," George concluded, "and
you will see how true it is that mankind really lives from hand to
mouth; that it is the daily bread of the community that supplies the
community with its daily bread."[7] With this insight George reached
the top of the first rise in his journey and caught a glimpse of his
goal: the self-regulating community of honest producers free from
artificial restraints and special privileges, world-wide in scope and
utterly simple in its workings. It was now time to confront the corollary of the wage-fund hypothesis, the population theory of Thomas
Malthus.

George attacked Malthus with the savagery of a prisoner trying
to escape the chains of iron law. Unable to challenge the statistical
methods of Malthus, he resorted to an attack on the motives of the
Malthusians. Why had such a vicious theory become so widely believed? Because instead of threatening vested interests, it reassured

them that they were safe from pernicious interference by the community. "For poverty, want, and starvation are by this theory not chargeable either to individual greed or social maladjustments; they are the inevitable results of universal laws, with which, if it were not impious, it were as hopeless to quarrel as with the law of gravitation."[8]

George's plan of attack was simple: without bothering to examine the statistical support for the theory, he proceeded straightway to a denial. Of all the cases of vice and misery cited by Malthus, not one of them could be attributed to an actual increase of the number of mouths to be fed over the power of the accompanying hands to feed them. In every case it was social ignorance or unjust laws or senseless warfare that accounted for human suffering. In India religious superstition and primitive social arrangements were sufficient causes of famine. The same was true of China, where "warfare, tyranny and oppression" flourished. In Ireland, England's rural slum, if the food raised by the peasants had been left for them to eat, "there would have been enough to support in bounteous comfort the largest population Ireland ever had."[9]

Life properly lived, George insisted, does not use up the forces that maintain life. Man, as the Malthusians and Darwinians never ceased to argue, might be an animal, "but he is an animal plus something else." If a metaphor were needed, man was the mythic earth tree with his roots in the ground and his topmost branches brushing the heavens. In a final blast at Malthus, George fell back on unsupported contrary assertion:

> I assert that in any given state of civilization a greater number of people can collectively be better provided for than a smaller. I assert that the injustice of society, not the niggardliness of nature, is the cause of want and misery which current theory attributes to over-population. I assert that new mouths which an increasing population calls into existence requires no more food than the old ones, while the hands they bring with them can in the natural order of things produce more. I assert that, other things being equal, the greater the population, the greater the comfort which an equitable distribution of wealth would give to each individual.[10]

Implicit in these affirmations was George's theory of social development. If increasing wealth accompanied increased population, that fact explained the greater advance of the settled eastern parts of the United States over the relatively empty frontier regions. New and undeveloped areas everywhere were marked by a natural equality but also by a lower standard of living. There might be fewer poor in a new country, but there was also less culture and fewer amenities. George was not prone to romanticize agrarian simplicity. He knew that economic growth and cultural advance were essential in all societies, and that growth depended on achieving a certain density of population that encouraged greater social efficiency. But the answer to the problem, he was now prepared to argue, was not the brutal Malthusian one of allowing nature to winnow the population of the presumably unfit, but one of carefully selecting the right mechanism for spreading population and wealth across the face of the earth.

It had required 150 pages and several months' hard work to reach this point in his analysis, but with the pitfalls of the wage-fund and population theories behind him George turned to explaining and correlating the laws of production with the laws of distribution—that is, setting capital, land, and labor in motion as interest, rent, and wages. Orthodox definitions did not correlate. Let us begin again, George urged, this time following the "natural order" of things. Labor, not capital, is the prime mover of all industrial and agricultural production. And land is its fundamental field of application.

> Labor is the active and initial force, and labor is therefore the employer of capital. Labor can be exerted only upon land, and it is from land that the matter it transmutes into wealth must be drawn. Land is the *condition precedent*, the field and material of labor. The natural order is land, labor, capital; and, instead of starting from capital as our initial point, we should start from land.[11]

Land, then, is the key factor in the *production* of wealth; rent is its equivalent in the *distribution* of wealth. Guided by Ricardo's theory of rent, which, in his view, possessed "the self-evident character of a

geometric axiom," George proceeded to explore the English economist's proposition that "the rent of land is determined by the excess
of its produce over that which the same application can secure from
the least productive in use." George was obliged to redefine rent in
more pointedly ethical terms as an exclusive nonproductive benefit.
"Rent, in short, is the price of monopoly, arising from the reduction
to individual ownership of natural elements which human exertion
can neither produce nor increase."[12] In other words, under any economic system based on private ownership of land, monopolistic rent
inevitably drains off the wealth-producing powers of a people.

At last George had uncovered his fundamental principle, the scientific law that to political economy was "what the attraction of gravitation is to physics." Its meaning he illustrated with a deft piece of
algebraic transportation.

$$\text{Produce} = \text{Rent} + \text{Wages} + \text{Interest}$$
$$\text{therefore}$$
$$\text{Produce} - \text{Rent} = \text{Wages} + \text{Interest}[13]$$

In bold relief stood his findings: wages and interest do not, as they
should, depend upon the total produce of labor and capital, but instead on what remains to them after rent is taken out. In effect,
George had borrowed from the classical economists the concept of a
fixed deduction and applied it to ownership of land in order to show
that the rewards assigned to labor and capital were those earnings
left over after the unearned increment of rent had been set aside for
the landowners. Rent, it was at last clear, acted as an enormous drag
on social development and the creation of wealth.

From this point forward in his analytical journey the traveling
grew easier as George's route became more clearly marked. He had
found the source of the present American economic plight and the
answer to the riddle of the Sphinx.

> Thus where the value of land is low, there may be a small
> production of wealth, and yet a high rate of wages and inter-
> est, as we see in new countries. And where the value of land is
> high, there may be a very large production of wealth and yet a
> low rate of wages and interest, as we see in old countries. And

where productive power increases, as it is increasing in all progressive countries, wages and interest will remain as before.[14]

The divided society that emerged from George's revision of classical political economy was dramatically different from the one depicted by Karl Marx. In effect, George had reintroduced the dual distinction so dear to the moral sensibilities of the Jacksonians—the division of society between a landed, unproductive old wealth, on the one hand, and ambitious capital together with deprived labor, on the other. In the picture of American society he drew for his readers, the venturesome capitalist and honest workingman were blood brothers, victims of the grasping landlord. Yet now, in the midst of an industrial depression, capital and labor, unaware of their common interest, were preparing to square off while the real villain—the landlord charging exorbitant rents—sat on the sidelines and offered to hold their coats. George's next task was to separate the combatants, conclude a truce, and direct their attention to the real danger of land monopoly.

The most difficult part of George's assignment involved explaining to American workingmen the true functions of capital and the legitimacy of interest. Return on money invested, he reminded his readers, was wholly justifiable. Capital performed a liberating function in the development of civilization: it released the energies of a people and discharged prodigious forces of production. Without it labor would remain at best inefficient, at worst inert.

None of this meant that there were not excesses or malpractices in the investment of capital or that there were not some kinds of interest like watered railroad stock that were wholly illegitimate. But these evils could be corrected. Corruption resulted, not from the natural operation of capital, but from the unnatural working of *concentrated* capital "acting on bad social adjustments" that allowed Astors, Vanderbilts, and Goulds to amass superfluous millions. In a normally functioning society, George argued, there was a "normal point of interest" that secured an adequate return to capital and security for labor. In George's refurbished eighteenth-century world there was an ultimate balance of contributions and rewards. If it were not for the greedy landlord, the partnership of labor and capital, "different forms of the same thing," would be perfectly reciprocal. To prove to both parties their mutual dependence George extended Ricardo's theory of rent to the analysis of interest and wages: as rents rise, interest and wages fall, since both depend upon Ricardo's margin of cultivation. The result of George's transfer was a stunning arrangement of symmetrical laws in a panel that told the story of economic development:

> Where land is free and labor is unassisted by capital, the whole product will go to labor as wages.
>
> Where land is free and labor is assisted by capital, wages will consist of the whole produce, less that part necessary to induce the storing up of labor as capital.
>
> Where land is subject to ownership and rent arises, wages will be fixed by what labor could secure from the highest natural opportunities open to it without the payment of rent.
>
> Where natural opportunities are monopolized, wages may be forced by the competition among laborers to the minimum at which laborers will consent to reproduce.[15]

At a stroke George had given the permutations of his law of rent and sketched his own account of American progress and accompanying poverty.

His analysis complete, George paused to survey his handiwork and pronounced it a marvel of economy and efficiency. Without introducing a single new principle or term he had repaired the machinery of classical economics and restored the reciprocal parts disarranged by his predecessors. "In the current statement the laws of distribution have no common center, no mutual relation, they are not correlating divisions of a whole, but measures of different qualities. In the statement we have given, they spring from one point, support and supplement each other, and form correlating divisions of a complete whole."[16] Nothing could be clearer than the conclusion that the failure of wages to keep pace with productive power was due to the increase of rent.

But how did his theoretical model actually work? How did the law operate in a given historical situation? Why, for example, in the current industrial crisis were wages drastically reduced? George located the cause for rising rent in the developmental process itself—in the myriad improvements in the arts of production; the perfecting of the political means of managing wealth; and the improvements in education, government, manners, and morals. First, the discovery and spread of laborsaving machinery increased the demand for land. When the supply of high quality land became exhausted, people were forced to cultivate poorer soils as the best land fell to the landlords. Then a chain reaction ensued as rents rose everywhere and land monopoly advanced. Now the United States confronted an imminent social crisis, for in increasing rents lay the seeds of an oppressed class, the yeomen dispossessed by land monopolists, rejected by industrial societies, declassed by the very forces of progress they themselves had unleashed. Already, George could see, the nation was pressing toward that final point of consolidation and concentration that announced the onset of social cataclysm.

Even more destructive of the body politic was the speculative rage that land monopoly brought to new countries, together with all the diseases afflicting older countries—tramps on virgin acres, a large class of paupers in the cities. He himself had witnessed this unnaturally rapid aging process in California. For George, as for Bellamy, there seemed to be a natural pace to life—personal as well as public—a measured seasoning of capabilities and resources. Land monopoly and speculation telescoped nature's timetable by compressing time, stimulating anticipation unduly, and triggering acquisitive instincts in Americans for whom instant gratification had become an obsession. A corrective, he now saw, would have to begin with land.

In proceeding from rent and monopoly to the theme of land and the fecundity of nature, George was invoking an agrarian mystique that the great majority of Americans understood. Land, he repeated, was the source of all real wealth, "the mine from which must be drawn the ore that labor fashions." The farmer was God's chosen instrument for extracting this abundance, and on him society's achievements ultimately rested. "It is not the storekeeper who is the cause of the farmer," he reminded readers in a cliché that William Jennings Bryan would soon use to rally the Populists, "but the farmer who brings the storekeeper. It is not the growth of the city that develops the country, but the development of the country that makes the city grow."[17]

At midpoint in the book George stopped to survey the ground ahead and behind from the imagined heights he had once given his California settlers descending the mountains into the rich interior valleys. "We have been advancing as through an enemy's country, in which every step must be secured, every position fortified, and every bypath explored; for this is hid from the great masses of men partly by its very simplicity, and in greater part by the widespread fallacies and erroneous habits of thought which lead them to look in every direction but the right one for an explanation of the evils which oppress and threaten the civilized world."[18] But now his way was clear, and the road to utopia lay open.

Between his present point of discovery and his final destination, however, lay an ideological no-man's-land over which warred a variety of contestants for their particular social nostrum. For one who had come of age before the Civil War, as George had, a loyal Democrat and scion of Andrew Jackson, the idea of a national consolidation of power in a vigorous central government was anathema. Even now, writing in the wake of a major depression, George was tempted to follow the time-honored directives of the Democracy for reducing the functions of government to a minimum. But was frugal government run by the "best men" enough? "Let me be clearly understood," he answered. "I do not say that governmental economy is not desirable; but simply that reduction in expenses of government can have no direct effect in extirpating poverty and increasing wages, so long as land is monopolized."[19] The demand for limited government, he noted, was most often heard from men of wealth and position who lamented their declining status. With their particular brand of conservatism he had little sympathy.

There was a second argument seemingly liberal but in fact deeply offensive which George dismissed out of hand. This was the view derived from Malthus and popularized by Social Darwinians like William Graham Sumner of poverty as the result of individual weakness curable only by enforced industry. The fallacy of this argument, "which at once soothes the sense of responsibility and flatters by its suggestion of superiority," was the assurance that every entrant in the great American footrace could win. His own fight against poverty told him that not everyone could even enter, let alone finish, the race. As for education as a corrective to indolence and sloth, it was properly the result rather than the cause of economic security. "To make people industrious, prudent, skillful, and intelligent, they must be relieved from want."[20]

Next George considered several collectivist proposals calling for the centralized control he instinctively disapproved. First came organized labor's answer to business consolidation, the argument that the exploitative power of the capitalists could only be checked by the solidarity of the workers. This argument for unionism gave George difficulty, and it would continue to trouble him for the rest of his life. Unions, he was forced to admit, might accomplish temporary good for their members, but they could never solve the problems of poverty and monopoly. The most serious objection to unions, however, was that they pitted the wrong adversaries against each other. Then too, because unions relied on coercion, they necessarily sanctioned strikes, walkouts, boycotts, and picketing, all of which deprived the individual workingman of his freedom. The prospect of a vast, impersonal industrial army, which Bellamy would find so compelling, appalled George. Unions, he warned, were agencies of class conflict, their strikes senseless battles that nobody won, their very existence a threat to national order and prosperity.

Another form of collectivism urged a vague "cooperation" between labor and capital in producer cooperatives, consumer leagues, and profit-sharing schemes. None of these designs, George complained, proceeded from a clear perception of the problem, which was not competition but monopoly. "Destroy this monopoly, and industry must become the cooperation of equals. Destroy this monopoly, and competition could exist only to accomplish ends which cooperation aims at—to give each what he fairly earns."[21]

Then in the parade of would-be reformers came the socialists carrying their bureaucratic baggage and blueprints for government management and ownership of the means of production. George, like Edward Bellamy and Henry Demarest Lloyd and their entire generation of social critics, was of two minds concerning socialism. Its ethical goals he accepted with enthusiasm. "The ideal of socialism is grand and noble; and it is, I am convinced, possible of realization; but such a state of society cannot be manufactured—it must grow."[22] In appealing for time and the gradual maturing of social altruism George joined a whole company of Gilded Age humanitarians and reformers who were convinced that they saw on the far horizon the millennial community toward which Americans were resolutely marching.

By the time George finished *Progress and Poverty* two variants of evolutionary reform thinking were emerging in the United States, the first a religious response to the science of evolution that quickly crystallized in the Social Gospel, and the second a secular modification of Darwinism by theorists like Lester Ward, John Wesley Powell, and WJ McGee, who were building careers and reputations as scientific reformers at the Smithsonian Institution in Washington. For both sacred and secular reform communities the concepts of evolution in the natural world and progress in the human one were complementary. The Reverend Washington Gladden, Bellamy's neighbor in Springfield who moved west to take a church in Columbus, Ohio, was already pioneering with the Social Gospel, which defined the mission of the church as fostering the steady growth of new forms of sympathy, fellowship, and service. Within a decade Gladden's original formulation was being refined and extended by a host of Social Gospelers, from Walter Rauschenbusch's Brotherhood of the Kingdom to William Dwight Porter Bliss's Christian Socialism and the radical labor theology of Henry George's friend, the Reverend J. O. S. Huntington. The secular reform tradition, nourished by the philosophy of Auguste Comte and homegrown notions of natural science and moral economy, pointed toward the creation of an evolutionary science of social control culminating in what Lester Ward called "the psychologic law, or law of the mind."

It was the socialists' means that George and his generation objected to—theories of materialism, doctrines of class conflict, and predictions of revolution. George singled out the loss of individual freedom inherent in any socialist scheme. The socialists, he observed, "attempt to secure by restriction what can better be secured by freedom." Any attempt on the part of government to impose a set of economic regulations was bound to end in "a Roman distribution of Sicilian corn." Then would follow the rule of the Imperator.

There was a last drastic remedy for poverty, one commanding support from the dispossessed all over the world and denounced, ever since the French Revolution, as "agrarianism"—the confiscation and forced redistribution of land to the little man. To this proposal George made the same objections he had to socialism: such draconian measures were regressive. Big agriculture could not be checked by force alone. "All the currents of the time run to concentration. To resist it successfully we must throttle steam and discharge electricity from human service." If the hands of the American clock could not be turned ahead to a socialist future, neither could they be set back rudely to a golden age.

In rejecting both individualist and collectivist solutions for the problem of poverty, George had placed himself squarely on the horns of a dilemma of his own devising. On the one hand, traditional liberalism with its hands-off heritage possessed a powerful appeal: the good society, he was convinced, must be a simple and permissive one allowing its members the widest range of freedom possible. But it was this very freedom degenerating into private selfishness which proved the undoing of liberalism. To prescribe a do-nothing government, to ritualize self-help and preach self-denial while giving full play to monopoly and privilege, was to destroy those conditions that the liberal society needed in order to survive. On the other hand, socialism involved coercion, and George bridled at the notion that society had the right to regulate his life.

How, then, could he invent controls on the ownership and use of land without enlarging the powers of government? Might there not be a simple device that would make land nominally common property but without sacrificing the individual freedoms attaching to the right of ownership? To put it most broadly, could he find the formula for neutralizing the socially destructive power of private property without at the same time unchaining the dogs of the modern state? Such an assignment required the offices of utopia.

George's utopian device—although nowhere in the book did he use the phrase—came to be known as the Single Tax, the appropriation of all ground rent through taxation. His case against the unrestricted right of private property rested ultimately on ethical grounds. Did his readers doubt the justice of a confiscatory tax on land? Let them consider the matter from the standpoint of natural rights. "There can be no ownership of anything, no rightful title which does not rest upon the natural right of man to himself." Nature recognized no claim but that of labor, and this meant that no man was entitled to the ownership of anything that was not the fruit of his labor. Precisely here lay the "great primary wrong" committed by the land-owner in appropriating to himself the means by which his fellow men must live. "For what are we but tenants for a day?" George asked, echoing Jefferson's plea for the land as belonging to the living. "Have we made the earth that we should determine the rights of those who after us shall tenant in their turn? The Almighty, who created the earth for man and man for the earth, has entailed it upon all the generations of the children of men by a decree which no human action can bar and no prescription determine."[23] No one was to be turned away from nature's banquet.

The Single Tax was designed to provide a complete solution to the problem of land, but one that avoided a choice between individualism and collectivism by retaining a nominal right of private property which left improvements on the land undisturbed while establishing once and for all the right of the community to the soil. George explained its operation in two distinct ways. First in the coolly abstract terms of political economy: "Thus if we concede to priority of possession the undisturbed use of the land, confiscating rent for the benefit of the community, we reconcile the fixity of tenure which is necessary for improvement with a full and complete recognition of the equal rights of all to use the land." And then in his famous declaration:

> I do not propose either to purchase or confiscate private property in land. The first would be unjust; the second, needless. Let the individuals who now hold it still retain, if they want, possession of what they are pleased to call *their* land. Let them buy and sell, and bequeath and devise it. We may safely leave them the shell, if we take the kernel.[24]

The Single Tax and the utopia it would create were the products of a romantic liberal imagination and a millennialist sensibility pushed to its limits and forced to improvise. George's dream of a transpolitical and transhistorical realm of social harmony issuing from the simple alteration of the distributive machinery of American life was the product of two contradictory perceptions—images that could not be reconciled on the plane of "realistic" social analysis in historical time but required a leap to the "fictitious" level of wish-pictures of the millennium. The primary perception, which George shared with Bellamy and Lloyd, together with a large number of social critics after the Civil War, was that of an essentially rural republic, pastoral, small-town, run according to village values. A way of life presented itself to each of them that was still eighteenth-century in its stress on balance, measure, proportion, scale, and symmetry—a view of America as a complex of crossroads and neighborhoods, rooted in the land, truly productive and wholly satisfying. George had first described this Jeffersonian paradise in the Millennial Letter as a haven from "the fierce struggle of our high civilised life," a hillside retreat "where I could gather those I love." Fifteen years later he still wanted to believe in the "promised Millennium" of Thomas Jefferson, and he still quickened to the prospect of recovered innocence in a natural order.

Yet ranged against this preference for the pastoral and contrasting starkly with its wish-pictures of a Jeffersonian recovery was a reality-principle resting in an acute sense of change that contradicted each of George's cherished fancies. In place of the stability of agrarian society, constant flux in a rapidly industrializing one. Instead of the rule of self-sufficiency, a new forced social interdependence. Displacing an old faith in a timeless natural order, a new sense of historical forces organically connected and demanding a new social intelligence for their management. In one mood George might regret the passing of the eighteenth-century intellectual order, but in another he was driven to admit the fact of modern complexity. The problem was how to combine these conflicting perceptions. Caught between two diametrically opposed propositions, he needed a way of reconciling them. That way was the utopia built by the Single Tax.

The beauty of the Single Tax, he explained, was its efficacy as a "simple yet sovereign remedy."[25] At one stroke it met all the tests of efficient taxation. It bore lightly on production. It was cheaply and easily collected. It afforded no opportunity for evasion. And it rested equally on the population. In short, it constituted "the taking by the community, for the use of the community, of that value which is the creation of the community," a measure that would make it possible to abolish every other form of taxation. This piece of magic machinery would raise wages, increase interest on capital, guarantee full employment, wipe out poverty, and "afford free scope to human powers, lessen crime, elevate morals, and carry civilization to yet nobler heights."

Lest his readers remain skeptical of the wondrous power of the

Single Tax, George devoted an entire section, Book Nine, to a picture of the resplendent American future awaiting the enactment of his simple law. Imagine yourselves, he seemed to say, transported into the twentieth century when the Single Tax has been performing its redemptive work for several decades. What kind of society do you see around you? Note, first of all, the extreme simplicity of the government. The withering away of the state predicted first by Adam Smith and subsequently by Marx has finally come to pass—a progressive atrophying of the regulatory arm of the government which the habitual good behavior of the citizenry has made obsolete. Gone are the complicated networks of courts for adjudicating disputes over land and titles. Civil as well as criminal dockets have been trimmed. Crime has been drastically reduced, and the system of criminal law "with its paraphernalia of policemen, detectives, prisons, and penitentiaries" has ceased to monopolize the attention of the American people.[26] Judges, bailiffs, clerks, custodians, and parasitical lawyers who formerly wasted public energies in legal subtleties have been replaced by a few impartial administrators whose evenhanded efficiency saves time and money.

With the disappearance of the repressive and corrective functions of government, legislative and executive work has also become "vastly simplified."[27] No longer are Americans burdened with a public debt and a standing army. There are no tariffs or subsidies, no pork-barrels or selling of votes. Politics has been purged of bosses and ward heelers; and good men, formerly victims of "political demoralization," have been returned to the few offices that are still needed to conduct public business.

No less striking in the Single Tax republic of the future are changes in the national economy. The price of land has plummeted, and speculation has received its death blow. No one seeks to own more land than he can use, and millions of acres have been opened to actual settlers who eagerly return to the soil. Orchards fill the waste places—shade trees line quiet city streets—vacant lots sprout new buildings—the demand for goods and services, once throttled by monopoly, respond to a beneficent nationwide competition. Unemployment has disappeared, and depressions have become a dim memory. The energies that once had been expended in maintaining public order have been released for more creative work. The government runs the railroads and the telegraph; builds and maintains roads; and supplies water, electricity, local transit systems, heat, sewage systems, garbage disposal, and all of the other services required by an integrated industrial society. The list of public establishments lengthens every day: "public baths, museums, libraries, gardens, lecture rooms, music and dancing halls, theaters, universities, technical schools, shooting galleries, playgrounds, gymnasiums." The ample public revenue yielded by the Single Tax is used in thousands of ways for the direct benefit of the people. Finally, it is not too much to claim that Americans have reached the goal of socialism *"but not through socialist means."* Government has changed its character and become simply "the administration of a great cooperative society."[28]

The material recasting of American society has triggered a chain reaction of spiritual effects that penetrate to the heart of the body politic. With the end of inequality and the spreading of wealth comes a new social intelligence and a new kind of citizen. Since no one fears poverty any longer, no one pursues wealth as the mark of status. Fear of want has been eliminated and with it the envy and hatred bred of insecurity. The most obvious sign of the relaxation of fear is a massive psychological slowdown which radically alters the style and the pace of life. The waning of the compulsion to beat the other fellow and to horde one's resources has freed the average American for the openhanded life that George imputed to the early Californians. Minds once engrossed with "scraping together riches" have been turned toward "far higher spheres of usefulness."

George offered his vision of a future America renovated and purified by the Single Tax with conscious educative intent: the good society would be the final product of measurable social forces whose operations could be scientifically predicted by his political economy. It was thus a question of *policy*, he insisted, the conscious selection of a specific measure calculated to produce predictable consequences. Within the "fiction," he was sure, lay a genuine alternative model of social and economic development which he presented in the belief that, once assured of its practicality, his readers would proceed to enact his program and halt the slide of the republic into despotism. The Single Tax was designed to strengthen and perpetuate an earlier nineteenth-century set of social conditions, even as it presumably adapted them to new industrial conditions and urban growth.

George's rescue operation depended on a counterrevolutionary strategy.

The economic base for the democratic-republicanism that George shared with Lloyd and Bellamy had been built by Jacksonian entrepreneurs and its superstructure had been inhabited by Whig-Republicans as well as the Democrats from whom he took his initial premises. In the model of economic progress that George inherited there was room for neither a proletariat nor inevitable class conflict. Economic distress and social dislocation were seen as transient phenomena beneath which lay the permanent substratum of a Christian moral order. In theory, individualism and the Protestant ethic promised unlimited opportunity and eventual independence to the American workingman while guaranteeing him a material reward for his ambitions. George had begun his career in California with this version of a freely operating decentralized economy organized on a regional scale, rationalized by a sectional politics, and dominated by small productive units. George's generation did not anticipate the rapid destruction of their way of life by industrialization and the growth of huge cities, and it was alarmed by the price computed in the arithmetic of the old republicanism. The urgent tone of the concluding sections of *Progress and Poverty* matched a middle-class mood and spoke to his readers' conditions as natural counter-revolutionaries. As George defined their task it was to strengthen and protect an inherited way of life that was fast becoming an adversary tradition confronting a dominant industrial capitalist system. Seen in this light, the Single Tax was a classical utopian fiction with an all-important difference: it was a model in the mind like Thomas More's original production, but it was also a delineation of means, a developmental grammar that crudely sketched the problem of restoration in ecological terms.

The key to the operation of the Single Tax was its performance as a balancing mechanism stabilizing the relationship between city and country, instilling in a people caught in the throes of rapid change a love of the land and respect for the way of life it supported. George saw his Single Tax as first and foremost a device for controlling population and establishing patterns of settlement, arranging people in economically and socially functional clusters, and spreading the benefits of civilization more evenly across the total population.

The destruction of speculative land values [by the Single Tax] would tend to diffuse population where it is too dense, and to concentrate it where it is too sparse; to substitute for the tenement house, homes surrounded by gardens, and fully to settle agricultural districts before people were driven far from neighbors to look for land.[29]

Despite the note of pastoralism in George's account, the American society created by the Single Tax was not to be antiurban. Behind his proposal for diffusing population lay his imaginary history of American settlement and community building, a fictionalized sketch of national growth from the arrival of the pioneer given land but isolated from the community which alone can sustain him. Cut off and imprisoned in his wilderness retreat, the first settler lives a rude and impoverished existence as a bountiful nature mocks his lonely efforts to create wealth and a satisfying life for himself. Only with the coming of neighbors and the beginnings of a society marked by division of labor and the pooling of effort does the individual fulfill his dreams. "Satisfactions become possible," George explains, "that in the solitary state were impossible. There are gratifications for the social and intellectual nature—for that part of man that rises above the animal. The power of sympathy, the sense of companionship, the emulation of comparison and contrast, open wider and fuller and more varied life."[30] The functionally balanced town and provincial city guarantee prosperity but also what George called "productiveness of a higher kind" in the creation of culture. "Here intellectual activity is gathered into a focus, and here springs the stimulus which is born of the collision of mind with mind." Here in the regional city can be found the universities, museums, libraries, and concert halls so vital to a healthy culture.

The true city, George concluded, contains a critical cultural mass unavailable in preindustrial societies but absolutely essential for republican achievement. Its natural size and normal scale are assured by the Single Tax; its dependence on and penetration by surrounding agricultural regions establish natural markets and a stable balance of urban and rural. The control made possible by ecological balance brings a major renovation to the nineteenth-century industrial city, with its grimy factories and huddled squalor. Tenement houses give way to neat single-family cottages, and citizens arrange themselves in neighborhoods where their voices can be heard and their votes registered. "The people in the cities would thus get more of the pure air and sunshine of the country, and the people of the country more of the economies and social life of the cities."

If the first nine books of *Progress and Poverty* presented a basically secular argument, Book Ten, "The Law of Human Progress," dominated by a powerful millennialist vision, described the mass conversion experience needed to deliver the American people. Only a national change of heart made possible by the Single Tax could save the United States from death and decay. The choice for George was clear: the millennium or oblivion. Great civilizations of antiquity had perished and left no trace. Why should Americans consider themselves exempt from the verdict of history?

That history rendered a verdict on mankind George was by now absolutely certain. He had read widely in the universalist historians of the nineteenth century as well as in Herbert Spencer's synthetic philosophy and Walter Bagehot's *Physics and Politics*, but all of these he used to argue his essentially ahistorical case for the law of human progress. Evolution and historicism, he was convinced, did not explain the dead ends and the gaps in history, the "arrested civilizations" that ultimately failed to progress. George viewed history as an unfolding sequence of progressions and retrogressions. Whether this rhythmic movement followed an ascending line that spiraled upwards, as the evolutionists had it, he doubted. The evolutionary model and the historicism it engendered failed to account satisfactorily for catastrophe and cataclysm. "The earth is the tomb of dead empires, no less than dead men," he reminded his readers. "Civilizations have died and made no sign, and hard-won progress has been lost to the race forever."

Civilizations, he theorized, are ripe for external overthrow when internal forces have weakened their will to survive. To support this observation drawn from classical history, George borrowed Herbert Spencer's law of integrative development from "an indefinite incoherent homogeneity to a definite coherent heterogeneity" and combined it with the nebular hypothesis in a cosmic analogy that helped explain historical options. Just as the heat and light of the sun will finally cease when atoms come into a state of equilibrium and immobility, so a community of people in life-sustaining motion evolves forces that produce the warmth and light of civilization only to die of inanition once they reach a state of equilibrium. The analogy pointed directly to George's law of human progress—"association in equality." This law rested on two postulates: first, that "mind is the instrument by which man advances"; and second, that the "mental power" in any society is a "fixed quantity."[31] When the mental energies of a people are devoted exclusively to maintaining life or when they are dissipated in social conflict, their society, like the solar system, loses the movement that spells life. But where association in equality is allowed to develop freely, progress toward Spencer's state of definite coherent heterogeneity is assured.

Yet precisely here lay the difficulty. In all the civilizations known to history, progressive integration had always been accompanied by its opposite, the contradictory fact of inequality. History, George was sure, showed that inequality, like a cancerous growth, first lodged in one organ of the body politic but quickly spread. Thus patriarchal societies in the ancient world had become depotisms, and the commercial wealth of the Italian city-states of the Renaissance had produced oligarchies. In every historical epoch the countertendency worked the same way: the unequal distribution of power and wealth checked and then reversed the equalitarian tendency making for social advance. Then the masses of men were driven to expend all their energies on survival, while the privileged classes devoted the accumulated fund of mental power to luxury, conspicuous consumption, and finally to the art of war. Modern Europe, built on the foundation of Christianity and the national state, had also proved vulnerable to these same disintegrative tendencies even though the Christian ideal continued to provide momentum. "Distorted and alloyed" as it once was, Christianity with its millennialist promise now offered the best guide for Americans in their search for association in equality.

> Political economy and social science cannot teach any lessons that are not embraced in the simple truths that were taught to poor fishermen and Jewish peasants by One who eighteen hundred years ago was crucified—the simple truths which, beneath the warpings of selfishness and the distortions of su-

perstition, seem to underlie every religion that has ever striven to formulate the spiritual yearnings of man.

With the appeal to the spirit of Christianity, *Progress and Poverty* suddenly shifts from an analytical to a millennial mode and visions of the apocalypse. The United States approaches a fatal turning point: "A civilization like ours must either advance or go back; it cannot stand still." The final act in the drama of prehistory was about to be played out in American cities where wealth and poverty contended for mastery. "There is no mistaking it—the very foundations of our society are being sapped before our very eyes, while we ask *how* it is possible that such a civilization as this . . . should ever be destroyed." Whence will come the new barbarians? "Go through the squalid quarters of great cities, and you may see, even now, their gathering hordes." American civilization, when it ceased advancing, would not retrace the path of its ascent. Relapse would be no orderly retreat by familiar historical routes but a terrifying pitch over the abyss into "imperatorship and anarchy." All the signs of social breakdown were now clear: pauperism, disease caused by over-strained nerves, undernourishment, squalid lodgings, and, hanging over the lower orders of society, an atmosphere of "brooding revolution."

In its final flirtation with the catastrophic, *Progress and Poverty* prefigured a fin de siècle obsession with cataclysm which in the next two decades swept across the whole of Western society. The forms of late nineteenth-century catastrophism were myriad: in Europe a delicious decadence and cultivated primitivism in the arts; a probing of the irrational and instinctual in literature; mysticism in religion; fascination with the idea of degeneration among social theorists. In the United States in the closing decades of the century, apocalyptic visions nourished imaginations as varied as Henry and Brooks Adams, Frank Norris, Alfred Thayer Mahan, Mary Lease, and Ignatius Donnelly, all alienated visionaries enchanted by the prospects of finality. For these and a host of other disillusioned prophets, Book Ten of *Progress and Poverty* prepared the way.

American fascination with catastrophe had survived the Enlightenment and continued to mount in a nineteenth-century millennialist society, captivating the otherwise sober fancies of an industrious people—in the formal didacticism of Thomas Cole's *The Course of*

Empire or in the fatal attraction for the popular mind of volcanic eruptions, steamboat explosions, Mississippi floods, and the countless fires that periodically laid waste to American cities. In touching this nerve, George played on a prevailing American taste.

Yet throughout modern history the catastrophic mode has flourished at the ends of centuries which were thought to mark in some mysterious way the onset of the last days. In America the waning years of the seventeenth century witnessed a preoccupation with witchcraft and satanism in a New England unwilling to accept the fact of religious declension. The 1790s saw another outbreak of millennialist visions and conspiratorial politics, offshoots of widespread fears of relapse following the great days of the Revolution. A late nineteenth-century generation of Americans proved equally susceptible to catastrophism, as the strains of rapid technological change required perceptual adjustments too drastic for many of them to make. George's Single Tax was both a product of these apprehensions and, in part at least, an answer to them—a utopian promise expertly designed to meet the psychological needs of a people undergoing the shock of massive change which they could not comprehend in terms of secular history. The Single Tax and the millennium it pictured offered an escape from the confinements of time and indeterminacy in a simple device for restoring strength and purpose by returning Americans to the soil.

George's sense of an ending, like that of his whole generation, centered on land and the fear of its loss with the closing of the frontier. His was a common American concern, keenest among agrarians but increasingly shared by the rest of society that fifteen years later responded with alarm to the explanation of a little-known historian from Wisconsin. Frederick Jackson Turner ratified for Americans their profound sense of loss of a way of life. Whatever the question of Turner's intellectual debts, it was George who first stated the frontier thesis in terms that the historian would make famous.

The public domain—the vast extent of land yet to be reduced to private possession, the enormous common to which the faces of the energetic were always turned, has been the great fact that, since the days when the first settlements began to fringe the Atlantic Coast, has formed our national thought. It is not that we have eschewed a titled aristocracy and abolished primogeniture; that we elect all our officers from school director to president; that our laws run in the name of the people, instead of in the name of a prince, that the State knows no religion, and our judges wear no wigs—that we have been exempted from the ills that Fourth of July orators used to point to as the ills characteristic of the effete despotisms of the Old World. The general intelligence, the general comfort, active invention, the power of adaptation and assimilation, the free, independent spirit, and energy and hopefulness that have marked our people, are not causes, but results—they have sprung from unfenced land. This public domain has been the transmuting force which has turned the thriftless, unambitious European peasant into the self-reliant farmer; it has given a consciousness of freedom even to the dweller in crowded cities, and has been the wellspring of hope even to those who have never thought of taking refuge upon it . . . In America, whatever his condition, there has always been the consciousness that the public domain lay behind him; and the knowledge of the fact, acting and reacting, has penetrated our whole national life, giving to it generosity and independence, elasticity and ambition.

Now the American advance had reached the Pacific and turned back upon itself. "The great fact which has been so potent is ceasing to be." The urgency of George's task in winning acceptance for his Single Tax was thus all the greater, for it amounted to no less than preserving the American land and its people.

George finished the manuscript in the spring of 1879, revising and recasting as he outlined his theory of history in Book Ten. As he neared the end his emotions rose to the pitch of a religious fever. "And when I had finished the last page," he recalled, "in the dead of night, when I was entirely alone, I flung myself on my knees and wept like a child. The rest was in the Master's hands." What he had first conceived of as a brief tract on political economy had grown in the course of two years into a massive personal testament and plea for Christian action. He confessed that the book had worked a psychological transformation approximating a religious conversion.

"That is a feeling that has never left me, that is constantly with me. It has made me a better and purer man. It has been to me a religion, strong and deep, though vague—a religion of which I never like to speak, or make any outward manifestation, but yet that I try to follow."[32] The Prophet of San Francisco had been born.

In March 1879 George sent off a copy of the manuscript to Appleton in New York and awaited the verdict which came soon enough. Though written with "great clearness and force," the publisher reported, the work was also "very aggressive," and its inflammatory message would be unlikely to appeal to many readers.[33] Harpers followed suit, rejecting it as openly revolutionary. Then, just as despair seemed to have settled permanently in the George household, an old California friend, William Swinton, now living in New York, arranged to meet with William Appleton, and the publisher agreed to bring the book out if George would supply the plates. Meanwhile George had given up his job as inspector of gas meters and returned to newspaper work. For a moment it seemed to be the old story all over again. After two years' hard work he was the possessor of a magnificent manuscript and now was told that if he wished to see it in print, he would have to find the means to prepare the plates. Then friendship came to the rescue a second time. A former partner on the *Post* offered his services as printer on credit. The entry in George's diary for May 17, 1879, reads: "Commenced to set type on book. Set first two sticks myself."

He continued to reshape the book as he supervised the preparation of the plates. As originally submitted, *Progress and Poverty* consisted of eight books. These he enlarged to ten by dividing the unwieldy Book Six into three chapters, and then as the printers rushed to keep up, added an afterword entitled "The Problem of Individual Life," in which the crescendo movement of the latter parts of the book ends in a clarion call to action. In his final word to the reader, George raised the same problem that Bellamy confronted in "The Religion of Solidarity." Linking the life of the lone individual to a social purpose meant acknowledging the fact that "unless man himself may rise to or bring forth something higher, his existence is unintelligible." Could Americans be made to understand this? "Ultimately yes. But in our own times, or in the times of which any memory of us remain, who shall say?" Surely not unless millions of readers recognized the truth he had shown them and, having seen it, were willing to "toil for it; suffer for it; if need be, die for it."[34] Having pointed, like Moses, to the promised land, he must now lead the way into it.

By summer the plates were ready, and an advanced "Author's Edition" had sold well enough to pay part of the cost of printing. He sent a copy to his father, now eighty-one, who must have marveled at his son's bold prediction of the fate of his book. "It will not be recognized at first—may not for some time—but it will ultimately be considered a great book, will be published in both hemispheres, and be translated into different languages. This I know, though neither of us may ever live to see it here."[35] After sending copies to Sir George Grey in New Zealand and Gladstone and Herbert Spencer in England, he indulged in another bit of puffing. At the risk of sounding immodest, he explained to John Swinton in New York, he was forced to admit that his book was the most important contribution to the science of political economy yet made. "The professors will first ignore, then pooh-pooh, and then try to hold the shattered fragments of their theories together; but this book opens the discussion along lines on which they cannot make a successful defense."[36]

The few California reviews of *Progress and Poverty* expressed incomprehension and amusement at the "hobby" of "little Harry George," but he was less concerned with his local reputation than with response in the East. In fact, there was nothing to hold him in San Francisco now, and in August 1880, leaving Annie and the children at home, he set out to reconnoiter New York. It was an apprehensive if still truculent author who arrived in the city to sample reactions to his book. In a sense he was returning East with no more money and scarcely brighter prospects than when he left Philadelphia a quarter-century ago. He was forty-one now, balding, his full reddish beard beginning to streak with gray, his small plump body already subject to the various infirmities of middle age. He carried with him a few letters of recommendation and a book of unknown merit. Yet the world would soon learn that he had discovered both a cause and a calling.

6

MUCKRAKING

IN THE MARCH 1881 ISSUE of the *Atlantic Monthly* the editor, William Dean Howells, recently arrived in Boston from the literary provinces, featured an article by another newcomer from the Midwest, "The Story of a Great Monopoly," by Henry Demarest Lloyd. Lloyd's sixteen-page indictment of Standard Oil marked the opening of a new market for popular reform journalism which a quarter of a century later President Theodore Roosevelt would denounce as "muckraking." To Lloyd's pioneer effort belongs the distinction of lifting the exposé to the level of serious social criticism designed for mass consumption.

Lloyd first submitted his article to the *North American Review*, whose editors rejected it as too sensational for their staid readers. Whereupon Lloyd passed it along to Howells, who immediately recognized in its slashing attack a chance to raise an important question of national policy and his magazine's circulation at the same time. Howells's estimate proved correct: the March number enjoyed six reprintings, and "The Story of a Great Monopoly" was soon being cited all over the country as the best single analysis of the dubious ethics of a new breed of industrial monopolists.

Lloyd's arraignment of Standard Oil was only the first in a series of articles in the early eighties in which he explained the danger of monopoly to an American public seemingly unconcerned with the effects of economic concentration. A year later Howells accepted "The Political Economy of Seventy-Three Million Dollars," a blistering review of Jay Gould's record of financial buccaneering. In 1883, the *North American Review*, belatedly acknowledging the power of Lloyd's brand of personal journalism, published "Making Bread Dear," a report on corners in wheat on the Chicago Board of Trade, and the following year, "Lords of Industry," a hasty compilation of the sins of the trusts and an estimate of the damage they were doing to traditional business practices.

The five years between the appearance of the Standard Oil article and Chicago's Haymarket Riot in 1886 were in many ways the most strenuous and exhausting of Lloyd's life. Having determined to stay on at the *Tribune* and accept Medill's leadership, he nevertheless began to challenge the editor's tired liberalism with his own unorthodox opinions delivered in an increasingly strident editorial voice. His collision course inevitably ended in a smashup. By 1885 the conflict between the "Chief" and his headstrong lieutenant reached a crisis, and Lloyd, buckling once more under the combined weight of Medill's ire and his own doubts, suffered a second emotional collapse and quit the *Tribune*. In the interval, however, he perfected a style of highly charged personal journalism and established a national reputation as a critic of monopoly.

Much of Lloyd's life from now on centered at the Wayside in Winnetka, where in an upstairs study overlooking Lake Michigan— "our Mediterranean," he and Jessie called it—he worked doggedly at reconstructing his political philosophy. Between them, he and Jessie also turned the Wayside into a haven for Chicago's growing community of artists and intellectuals, transforming it into a way station and weekend retreat which Jane Addams later described as "an annex to Hull House." In the beginning, however, it served chiefly as the focus of a bustling domesticity that helped relieve the tensions and anxieties of an uncertain career. Lloyd delighted in his children— William Bross Lloyd, born in 1876, Henry Demarest, Jr., "Hal," two years later, and "Jack," the baby of the family in 1885. Like Henry George, he was a model late-Victorian husband and father, idolizing a wife on whom he increasingly depended to manage the household, raise the children, and guard his frail health. Jessie accepted her assignments and ruled her domain with a quiet efficiency and the help of the servants her father's money provided.

Intentionally Lloyd made his home the core of his emerging social philosophy and the staging area for his forays into the reform world. Although he constantly enlarged his group of casual friends and acquaintances as he joined the causes that took him away from home, there remained a part of him that needed to draw that world to his own doorstep and to gather his friends into a movable extended family. His private notions of home and family, though they never obscured his vision of the larger community, nevertheless remained integral to it. Some of his guests—shopgirls from Marshall Field's or young factory operatives come for a weekend in the country—made few demands and answered a simple need for sharing with the less fortunate. But there were also friends and colleagues who visited in increasing numbers—Florence Kelley, Eugene Debs, Jane Addams, George Trevelyan, Charlotte Perkins Gilman, Ignatius Donnelly, Booker T. Washington, John R. Commons, Richard T. Ely—invited for a weekend in the expectation that they would add to the bill of fare at their host's intellectual feasts. For it was conversation, varied, sparkling, earnest, and endless, that Lloyd's friends remembered best about the Wayside. Spirited debates at the dinner table. Long ruminative discussions around the fire. Or a lecture from Lloyd while tramping the woods or the lakeshore. Talk and still more talk on subjects ranging from anarchism to child labor, Mazzini to William Morris, trusts to the Social Gospel.

In describing the Wayside as an adjunct to her own collective family at Hull House, Jane Addams hardly exaggerated, for Lloyd's ideas on the family and community were strikingly like her own. His ideal was the communal family incorporating different generations like the Washington Square home of his boyhood and reaching out to neighbors, associates, and occasional outsiders in a fluid relationship, a lively procession of minds and personalities. At the center of this domestic figure he placed himself in the shifting roles of husband, father, adviser, confidant, playing each with sensitivity and skill. Lloyd was determined to fight the demands of a narrowing professionalism and the compartmentalizing of modern life, whether because of his own vocational dissatisfactions or because he sensed the loneliness of nuclear families. For whatever reason, he began to comtemplate building a society in which this network of extended familial relationships defined a wholly new kind of individualism based on the social creation of personality. He came to view the family as a vital, if small, collectivity—a miniature settlement house complete with school and playgrounds and possessed of vast socializing powers that connected individual members to the outside world. When ten years later in *Wealth Against Commonwealth* he pointed to the need for a new individualism to be achieved only by "submitting to be bound by others," it was in large measure to his own life at the Wayside and its regimen that he referred. "We extend our freedom," he explained, "only by finding new laws to obey . . . The isolated man is a mere rudiment of an individual. But he who has become citizen, neighbor, friend, brother, son, husband, father, fellow-member, in one is just so many times individualized."[1]

Lloyd's ideal community as it rose out of his social theory in the next two decades was decentralized and family-centered, his primary institution the open household where love and intellectual friendship formed the bridge from self to society. The social worker Vida Scudder, who once visited the Wayside, noted her sense of relief at escaping for a few days the average American home where ideas and social theories were treated as "dangerous vagaries or absurd fallacies." "To pass from an atmosphere charged with incredulous perplexity to one full of friendly tranquil comradeship is an experience one does not forget; the Lloyds' home must, I should think, have afforded such a haven to many a solitary soul." Not all of these possibilities were clear to Lloyd in his early years at the Wayside, but gradually he came to build his case for social reconstruction on a hierarchy of communities—neighborhood, village, city—that rested on the institution of the family as the one cohesive unit in an age of disintegration.

In overhauling his antiquated liberalism Lloyd proceeded systematically, starting with the revisionist school of English economists and rapidly broadening his reading to include the new historians and sociologists. His was less an original than an eclectic mind, one that borrowed freely and adapted other people's ideas to strengthen his own impressions of the current intellectual crisis. He read Leslie Stephen's *History of English Thought in the Eighteenth Century* to gain a clearer understanding of the historical forces that had produced an Adam Smith. From Sir Henry Maine he acquired new concepts of the organic growth of the law, and from the economists Stanley Jevons and J. E. Cairnes a critique of the methodological shortcomings of their predecessors. Together he and Jessie reread Carlyle and Ruskin. He investigated Comte's positivism and plowed through Bagehot's *Physics and Politics* searching for scientific analogies with which to strengthen his growing inclination toward state power. Finally, he returned to Adam Smith, Bastiat, and the two Mills, studying their works in the light of Wilhelm Roscher's historical economics and Emil deLaveleye's account of primitive societies. Out of a two-year course in recent scholarship, first in scattered impressions scribbled in his journals and then in finished editorials and articles, came the outlines of a new social philosophy.

Lloyd began, as Henry George did in the opening sections of *Progress and Poverty,* with an account of the rise and fall of Adam Smith's theories. But Lloyd singled out for criticism precisely those abstract deductions which George considered Smith's strengths. Smith and his followers, Lloyd now saw, had proceeded from a false psychology: "they claim to know not only that the love of gain is the impelling force in business, but just how it acts." George dismissed the nineteenth-century followers of Adam Smith as false prophets of the true gospel; Lloyd discarded the gospel itself. His notebooks began to fill with summaries and quotations from his new mentors, interspersed with his own pointed comments on the insufficiencies of classical theory.

> Great point proved by Maine, de Laveleye etc. is that ownership, property has assumed various forms. Hence arises moral certainty that it is still to undergo changes.

> T. E. Cliffe-Leslie ... shows that chain of consequences deduced by orthodox Political Economy from the general love of money is defective in every link ... Political Economy ignores the family, and the community, the social influences and the state as a juridical and political and fiscal influence.

> A[dam] S[mith] did great work in releasing individual liberty from incubus of constraint and unintelligent interference. But time has now come to admit that natural liberty must be at least controlled in the interest of the community, that the lib-

erty of cooperation through incorporation must be more and
more controlled by law . . . and hence the great need today is
a Political Economy of Regulation—not as in A S's day of liberty.[2]

With the help of modern social scientists Americans could now
construct new mechanisms of social control. Already, Lloyd realized,
lawyers and legal theorists were making a revolution in jurisprudence in the name of indeterminacy and instrumentalism. "Same
revolution must take place in Political Economy," he noted in the tel-
egraphic style of his journals. What was needed first was a "natural
history" of political theory with which to make educated guesses as
to the best solution to the problems of industrial society. No longer
could statesmen simply appeal to "some Great and vague tribunal of
reason."[3] They must know their history and the point to be made
of it.

The most dramatic example of this need was the record of Standard Oil's dealings that Lloyd uncovered in "The Story of a Great
Monopoly." His article opens with a brief and not altogether accurate account of the rise of the Rockefeller enterprise, from an obscure partnership between "a former bookkeeper in some interior
town in Ohio" and Samuel Andrews, "owner of a ten-barrel still," to
its present domination of the market.[4] By 1880 Standard Oil had
come to rule the oil industry with an iron hand that had destroyed its
competitors. Lloyd's difficulties in discovering what in fact Rockefeller had been up to resulted from the company's carefully contrived policy of secrecy. "Just who the Standard Oil Company are,
exactly what their capital is, and what are their relations to the railroads nobody knows except in part." Since the Company's officers
had refused to testify before the Supreme Court of Pennsylvania and
again before a Congressional investigating committee, a conspiracy
between Rockefeller and the railroads could only be inferred. This
inference Lloyd proceeded to make in his account of the South Improvement Company, Rockefeller's secret scheme for doubling the
freight rates for his rivals while arranging rebates for himself. The
South Improvement Company died a richly deserved death, Lloyd
declared, but Rockefeller's monopoly continued to prosper. "He
made no more tell-tale contracts that could be printed."

On the assumption that silence gives consent Lloyd accused the major trunk lines—wrongly as it turns out—of joining a new Rockefeller conspiracy. But his picture of the Standard "octopus" with its tentacles wrapped around the nation's railroads was essentially accurate. "The railroads create the monopoly, and then make the monopoly their excuse." With these results: control of the market by the producers of one-fiftieth of the country's oil; unnaturally depressed prices; the destruction of the independents.

Lloyd's heroes in the war for control of the oil business were the little men—independent producers and refiners—who were being bludgeoned and battered by Rockefeller. "All that men could do who were fighting for self-preservation was done," but to no avail since "the plundered found the courts, the governor, and the legislature of their State, and the Congress of the United States" had become the "tools of their plunderers." The current truce between the company and the remaining independents was in fact a victory for the monopoly because it allowed the railroads to continue granting rebates to major shippers. "The Standard holds its vantage ground, and America has the proud satisfaction of having furnished the world with the greatest, wisest, and meanest monopoly known to history."

Lloyd readily admitted that he had isolated only one part of the problem, but he also realized that he had discovered the primary target for the regulatory policy called for by his new political economy. The active role played by the railroads in fostering a monopoly in oil meant that public control must begin with them. Railroad pools would have to be broken up or controlled: "The cat must be killed or belled." As a start he recommended federal enforcement of reasonable rates set by an independent commission given broad powers of review. Not until his death over twenty years later would the Interstate Commerce Commission give even the promise of fulfilling his demands.

As the first national exposé of Standard Oil, "The Story of a Great Monopoly" was perfectly timed. The depression of the seventies had produced a crop of corporate consolidations as businessmen in all the major sectors of the economy began to weigh the advantages of stability and predictability and to seek salvation through combination. The Muckraker Charles Edward Russell exaggerated

when, after the opening of the new century, he recalled Lloyd's article as "a turning point in our social history," but he was right in giving Lloyd credit for first calling public attention to the new "oligar-
chy of capitalists." The article immediately received extravagant
praise and unsparing criticism, and the accuracy of his analysis was
widely debated just as today it continues to intrigue students of the
corporate revolution. How informed were Lloyd's judgments? Was
he, as his defenders argued, a sharp observer and a good historian?
Or was he, as his detractors have charged, a reckless and irresponsible libeler of America's pioneer industrialists?

These questions raise the issue of moral publicity and the right of
the people to know. Lloyd was only the first of the critics of monopoly who found access to corporate information always difficult and
frequently impossible. From the beginning Standard Oil proved the
most secretive and uncooperative of modern businesses. Lloyd was
forced to resort to the very limited information about its activities
available to the public: the five-volume Hepburn Report, trial
records, and the restricted findings of state investigatory committees.
The cries of outrage and charges of misrepresentation issuing from
Standard Oil headquarters echoed Rockefeller's conviction that "it is
not the business of the public to change our private contracts." "We
will do right," he assured his wife, "and not be nervous or troubled
. . . and leave future events in the business to demonstrate our intentions and plans were just and warranted."[5] It was Lloyd's insistence
that the "future" would be too late to check on Standard Oil's dubious "intentions" that so nettled Rockefeller and his managers.

With his scanty knowledge of secret contracts and backstairs
deals Lloyd could be only partially accurate. Some of his alleged
"facts" were wrong. Standard Oil and Tom Scott's Pennsylvania
Railroad had not plotted the Pittsburgh riots during the Great Railroad Strike of 1877. Not all of the fifty-eight refineries operating in
Western Pennsylvania after the Civil War were the victims of Rockefeller's rapacity. Many of them were fly-by-nights unable to order
their own affairs or solve the problem of overproduction. Lloyd also
played carelessly with statistics, not doctoring them but arranging
them for dramatic effect. In calculating the profits on each barrel of
oil shipped by the company, for example, he conveniently overlooked such factors as plant investment, overhead, and depreciation.

But Lloyd was neither a historian nor an economist but, at bottom, a moralist to whom data and statistics were useful principally as frames for the many aphorisms that decorated the article.

> The Standard has done everything with the Pennsylvania legislature except refine it.

> Publicity is the great moral disinfectant.

> Only the rich can get justice, only the poor cannot escape it.

Finally, however, Lloyd's verdict is unassailable: "The Standard killed its rivals, in brief, by getting the trunk lines to refuse to give them transportation." The exact details of the plots were less important to the moral publicist than the questions they seemed to raise for American consumers. What did the coming corporate revolution mean? Was it inevitable? Would it deliver on its promise to order a national economy? Or was the monitored competition of smaller productive units a better solution? Lloyd knew none of the answers yet, and he would continue to waver between the principles of trust-busting and regulated consolidation. What he did know—and what he told the readers of his first national article—was that the coming of monopoly had ended a way of life they had taken for granted.

Lloyd pursued his investigations in a second article written for the *Atlantic* a year later. "The Political Economy of Seventy-Three Million Dollars" carried the weight of a confessional in which he dismissed his own outworn economic beliefs.[6] Who could mourn the passing of a pseudoscience in which wealth was the sole subject, desire for wealth the motive, competition the regulator, supply and demand the rule, and private profit the result? Classical economics had made machines of men, robbing them of their humanity and turning them into cool calculators of personal advantage.

Suddenly Lloyd moves from arraignment to caricature in setting the dismal science in motion with a hilarious account of the strange career of Jay Gould, the "mouse-trap" man, and his quest for $73,-000,000. Jay Gould is a demonic Horatio Alger, a "slender, black-eyed, black-haired boy" who comes to the big city and succeeds in becoming "the greatest mouse-catcher of America," whose predatory career is "the envy of every man of feline aspirations." Lloyd's

account of Gould's escapades begins with the raid on the Erie Railroad:

> At once there began to turn before the eyes of the stockhold-
> ers and the public a kaleidoscope of ruin: shower after shower
> of stocks and bonds issued to run the road, while the trustee
> and his pals—pal is Old English for fellow-trustee—drank
> dry the stream of earnings; a devil's dance of lawyers, judges,
> legislators, governors, and Tammany politicians, flinging
> themselves into every attitude of betrayal of trust—an orgy of
> fiduciary harlotry, led by the great law reformers; a tangled
> web of injunctions and counter-injunctions, and more in-
> junctions, contradictory orders of courts, perjured affadavits.

Lloyd follows Gould's triumphant course through the Great Gold
Conspiracy, "no ordinary trap" but a gigantic corner in gold that
snared Sub-Treasury officials, members of the Stock Exchange, New
York bankers, and friends of President Grant. When this "conjuror
of the irresistible laws of trade" is once again discovered, he coolly
invokes the law of self-preservation in deciding to betray his cronies
by destroying his own corner. "I had my own views about the market and my own fish to fry." Gould's latest exploit, the one that seals
his fortune at $73,000,000, is the Manhattan Elevated mousetrap, an-
other ruse from which he emerges richer than ever. "Seventy-three
millions, and more," Lloyd marvels, "accumulated by an enthusiast
in competition in twenty-nine years of office work."

Both of Lloyd's *Atlantic* articles focused on individuals—the sinister Rockefeller and the devilish Gould—and both were purely descriptive. In a third article, for the *North American Review*, "Making
Bread Dear," he examined the transactions of the Chicago Board of
Trade and once again pointed to the failure of orthodox political
economy to explain the frenzied speculative behavior of the traders.
The members of the Board of Trade, like their powerful counterparts
on the Stock Exchange in New York, were engaged in manufacturing, not goods but prices. "The Exchanges are cosmopolitan legislatures. Their enactments are prices, and their jurisdiction extends beyond that of Congress, Parliament, the Assembly, and the
Reichstag."[7]

For Lloyd as well as for George and Bellamy it was not the occasional moral lapse of speculators operating in the shadows that was so disturbing, but the bland innocence of such predators. All three men were convinced that speculation was unnatural and hence destructive, and all three were forced to make some very fine and not altogether convincing distinctions. Lloyd considered the Board of Trade a useful mechanism for securing order. Corners, on the other hand, were the devil's work that crippled legitimate business. The Board of Trade, he reasoned, ought to be dealing with real hogs and actual staples, but under the evil influences of the speculators it played games with spectral wheat and fictitious pork. To correct these abuses, however, Lloyd could only suggest a body of administrative law, "tribunals composed of disinterested men" and "official arbitrators."

The final article in this first series, "Lords of Industry," which appeared in the June 1884 issue of the *North American Review*, surveyed the new industrial monopolies and pools—some fifty of them—and denounced their "war against plenty." The National Burial Case Company secretly agreed to limit production of coffins "lest mortality should be discouraged." The Empire Pipe Company controlled output "to prevent the calamity of too much pipe." Textile pools curtailed production "to cure the devastating plague of too much cotton cloth." "These combinations," he warned, "are not to be waved away as fresh pictures of folly or total depravity. There is something deeper than that." If concentration and combination were inevitable, then there would have to be a controlling moral purpose to sanction them. What worried Lloyd was the half-life of obsolete ideas, one of which was the illusion that a frontier society needed no social policy. "Our young men can no longer go west; they must go up or down. Not new land, but new virtue must be the outlet for the future."[8]

Both Lloyd and George understood that the closing of the frontier would bring a social order markedly different from the old antebellum community of their boyhoods. But whereas George sought to slow the development process in the United States with a counter-modernization scheme, Lloyd began to search for different "moral inventions" latent in the collective mind of the American people. The end of the frontier, he was convinced, meant the end of a morality of privatism and the dawn of a new religious age.

In practical terms, however, it was not clear to Lloyd just what the new "moral inventions" ought to be or how they should be applied. Enthusiastic letters from readers of his article on monopoly were all very gratifying, but some of them mixed congratulations with perplexity. "You put all this as terribly unsatisfactory, & *so it is,*" wrote one correspondent. "But what then?"

> Unlimited, unrestrained *competition* is hardly less mischievous—which indeed was the point of a previous article of yours wasn't it? I write because you seem to touch the only possible remedy when you say "not new laws, but new *virtue,*" "competitive morals" etc.—and yet you seem to touch it hesitatingly, as if feeling that this doesn't amount to much.[9]

The same complaint came from an English correspondent, William Clarke, a disillusioned liberal who would soon take up Fabian socialism. "Now cannot you follow this up," Clarke urged, "by showing us some of the first things to be done and by indicating how social control of monopolies is to be effected?"[10]

These questions touched a sensitive nerve, for Lloyd had no very clear ideas about how to control monopolies. Obviously some form of coercion was necessary. "Appeals of Church, Christian Socialists, pamphleteers, etc. etc. and heads of Labor Bureaus, Legislative Representatives, etc., to sympathy of ruling classes are futile beyond exciting a little piecemeal philanthropy . . . Force must be used." But force employed to what ends? Puzzled by these questions, Lloyd compiled a list of functions properly belonging to the state that paralleled the assignments Bellamy would give his utopian society in the year 2000.

> The playing of unemployed against employed labor, constantly cutting down wages, could be prevented by enrolling and licensing all workers, each in his trade, classifying industries into guilds, compelling all contracts for employment to be made with guild, making guild responsible for breach of contract, preventing monopoly by providing for instruction— technical—in public schools and giving graduates place in licensed trade. Unskilled laborers could be protected by law that no dismissal or reduction should be made except under

cognizance of some representative of the state—specially qualified officials could be created for that purpose.[11]

Next on the list of national reforms came a revised tax structure designed so that "stocks and bonds and corporate property etc. shall pay its proportion." And, if necessary, government should own and manage transportation and communications. Add to these a national child labor law, tenement house legislation, safety regulations for industry and railroads, court reforms trimming the power of judicial review, referendum and initiative, and the municipalization of public utilities—in short, the complete agenda of reforms that a Progressive generation would take up twenty years later.

Such unprecedented measures would have to be justified to the American public. How? Lloyd found his answer in what he called "fictions," useful myths with which to arouse the will to social action. "Mass of mankind need general statement to help understand because general statements are simple," he remarked in his notebooks. Myths put proposals for reform into circulation as packaged truths. The myth of natural equality, which Henry George now sought to perpetuate, seemed to Lloyd to have served its historical purpose. "It is now necessary to move a step further and while retaining benefits of fiction to recognize the inequalities which call for intervention."[12] Intervention necessitated a new myth of the state. "The State is the organ of self-consciousness of peoples," he wrote, groping for a formula for mythmaking. "Dominating all as the noblest, strongest, best passion and force is that which acts through the state, through government, to curb the too strong, and protect the weak to preserve the common weal."[13]

The heady notion of the state as the highest spiritual entity, the very "mirror of the civilization of its people," which had begun to direct Lloyd's thought, was alien to most Americans, and Lloyd himself was still not altogether comfortable with it. Yet for a handful of Americans and a much larger group of European theorists in the late nineteenth century, the myth of the state was crucial for the spiritual counterrevolution they planned for Western society in opening up a whole range of alternatives to the reign of materialism and commercialism. To Lloyd it seemed that the new doctrine of the state synthesized all the partial insights he had gleaned from Carlyle, Ruskin, and Mazzini. The role of the state was to supply higher values and worthier goals than those of a competitive individualism. "Is it necessary," he asked himself, "that man should always pursue wealth as now? That labor can never be organized on a basis in which the provision of homes, comforts for all being a matter of course, involving no mutual strife, the concerted effort of men may be aimed at the production of Beauties, moral, artistic, etc.?"[14]

In putting to himself the same question that Bellamy had asked his lyceum audience and that George posed in the Millennial Letter, Lloyd envisioned communal harmony as the creation of the state acting as the agent of a "compulsory publicity" that could command a declaration of intentions from its citizens and compel full disclosure of their activities. This definition, he admitted, carried the idea of citizenship far beyond the boundaries of Emersonian individualism. Emerson had sought to make the self-sufficient individual the highest social good. "But there is something higher than that—it is the fusion of perfected individuals in social action—the melting of the grains of sand into the perfect glass."[15] Only the state could complete the union of family, neighbors, and citizens, and strengthen those "sentiments of our religions" that harked back to the "communal period of one hearth, one table, one family." This frankly mystical view of the state, he mused, was "intimately allied with the power of dreaming, seeing visions, idealizing" as it called forth "inspirations" and "intuitions" of the millennium from the collective unconscious. The state in its religious aspect could first evoke and then fulfill the ancient longings for solidarity with "conceptions of Fatherhood, brotherhood, etc. widening (not revolutionizing) into applications and extensions affecting men as participants in all life."[16]

Just as these ecstatic visions threatened to plunge Lloyd over the brink into religious mysticism, a series of sharp encounters with Joseph Medill pulled him back to the more mundane matter of editorial freedom. His *Tribune* editorials had kept pace with the growing militancy of his attacks on monopoly in the *Atlantic* and the *North American Review*. One of them, "American Pashas," which appeared in December 1881, singled out John D. Rockefeller, Jay Gould, and Commodore Vanderbilt as new social types whose sultanic disregard of their American subjects called for new legal restraints. Each new monopoly had its own "pasha," and all of these "Mehemet Alis" ruled their domains as oriental despots. In the next four years there followed a procession of similar diatribes, each more astringent than its predecessor—a savage account of Jay Gould's takeover of Western Union; a deft and deadly caricature of James G. Blaine, Plumed Knight and presidential contender with his broken sword and tarnished shield; an exposé of New York City's gas monopoly; and a tale of mismanagement by Wall Street brokers of other people's money. Lloyd's heady notions of the state and a mounting disgust with sharp business practices were combining to lead him further and further away from the well-worn liberal paths trod by the editor of the *Tribune*.

Recently Lloyd had read *Progress and Poverty*, and though he was tempted to dismiss George's "lunar theories" on land and rent, he could not help agreeing with the Californian's predictions of a coming social crisis. Exactly how American workingmen were to win their industrial freedom, he scoffed, "only quacks like Henry George pretend they can see." Yet misguided as George might be, and nonsensical as his Single Tax might appear, his estimate of present tendencies seemed to Lloyd close to the mark.

Lloyd's objections to the one-dimensional features of Henry George's analysis, the exclusive emphasis on land, never changed. He distrusted George's dependence on classical theory and his fascination with formal systems. George, it seemed, lagged a century behind the rest of the world, dawdling along bemused with antique laws of production and distribution instead of paying attention to present trends or developments. Out of this closet world came his ridiculous formula—the *impôt unique* of the Physiocrats masquerading as the Single Tax. Lloyd could agree that land monopoly was one feature of the American economic transformation, but it was only one among a host of related problems calling for direct government interference. George's shopworn beliefs in competition and little government Lloyd dismissed as tired Jacksonian prejudices.

At another level, however, Lloyd and George shared similar religious values, as they would come to realize. Lloyd's distaste for mechanical solutions and his fascination with theories of the state masked ethical concerns and millennialist hopes that were fully as pronounced as George's. Both men had developed a grammar of politics that was studded with normative assumptions: monopoly in all its forms was evil; party government was corrupt; the people must be converted to righteousness. George sought to secure the principle of competition by freeing it from land monopoly; Lloyd, to purify it with a new public conscience that would regulate individualism without destroying it. Both men, moreover, sought the same ethical goals. Their distrust of socialism, their heavy reliance on Christian ethics, and their essentially millennialist view of the world should have made them brothers-in-arms in the reform battles of the late Gilded Age. Much of the time, however, they remained competing critics, interested but wary observers of the other's ideas and programs.

Lloyd's attacks on monopoly and political corruption were propelling him toward confrontation with Medill and an emotional collapse. By 1884 the psychological costs of his crusade had become prohibitive, and his health broke. There were persistent headaches that sent him to New York for a series of osteopathic treatments. Then it was "nervous prostration" that brought on a high fever. Then sciatica and with it the return of insomnia that had plagued him in his earlier crisis. His battle of wills with his boss, he admitted, was taking its toll. "I have gone to the edge of an abyss, but I have not gone over," he reported to his mother. "The battle has left me weak and sore. To whom should a man confess if not to his mother? Pray for me, and that the strength wasted on unnecessary temptation may somehow be given to me again for my work."[17] To his friends he admitted that he was "not well."

The final scene of his encounter with Medill opened with the presidential election of 1884 and his refusal to join the Chief in supporting Blaine and his financial backer, Jay Gould. Medill quickly confined him to editorial quarters by insisting that he stick to financial subjects for the duration of the campaign and leave politics alone. But the senior editor ought to have known his fractious lieutenant better than that. Under the pretense of analyzing the workings of monopoly, Lloyd continued to let fly at "the masters of all great business" who had invaded the political arena. Though he refused to vote for Cleveland, whose moral lapses he disapproved, he could not refrain from publicly rejoicing at Blaine's defeat and reminding Medill of the unseemly antics of the *Tribune*'s pals.

The war of nerves culminated in an editorial of Lloyd's exposing the activities of the Union Pacific lobby in Congress. When one of the railroad's directors complained to Medill of the "communist" he harbored on his staff, the editor made the mistake of reporting the complaint to Lloyd, thus presenting him with the issue he sought. Lloyd's rejoinder was "Wall Street Nihilism," in which he denounced the "boundless impudence" of the mousetrap men who tried to smear anyone with the courage to uncover their "scandalous railroad robberies." Next, as if to invite dismissal, he wrote a series of editorials on the labor question in which he defended labor unions as the best check on the depredations of big business. "To forbid the trades-unions," he warned, "is to feed conspiracy."[18]

Finally, in February 1885 Lloyd launched his last missile at the Gould syndicate, "The Mouse-Trap Men's Lobby," lambasting railroad lobbyists and attributing the lack of congressional enthusiasm for railroad regulation to their secret success in Washington corridors. In openly denouncing the management of the Union Pacific and the Gould lines, he resurrected William Lloyd Garrison's old abolitionist charge—"the sum of all villanies." If Medill needed a reason to fire him, here it was! In fact, the Chief moved cautiously and tried to avoid a breach. He knew that Lloyd was an able stylist whose articles sold newspapers. With his Bross connections he would not be easy to dismiss. Medill offered Lloyd a year's leave-of-absence in which to consider his future with the *Tribune*. He was perfectly free to stay or go, Medill made clear, but if he remained, he must make himself more amenable to editorial supervision. Here at last was the moment Lloyd had been waiting for, the choice put in the stark terms he preferred. He agreed to the leave, and in February 1885, he and Jessie set out for New York and a year abroad. Lloyd professed to be undecided as to his future course, but no one, least of all Jessie, doubted that he would quit. The Deacon saw them off with misgivings, for it was clear that his son-in-law was headed for another breakdown.

For six weeks Italy promised to restore his shattered nerves as he and Jessie toured its cities and studied the art and architecture they had read about in Chicago. Then in Venice, Jessie fell seriously ill with typhoid, and Lloyd spent another anguished six weeks nursing her back to health. Recovered but exhausted, she was sent back home while Lloyd reluctantly agreed to finish the tour alone.

His summer in England, despite Jessie's absence and worries about the future, proved to be the intellectual turning point in his life, supplying him with a set of new friends and ideas that he retained for the rest of his life. London he found seething with reform societies and projects that were still unknown in Chicago. His new English friends served as models of power without obligation, disinterested critics with an established constituency that was yet unavailable in the United States. The most congenial of these new friends was William Clarke, the Fabian whose conversion to moderate socialism provided Lloyd with an example to follow. In London he also met James Bryce, Charles Stuart Parnell, and, the most striking figure among his new acquaintances, William Morris, whom he described to Jessie as "a Norse god style of fellow, big, broad, hairy, loud and kind." At a socialist meeting he attended Morris held forth on matters ranging from industrial cooperation to sexual liberation, his outspoken views on the latter causing Lloyd some distress. "I was positively startled to hear Morris enunciate doctrines which would reduce love to the miscellaneous intercourse that would keep mankind on the level of a herd of wild dogs," he reported to Jessie. "It is a curious thing to note, that just as at the time of the French Revolution, so here the broadest ideas of free love are going hand in hand with other anarchies." For such loosening of the sexual bonds Lloyd, like Bellamy and George, had no tolerance. "To live purely until you find your mate—to live faithfully in love after you have found him or her—there can be but one law for both—that is real free love," he assured his wife. The great reforms he now dreamed of would leave untouched the institution of marriage and the "noble, tolerable animalism" it sanctified.[19]

In London, Lloyd also discovered a vital if inchoate labor movement, and took time to examine the new working-class cooperatives springing up in the city and the outlying towns. He attended the House of Commons and discussed the Irish problem with Parnell. "Meeting Englishmen like Bryce and Rogers and Morris and seeing the individual and powerful work they do makes me long to be my own man, and devote myself wholly to the work I have to do," he admitted.[20] With his brother David Demarest he made a quick trip through Scotland, taking with him George Eliot's autobiography which, he explained, taught him how best to manage a tempestuous talent. "One thing she has taught me over again, and that is that one can do one's life-work despite gravest physical limitations. Her way of working through headaches, prostration, nervousness, and all kinds of ills was heroic."[21]

He had nearly decided to leave the *Tribune* and strike out on his own. "I doubt whether I go back to the *Tribune*, I shall not decide until I have been able to talk it over with you and father," he wrote Jessie:

> I think perhaps the time has come for me to devote myself to a larger constituency—a constituency I already have. I cannot work for both. That did well enough when I was willing to burn my candle at both ends in my enthusiasm, but I must choose one to serve and follow ... And thanks to Father's more than fatherly kindness to me I do not see there is any reason I should do that. Mother Lloyd wrote me that Father [Bross] had said to her that it seemed to him it might be best for me not to return to the *Tribune* so that I see his mind is working in the same direction ... The future presses close with its work calling to be done by true nerves and fresh brains.[22]

The Deacon's approval, however, was itself half the problem: Lloyd could keep his financial independence at the price of his editorial freedom; or he could retain his freedom at the expense of his standard of living. It was an unenviable choice, and in making it he suffered the collapse his father-in-law had predicted.

His decision to retire was followed by a hurried visit to the Lake Country. From there, after a five-mile walk in the drenching rain, he returned to London, a trip made unbearable by the state of his nerves. In London he took to his bed, his physical energies drained and his mind a whirl of conflicting emotions. He was reduced to taking drugs in order to sleep and required the constant care of his brother. "I was ... more ill than I knew," he recalled, and "the reconquest of fair command of nerves, sleep, working power" proved "very slow."[23] After a month in bed he had apparently recovered enough to discontinue the bromides and make plans for returning to Winnetka. In the fall of 1885 David Demarest, having arranged for someone to meet him, put him on the boat for New York. Back home at the Wayside he seemed recovered, but whether because of lingering doubts or the need to make his departure from the paper official, he suffered a relapse. "As day after day goes by, and Henry has not been able to go back to work, but still has sleepless nights and terrible headaches by day, I don't feel sure that our hard pull is

over yet," Jessie confided to a friend. "It will take time and patience
and courage for the poor fellow to pull through, but I believe he will
come out well, and be able to do the world's work so near his heart.
We have given up all social and worldly ambitions I really believe.
This year of sore trial, of nearness to separation, has almost seemed
to alter our life and thought."[24]

His father-in-law's purchase of the Winnetka property for him
and a gift of ten shares of *Tribune* stock brought a measure of security, and under Jessie's care he slowly began to recover. By January
1886 he was able to promise Henry C. Adams, the liberal economist
who with Richard T. Ely was busy organizing the American Economic Association, that as soon as he was back in "fighting trim" he
would help publicize their new ideas, which he admitted to liking
"very much," even though he abhorred the word "economic."[25]

His first article after his recovery was an enthusiastic report on
the English labor movement, in which he summarized for the trade
paper *The Age of Steel* his impression of the enormous advance being
made by British workingmen. "Their remedy seems to me to lie in
combination—combinations to make better contracts with their employers, combinations like the supply stores of England, to buy their
goods in quantity at wholesale prices, combinations to enable working men to engage in productive enterprises on their own account,
and as their own capitalists and employers."[26] With all of these good
works, Lloyd declared, workingmen on both sides of the Atlantic
would continue to gain the sympathy and support "of the thinkers of
the world and of the lovers of mankind." Then, as if to give the lie to
his prophecy, came Chicago's Haymarket Riot in the spring of 1886
and the chance to act which he had denied himself until now.

7

CLOUD PALACES

AND PRACTICAL MEN

BY THE EARLY EIGHTIES, Henry George, his book finished, had abandoned California for the East and the work of spreading the gospel of the Single Tax in a missionary effort that would take him, first to Ireland, and then back to New York City in time for the frenzied mayoral campaign of 1886. In a different assessment of the costs of modernization, Henry Demarest Lloyd moved toward an open break with the American political establishment that would drive him into an alliance with farmers and workingmen to form a new political party. Edward Bellamy, having retired from the *Union* because of his failing health, was engaged in writing pale romances seemingly wholly divorced from the American social scene. None of the genteel readers of his fantasies and fables, least of all their author, could have guessed that before the eighties ended he would have joined George and Lloyd in playing out the climactic scenes in a nineteenth-century drama of moral politics.

Bellamy had returned from Hawaii mended in spirit but with a body still ravaged by tuberculosis. "I never weigh myself but am fatter than formerly," he dutifully reported to his parents from San Francisco while waiting, homesick and impatient, for his brother

Fred "to see the last dog hung" before coming home.[1] Back in Chicopee Falls, he took advantage of his new freedom to continue his explorations of Might-have-been-land. In 1878 he arranged for the printing of a limited edition of *Six to One: A Nantucket Idyll*, a fictional attempt to capture the evanescent moods of the Religion of Solidarity. The following year he published in serial form in the *Union* a second fantasy, *Dr. Heidenhoff's Process*. In 1884 came *Miss Ludington's Sister*, a third fable, subtitled *A Romance of Immortality*. These novellas, together with a number of short stories for *Scribner's* and the *Century*, comprised the bulk of his literary output before the appearance of *Looking Backward* in 1888.

Bellamy constantly complained of his difficulty in putting his ideas on paper. "In writing I am plagued infinitely by a sense of the insecurity of foundations," he explained. "I start on one stratum of thought, say the vulgar. Suddenly that seems to me superficial and I drop into the philosophical, from that I descend to the metaphysical, and finally deeming the idea too great for any fitting definition or expression, I relapse into the Indian Fakir's attitude of mere contemplation. Continual refinement in search of the ultimate generality."[2] All of his fiction, in fact, bore the marks of his obsession with abstract design, as characters in a slow conversational procession carry their ideas and messages about with them like so many placards.

This variety of fable he cultivated in the quiet atmosphere of his parents' home. Rufus Bellamy presided with amiability over the household, but it was the precise and exacting Maria who ruled it. In the last years of a long and untroubled ministry Rufus suddenly became embroiled in a dispute with his congregation over the existence and precise location of hell, and in 1882 his parishoners responded to his quiet remonstrances by dismissing him. Edward took the occasion of his father's resignation to break his own slender ties with organized religion. From now on he was free to indulge his scorn for sectarian prejudices as well as his taste for the whiskey the doctor prescribed. Once, coming home from the drugstore with an unwrapped bottle in hand, he was accosted by one of his father's deacons who remonstrated with him for tippling. The medicine, he reminded the local worthy, was a prescription, but even if it had not been, he and John Barleycorn would have struck up a warm friendship. "I am not like you deacons. I go in the front door and get it."[3] When the weather allowed, he could be seen by Baptist elder and curious neighbor alike ambling along the railroad tracks behind the house, flask in his hip pocket, a sheaf of papers clutched behind his back. Presently he would pause, fix his stare on the horizon, reach for the flask and tip it up, scribble a few notes, and resume his stroll.

By 1880 a quiet, courtly bachelor, he had settled into an ascetic routine. He neither danced nor played cards and volunteered little in the way of conversation, although when put a question that intrigued him, he would answer at length in a low, melodious voice, never groping for words and always arranging his thoughts in logical sequence. His favorite reading remained the Bible and the growing pile of novels, good and bad, he collected. He enjoyed solitary rambles in the woods nearby and usually took his gun along, although he was never known to bring any game home. Reserved, even taciturn, he nevertheless enjoyed the lively discussions around the supper table when his father provoked a good-natured debate. As the argument grew heated, he would jump up and stride around the dining room, rubbing his hands together and shouting, "If there is anything I like, it's a good mill."[4]

Only with his mother was he in intellectual accord, and only to her did he ever unburden himself. He was habitually untidy in his dress and seemingly oblivious to matters of style. He disliked stiff collars and was apt to wear the same soft blue shirt, until reminded to change it, and an unpressed blue or black serge suit spotted with grease. His lack of manual skills was a standing joke among members of the family, who complained that "Ed" could barely manage to light a fire. He was fascinated with gardening and considered a flower or vegetable patch one of the few pleasures left in a world of encroaching urban blight. In all outward appearances the author-recluse resembled no one so much as one of the introverted characters he created, and the settings in his fiction faithfully reproduced the placid flow of small-town New England life.

In 1880 Bellamy, his health slightly improved, decided to join with his brother Charles in launching their own experiment in personal journalism, like the one George had conducted with the San Francisco *Evening Post* and Lloyd with the *Pictorial Tax-Payer*. Charles Bellamy, who was to publish some half-dozen books of his own, had also reached pessimistic conclusions about American industrial growth, impressions he first collected in *The Breton Mills*, a novel published the same year as Edward's *Dr. Heidenhoff's Process*. Four

Edward Bellamy in the 1890s.

Emma Sanderson Bellamy at the time of her marriage in the early 1880s.

years later Charles published a second book, *The Way Out*, in which he advanced moderate proposals for social insurance, antimonopoly laws, an eight-hour day, and the nationalizing of land.

Although Bellamy was less interested in Charles's piecemeal reforms than in the psychological underpinnings for the good society, he joined him in vesting $1,200 in the Springfield *Penny News*, a tri-weekly sheet whose editorial content he supervised while his brother managed the finances. The brothers billed their venture as "The Largest and Oldest One Cent Paper in New England," but otherwise it bore the stamp of Edward's low-keyed style. "We mean to interest our readers, but we shall not seek to do so by spicing our columns with questionable personalities," he warned. "*The Penny News* means to be a gentleman."[5] True to his promise, Bellamy wrote measured commentary on subjects extending from working conditions in local mills to the terrorism of Russian nihilists, all of them treated in a flat, unvarnished style that had become habitual. He had always deplored the tendency to overstatement, and had insisted on "the partial degree of comparison" as distinct from the "wild statements" of even reputable journalists like Henry Demarest Lloyd. Now he practiced what he preached, dressing his editorials in the gray garb of a conversational style.

Surprisingly, *The Penny News* prospered, and within six months the brothers expanded it to a daily. But Edward, who found the return to a rigorous schedule exhausting, had begun to lose interest when the printing plant burned and the future of their venture grew doubtful. The partnership was finally dissolved over a friendly game of billiards, and he was free once more to pursue his elusive muse with proven strategies and seek a wife with new ones.

In the early seventies Rufus and Maria Bellamy had brought into their home a young girl of eleven, Emma Sanderson. Emma recalled her first glimpse of Edward, when he met her at the station to bring her home, as a "pimply young man with wild looking hair, very grave and preoccupied, but possessing a courteous manner and owner of a warm smile." Rufus, with a full complement of sons but no daughters, took to the good-natured girl immediately. "Emma," he once told her, "you're so comfortable. Everybody else in the house is always finding fault with me."[6] In 1873 he and Maria adopted her. For Maria, the girl was more a willing apprentice than a foster daughter, a cheerful domestic to be sent on errands or set to household chores. For her part, Emma developed a deep affection for the aging parson, stood in considerable awe of his wife, and was puzzled by the mixture of reserve and attachment she recognized in their son. Gradually Emma and "Ed" came to feel an affection for each other stronger than mere attachment, though Emma always complained good-naturedly that he treated her like a child. As the girl came of age and Bellamy, now thirty, accepted his need for a wife and children, the man whom his brothers accused of chronic indecision began to declare his love in secret notes chiding her for forgotten kisses. Emma was no intellectual and must often have been discomfited by her bashful suitor's reserve, but her simple affection more than matched Bellamy's more complicated feelings. In 1882, to the relief of Rufus Bellamy, who feared losing his foster child, and to the consternation of Maria, who feared a misalliance, Edward and Emma were married.

The events of the years leading up to his marriage were refracted through Bellamy's rambling, disjointed, and finally unfinished autobiographical novel dealing in one of its several versions with a "hermit" named Eliot Carson. His hero in all the guises given him objectifies his creator's inner life and hidden fantasies. In one version it is Eliot himself who is dying of consumption; in others, a friend whom he cherishes and mourns. In the various manuscripts Eliot Carson is a disillusioned lawyer, tired businessman, and jaded journalist, but in each of these roles he makes the same decision to turn his back on a false world and become a recluse who spends his days fishing and philosophizing. Eliot's decision proceeds from the same vocational crisis described by both Bellamy and Henry Demarest Lloyd at the outset of their careers, the conviction, as Eliot explains, that "the life he was leading deducted to routine physical and mental work ten hours a day was not worth having." Reserving suicide for a last resort, he plans his escape from a workaday world. "What could he do? Was there any way out of this bondage? What deliverance was there for him, a serf of civilization, whereby he might escape this treadmill existence and get air for his soul and mind?"[7] Journalism? "It is a good trade," Eliot muses, "when a man controls the paper he edits and can say what he will." Yet newspapers require capital, and capital means meddling. In fact, Bellamy's alter ego concludes, all professions are "states of involuntary servitude." Accordingly, Eliot, "educated, of high character, with the culture and manner of a gentleman and the practical line of a man of business," is a paragon without prospects, a dropout who takes his meager investments into the woods, there to drive life into a corner.

Eliot Carson is a prophet without disciples until he meets Edna Damon, whose teacher, confessor, and eventual lover he becomes. Edna Damon is only the first of a series of Bellamy's ideal mates, the fashionably liberated but genteel young woman, endowed with high seriousness, intellectually tenacious though socially demure, open and straightforward but vulnerable to a paralyzing doubt and dread that only Eliot can remove. She has lost her faith and with it her will to endure the "blind brutality, the hideous cruelty of life." Hers is a spiritual sickness unto death, and she prefers a life of "social quarantine" to one of pretense. Dismissed from her church as a "female infidel," she retires to the country to recover her "moral tone" and there encounters Eliot, a latter-day Lazarus who tells her that he too has just "risen from the dead" and begun "the better life."

In all of Bellamy's tales the dialogue becomes the "plot" as his characters exchange philosophies in a confessional drama. The discourse between Eliot and Edna (with the exception of an original boating accident there is no other action) is the work of Bellamy's double consciousness as they earnestly debate the meaning of life. Eliot is the masculine half of the author's persona—"rather tall and powerfully built but with the outlines of a sensitive mouth and chin." And like his creator, Eliot is painfully shy in front of the ladies, ill-at-ease and with no knack for mincing words "as if I were cutting up cat's meat." In joint retreat from the world, Eliot and Edna find in each other the completion they seek, and together they become the question and the answer, the knower and the known.

In the beginning Edna is wholly concerned with the damaged state of her soul, as Eliot brings his liberating message to her in the form of a question: "Is there anything else more worth while on earth than the enlargement of oneself, the extension of the limits of one's conscious being?" With that cosmic question she is launched on wings of metaphysical flight with Eliot as her pilot.

Edna is fully equal to the demands of an intellectual courtship and more than willing to take on her share of its burdens. Thus Eliot is spared—much as his creator managed to avoid—the torments of wooing and winning a young woman who is perfectly willing to speak for herself. But Edna desperately needs the succor that only

Eliot's Religion of Solidarity can provide. The heart of their uninter-rupted discourse concerns questions of immortality, the dual self, and the conscious cultivation of a state of impersonality. Edna's cure lies in the conversion experience already undergone by her lover, who lectures her and prophesies the coming of a new race of serene and selfless people. "This is the new religion I have to offer you . . . a religion which . . . tells you that you are more god than man, and makes your manhood a trifling thing, compared with the cultivation of your godhead." At last Edna learns the truth of Eliot's belief that "the dungeons men build out of stone or dig underground are noth-ing to the dungeon that man's own individuality necessarily is to him," and she is ready to join him in a life of solidarity.

It was not difficult for Bellamy to recognize in his truncated ro-mance the conflicting demands in his own life: an obsession with death countered by a rage for life; a conviction of physical and per-haps sexual inadequacy combined with a hunger for experience; and weariness with a world that perversely demanded even greater in-volvement. His Religion of Solidarity had originally been designed to help him avoid bruising confrontations. In this sense, even though he could not resolve the paradox posed by his philosophy or, indeed, finish the novel, in opting for the union of his twin personalities, he had at least opened the door to meaningful action. Like his creation Eliot Carson, he was freeing himself to preach the message of soli-darity.

Emma Sanderson was no Edna Damon, and Bellamy's marriage never generated the intellectual passion of his fictional search. If life with Emma lacked the philosophical intensity of his ideal matrimo-nial state, it was nevertheless filled with quiet companionship, chil-dren, and a placid wife who understood his needs and loved and cared for him the rest of his life. For the next year the young Bel-lamys continued to live with his parents until they found a house of their own down the street. There in their new home a son, Paul, was born in 1884, and a daughter, Marion, two years later. At least part of the crisis of the inner man had been resolved, and Bellamy settled to the task he had given Eliot Carson of spreading the gospel of soli-darity in the novels and short stories he began to publish. Money was a constant problem, since his decision to free-lance meant re-duced circumstances. Marion remembered living "very abstemiously" as a child, but Bellamy never objected to the lack of amenities in his Thoreauvian household.[8]

There was no politics in Bellamy's fictional world and very little social texture as he concentrated, instead, on scrutinizing the motives of his emblematic characters. His conservatism, moreover, was not easily set aside, and his distaste for professional reformers was still strong. "Mistake of abusing the rich," he noted in his journal, "those who profit by present count. Nobody profits by it . . . We are all in one condemnation." As for selfishness, "one class is just as selfish as another."[9] The desire for wealth, as he analyzed it, consisted of three distinct motives: an appetite for comforts and luxuries; a hunger for distinction; and a longing for power. The problem for modern society was to secure the first condition for everyone by indulging a universal craving for abundance while at the same time curbing the individual drive for distinction and dominance. In planning the society of the future the Eliot Carsons of the world should practice a form of stewardship, voluntarily sharing their wealth with the less fortunate. A recurring theme in the notebooks concerned the new hero with his modern magic wand who distributes his money out of sheer impulse and with a view to his own amusement. "Of course he will do good rather than evil, but it is in the fun to be gotten out of the experiment with their lives rather than the mere business of almsgiving that he is to find satisfaction and reward." In an added comment Bellamy supplied the moral: "How the romance of fairy land would return if rich men did likewise."[10]

The fairylands of the future would be arranged to avoid too-frequent interference with private lives and to discourage the overgrowth of the affections. Love and loyalty were not to be repressed but redirected away from personalities toward ideals. Life would be lived on a plateau of the senses where families avoided both the heights of emotion and the depths of depression.

> Therefore it is resolved [in such a depersonalized society] that parental love shall be modified by circumstances as to be greatly restricted by its present development. Mothers shall indeed nurse their infants but be relieved of nearly all other care of them, and fathers shall have no intimate relations with them.[11]

Children in such a world would be educated and maintained by the state, which is best equipped to provide for their welfare, and parental love would become "an effete survival, an aching root of a tooth no longer useful." In the good society there would be no more parental interference and none of the close family ties that had bound him as a child. Future Eliot Carsons would appear *ab novo* on the American scene—new men stepping out of an anonymous past into an impersonal present.

The modern magic wand was only one of the metaphors with which Bellamy began to trace the "sudden transformation of an otherwise hopeless situation." Nearly all of his stories and novels center on the conversion experience—an acho of the Reverend Joseph Bellamy's call for the millennium—that brings retrieval from disaster or escape from Nemesis through magic. The "fatal fact" in his stories is a paralyzing confinement in the personal and the private.[12] Magic marks the passage from self to society by disclosing a larger social possibility and indicating an escape route from isolation to community. In all his fiction from now on Bellamy would touch his characters with a magic wand that completed their lives by revealing to them the way to the blessed community.

In an early short story, "Two Days Solitary Confinement," the illusion is the false sense of guilt hypnotically induced in a morbid young man who convinces himself, without a shred of evidence, that he has killed a tramp. The story records the rapid deterioration of family affections as the would-be murderer's brother and his wife become convinced of his guilt. "There was a constraint between them like that between strangers, but stronger and more chilling by far than ever that is. There is no chill like that which comes between friends, and the nearer the friends, the more deathly the cold." Paralyzed by guilt, the protagonist can offer no convincing explanation of the crime, or clear himself from the charge which he is convinced is true. Just as he is driven to the verge of insanity and clamors to confess, the police find the real murderer, and he experiences freedom for the first time, announcing to his family that he feels "as if I had just been dug up after being buried alive."[13]

In another short story of family relations, "The Cold Snap," magic functions as the mystical regeneration of the spirit through the ritual of prayer in a world caught up in the "eternal clutch" of

"God's cold." The narrator and his wife have just returned to the family homestead in a small New England village when a "cold snap," as they first think it, sends the temperature plummeting far below zero. Dimly the husband senses "how wholly by sufferance it is that man exists at all on earth," but his fears are forgotten in the temporary exhilaration of suspended routine. Slowly, however, as the cold deepens into catastrophe and the farmhouse fills with a glacial silence, bravado gives way to anxiety and then to paralysis of the will, until the family unit has disintegrated under the stupefying effects of the cold. Communication with the outside world is cut off: the members of the family are imprisoned by a deadly enemy intent on undermining their wills. "Other forces of nature have in them something of the spirit a man can sympathize with, as the wind, the waves, the sun; but there is something terribly inhuman about the cold . . . a congenial principle brooding over the face of chaos in the aeons before light was." The cold snap, by now a terrifying hint of a cosmic heat death suggestive of Henry George's fear of entropy, also threatens the death of the heart. With a seemingly diabolical indifference, the cold detaches the family one by one from a life-sustaining communion and quietly awaits the capitulation of each individual will to live. Finally, in a last desperate act of defiance, the family comes together to pray. Always before, the narrator reflects, praying had seemed simply "a fit and graceful ceremony" from which no one expected anything in particular. "But now the meaning so long latent became eloquent . . . There was a familiar strangeness which touched us all." It is not divine intervention that saves the narrator's family but the mystical renewal of quiet affection and with it the will to live that ritual effects. The rediscovery of Christian habit in the ceremonial act brings the family back from the margins of dissolution and death, and the next day the cold snap breaks.[14]

Where Henry Demarest Lloyd envisioned the ideal family as a bustling and even collisive group of individuals happily engaged, like his own, in playing the social roles that expand their personalities and extend their commitments, Bellamy's family is contemplative and dispassionate, a union of souls joined in a state of perfect impersonality. Seldom did his plots come to him through observation of the life around him, but appeared instead as fragmentary propositions or odd situations to explore:

Man sensitive to touch at a distance without contact or to feel with extraordinary intensity.

Story. Case of a rich miser caught himself in a burglar trap in his own vaults, starving to death, welcomes approach of burglar as his only chance for life.

To describe the mood ... as escaping from a narrow place into a large one that the close impression of story shall not be pacific but exhilarating.

"Scaling the Heights." Title of the subjective-objective story of the man who sought to raise himself to the divine state by attaining the combination of subjective-objective in himself.

The next stage in the process of composition was the solidifying of these impressions and their arrangement in an argument:

Story of coming race. How pessimism had so theorized on the evil condition of the race that suicide was the fashion, and a school of thugs was established. The most cultured of the race also as solemn duty took life whenever they could out of sheer compassion. A convention called, which declares that the pessimists are right as the world stands, but if men were physically, morally, mentally what they ought to be, life would be more enjoyable. They also decide that none of the reforms, political or social, which have been agitated since the beginning as means of ameliorating the race, have any chance of success until men are more moral and intelligent. The experiment of stirpiculture is attempted. Hope is born again among men. They see a future for the race and devote themselves with enthusiasm to the new cult.[15]

Out of these sketches and outlines came the finished fable. There is a foreground in Bellamy's tales—the thinly disguised village life of Chicopee Falls—and in the distance clouds charged with moral mysteries hang heavy and portentous over the pastoral scene. But the middle ground of social exchange, the depiction of character and the unfolding of drama, is conspicuously lacking. Where the gap between conception and execution is widest, the result is sentimentality. Bellamy's first novel, *Six to One: A Nantucket Idyll*, his first major attempt to apply the Religion of Solidarity and explore the impersonal, is a case in point.

Six to One is the most directly autobiographical of Bellamy's novels. The "one" is Frank Edgerton, a New York newspaperman suffering from nervous collapse, who comes to Nantucket to recuperate. The "six" comprise a band of feminine healers of the spirit for whom the arrival of an eligible male is an occasion for merriment and matchmaking. Edgerton is restored to health by their combined ministrations which include clambakes, sailing expeditions, and hours of desultory conversation. Frank falls in love with one of the girls, rescues her from drowning, and marries her with the intention of saving her from a lonely life by the sea. At first glance the tale seems a simple reverie peopled with all-too-charming types dawdling toward an entirely predictable conclusion.

From the outset, however, it is clear that Edgerton and Addie Follett, his sea-bride—like Eliot Carson and Edna Damon—are projections of their creator's dual consciousness, the one a representative of the personal, the other of the impersonal, state of mind. The story with its dialogue framed as a debate and the action determined by opposing philosophies is an extension of Bellamy's continuing controversy with himself. Edgerton, by his own definition, is a "broken-down man," a victim of recurrent fits of depression. As a newspaperman he has been completely engrossed in the personal, "transmitting the sensations of a world through his nerves every day" until he realizes that the hectic pace and the meaninglessness of modern life have made him a "mental invalid."[16] He needs the restorative power which only the sea can provide.

Addie Follett is a "nun of the sea" who has renounced the world and devoted herself to cultivating the impersonal aspects of consciousness. "There are personal and impersonal eyes," Edgerton reflects, "personal eyes that are full of an importunate individuality, and impersonal eyes that are serene meeting-places of souls. When you looked into this young lady's eyes you did not see her at all; she seemed to leave herself behind to come and meet you there." Unlike the other girls, Addie is content with her island existence. The sea, she tells Edgerton, confesses and shrives her. Edgerton, who prefers his nature domesticated and companionable, replies that the sea is as incomprehensible as the modern God, while rivers and lakes are like demigods and lesser divinities with a touch of humanity in them.

"You complain," Addie counters, "that the sea doesn't give a rap whether we live or die, but that's precisely the key to the highest sort of sympathy we mortals have with it, for it is an impersonal sympathy, in which we as much forget our personalities as it ignores them."

To Edgerton the sea at first seems a source of spiritual renewal, its incomprehensible vastness soothing his shattered nerves. "His eyes felt as his muscles would, were the attraction of gravitation suddenly annulled and the body made weightless . . . He seemed resting on the heaving bosom of infinity." Yet Edgerton also senses in the sea a jealous rival dominating the girl with its capricious moods, its waves "sullenly" feeling their way through the darkness to enclose her, and "moaning" and "muttering" on the beach. Then in a figure which was beginning to recur to him with increasing frequency Bellamy attributes to the sea a martial valor and stoic selflessness from which men can learn the meaning of life.

> The waves sweeping across the unbroken breadth of the Atlantic, tripped and fell thunderously at their feet. The hemispherical journey of each of them represented an achievement of Titanic power that gave a startling impression of the prodigality of force in nature. With such momentum the interminable succession of rollers came on, that the word of God seemed freshly needed to stay each one with its "thus far and no further." The invisible reins of Omnipotence must needs have been upon the necks of these mighty white-maned coursers to curb them at the critical moment.

The significance of the scene is lost on neither readers nor the spectators, one of whom exclaims: "The sight of these brave waves pouring so steadily on to certain destruction, one after another in endless ranks, merely to wash away a mile or two of land in a century—what an example of self-sacrifice it is. If I were a general, I'd bring my army down on the beach before leading them into battle." To which another of Edgerton's young companions adds: "And they die so gayly; that's what I like. Your sour heroes I never could fancy." But it is left to Edgerton to summarize the lesson: "Surely death is after all the supreme function of life, its consummate act. And yet in what a shabby, broken-spirited, draggle-tail fashion most people die." When it comes his turn to die with Addie after failing to drag her out of the undertow, he decides that it would be manlier to die voluntarily rather than wait for utter exhaustion. In Bellamy's magic kingdom, however, the moment of submission is instantly followed by providential rescue. As for Julian West in the year 2000, so now for Frank Edgerton—with capitulation to the impersonal comes the magical release to the forces of life. Just as he gives up his struggle a boat arrives, and he and his sea-bride are saved.

Attempted rescue takes a fatal turn in *Dr. Heidenhoff's Process*, a science-fiction fable of guilt and redemption woven like *Looking Backward* around the dream. The central concern of the novel is Henry Burr's unrequited love for the proud Madeline Brand. Out-maneuvered by the villain, Henry goes off to Boston and a new job while Madeline is disgraced by the loss of her virtue. Presently she appears in Boston, and Henry finds that his love, now elevated by pity, is stronger than ever. But Madeline is consumed with guilt, and Henry grows desperate to the point of madness at his inability to free her from the past. Late one evening after a painful interview punctuated by a farewell kiss, he returns to his lodging, takes a large draft of sleeping powder, and falls into a deep sleep.

The next day Henry seemingly discovers the magic formula for redemption in a newspaper advertisement announcing an "Extirpation of Thought Process" invented by one Dr. Heidenhoff. A visit to the good doctor reveals that he has indeed solved the mysteries of "galvano-therapeutics" or mechanical brainwashing, which obliterates the "obnoxious train of recollections" that heretofore have "wielded their cruel scepters over human lives." Henry produces a willing Madeline for experimentation, the operation is performed, and while she recovers on the couch, the doctor expatiates on the larger moral implications of his invention which is clearly Bellamy's major interest.

Thought extirpation, Dr. Heidenhoff assures Henry, will bring a moral revolution. Crime and revenge will disappear with the forgotten slight. Friendship will no longer be threatened by remembered disservices. Eventually, the doctor explains as Madeline stirs on the couch, his memory-extirpation machine will bring a new understanding of the discontinuous nature of the personality. Consciousness exists only in the present, and "it is in that moment only that the individual exists." In an eternal present true solidarity will at last be possible. Someday, the doctor predicts, there will come an entire society of supermen who can accept the discontinuity of personality and exchange bondage to the past for the freedom of utopia.

Henry Burr and Madeline Brand, however, have not reached utopia, and the magic transformation fails to arrive. Her cure is the product of her lover's morphine dream, and Henry awakes to see the "clear, hard lines of reality" replacing the "vague contours of dreamland." A note arrives from Madeline telling him of her decision not to marry him for fear that his happiness would be contaminated by her guilt. "Is it only when death touches our bodies that we are called?" she asks. "Oh, I am called. I am called indeed!" The magical liberation disappears with the dream, and the passage to utopia is blocked.[17]

Dissociation of personality, which would serve as one of the main psychological props for Bellamy's utopia in *Looking Backward*, also provides the theme of the last of his fantasies, *Miss Ludington's Sister*, subtitled *A Romance of Immortality*. Here the situation is determined by the longing, not to forget the past, but to capture and hold it. Miss Ida Ludington is a middle-aged spinster who as a beautiful young girl suffered a disfiguring disease which left her hideously seamed and scarred. Though she craves some kind of external permanence to compensate for her lost beauty, she is forced to witness the destruction of her pastoral village of Hilton by the invasion of the machine. She leaves the town and with her sizable inheritance buys a large plot of land on rural Long Island where she builds a replica of her childhood Hilton down to the last brick and nail. There in lonely splendor she relives her childhood, visiting the schoolhouse, sitting in the back of the church, and wandering the empty elm-shaded green of her duplicate town. The reigning princess of her fantasy world is the young girl in the portrait hanging over the mantelpiece, the seventeen-year-old Ida who, so the aging spinster believes, governs the dispossessed spirits of her neighbors, in real life long dead.

Miss Ludington is joined in her haven by the son of a distant relative, Paul deRiemer, whom she adopts and raises in her ghost town. The boy promptly falls in love with the girl in the picture whose history and secret life Miss Ludington relates to him. Paul grows to manhood and goes off to college but returns with no serious thoughts of a vocation, wholly content with his passion for the spirit

Ida. To justify his misplaced devotion he invents a philosophy of immortality which he teaches his foster parent. What people consider simply stages of growth, he tells her, are in fact distinct personalities in themselves. Thus Miss Ludington's former self—the lovely lost Ida of her childhood—is not really lost at all but is as immortal as her present self. So obsessed is he with proving his theory that he gives himself completely to the worship of the "spirit-child" Ida and eagerly awaits the reunion which death will bring. Throughout the romance there are parallels between the author's life and that of his young hero: a prolonged vocational crisis; an anguished search for emotional security; an excessive "ideality" dictating a retreat from society; and a self-induced impotence. But Bellamy, like his alter ego, was seeking escape from inaction, and again magic supplies the means. As Paul grows increasingly dissatisfied with this emasculating love, he and his guardian visit a famous medium in New York City who produces the youthful Ida briefly in spirit form. At a subsequent materialization the medium, who conveniently suffers from a weak heart, dies in the midst of the translation. Her life passes into the spirit-form of Ida, who promptly steps forth from the shades and into the life at Hilton.

The rest of the labored fantasy involves Paul's painful extrication of himself from the trammels of adoration. Finally he declares his love to Ida, whereupon the all-too-full-bodied maiden runs away leaving a letter in which she confesses all. Alas, she is not what he supposed her! The whole business has been a monstrous hoax. Undaunted, Paul rushes after her, wins her, and, after the timely death of Miss Ludington, brings her home to his pastoral paradise, a deserted village which they can now fill with life.[18]

By 1886 the real world of industrial ugliness and labor strife was closing in on Bellamy as marriage and the arrival of children brought new responsibilities and uncertainties. After the birth of their son, Emma was subject to bouts of depression which were not improved by the discovery that she was pregnant again. Her husband, sympathetic and anxious, promised to "try to make it easier for you . . . and to provide more recreation for you." "Poor little duck," he wrote on one of his rare absences from home, "I should like to know that you are feeling more cheerful just now." When Emma's vacation came, he took over the management of the children, assuring her that now he realized "how it is to be a bachelor once more," he saw plainly "that I did a very sensible thing when I got married." Man was not meant to live alone.

One sign of his contact with the jarring life of industrial society was the confession he provided Eliot Carson in a final section of the unfinished manuscript he was about to lay aside. "Then his child came, not anticipated with much pleasure. Submitted to. With it comes the revelation of his oneness with mankind. He cannot thenceforward bear the thought of leaving his children, any man's, anybody's children to struggle in such a horrid world as this. Cured once and for all of Hermitism and self-absorption, he plunges with enthusiasm, with tremendous earnestness into the study of social conditions and develops nationalism." In a second and even more pointed revelation given to his protagonist—here significantly called "Caesar"—Bellamy explained his own sudden conviction of the need to act.

> I have children; the future America is more to me for their dear sake than the present America. Yes, and not only for my children, for the look ahead to some mysterious tie that makes my life one with my children, makes it one with the race of men, for we are bodies of one another. I was, I admit, dull of mind and slow of heart not to see and understand this before. Quicker men would not have needed the example of the child to teach them, but I have learned now once for all that selfishness is suicide, the only true suicide.[19]

Bellamy's own conversion to reform was less sudden and dramatic than his alter ego's, but it too stemmed from the discovery recorded in the journals that "meditation, introspection, is not alone the avenue to realization of Solidarity, but rather deeds of generosity and self-devotion. These are better than fasting and prayer." Solidarity, he had now concluded, was a moral state of grace to be won by purposive social action. This much his "fictions" were disclosing to him.

If Bellamy had acquired a new understanding of the need for reform, he had not at the same time learned how to proceed. As he readily admitted, he had grown up quietly in a "thriving village" in rural Massachusetts "where there were no very rich and very few poor, and everybody who was willing to work was sure of a fair living." He recalled his trip to Europe as a young man and the shock of ugly cities and teeming ghettos that formed "the blue background of misery" for working-class life. But it was his return to a Chicopee Falls transformed by technology that had first shown him "the inferno of poverty beneath civilization." Even so, he had been driven by the "sordid and selfish necessity" of earning a living to continue turning out "in a desultory way" seemingly escapist fiction.

> In none of the writings of the period [he recalled after the publication of *Looking Backward*] did I touch on the social question, but none the less all the while it was in mind, as a problem not by any means given up, how poverty might be abolished and the economic equality of all citizens of the republic be made as much a matter of course as their political equality. I had always the purpose, some time when I had sufficient leisure, to give myself earnestly to the examination of this great problem, but meanwhile kept postponing it, giving my time and thought to easier tasks.[20]

This explanation, written later, told little of his ten-year struggle to adapt the Religion of Solidarity to the real world, and it said nothing of his initial retreat to privatism or the extended moratorium he had allowed himself. The key to his explanation was the phrase "social question," implying as it did a unitary problem detached from complications and interdependencies and requiring for its solution only good intentions and singleness of purpose. Bellamy, like George and Lloyd, was resorting to an inherited evangelical glossary to help explain and locate the problem of social control where most Americans still believed it belonged—in the moral consciousness of the people where a collective change of heart might be induced. It was this conviction that explained a second bias, an aversion to programmatic reform and political alliances. "I had never, previous to the publication of the work [*Looking Backward*], any affiliation with any class or sect of industrial or social reformers," he admitted, "nor, to make my confession complete, any particular sympathy with any undertaking of the sort."[21]

Again, he agreed with Lloyd and George in holding fast to the principle of private property and acknowledgments of natural inequality. Quarrels between labor and capital, he had written during the Great Railroad Strike, were as old as the discrepancy between wealth and poverty. "There is no remedy for this state of inequality by any positive provision of government or society, for these contracts in what men have or have not are just as natural and unavoidable as are the differences in people's height or weight or the color of their eyes." No rights were more sacred, he had concluded, than those of property. "They are the underpinnings of all possible social and civil organization from a township to a nation."[22]

His earlier pronouncement, he now admitted, had been exaggerated, but had he really changed his mind? How could he build a society based on solidarity without recourse to the collectivist blueprints of radicals who denied all rights of property? Such questions strengthened his preference for fiction as the vehicle for his ideas. If fables and fantasy could serve for private explorations of the Religion of Solidarity, they might also help to investigate utopia. "Nothing outside the exact sciences has to be so logical as the thread of a story if it is to be acceptable," he reminded himself. "There is no such test of a false and absurd idea as trying to fit it into a story. You may make a sermon or an essay or a philosophical treatise as illogical as you please and no one will know the difference, but all the world is a good critic of a story." Since giving up *The Penny News* he had been toying with the idea of writing a fantasy in the tradition of Sir Thomas More's *Utopia* as a simple description of an ideal society. In one of the early sketches in his journal he outlined an imaginary society called Antononna, a meritocracy run by a community of elders:

> There were no popular elections in Antononna. No one under the age of forty was eligible for any public office. The men most eminent in their several professions of medicine, great inventions and men who in any way had worthily served the State constituted a class of eligibles, from whom the governors were chosen by lot in order to avoid all possibility of emulation or self-seeking and rendering pride in emulation absurd . . . For lower offices lots are drawn of the whole body of citizens for the council of the entire State. No taxes. Everything is the State's.[23]

By 1886 the combined pressures of the Haymarket Riot and a series of railroad strikes led by the Knights of Labor gave Bellamy's musings a new clarity. From the bag of fictional tricks supplied by the "modern magic wand" he drew his solution to the problem of utopian entry—"an extremely simple method of reflexive hypno-tism, a self-magnetization, which while leaving the patient in full possession of all his powers of mind and body, and apparently in a perfectly normal state, practically suspended his consciousness of the passage of time." Though he was unaware as yet of the imagina-tive lengths to which his use of time would carry him, he had in fact replaced the classical concept of *utopia*, "the good place," with the prophecy of *euchronia*, "the good time coming," a conceptual shift that would make all the difference.

In undertaking a utopian novel, however, Bellamy did not envi-sion at first a serious contribution to social thought like Henry George's *Progress and Poverty*. *Looking Backward* was originally con-ceived as a simple fable of social happiness, a glimpse of earthly paradise whose arrival mankind could await but not hasten. "There was no thought," he later confessed, "of contriving a house which practical men might live in, but merely of hanging in mid-air, far out of reach of the sordid and material world of the present, a cloud-pal-ace for an ideal humanity." To gain the needed scope for the imagi-nation he first unfolded his story in the year 3000—measuring time in the millennia so appealing to the religious sensibility—and set it in Asheville, North Carolina, the provincial capital of a world state. His scene opened on an enormous parade of a departmental division in the world industrial army marching toward its annual muster-day ceremony, where new recruits to the universal work ethic took the oath of duty before the world standard, and veterans were demobi-lized with the thanks of humanity. In constructing this initial scene, Bellamy had been struck with the martial order he described—"each battalion with its appropriate insignia, the triumphal arches, the gar-landed streets, the banquets, the music."[24] The whole meaning of solidarity seemed to rest on such ceremonies of rededication and re-vitalization.

Then suddenly, as he reread his description suggestive of Civil War parades, there came one of those moments of insight that change the entire concept of a work. The industrial army, which in its anonymity and spirit of dedication had at first seemed to him sim-ply a rhetorical analogy to the military, now appeared as an organiz-ing principle for reforming society, "a complete working model . . .

the unanswerable demonstration of its feasibility drawn from the actual experience of whole nations organized and maneuvered as armies." His discovery led to an immediate recasting of the novel. "Instead of a mere fairy tale of social perfection, it became the vehicle of a definite scheme of industrial reorganization." The analogy which he admitted "had been floating in my mind, for a year or two" underwent a drastic transformation, and the original myth of an earthly paradise out of time and beyond the reach of history quickly became a model for social planning.

> The form of the romance was retained, although with some impatience, in the hope of inducing the more to give it a reading. Barely enough story was left to decently drape the skeleton of the argument and not enough, I fear, in spots for even that purpose. A great deal of merely fanciful matter concerning the manners, customs, social and political institutions, mechanical contrivances, and so forth of the people of the thirtieth century, which had been intended for the book, was cut out for fear of diverting the attention of the readers from the main theme. Instead of the year A.D. 3000, that of A.D. 2000 was fixed upon as the date of the story. Ten centuries had at first seemed to me none too much to allow for the evolution of anything like an ideal society. But with my new belief as to the part which the national organization of industry is to play in bringing the good time coming, it appeared to me reasonable to suppose that by the year 2000 the order of things which we look forward to will already have become an exceedingly old story.[25]

His purpose had completely altered. Henry George experienced his conversion riding alone in the Oakland hills. Revelation came to Henry Demarest Lloyd as he read newspaper accounts of the Great Railroad Strike. Now Bellamy had been touched by his own modern magic wand and was about to throw his lot in with the reformers.

8

THE PROPHET FROM SAN FRANCISCO

HENRY GEORGE stepped off the train in New York in the summer of 1880 with a suitcase, a handful of introductions, and the conviction that the spell had been broken and he had at last found the road to success. He was forced to admit, however, that his transcontinental trail lay strewn with unpaid debts and that he had left Annie and the children to manage on the slimmest of margins. Soon, in fact, Annie wrote that the family had given up the little house on First Street for a boardinghouse and that she had settled her husband's bills by selling part of his library. "It is at such a time as this a man feels the burden of a family," George admitted. "It is like swimming with heavy clothes on." To economize still further he took lodgings on the Lower East Side and began feverishly hunting for a job. The enthusiasm of the prophet was waning. "I did feel depressed when I wrote you," he confided to one of his friends in recalling the "darkest hour" of his new life. "But it was not so much on account of circumstances. I am in the way of being a good deal of a Stoic. Adverse fortune does not depress me—what always worries me is the thought I might have done better, that it is that to blame, and it seemed to me then as if I had been fooling my time away very largely."[1]

Such momentary misgivings seemed the sharper because George had arrived in New York with a mission. He was convinced that the reform of American society awaited the mass conversion of the nation's middling ranks of sensible citizens, whose Christian beliefs and conservative social views could be marshaled by an educative politics for a final stand against the forces of monopoly and privilege. To Charles Nordhoff, a reporter for the New York *Sun* and fellow observer of the reform scene, George stated his conviction that "successful efforts can come from the class above, not below."[2] Concepts of Christian service and middle-class stewardship, which studded the final chapters of *Progress and Poverty*, now defined for him a role as prophet, the clear-eyed man of vision who, like Bellamy's Perez Hamlin, could rise above class appeals and partisan concerns to teach an entire generation the ways of social righteousness.

These millennialist sentiments, which supplied George with a set of simple categories and a moral glossary, also dampened his enthusiasm for conventional party politics and the upcoming presidential election. But when Democratic party stalwarts in New York, mindful of his services in California, sought to enlist him, and, for the moment, there was nothing better in the offing, he agreed to take to the stump on issues of his own choosing. These, it quickly appeared, were too explosive for the professionals who had not reckoned the Single Tax among their party's most cherished principles. "Well," George wrote in recounting his one performance, "the audience applauded, but you should have seen the men on the platform there; and I went off without a man to shake my hand."[3] That evening, on route to his next speaking engagement, he received a telegram from the state committee thanking him profusely for services rendered but canceling the rest of his tour. From then on George was free to perfect a new political independence.

Still floundering professionally and financially, George became desperate as 1880 drew to a close. "I shall not go back to California, unless for something," he wrote to a friend on the West Coast. "I don't know precisely what I shall do . . . I shall go to work if I have to go to the case."[4] Meanwhile he was reduced to borrowing, an expedient that depressed him but did not deter him from dunning his friends. "It is not so much the want of money," he complained to one of the lenders, "as the mental effect it produces—the morbid condition." Those who had never known poverty could not understand the appeal of suicide that had recently "weighted" his mind.[5]

Then came an offer of a temporary job ghost-writing a congressional committee report for Congressman Abram S. Hewitt, whom the fates were reserving for the role of George's victorious opponent in the New York City mayoralty contest of 1886. Hewitt offered George fifty dollars a week to write the report, but his disapproval of the first draft coupled with George's request for a hundred-dollar advance ended the relationship. In 1886 each would recall the incident differently, George denouncing the congressman as a shameless exploiter of talent, and Hewitt dismissing the prophet from San Francisco as a penniless scribbler and an ingrate.

With the new year George's fortunes mended. The reviews of his book, though not always favorable, attracted the attention of New York's journalistic community, and presently George placed two articles, one on taxation in the prestigious *North American Review*, which had just rejected Henry Demarest Lloyd's exposé of Standard Oil, and a second with *Appleton's*, which was already publishing Edward Bellamy's short stories. By the spring of 1881 he had saved enough to bring on Annie and the children and settle them in a porter's lodge in Kingsbridge Road in the outlying Fort Washington section of the city. Then a hurried trip across the continent to settle his debts and learn in San Francisco that he had received two votes for the United States Senate in the upper house of the state legislature, "about as near," he joked, "as I shall ever come to being elected to anything," a not wholly accurate prediction but a measure of his sudden disinterest in conventional politics.[6]

Progress and Poverty continued to make slow headway against unfavorable reviews and noncommittal notices, as its author waited despondently for the serious reading he knew it deserved. Instead he received a stinging rebuke from the crusty William Graham Sumner, who dismissed his ideas as beneath contempt. "The thing begins to draw fire," George commented ruefully. Patrick Ford's *Irish World*, the largest Irish-American newspaper in the country and now embroiled in Land League politics on both sides of the Atlantic, puffed the book handsomely, if with an occasional sigh over the author's neglect of interest rates and excess profits. But the New York *Times* damned *Progress and Poverty* as downright heresy, and the *Nation,* while alotting several columns to it, concentrated exclusively on its presumably faulty logic. In fact, George complained, none of his reviewers bothered to explore the book's larger argument. Then as if responding to his pleas for a hearing, Michael Davitt, the veteran Fenian leader and organizer of the Irish Land League fresh from prison, arrived in New York on a fund-raising expedition and changed the course of George's career, opening the way to the recognition abroad that was still denied him at home. "The Irish land question," George observed, "has educated a class of our people who might not for years have been reached by any other influence." In the Irish-American supporters of the Land League, George found his first major constituency.

The Irish Land League, organized in 1879, was the radical response to agricultural depression and two successive crop failures in Ireland that stirred memories of the Great Famine thirty years earlier. Within a year the League had compiled a list of demands for land reform, established 1,000 branches with some 200,000 members, and dispatched Davitt together with Charles Stuart Parnell on a fund-raising tour of America. Following Parnell's return to Ireland to stand for election to Parliament, Davitt continued to barnstorm the country from coast to coast, raising thousands of dollars and organizing 1,500 American branches of his Land League.

In New York the leading supporter of the Land League was Patrick Ford, the editor of the *Irish World* and a highly vocal advocate of nationalizing land both in Ireland and the United States. Ford, born in Galway in 1837, had come to America as a boy and worked for a time setting type for William Lloyd Garrison's *Liberator* before editing an antislavery paper of his own in the 1850s. In 1870 he moved to New York and established the *Irish World* which soon acquired a circulation of 35,000. In addition to apprising readers of developments in Ireland and urging them to vote Greenback-Labor, Ford's editorials pronounced the American economic system "hopelessly corrupt" and called for an eight-hour day, a federal income tax, and "Land to the People." His office at the *Irish World* served as the organizational center of the Land League in the United States, and it was here that George met the labor leaders who would make him a workingman's hero.

Michael Davitt's partnership with Patrick Ford quickened George's interest in the Irish land question. Before coming East he had written a short article for Land Leaguers in San Francisco, and now, under Davitt's urgings, he expanded it into a pamphlet—*The Irish Land Question: What It Involves, and How Alone It Can Be Settled.* The "unpalatable truth," he announced in the opening section of the 100-page pamphlet, was that the land problem in Ireland was no worse than in the rest of Europe or the United States.[7] The Irish were suffering under "essentially the same land system which prevails in all civilized countries." If land titles in Ireland rested on force and fraud, so did the claims to millions of acres of western lands in the United States. Nor was famine unique to Ireland. The recent "starving times" did not constitute a true famine arising from a scarcity of food, but only a "financial panic" caused by underconsumption and poverty. This meant it was a mistake to approach the land problem as a national question indistinguishable from home rule. Yet just such an illusion, George complained, continued to bedazzle Irish reformers, hanging over the countryside like a whiskey haze. Confiscation of all ground rent—in effect his Single Tax—offered the only genuine solution to Ireland's problems. "This," he insisted, "is not radicalism in the bad sense which many attach to the word. This is conservatism in the true sense." Land was the primal workshop and storehouse for all men in all ages. Land meant not crops merely but cities and consumers, not just staple production but commerce and manufactures, not simply Ireland with its rack-rented peasants but the whole world with its uprooted peoples. "The cause that in Ireland produces poverty and distress—the ownership by some people of the land on which and from which the whole people must live—everywhere produces the same results." And those results—exploitation and alienation—he meant to attack wherever he found them.

Thus Michael Davitt and Patrick Ford encountered no difficulty in recruiting George to the cause of the Land League. In September 1881 Ford offered to send him to Ireland as a correspondent for the *Irish World* and to pay his and Annie's passage and sixty dollars a week for a series of letters. George jumped at the chance as "a big thing . . . the biggest I have had yet."[8] Visions of kings and queens, lords and dukes danced through their heads as he and Annie arranged to keep Richard in school and young Henry at work on the Brooklyn *Eagle.* "Going to college," he advised Henry, "you will make life friendships, but you will come out filled with much that will have to be unlearned. Going into newspaper work, you will come in touch with the practical world, will be getting a profession and learning to make yourself useful." Leaving his son to ponder the uncertain meaning of his own career, George, together with Annie and their two young daughters, boarded the steamship *Spain* bound for Liverpool on October 15, 1881.

He had accepted Ford's offer because he considered conditions in Ireland as the perfect test of his principles, the rent war and ensuing political crisis affording an ideal laboratory for proving the worth of the Single Tax. As a first-hand observer, he reasoned, he could popularize his general theory at the same time he developed a political strategy for applying it. "It will be a big thing for me," he exclaimed, the use of Ireland as a staging area for a worldwide peaceful revolution.

Conditions in Ireland in 1881 admitted of no such optimism as that with which George disembarked at Queenstown. The conflicting political and economic interests that would make a common Irish cause impossible were embodied in the two key figures who dominated events at the time of his arrival—Charles Stuart Parnell and George's new friend Michael Davitt. Thirty-five years old in 1881, Parnell was a wealthy and accomplished Irish landlord who had been converted to home rule and moderate land reform. He had been elected to Parliament six years earlier and had since perfected a "policy of retaliation" by obstructing the business of the House of Commons and defying British public opinion in the name of his Home Rule party. Michael Davitt, the son of an evicted tenant farmer in County Mayo, had grown up in Lancashire and lost an arm working in one of its cotton mills. Also thirty-five in 1881, a veteran Fenian who had been imprisoned for smuggling arms into the country, Davitt had emerged in 1877 to win the support of the peasants for his Land League, founded two years later. A mercurial but economically conservative landowner and a veteran professional agitator, Parnell and Davitt represented different classes and divergent tactics as the brief history of the Land League would make clear.

The land problem in Ireland confounded moderates and radicals alike. Gladstone's limited reforms of a decade earlier had failed to correct the worst features of the tenancy system. When prosperity in Ireland came to an end with a series of poor harvests beginning in 1877, food prices and the number of evictions soared. Driven off the land, tenants, combining the principles of land reform and home rule, joined the Land League, which promised to put a stop to rack-renting, evictions, and other forms of landlord oppression, and, somewhat more equivocally, "to effect such a radical change in the land system of Ireland as will put it in the power of every Irish farmer to become the owner, on fair terms, of the land he tills."

The Land League dominated Irish political life for nearly two years, capturing a majority in the general election of 1880, applying a new tactic of boycotting, and countenancing if not actually sponsoring terrorism in the countryside in what quickly became known as the Land War. By the time Henry George arrived on the scene the number of violent incidents had exceeded the figure for any year during the Great Famine of the 1840s. Parliament, in a series of retaliatory measures, suspended habeas corpus and continued to ponder the contradictory findings of its several investigatory commissions. By 1881 matters in Ireland appeared at an impasse.

Yet even as George arrived, the forces of conciliation in Parliament were attempting to accommodate Parnell and the moderate wing of the Land League with still another of Gladstone's propitiatory gestures, the Fair Rent Act, which established the so-called "three F's"—fixity of tenure, fair rent, and freedom of sale. When the new law failed to provide any of the three forms of relief, evictions and reprisals mounted. The government, sensing that the time had come to break Parnell's power and destroy the Land League, arrested him and began to enforce repressive measures in the countryside. The League struck back with its No Rent Manifesto urging tenants to withhold payments until British "terrorism" ceased. But within the League the split between moderate and radical wings continued to widen. In May 1882, as a provision of his release from jail, Parnell agreed to support Gladstone's efforts to put down resistance and accepted his conservative plan for peasant proprietorship. Parnell's defection left Michael Davitt and his relative handful of followers, including George and Patrick Ford, with the task of spelling out the terms of their own scheme for "nationalizing" the land through taxation. In taking up Michael Davitt's cause, George had joined the losing side.

George's dispatches to the *Irish World* were appropriately belligerent, as he castigated English rule as "a despotism sustained by alien force, and wielded in the interests of a privileged class."[9] Hurrying to Dublin, he saw for himself "the most damnable government

that exists today outside of Russia." George, however, was less interested in home rule than in land monopoly, and when, as frequently happened, the former obscured the latter, he was properly
bewildered. Privately he reported to Ford that his arrival had come
"at a most unfortunate time for my purpose" and that accordingly he
had experienced difficulty in getting his feet down. His letters were
sharpest in contrasting the opulent life-style of the Anglo-Irish landlord with the desperate poverty of his tenants. The political intricacies of the land question, on the other hand, baffled him. It was impossible, he complained, for an outsider "to get to the bottom" of the
connected problems of land and liberty. He approved the Land
League's No Rent Manifesto and dutifully condemned the scheme
for purchase and peasant proprietorship. Yet he grew disillusioned
with the infighting among the Land Leaguers and complained to Ford
of the "lack of management" and the "waste both of opportunities
and resources." "Sometimes it seems to me as if a lot of small men
had found themselves in the lead of a tremendous movement, and
finding themselves lifted into importance and power they never
dreamed of, are jealous of anybody else sharing the honour."[10] To
make matters worse, he himself was now widely regarded by those
moderates he hoped to convert as an interloper and dangerous agitator. Still, "in spite of everything," he insisted publicly, "the light is
spreading."[11]

In fact, George's principle of appropriation of rent had won little
approval. He found the Land League deeply divided and its power in
the countryside dwindling. All of a sudden Ireland seemed much too
complicated to be understood by an outsider. Almost no one, it
seemed to him, had a just appreciation of the real issues:

> There is a great amount of "whigging" in the Land League
> movement, more than I thought before coming here. And I
> think this is especially true of the leaders. With very many of
> those for whom it is doing the most, the "Irish World" is any-
> thing but popular. And I have felt from the beginning as if
> there was a good deal of that feeling about myself.[12]

The longer he stayed the more confused he became, increasingly
dissatisfied with his letters to the *Irish World* and "all in a heap" in
his estimate of men and events. From New York came advice from
Ford to undertake an extensive lecture tour of the country, but

George refused. "I am willing and anxious to do all I can, and have done all I have been asked to do," he replied, "but you must remember I am not an Irishman, and these people are jealous of advice or interference from an outsider."[13] By summer he was ready to abandon Irish politics, which he described as "a great blind groping forward," and move on to England where he could see "the beginning of *the revolution* sure."[14]

Instead he encountered socialism in the person of Henry M. Hyndman, the wealthy disciple of Karl Marx, who together with William Morris had recently founded the London Democratic Society to spread the word of the master. Hyndman, who admitted to being impressed with George's powerful if finally unpersuasive argument for the Single Tax, was only the first of a growing number of British socialists, labor leaders, and left intellectuals—George Bernard Shaw, Beatrice and Sidney Webb, H. G. Wells, J. A. Hobson, Keir Hardie, Tom Mann, Lloyd George—who drew freely from the American prophet's moral funds in the next two decades, while they firmly rejected his economic analysis.

Marx himself had set the tone of socialist response to George's ideas when, after reading *Progress and Poverty*, he denounced its author as "utterly backward" in his analysis of modern capitalism. Since George was ignorant of surplus value, Marx pointed out, he had failed to understand that the appropriation of ground rent by the state was regressive. *Progress and Poverty*, Marx scoffed, was "simply an attempt, decked out with socialism, to *save capitalist domination* and indeed to *establish it afresh on an even wider basis* than its present one."[15] George's book, significant though it was as the first widely read attack on orthodox political economy, was all the more dangerous because it was a piece of pseudoanalysis by an American amateur "with a talent for Yankee advertisement" and the "repulsive presumption and arrogance" of promoters of panaceas the world over.[16]

Hyndman, less categorical in his dismissal, also took note of a "bump of reverence" of "cathedral proportions" on the head of his American friend.[17] For his part George deplored the sinister "mental influence" of the revolutionary Marx, and accepted an invitation to visit Hyndman with the intention of converting his host to the Single Tax. Hyndman countered with a copy of Thomas Spence's "The Real Rights of Man," a lecture delivered to the Philosophical Society of Newcastle in 1775 in which the author declared land common property by natural right and called for the taking of it through taxation. If Hyndman hoped to convince his guest of the obsolescence of his social views, he failed. George was delighted to find precedents for his own analysis. It only proved, he assured Hyndman, that eternal truths were indestructible.

It was at a reception in Hyndman's sumptuous townhouse in Portland Place among a "London crush" of notables that George met with opposition from one of his intellectual heroes, the portly Herbert Spencer, grown waspish with the years and repentant of his youthful pronouncements on land as common property. George remembered vividly the argument in *Social Statics* against private property in land and now sought Spencer's blessing on the Land Leaguers. "They have only got what they deserved," Spencer retorted. "They are inciting the people to refuse to pay the landlords what is rightfully theirs—rent." Disconcerted by the seeming reversal, George could only argue the more clumsily for uncompensated appropriation upon which Spencer rejoined: "It is evident that we cannot agree on this matter," and turned on his heel. George never forgot either the apparent betrayal of early humanitarian sentiments or the personal slight, and when some years later he undertook to demolish what was left of Spencer's reputation, the memory of this meeting returned to give his attack a savage personal edge. Now, however, he simply advised his American friends to "discount" Spencer altogether. "He is most horribly conceited, and I don't believe most great men are."[18]

Dinner at the Reform Club with the aging John Bright and Joseph Chamberlain, Radical member of Gladstone's cabinet, raised George's hopes for a hearing in England. Chamberlain, who had read some of his letters to the *Irish World*, warned him playfully against getting arrested as a "suspected person" on his return to Ireland. To boost sales of his book George arranged for a three-penny edition of the pamphlet on the Irish Land Question. "The big stone is really moving," he wrote to an American benefactor who had sent him 300 pounds to cover the publishing costs. "All it wants is a little push to start it rolling. And that, I think, we are about to give."[19]

However, the futility of returning to Ireland to preach radical land reform was forcibly brought home to George when he was arrested there in the summer of 1882, not once but twice on successive days as precisely the "suspected person" Joseph Chamberlain had jokingly called him. In August he started out in the company of a young Oxford don to tour the western counties, hoping to overcome resistance to his scheme of "nationalization." Stopping briefly in the crossroads town of Loughree, the pair were accosted by the local constabulary, detained in barracks for three hours, and brought before a choleric magistrate who harangued them before releasing them. The comedy of errors was not lost on George, who found the affair "so infinitely ridiculous" that he lost "all sense of annoyance."[20] A repeat performance the next day, when they were haled before the same local Dogberry, was less amusing. Eventually George's complaint to the American minister, James Russell Lowell, triggered an embarrassing parliamentary question, which yielded an apology from Her Majesty's Government. Meanwhile George returned to New York in October 1882 convinced that he had "kindled the fire in England, and there is no human power that can put it out."[21]

George came home to New York to find that his reputation, negligible a year earlier, had grown to sizable dimensions, particularly among Irish-American workingmen in the city for whom the land question in Ireland and the United States figured prominently as a major social issue. His new friends urged a triumphal entry into politics, but George, already considering a profitable lecture tour, vetoed the plan. "I think I can be quite as useful outside of Congress as in," he replied to Charles Nordhoff, who had suggested a career in politics, "and I should not now seek a nomination in any way." A small inheritance left him by his benefactor, Francis Shaw, father of the Civil War martyr Robert Gould Shaw, helped meet his financial needs, at least temporarily. "What a curious life mine is," he mused, "literally from hand to mouth; and yet always a way seems to open."[22] Shaw's bequest now opened the way to an educational crusade for which he would need allies. He discovered the first of these in the spirited president of the Knights of Labor and another in a charismatic Catholic priest.

When George accepted Terence Powderly's invitation to join his organization in 1883, the Knights of Labor were enjoying a period of rapid growth, "only one indication," George agreed, "of the general change that is going on."[23] In many respects the Knights were the institutional embodiment of George's economic views and faith in educational politics. From their inception in 1869 the Knights of Labor comprised a huge, sprawling industrial union whose leadership rejected the strike as a "relic of barbarism" and sought to transform industrial America with an educational campaign that would teach workers to replace cutthroat competition with cooperation and shopfloor comradeship. Within a ramshackle organizational structure, mixed and pure craft unions were linked together tenuously in loose federation, an arrangement that made centralized control always difficult and sometimes impossible. A definition of "working classes" and "true producers" that excluded only distillers, bankers, stockbrokers, and professional gamblers was reminiscent of an earlier day of Hard Money and Antimonopoly, artisanal societies and self-improvement. The program of the Knights of Labor, like the core of *Progress and Poverty*, consisted of doctrines of voluntary union, natural cooperation, equal rights to the land, and Christian service— a combination summarized in President Powderly's dictum that "the aim of the Knights of Labor is to make each man his own employer." The means to this end, for both Powderly and George, were simple: the breakup of all monopolies wherever feasible and the nationalizing of those "natural monopolies" that remained; recognition of land, in the language of the Knights' Declaration of Principles, as "the natural source of wealth . . . the heritage of all the people"; and the call for a simpler economy achieved through the yoking of individual responsibility and social brotherhood.

Powderly himself exemplified the connection between the Irish Land League and the American labor movement in the early 1880s. The Grand Master Workman of the Knights had been elected to the Land League General Council in the United States, and he firmly believed that the key to both the Irish problem and the American labor question was land. "The land," he maintained, "is the question." In joining the Knights of Labor, George cemented a symbolic alliance with other "hard-fisted mechanics" like himself, many of them Irish-Americans working in the mines and mills of the Northeast, and nearly all of them true believers in the old doctrines of producerism, which they sought to assemble in an oppositional culture to a dominant industrial capitalism. These were the men who agreed with George and accepted him as one of their own.

George's second ally was a product of the Catholic social gospel. While he was canvassing the Irish countryside, he had acquired a convert and a comrade in Father Edward McGlynn, one of the principal spokesmen for the Irish-American Land League in the United States. Two years older than George, Father McGlynn was born in New York City, became a protege of Archbishop John Joseph Hughes, received orders in Rome, and returned to take over the sprawling working-class parish of St. Stephens in lower Manhattan. When Michael Davitt arrived in the city on his fund-raising expedition, Father McGlynn had already read *Progress and Poverty* and was ready to join Davitt and George on the stump for the Land League. When his superiors warned him against ill-advised connections with radical reform, he retorted that "lest any timid, scrupulous soul might fear I was falling into the arms of Henry George, I don't know a man whose arms I should be more willing to fall into than into the arms of Henry George." He nevertheless agreed to give no more speeches in behalf of the Land League, "not because I acknowledged the right of any one to forbid me, but because I knew too well the power of my ecclesiastical superiors to impair and almost destroy my usefulness in the ministry of Christ's Church to which I had consecrated my life."[24] Father McGlynn, like the man he so greatly admired, was a latter-day "come-outer" and seeker after social justice who also chafed under institutional restraints and instinctively sought a purer freedom in independence and principle. The Priest and the Prophet were kindred souls. From the moment he met the outsized, shambling, genial priest in St. Stephens parish house, George welcomed him as another Peter the Hermit bringing an army with banners. And Father McGlynn marveled at his new friend's "lofty intellectual and virile character," which combined oddly, he thought, with "something feminine," best defined as the innocence of a child. "Already captured by 'Progress and Poverty,' I was now captured by its author."[25]

George came home to two projects, the first an unfinished manuscript on the tariff question which he had set aside once he realized that his real purpose in discussing the tariff was "to show the workingmen that *the* great question is the land question," and the second a casting-up of accounts on his travels in Ireland. He had already started work on tariff reform when he was invited to submit a series of articles to *Frank Leslie's Illustrated Newspaper* on the "social question" for a fee of $100 an article. The collection, which he subsequently published under the title *Social Problems,* was intended as a rejoinder to the chronic nay-sayer, William Graham Sumner, whose series, "Problems of the Times," running in *Harper's* warned all right-thinking Americans against tinkering with their social system. George announced it as his intention to point out "the momentous social problems of our time, unencumbered by technicalities, and without that abstract reasoning which some of the principles of political economy require for thorough explanation."[26]

The very title of George's series—"Social Problems"—was a phrase that had already become one of the late nineteenth century's most serviceable clichés for urban middle-class readers beset with anxieties and fears. The Achilles heel of modern civilization, George agreed, was the metropolis, where, "let civil conflict break or paralyze the authority that preserves order," and the people become a mob "without point of rally or principle of cohesion."[27] Under the skin of civilized man lurks the selfsame savage who in darker ages drank fury with blood in primeval forests before venturing forth to lay waste to empires. Such men, George warned his readers, were to be met daily in city streets. *Progress and Poverty*, conceived and written from a California perspective and time frame, anticipated the triumph of urban America. *Social Problems*, hastily compiled from recent New York impressions, recorded that triumph and warned of imminent dangers in the familiar terms of the frontier.

For George's generation of social gospel and social justice reformers, the city figured as a modern wilderness, an inverted image of the frontier as a terrifying wasteland where, as George put it, "he who seeks isolation may find it more truly than in the desert."[28] In the great industrial and commercial cities of the modern world, wealth and poverty are cruelly juxtaposed—"one revels and another starves within a few feet of each other." Without "social settlements," lacking the neighborhoods and social groups necessary for civic responsibility, cities, George argued as Bellamy had before him, breed spiritual as well as material poverty for the many, even as they provide wealth and privilege for the few. Cities could only be understood in catastrophic terms: "Symptoms of danger, premonitions of violence, are appearing all over the civilized world. Creeds are dying, beliefs are changing; the old forces of conservatism are melting away. Political institutions are failing."[29]

More insistent now than in *Progress and Poverty* sounded the note of determination to hold the line along a middle course against the plutocracy on one side and the mindless masses on the other, to check monied pretension and power but also the atheism and envy they bred in the lower classes. More clearly than ever, George began to see his historical task as defending the center with a strategy of "social intelligence" against incursions from both the right and the left, above and below.[30] The concept of social intelligence as George, Bellamy, and Lloyd invoked it from now on signified a religious rather than a secular approach to society and postulated an instinctual wisdom fed from sacred sources rather than scientific understanding of cause and effect. All three reformers inherited from mid-century an assumed harmony of religious truth and social fact, an identification which they, in turn, bequeathed to the first generation of Progressives who came to maturity after the turn of the century. As it developed after 1900, Progressivism gradually secularized the concept, stripping it of its specifically Christian connotations and substituting for a vague "social sympathy" an informed "sociological intelligence" taught by instrumentalism and bureaucracy alike. But as it emerged from the work of these three reformers and their followers in the 1880s, "social intelligence," like the "social problem" it was charged with solving, meant self-evident Christian ethics and commonsense altruism. As George explained his new term, "It must be animated with religious sentiment and warm with sympathy for human suffering. It must stretch out beyond self-interest, whether it be the self-interest of the few or of the many."[31] In this view genuine reform depended upon the spread of an essentially spiritual power among the masses of people. Professional politicians in both major parties concerned themselves with loaves and fishes, while on the outskirts of the political establishment stood Greenbackers with their queer currency nostrums. Even the labor unions could think of little more than winning the eight-hour day and outlawing prison contracts. "All this shows want of grasp and timidity of thought," George insisted.[32] Root-and-branch reform awaited a national change of heart and the will to make a new heaven and a new earth.

Once again George's utopia of the middle way emerged from two quite different perceptions of the good society and the best way of creating it. There was his old dream of a Jeffersonian paradise of little government that combined neatly with the Jacksonian world of

Dodge and Bragg. Common to both was the notion of the sacro-sanctity of property. "Instead of weakening and confusing the idea of property, I would surround it with stronger sanctions," George announced.

> For my part, I would put no limit on acquisition. No matter how many millions any man can get by methods which do not involve robbery of others—they are his: let him have them. I would not even ask him for charity, or have it dinned into his ears that it is his duty to help the poor. That is his own affair. Let him do as he pleases with his own, without restriction and without suggestion.[33]

This picture of a lost entrepreneurial world afforded no room for governmental interference or a policy for distributing wealth equita-bly. In the libertarian half of George's vision, the test of a good gov-ernment was precisely the services it could do without—a standing army, a "burlesque of a navy," and a diplomatic corps "servilely copied from the usages of kings." Next in the process of pruning the political plum tree would come the elimination of a cumbersome legal system. "The best use that could be made of our great law li-braries," George crowed, "would be to send them to the paper-mills." Here spoke the archetypal American "come-outer," drawing on a Christian perfectionist tradition as old as Roger Williams: "It is not the business of government to make men virtuous or religious, or to preserve the fool from his folly."[34]

For George, in this frame of mind, American liberties remained indissolubly linked with small towns and local self-government, to which, he argued, the people would cling "with the more tenacity" as they came to realize that "in things which concern only them-selves, the people of each political subdivision—township, ward, city or State, as may be—[should] act for themselves." Just as he de-plored the concentration of economic power in monopolies, so he feared political consolidation, calling instead for home rule and de-nouncing all attempts "to govern great cities by State commissions and . . . making what properly belongs to County Supervisors and Township Trustees the business of legislatures."[35]

Yet George's preference for an unfettered American develop-ment was contravened at every point by a reality-principle rooted in

city life that defined with cold precision a new kind of industrial existence—interdependence, integration, management, and planning.
As modern society continues to develop, he was forced to admit, a
higher and higher degree of social intelligence will be required "as
the well-being of each becomes more and more dependent upon the
well-being of all—the individual more and more subordinate to society."[36] Despite his initial preference for local autonomy, small
business, grassroots decisionmaking, and cultural autonomy, George
could see that all the signs of the times—every one of the social
problems he identified in his articles—called for the abandonment
of his eighteenth-century model.

With the shift in perspective came a change in vocabulary in the
second half of *Social Problems*, a glossary fashioned from science and
history. "As in the development of species, the power of conscious
coordinated action of the whole must assume greater and greater relative importance to the automatic action of its parts, so it is in the development of society." Viewed in the light of historical development,
political and economic consolidation was simply the price for the
advance of civilization. "It is not in itself evil. If in anything its results are evil, it is simply because of our bad social adjustment."
Seen as segments of a larger historical continuum, the pastoral stage
of Jefferson's fee-simple empire and the new-money scramble of the
Age of Jackson had been the results of temporary frontier conditions
no longer controlling. "This is the truth of socialism," George concluded, "which, although it is being forced upon us by industrial
progress and social development, we are slow to recognize."[37]

Exactly here lay George's dilemma. Caught between a strong
preference for a decentralized society and his newly acquired sense
of history, he needed a way of reconciling opposites. That way, in
Social Problems as it had been in *Progress and Poverty*, was utopia set in
an American middle landscape and reached through mass religious
conversion. Reduced to mythic dimensions, the articles that he wrote
for *Frank Leslie's Illustrated Newspaper* comprised a long sermon that
unfolded a religious drama of initial innocence, disobedience and
degradation, and ultimate salvation. George was putting on the
prophet's mantle for good. The American Adam, by his calculation,
had been given two centuries in which to cultivate the Garden of the
World according to God's plan, but had willfully committed the
original sin of waste. "We do not return to the earth what we take

from it; each crop that is harvested leaves the soil the poorer. We are cutting down forests which we do not replant; we are shipping abroad, in wheat and cotton and tobacco and meat, or flushing into the sea through the sewers of great cities the elements of fertility that have been embodied in the soil by the slow processes of nature, acting for long ages."[38]

Expelled from Eden for their sins against divine order, Americans have taken refuge in cities, the sinkholes of corruption and crime. If for his version of paradise George borrowed from Jefferson and the Physiocrats, his picture of hell owed its power to Carlyle's descriptions of the nineteenth-century industrial city. George's Everyman enters cavernous factories to find the "din and clatter, and whir of belts and wheels" that make industrial labor intolerable: "Here you find men doing over and over the self-same thing—passing, all day long, bars of iron through great rollers; presenting plates to steel jaws; turning, amid clangor in which you can scarcely 'hear yourself think,' bits of iron over and back, sixty times a minute, for hour after hour, for day after day, for year after year."[39] Work habits have been routinized, natural rhythms flattened by the machine whose slave the worker has now become, powerless to vary the pattern, trained to his single task, locked into a rigid schedule. "In all occupations," George noted, "the workman is steadily becoming divorced from the tools and opportunities of labor; everywhere the inequalities of fortune are becoming more glaring. And this at a time when thought is quickened; when the old forces of conservatism are giving way; when the idea of human equality is growing and spreading." Nor is the factory worker the only one suffering from alienation. The American farmer also has grown dissatisfied with a life that seems hard and barren. Like the captive worker in the industrial city with whom he must now make common cause, the farmer faces elimination unless the course of history can be reversed.

Yet how reverse history without revolutionizing property relationships or overthrowing capitalism? George's instincts continued to assure him that he had no fundamental quarrel with the capitalist system or much faith in a socialist alternative. "The ideal social state," he concluded, "is not that in which each gets an equal amount of wealth, but in which each gets in proportion to his contribution to the general stock."[40] All that was needed to secure a fair distribution of wealth was the equal opportunity to compete with others and at the same time to cooperate with them in building the blessed community.

Here, then, was the middle way between corporate consolidation and stultifying socialism in an idea of competitive cooperation secured by natural altruism and an educative politics. These, George was now convinced, would serve as the weapons of a vanguard of "thinking" citizens whom circumstances had placed above the class-bound interests of workers. Power ultimately rested with the masses, he agreed, but until they had been taught to use that power for the good of all, no permanent social advance was possible. The duty to educate the workers of the world fell to that small minority willing to risk large toughts, fiery language, and great deeds. "Whoever becomes imbued with a noble idea kindles a flame from which other torches are lit, and influences those with whom he comes in contact, be they few or many."[41] Here George stopped to review the commandments of his new social gospel:

> And I am firmly convinced . . . that to effect any great social improvement, it is sympathy rather than self-interest, the sense of duty rather than the desire for self-advancement, that must be appealed to. Envy is akin to admiration, and it is admiration that the rich and powerful excite which secures the perpetuation of aristocracies.

> And as man is so constituted that it is utterly impossible for him to attain happiness save by seeking the happiness of others, so does it seem to be of the nature of things that individuals and classes can obtain their own just rights only by struggling for the rights of others.

> Hence it is . . . that it is around the standard of duty that men must rally to win the rights of man. And herein may we see the deep philosophy of Him who bade men love their neighbors as themselves.

George envisioned his band of brethren as preachers securing a massive psychic change in American life which would prevent the need for more drastic action. His vanguard was charged with the work of distributing amenities and social distinctions more evenly by knitting a pastoral pattern back into American life. "This life of

great cities is not the natural life of man. He must, under such conditions, deteriorate, physically, mentally, morally."[42] In language
similar to Bellamy's editorial indictments and with images that anticipated those of the Southern Agrarians and the regional critics of industrialism in the twentieth century, George pictured a wasteland
city where masses of downtrodden men and women never "press
foot upon mother earth." The evils of urban concentration, he
added, do not stop at the city limits. Like a wen or a tumor the city
draws the wholesome juices of the social organism into its poisonous
vortex. The countryside fails to keep pace with urban growth and
becomes a lonely backwash filled with bitter men. In a passage given
point by his recent tour of Ireland but also depicting an American
scene on which Hamlin Garland would soon concentrate, George reported on what was already being called "the farmer's plight":

> Consider the barrenness of the isolated farmer's life—the dull
> round of work and sleep, in which so much of it passes. Con-
> sider, what is still worse, the monotonous existence to which
> his wife is condemned; its lack of recreation and excitement,
> and gratifications of taste, and the sense of harmony and
> beauty; its steady drag of cares and toils that make women
> worn and wrinkled when they should be in their bloom. Even
> the discomforts and evils of the crowded tenement-house are
> not worse than the discomforts and evils of such a life.[43]

It occurred to George once more, this time even more forcibly,
that the genuinely "healthy life" was not the city but the village life,
receding into legend but perhaps not irrecoverable. Here was the
Elizabethan hamlet where Shakespeare and his companions frol-
icked, where commons and greens sported maypoles and "the
cloth-yard arrow flew from longbow to the bullseye of the butt."
Here stood churches as lordly reminders of ancient duties. Here
could be found Abbot Sansom's priory of Carlyle and Ruskin's original Guild of St. George and William Morris's Nowhere, a lost land
for late Victorians but also a dream of recovery on which Ebenezer
Howard would build his Garden Cities of Tomorrow. When the
Single Tax returned common rights to the soil, George predicted, the
huddled masses of the cities would be dispersed and the scattered
population of the countryside grow denser. In place of huge half-

cultivated bonanza farms lying at great distances from each other, individual homesteads would spring up in clusters. Settlers would not
have to travel thousands of miles through unused acres in order to
find their natural communities.

> The use of machinery would not be abandoned: where cul-
> ture of a large scale secured economies it would still go on;
> but with the breaking up of monopolies, the rise in wages and
> the better distribution of wealth, *industry of this kind would as-
> sume cooperative form.* Agriculture would cease to be destructive
> and would become more intense, obtaining more from the
> soil and returning what it borrowed. Closer settlement would
> give rise to economies of all kinds; labor would be far more
> productive, and rural life would partake of the conveniences,
> recreations and stimulations now to be obtained only by the
> favored classes in large towns. The monopoly of land broken
> up, it seems to me that the *rural life would tend to revert to the
> primitive type of the village surrounded by cultivated fields, with its
> common pasturage and woodlands.*[44]

The restoration of community accompanying the revival of the
village, George predicted, would return a lost wholeness to the industrial world. Cities too would feel the effects of the Single Tax restorative in a massive dispersal of its inhabitants so that:

> the masses now festering in the tenement-houses of our cities,
> under conditions which breed disease and death, and vice and
> crime, should each have its healthful home, set in its garden
> ... that home should be replete with all the conveniences yet
> esteemed luxuries ... that his family should be free to li-
> braries, and lectures, and scientific apparatus, and instruction
> ... that, in short, not merely the successful man, the one in a
> thousand, but the man of ordinary parts and ordinary fore-
> sight and prudence, should enjoy all that advancing civiliza-
> tion can bring to elevate and expand human life.[45]

George concluded his sermon with a glimpse of the altruistic life
consummated in a universal Christian ethic:

Men trample over each other from the frantic dread of being trampled upon, and the admiration with which even the un-scrupulous money-getter is regarded springs from habits of thought engendered by the fierce struggle for existence to which most of us are obliged to give our best energies. But when no one feared want, when every one felt assured of his ability to make an easy and independent living for himself and his family, that popular admiration which now spurs the rich man still to add to his wealth would be given to other things than to the getting of money. We should learn to re-gard the man who strove to get more than he could use, as a fool—as indeed he is.[46]

With the image of Dives as God's poor fool, George showed just how little his basic assumptions had changed. *Social Problems* restated the solution rather than redefining the problem. In writing the book, George had spent most of his analytical reserves and, as though in acknowledgment of that fact, turned in the closing sections to per-fecting the arts of prophecy and persuasion. Although he would write several books and many more articles on subjects ranging from Herbert Spencer's synthetic philosophy to his own last great state-ment of the truths of political economy, from this point on he con-centrated on refining his original insights and rearranging his proofs. The conviction that he had reached his goal he explained to a friend with an engaging candor: "I was firmly convinced of the truth of the views advanced in 'Progress and Poverty' when I wrote it. I came to them slowly and carefully, and had tried them by every test that I could apply. I have seen how utterly impossible it seems for anyone to controvert or shake them."[47] Thus George returned to England and Scotland on a second mission in the winter of 1883 as a preacher bearing the truths of the man of faith rather than the provisional findings of the social scientist.

Plans for a lecture tour through the British Isles were interrupted by the death of his parents. Richard George had written his son on his eighty-fifth birthday, just before he died, of his complete satis-faction with Henry's career. "By-gone days come back to me as if it were only last week when you came to me saying that you would go to California and that you would try your fortune there. I did not object; and now the result has been all I could have wished."[48] George's mother survived her husband by a week. The double loss brought intimations of his own death. One day in the middle of a stroll with his son Richard he stopped, mused for a moment, then turned and said: "I was thinking that I could die now and the work would go on." His great reform, he continued, was no longer a one-man enterprise but a growing network of "many men in many lands." "I can help it while I live; but my death could not stop it. The Great Revolution has begun."[49] Taking his older son, Harry, with him as secretary-companion, George sailed for England in December 1883 to inspect the progress of the Great Revolution.

By the eighties social reform in England had reached a crisis which, while advertising the "social question" widely, had yet to acquire agreed-upon ideological directives. Marxists, Christian Socialists, Social Gospelists, Land Reform Unionists, Fabians, all agreed on the need to repair the industrial order and acknowledged the importance of the "land question" while disagreeing on its centrality in their own program and on the efficacy of the Single Tax. But George was assured of a respectful hearing from most middle-class groups and a majority of working-class reformers who recognized the symbolic significance of the land question and accepted the moral exhorter from the States as one of their own.

The experience of young George Bernard Shaw was typical. One evening soon after George's arrival, Shaw, a brash young reporter of twenty-five, dropped in late on George's first lecture to Alfred Russel Wallace's Land Nationalization Society. Shaw immediately identified the speaker as an American because he pronounced "necessarily" with the accent on the third syllable and also because he was "deliberately and intentionally oratorical," appealing frequently to such unfashionable abstractions as Truth, Justice, and Liberty. Shaw confessed to being moved by George's eighteenth-century superstitions. "I noticed also that he was a born orator, and that he had small, plump and pretty hands." Some of his colleagues, Shaw admitted, found George as an American "about fifty years out of date," yet only an American could have seen in a single lifetime "the growth of the whole tragedy of civilization from the primitive forest clearing." Shaw also noted that George illustrated his theory with references to urban land values and London's prohibitive rents, hard

facts and no highfalutin language. Then and there Shaw enlisted as
"a soldier in the Liberative War of Humanity."

> The result of my hearing the speech, and buying from one of
> the stewards of the meeting a copy of *Progress and Poverty* for
> sixpence (Heaven knows where I got that sixpence!) was that I
> plunged into a course of economic study, and at a very early
> stage of it became a Socialist . . . And that all the work was not
> mere gas, let the feats and pamphlets of the Fabian Society
> attest. When I was thus swept into the great Socialist revival
> of 1883, I found that five-sixths of those who were swept in
> with me had been converted by Henry George.[50]

There were others who, while discounting George's specific remedy, responded to his Christian message with enthusiasm. It was all
very well, the future Fabian Sydney Olivier declared, to poke fun at
George for his "deduction of the immortality of the soul from the
sound theory of property in land," but that was to miss the point. For
all this "rhapsodical and unchastened style, strongly suggestive of
the pulpit," George had at least brought the social question "into
general notice of others than readers of Mill and Spencer, and for
that I think he is to be thanked."[51]

Assessing George's contribution to English reform after more
than a decade, the socialist J. A. Hobson recalled the Prophet of San
Francisco as "keenly intelligent, generous and sympathetic," though
blessed with more than his share of obstinacy. His peculiar effectiveness Hobson attributed to George's ability to make abstractions pal-
pable and to give definiteness to vague feelings of dissatisfaction by
"assigning an easily intelligible economic cause." Part of his appeal
was the very real grievance of agricultural depression in Britain, but
even more important was George's skill in utilizing "that advantage
which land grievances possess over other economic issues, their sus-
ceptibility to powerful concrete local illustration." Hobson understood George's symbolic significance for a wide variety of working-
class people in the British Isles who were prepared to give full assent
to his proposition that unqualified private ownership of land was
"the most obviously unjust and burdensome feature in our present
social economy." Everywhere Hobson traveled in England he encountered little knots of men "largely self-educated, keen citizens,

mostly noncomformists in religion," who carried forward a radical, freethinking tradition whose roots lay in an eighteenth-century moral economy.[52]

George was quick to realize his power over this kind of popular audience. His speeches were sermons complete with text and demonstrations. "I have at last attained what I have always believed in my power," he wrote glowingly to Annie. "This trip has aided in my development and I think that I am now a *first-class* speaker." No sooner had he unpacked in London than he realized he had arrived as an international figure. "I can't begin to send you the papers in which I am discussed, attacked, and commented on—for I would have to send all the English, Scotch and Irish papers." For his maiden performance at St. James Hall in London sponsored by the Land Reform Union he prepared thoroughly, staying up all the previous night revising and simplifying his speech. He gave instructions to Thomas Walker, the wealthy Birmingham manufacturer who had been assigned a place on the platform behind the speaker, to tug on his coattails if he spoke too long. "When I get thinking, ideas come with a rush; so that when I am on my feet I lose the sense of time."[53] The 4,000 people who packed the hall were treated to a rousing performance. Ruskin, who had called *Progress and Poverty* "an admirable book," was unable to attend, but on the platform sat Michael Davitt, Stewart Headlam, Philip Wicksteed, and Frederick Harrison, an odd mélange of Fenians, Social Gospelists, and Positivists who listened attentively to "George the Fifth" as he expounded the lesson with parables drawn from life in the nearby London slums. He finished with a flourish and fielded questions from the floor with agility, truly the "man with a mission, born to set right in a single generation the errors of six thousand years," as the Tory *Standard* dubbed him the following morning. To Annie he boasted, "I certainly have attained fame at last." And Harry remembered a scene in their hotel room the next day when the newspapers arrived and his father, after studying each account, murmured, "At last, at last, I am famous."[54]

Large crowds turned out for "telling successes" in Plymouth, Cardiff, and Bristol, and cheered as he explained why he refused to compensate the landowners for confiscating their rents. By now he had perfected what he openly called his "missionary style" of speaking without elaborate notes and of concentrating on a few simple points, counting on the inspiration of the moment to launch him in oratorical flight. In Birmingham and again in Liverpool he was heckled, and for the first time felt the wrath of conservative audiences frightened by his proposals for nationalizing land. Unruffled, he fenced with hostile questioners, turning their barbs aside with a withering sarcasm. "The consciousness of opposition," he explained in the spirit of Bellamy's young reformer, Joseph Claiborne, "gave me the stimulus I needed to overcome physical weakness."[55] He had now mastered all the old abolitionist tactics—exhortation, ridicule, invective, prayer, and a final vote on the question. Wendell Phillips would have marveled and applauded.

George's missionary style proved most effective in covenanting Scotland, where he barnstormed for the Scottish Land Restoration League from John O'Groat's to the Lowland cities. In Scotland, enclosures, the brutalized state of the crofters, and the steady siphoning-off of rent for wealthy absentee landowners who still possessed the remnants of feudal rights made for embittered and radical audiences willing to take George's prescription straight. He was right in thinking Scotland better prepared for his ideas than England, for there the grimy industrial cities encrusted with slums had been grafted on a countryside with a land system that had changed little since the sixteenth century.

In the industrial towns in the Midlands it was a different story, and he began to draw fire from all directions—from a Tory right with its complement of outraged gentry; from a socialist left irked by his refusal to condemn capitalism; and, most ominous of all, from a new contingent of academicians and professional economists with their guns already trained on the crumbling citadel of natural law. The neoclassical English economist Alfred Marshall was only one of these formidable adversaries, university trained, complete master of the classic theory that George claimed as his own, and eager to destroy every one of the presumed fallacies in the American prophet's reasoning. At Bristol, Marshall gave three lectures specifically designed to discredit the Single Tax. In the course of his analysis he submitted statistics to show that only 75 million pounds—about 7 percent of the total national wealth in Britain—constituted payments of rent, while some 250 million pounds made up the interest on invested capital and over 800 million pounds went directly to labor in the form of wages. Like the American neoclassical economist Francis Walker, who was making it a second profession to disabuse the reading public of the utopian notions of Bellamy, George, and Lloyd, Marshall represented, at its best, the modern university tradition of disinterested scholarship and, at its worst, the conservative smugness of the vested interests on which higher education increasingly depended. Once before, George had denounced the economic privilege and callousness of university life and warned students against the selfishness and indifference bred in a leisure class. In bringing this charge to Balliol, where Marshall and the academicians held court, George was following Daniel's footsteps into the lions den.

The Oxford speech bore all the earmarks of disaster from the outset. George knew full well how crucial the appeal to professionals and academicians was for the acceptance of his ideas. Nervous, worn out by a nonstop schedule, and apprehensive lest he fail to impress the Oxford dignitaries, he succumbed to his old enemy insomnia. "I hardly got any sleep last night," he complained to Annie, "have been like a drowned rat all day and now tonight it is as bad as ever until in desperation I have got up and started to write."[56]

The following night, before a packed assembly at the Clarendon Hotel, Oxford, a bone-weary and irritable speaker confronted not simply hostile socialists and academic skeptics but a clique of Tory undergraduate rowdies who jeered and cheered ironically as George attempted one of his old-fashioned moral exhortations, ill-adapted to a university audience. He had labored all day on the text but was relying on a number of local references to upper-class privilege for dramatic effect. To this kind of scolding the undergraduates took immediate offense and responded in kind. Driven to the edge of exasperation by repeated catcalls and groans, George cut short his prepared speech to ask for questions, a tactical blunder made painfully clear to him when his first questioner turned out to be none other than Alfred Marshall, his recent adversary at Bristol. Marshall rose and observed sententiously that he had not heard a single idea that was both new and true, for what George had just offered listeners— his argument for land nationalization—was not true, and what was true—his indictment of inequality—was hardly new. Marshall was offended by George's presumption and sought to defend his discipline from such a well-meaning but confused meddler. With maddening condescension he absolved the speaker of all responsibility for his heresies on the grounds of incompetence. George had neglected factors of productivity and thrift. He defined land purely in terms of location rather than use. He misunderstood the nature of monopoly. He possessed no grasp of competitive markets. He lacked both a science of statistics and a sense of history. After tossing a handful of loaded questions at a now thoroughly discomposed speaker, Marshall retired in favor of an undergraduate who denounced the "nostrum" of nationalization as "scandalously immoral." George, goaded beyond endurance, turned on his young tormentor with the question, "Sir, are you a member of this university?"—unwittingly using the stock interrogatory phrase put by college disciplinarians to undergraduate offenders. The slip produced a burst of hilarity incomprehensible to George who was conscious only of having irretrievably lost his audience. Shouting over his shoulder that this had been the most disorderly meeting he had ever addressed, he stomped off the platform to a rising chorus of hisses and groans.

At Cambridge, where he spoke a few days later, he was less roughly handled although neither students nor their elders professed much sympathy for land nationalization. Gladstone's daughter Mary, who attended the lecture, wondered whether George would be "up to the mark" after his drubbing at Oxford, but admitted that she detected in him "the divine spark" of "a man possessed [who] often carried one away." It was George himself, however, who nearly had to be carried back to London after a fortnight's sleeplessness, but with a doctor's prescription and a few days' rest he was ready for a final swing through Scotland before leaving for Dublin and the steamer back to America.

George's skirmishes with the new intellectuals at Oxford brought to an end a phase of his career. As his more attentive listeners noted, he had become "a man possessed," an evangelist bent on spreading his own "great awakening," a zealot of "singleness and height of aim." "I don't think we made the faintest impression on him,"[57] one of his critics remarked to Mary Gladstone after an evening's discussion of political economy. Henceforth there would be no fruitful exchange between George and his critics, no reciprocal refining of ideas and concepts. Convinced that he possessed the truth, that his premises marched out in strict logical procession from an impregnable fortress of first principles, George increasingly closed his mind to objections and corrections.

Thus for scholars on both sides of the Atlantic he came to repre-

sent the stubborn dogmatist who would have to be disabused or discredited. Alfred Marshall, only one of George's academic critics,
whose numbers would increase in the next twenty years, was both
amused and annoyed by George's confusion of ethics and economics. George argued that progress caused poverty. Marshall used national income statistics to show that labor's share of the total national
income had been rising slowly but perceptibly for two centuries and
suggested that real wages had likewise increased. George ignored the
empirical evidence for greater "progress"; Marshall identified the
sources of diminishing poverty. But it was at the level of theory that
the differences between the amateur moralist and the professional
economist were greatest. George offered a single-factor explanation
in making the determination of wages wholly dependent upon land
rents. Marshall devised an altogether different analytical model, a
general theory of competitive markets that was more flexible and
functionally satisfactory than George's land-based "law" that interest and wages are always high and low together. In the last analysis,
George's reforms rested securely on an ethical base; Marshall's, on a
more sophisticated use of theory and empirical data. No meeting of
minds could follow from such an encounter as theirs.

George's quarrel with the academicians began as a skirmish at
Berkeley, flared into a pitched battle at Oxford, and would end in
intellectual isolation, as one by one his outposts were overrun by the
forces of modern economics and sociology recruited in the universities. The tone assumed by his academic critics—Francis Walker,
Simon Patten, Arthur Twining Hadley, John Bates Clark, Edwin Seligman—was invariably and often insufferably condescending, as
they dismissed George as a simpleminded moralist dabbling in a science he could not understand, a well-meaning but misdirected
preacher whose nostrums only cluttered the professionals' reform
calendar. History, the younger generation of intellectuals and specialists insisted, had left George stranded on the far shoals of the
eighteenth century.

To the mounting charges of obsolescence George would reply
with increased annoyance, employing a variety of countercharges,
some of them old Jacksonian prejudices but others reasoned objections to the commercialized world of the professionals and the moral
accommodations they practiced. As a graduate of the frontier school
of adversity, he resented and feared the American university's de-

pendence on big money and its tendency to teach dominant business values. His latent anti-intellectualism betrayed him most obviously in his distrust of the concept of disinterested learning as it was being enthusiastically pressed into service by a younger generation of Progressive intellectuals. Despite his muscular intelligence and the power to forge simple but compelling ethical arguments, George's basic perceptions remained rooted in an earlier age of producerism and the moral economy. He disliked the idea of special freedom given to a minority of privileged intellectuals to distance themselves from the rest of society and seeemingly to shirk their responsibilities to the common people.

Confronted with an alien and increasingly hostile educational community whose motives he could not credit, George decided on his return to New York in 1884 to cultivate the talents and seek the support of those "divine average" men who agreed with him in condemning the present economic system and seeking a better one. The reformer, he told himself, could not afford to be neutral but, as Emerson and Whitman had urged, must play the hero in history, marshaling, educating, guiding his fellow men toward goals that both reason and faith pronounced attainable. The social critic, as George, Bellamy, and Lloyd had come to define him, was the old humanitarian reformer, his intellectual convictions given force by Christian conscience. It was conscience that allowed the reformer to identify his enemies and his allies. The enemy was privilege and selfishness in all its guises, even the academic regalia of the universities. The reformer's allies, George concluded, were the plain people—hard-working, self-denying, God-fearing workingmen like himself. If he could rally recruits like these around a new concept of politics, they could march to the millennium together.

9

UPHEAVAL

A FEW MINUTES after 10 o'clock on the night of May 4, 1886, in Chicago's Haymarket Square, an anarchist named Samuel Fielden was just finishing his speech to a crowd of workingmen. They had answered a hurried call for a meeting to protest police brutality the day before in breaking up a strikers' demonstration against the McCormick Harvester Company. Ten minutes earlier a brisk downpour had thinned the crowd, and Fielden, as he climbed up on the delivery wagon that served the anarchists as a platform, intended to finish his harangue quickly. He picked up the threads of his argument by warning his audience to have nothing to do with American law except to lay violent hands on it. "Keep your eye upon it, throttle it, kill it, stab it, do everything you can to wound it—to impede its progress." What did it matter, he demanded, whether his hearers killed themselves with overwork or died on the barricades fighting their capitalist enemies? "What is the difference?"[1]

Fielden never answered the question, for at that moment a company of police, 180 strong, led by Captain John Bonfield, came pouring out of the nearby Des Plaines Street station and surrounded the wagon while Bonfield commanded speakers and audience to disperse. Explaining that theirs was a paceable gathering, the anarchist leaders nevertheless descended behind their chief spokesman, Albert R. Parsons, who earlier in the evening had urged his fellow workers, "in the interest of your liberty and your independence," to arm themselves.[2] Suddenly, from a direction and hand unknown, a dynamite bomb, its fuse giving off a shower of sparks, came spiraling in and, landing at the feet of the policemen in the front ranks, exploded, killing Patrolman Mathias J. Degan instantly and mortally wounding several other officers. As the smoke drifted upward and the sound thundered off the walls of the warehouses nearby, the police quickly reformed their ranks and, with revolvers drawn and nightsticks at the ready, charged into the crowd, clubbing and shooting. When it was over, the Square lay strewn with bodies—one officer dead, six others dying, and dozens of battered and bleeding workingmen.

Overnight the shock waves of the Haymarket bombing went rolling across the country, as an outraged public denounced the anarchists as "vipers," "hyenas," "curs," and "serpents" and called for swift and summary justice. In New York, *Bradstreet's*, the businessman's bible, seemingly spoke the national mood in warning that the bomb proved beyond question that the anarchists' threats were "no mere idle vaporings." "There are individuals in the United States prepared to act upon the teachings of the anarchists' leaders . . . In time of disturbance like the present desperate men have a power for evil out of proportion to their numbers."[3] As though in agreement, Chicago police rounded up over 200 of the city's known radicals and carried out hundreds of illegal searches for weapons and incriminating evidence. On May 27th thirty-one persons were indicted by the grand jury, a number that was soon reduced to eight men—August Spies, Michael Schwab, Samuel Fielden, Adolph Fischer, George Engel, Louis Lingg, Albert Parsons, and Oscar Neebe—the presumed ringleaders of the plot to throw the bomb. The eight anarchists were charged with sixty-nine counts as accessories before the fact and with general conspiracy to murder. The date of the trial was set for June 21, just six and one-half weeks after the bombing and five days after the death of the seventh policeman.

The Haymarket defendants were members of a small group of anarchists, most of them German immigrants, who had followed their European compatriots in breaking with Marxism on the issue

Henry George's producerist circle: A Knights of Labor poster, 1886. George is at seven o'clock.

Haymarket Square by day.

of "propaganda by deed," the use of terrorism and armed uprising to destroy the capitalist system. Disorganized and doctrinally confused, these anarchists had virtually no connection with a native-American perfectionist tradition of philosophical anarchism and had struck few roots in the American working class itself. The anarchists' fatal weakness was their obsessive fear of any and all organization—"the poisoned tree of centralization"—which severely limited their effectiveness. Over the protests of August Spies and Albert Parsons, two moderate strategists who sought to infiltrate the trades unions and form the "advance guard of the coming revolution," the International Working People's Association, formed by a "national convention" of twenty-six delegates in Pittsburgh in 1883, began to preach direct action.

With their instruments of violence set aside, however, the anarchists and their Pittsburgh Manifesto looked surprisingly like the Knights of Labor and their platform of voluntary cooperation, the free exchange of equivalent products among producers, and the management of society by free contract between independent and autonomous communes. For most Americans, however, the anarchist appeal to violence made all the difference. "By force our ancestors liberated themselves from political oppression, by force their children will have to liberate themselves from economic bondage."[4] This was the message that Parsons, Spies, and their fellow agitators brought to Chicago's restive labor organizations in the spring of 1886.

By 1886 the labor movement in the United States was beginning to change its character and purpose. Earlier in the decade the organizational task had fallen to older workers in the skilled trades with their principles of craft unionism. But the economy took a sharp downturn in 1884, which was registered in declining profits and sharp wage cuts ranging from an average 15 percent in industry to a frightening 40 percent in the coal mines, where Irish-American Land Leaguers rallied behind the principle of nationalization. Although unemployment remained relatively low, the American worker's standard of living dropped dramatically. Soon it was as clear to the workers as it was to the editors of *Bradstreet's* that "where trade unionism is strongest contract rates and united resistance have combined to retard the downward tendencies of wages." The sudden increase in the number of strikes, walkouts, and lockouts testified to a new labor militance and the determination of management to check it. The question for American workingmen was how best to counter the attacks of management on a living wage—whether through political parties, craft unions, industrial unionism, or direct action. What was already clear to all students of the labor problem, however, was the fact that industrialism had set in train an organizational revolution that could no longer be contained by the paternalist strategies of American business.

At the time of the Haymarket Riot this organizational revolution was already in full swing, as the forces of technology combined with demographic shifts and the completion of a transportation network to create the rudiments of a national society. Rapid modernization after 1880 had two dimensions: the *making* of an integrated industrial economy and the increasingly complex problem of *managing* it. The business community in the years following the Civil War had been the first to learn the new organizational logic, as overproduction, declining prices, and cut-throat competition pointed to the urgent need for stability and predictability. In the last quarter of the nineteenth century, pioneers of big business like John D. Rockefeller and Andrew Carnegie began to introduce functional and structural changes in their industries, reforms extending from more efficient methods of production and laborsaving inventions to new schemes of vertical and horizontal integration with which to assure a measure of control over their enterprises. By 1886 many of their innovations—centralized business management, better bookkeeping methods, a more efficient sales force—as well as new organizational forms like the trust were becoming conspicuous in major sectors of the American economy.

Modernization and the new social perceptions it fostered, however, had not yet touched all aspects of American economic and political life. While business and finance were intent on mastering the principles of technological society, farmers and industrial workers were just beginning to examine their implications for a tradition of producerism that was comfortably individualistic, voluntaristic, and cooperative. But the panic and depression of the seventies and, more recently, the economic recession of the early eighties had focused the attention of farmers and workers on the need for organizational unity. It was this recognition that was already driving farmers in the Middle Border and beyond the Mississippi in the years of agricultural depression to abandon the purely social aims of the Patrons of Husbandry for regional organizations like the Agricultural Wheel and the Alliance movement. By this time too the organizational liabilities of the Knights of Labor were becoming clear to a younger generation of leaders who began to experiment with ways of exerting greater control from the center.

Still, the business community refused to accord to labor and agriculture recognition of their need for the same means of control it deemed essential for itself. Pools, gentleman's agreements for limiting output, railroad rebates, trusts, and mergers to consolidate directive power—all these seemed to businessmen entirely legitimate ways of ordering their world. But unions, strikes, boycotts, and collective bargaining for workers, and marketing organizations and low interest rate demands for farmers—these, in the eyes of the same businessmen, big or small, seemed dangerous forms of coercion. Still, businessmen, farmers, and workers could agree in condemning anarchism as a violation of both the economic and the moral order. The anarchists, most Americans believed, would have to be discredited and their power for evil destroyed.

Thus the Haymarket trial took on all the trappings of a ritual of retribution. The special bailiff appointed to summon additional veniremen was overheard promising that "those fellows are going to be hanged as certain as death."[5] The prosecution invoked the War of the Rebellion in indicting the anarchists' "insidious, infamous plot to ruin our laws and our country." Judge Joseph E. Gary lent full support to the prosecution, first by coercing jurors and overruling legitimate challenges for cause, then by handcuffing the defense in its attempt to discredit the conspiracy theory, and finally by instructing the jury that if indeed the defendants had ever advocated bomb-throwing, "then all such conspirators are guilty of murder." The verdict was a foregone conclusion: all eight men were found guilty, and seven of them were sentenced to hang while the eighth—Oscar Neebe—was given fifteen years in the penitentiary.

Henry Demarest Lloyd was at home in Winnetka recovering his health when the Haymarket trial opened. At first he was wholly sanguine as to the defendants' chance of a fair trial. "As I am informed, the Chicago dynamitards have secured able counsel who will employ all the resources of the law in their behalf," he assured Henry George's friend John Swinton.[6] Lloyd's own hopes for the American labor movement rested with the eight-hour drive of the Knights of Labor and the trade unionists. The anarchists he dismissed as a handful of misguided fanatics capable of nothing but mischief. As the trial wore on through the summer of 1886 and Judge Gary's hostility to the anarchists became too obvious to ignore, Lloyd realized that the defendants were being prosecuted simply for "the violent insanity of [their] public speeches." Chicago's businessmen and bankers, already organized to fight the unions, were using the bombing to discredit the entire labor movement, and with Judge Gary "acting as prosecuting attorney on the bench" they had a powerful friend in court. When the inevitable guilty verdict came in and the defendants were sentenced to hang, Lloyd prepared to join with liberals, churchmen, and labor leaders across the country in the attempt to save their lives.

Lloyd's attitude toward the condemned men remained equivocal throughout the long ordeal. On the one hand, he flatly refused to condone violence or the language of violence. Louis Lingg, one of the anarchists, recalled a lecture from Lloyd through the bars of his cell on the superiority of English parliamentary methods to revolutionary French ones. On the other hand, Lloyd knew that the men had not received even the semblance of a fair trial—that the proceedings from beginning to end had been an act of revenge. "Shall we be safe," he asked in his appeal to the governor of Illinois, "in setting—by the State—the precedent of arrest without warrant, search without warrant, and condemnation to death for being 'leaders'?" No doubt the anarchists were misguided fools, but they were also weak and helpless like "those for whom however mistakenly they acted." There was no need for panic: "The country is perfectly safe."[7]

These contradictory impressions converged in Lloyd's mind on the tactical problem of saving the defendants from the hangman's rope. He tried to explain the difficulties of his position to his father-in-law, who remained convinced of the anarchists' guilt and was infuriated by Lloyd's attempt to win a commutation of their sentence. "My point," Lloyd patiently explained to his own father, "was simply that all the circumstances raised so fair a question as to whether there was in the minds of the condemned, none of whom threw the bomb, an intent to malicious murder that justice demanded something less than hanging should be the penalty." As for his own motives, "I undertook this because the condemned were connected with the agitation of the great social question of the day." He hoped he could always be found on the side of the underdogs because they were usually right. "The agitators on that side make mistakes, commit crimes, no doubt, but for all that theirs is the right side. I will try to avoid the mistakes and the crimes, but I will stay by the cause."[8]

The anarchists' cause, he was convinced, could only be served by an appeal for commutation, and this involved wringing from them an admission of guilt and a promise to renounce violence. To this uninviting task Lloyd and the committee of appeal reluctantly turned, but only three of the men—Spies, Schwab, and Fielden—agreed to his terms. For the rest recantation was too high a price to pay. Lloyd's efforts during the next year grew desperate, as he helped prepare one appeal after another. He appeared as a spokesman for a group of Chicago businessmen and argued that the defendants had forsworn violence for constitutional means. Then he returned to Springfield a second time to warn that hanging the anarchists would only "tell the world that power and privilege, culture and ease, will debate in blood the questions between them and the poor and unprivileged, the unlearned and desperate." In a last-ditch appeal he stood before the governor with a group of labor leaders and personal friends of the condemned to plead for clemency. Grudgingly the governor agreed to commute the sentences of Fielden and Schwab but upheld the death penalty for the rest. On the night of the executions, worn out and distraught, Lloyd retired to the Wayside to hold his own private ceremony for the victims, singing with his family the "Hymn to the Gallows" he had written—"Silenced voices wrong shall shake/ More than the gallows take"—and bursting into tears.[9]

The costs of his campaign to save the anarchists were social and financial as well as emotional. Friends snubbed him on the street; the *Tribune* closed its columns to him; and the Deacon cut him out of his will. When Bross died in 1889, still unreconciled to his son-in-law's betrayal of his class, Lloyd learned that he had left his fortune (worth $6 million by 1910) in trust to his four grandsons, with an annuity for Jessie of $10,000 a year. Still, Lloyd was scarcely bereft since he continued to receive $10,000 of his own from *Tribune* stock and now owned real estate in Chicago worth hundreds of thousands of dollars. In 1888, he bought forty acres on Sakonnet Point in Little Compton, Rhode Island, and the following year built the Watch House, a magnificent shingled summer home in the Richardson manner.

The Haymarket crisis, like the Great Railroad Strike a decade earlier, drew Lloyd out of himself and into public affairs. By 1888 he could report to his friends that "for the past year it has been impossible even for me to doubt that my feet were traveling firm ground again."[10] Yet, he was in no hurry to take up his pen, even though he was being bombarded from all sides with advice as to suitable subjects. His new friend "Bert" Stewart, the Knights of Labor editor, urged him to finish his study of monopoly "even if you do not think it is the highest trump to play." From his brother David Demarest came conflicting advice to "combine with your theoretical work, a practical branch" of reform such as factory legislation or child labor. Lloyd was still torn between the pull of active participation and the appeal of a distanced approach. Taking his brother's advice meant playing the gadfly, while following Stewart's course risked isolation and political impotence. For the moment at least he preferred to remain one of the "deliberate ones" who acted with circumspection. "The unattached," he reminded himself, "often have the message."[11]

The figure of the "unattached" prophet was Lloyd's old dream of power without obligation in new garb. The appeal of freedom from all kinds of partisanship was still strong for a man unaccustomed to restraint and driven by the compulsion to do great work. But at a deeper level the principle of moral autonomy connected Lloyd with one of the main intellectual currents in Western society at the end of the nineteenth century. Like all intellectuals in the Anglo-American world after 1880, Lloyd was disturbed by the widening gap between community and organization, the increasingly sharp division between preindustrial values of fellowship, fraternity, intimacy, and cooperation, and the impersonal strategies and organizational structures demanded by industrialism. Community pointed toward a recovery of the past and a return to holistic principles and organic relations. Organization, on the contrary, called for new functional forms of planning and management with which to achieve rationality, stability, and predictability. By the end of the nineteenth century these two modes of social thought had diverged to the point where they offered seemingly clear-cut alternatives. From this point on theorists and reformers joined one camp or the other, following the mid-century romantics in their search for the spiritual values and affective ties of the High Middle Ages or making common cause with modernists in devising new controls for industrial society. Lloyd, Bellamy, and George were caught between these contending intellectual perceptions, and they discovered in the role of the "unattached" a means of transcending them by reinvoking for a secular age the idea of the sacred.

Lloyd was equally responsive to the idea of community and to the principles of organization. From his newly acquired fifteenth-century perspective the making of the modern world could only be computed in losses. "The harmony of association in the guild . . . has been lost. The land has been lost, exchanged for the tenement house . . . and the right of the workman to his position has been lost."[12] His reading of Carlyle, Ruskin, and, more recently, the English historian Thorold Rogers suggested employing the moral authority of the medieval world to knit back together those primary relationships severed by modernization. The task confronting the working classes in the West could thus be seen, at least in part, as restoring the spiritual order of a preindustrial world. Theirs would have to be a conservative undertaking, simply a demand for the return of their old rights which would "put them back where their predecessors were three or four hundred years ago."

There were distinct limits, however, to the use of the past to authorize present attempts to reform industrial society. What, Lloyd asked himself, if the celebrated moral solidarity of the Middle Ages turned out to be a myth? What if, as seemed entirely probable, the medieval community lay beyond recovery? History, after all, was powered by a progressive principle. "In each cycle or period of civilization, from simple relations in the earlier stages with an almost ideal equality between the different members of the Highland clans, the English community, the New England Puritan settlement—there must be a progressive change to more complicated relations, greater distances between social centers, great wealth, great poverty—each tendency growing stronger and its effects more rigid until the civilization breaks down, and new arrangements are made."[13]

"New arrangements" meant modern organization, and Lloyd, caught between an idyllic past and an unsettling present, recognized the need for a new policy of control. The list of regulatory functions he was prepared to assign the state lengthened every day:

> The force of state [he noted in his journal] can be used against capitalistic slave-drivers by reforming taxation . . . Also by controlling and confiscating all lines of transportation, all common carrier business thereon . . . also by system of pensions to disabled or aged workmen; also by explicit laws against all forms of fraud and adulteration . . . also by extension of civil-service system . . . also by fully proportionate, if not progressive, income tax . . . also by repeal of all laws giving special privileges in banking, currency, etc. . . . also by repeal of forfeitable land grants . . . also by prohibition of all child and wife labour; also by universal eight-hour laws; also by enforcing to full the police prohibition of all letting of unhealthy and unsafe tenements, and by complete sanitary code with penalties.

Lloyd's list—a calendar of Progressive reform—was an open invitation to the managers of modernization—specialists, experts, technocrats, and bureaucrats—to reorganize industrial society. The accompanying risks of specialization and disruption of community, however, were high, and they would have to be met by returning the nation to the idea of the sacred. The softening and spiritualizing of the industrial regime, Lloyd now saw as a new calling for the "unattached" prophet with his plea for a "new conscience."

As the chief agent in the process of transcending the conflicting categories of community and organization, Lloyd's prophet was assigned a mediational role. "Through this mediator of mankind, a mediator who has sinned as well as suffered, a completer sympathy than any yet known will be established between men and God." Through the offices of the mediator-prophet mankind could at last complete the transit between two worlds—"Eden of the past and Heaven of the future." In combining his search for the sacred with the idea of mediation, Lloyd joined Bellamy and George and a whole generation of late-nineteenth-century intellectuals and reformers in fashioning the Social Gospel, the response of organized Christianity to the inequities and dislocations of rapid industrialization. Churches and seminaries in increasing numbers after 1886 dispatched their members to new city settlements to minister to the poor, and congregations initiated a variety of social services, from employment bureaus to playschools, reading rooms, and model tenements. Ministers in a line of descent from Washington Gladden to Walter Rauschenbusch turned away from seemingly unprofitable theological discussions to preach a doctrine of works based on the immanence of Christ. With their strong evangelical backgrounds, all three utopians proved willing recruits to the Social Gospel. George's "social intelligence," Bellamy's "Religion of Solidarity," and now Lloyd's "new conscience" were similar statements of intent to apply a new set of sacred categories in analyzing the modern world.

Lloyd's figure of the mediator solved the problem of thought and action by locating both in the "outsider" who avoided identification with any particular class or segment of society and performed his redemptive assignment on his own terms. The mediator's power lay in the new conscience, an ethical force that dispensed with time, history, and all secular agencies of change and replaced them with the transhistorical terms of millennialism. First came warnings of impending catastrophe: "Will the leaders of our society as at present constituted lead us out of our present ills?" Lloyd asked. "If they do not, others will ... Here is the great danger." Then came the redemptive promise inherent in mass conversion and the power of the charismatic leader: "A Christ who has sinned and repented and could claim the attention of mankind because he knew and could sympathize with the suffering of sin as well as sorrow and pain, might easily if he had the ethical inspiration and literary ability of Christ of Bethlehem, have a greater following and do more good." And finally, the charismatic leader's sacred prophecy: "A new sunburst, a new resurrection, a new flood of the divine spirit, a new welling up of love for men out of some infinite inspiring heart."

The Haymarket tragedy convinced Lloyd that the American labor movement's greatest need was for a "prophet-counsellor," an adviser willing to lead the workers in the peaceful historical task of checking the revolutionary forces of big business. When Chicago's labor leaders approached him with a request to head their third-party ticket in the congressional election for the Fourth Illinois District in 1888, he agreed to stand though not to run for office. In declining to campaign and retreating instead to the Rhode Island coast for the summer, Lloyd made it clear that he had no intention of joining the city's politicians in a game of rough-and-tumble. Still, in accepting the nomination he meant something more than a ceremonial gesture. His candidacy represented the first tentative step in the direction of a new expressive politics that had already drawn Henry George into a mayoralty race in New York City and would soon attract Edward Bellamy to Populism. With no hope of winning and no interest in building a machine, Lloyd was nevertheless putting his mediational concept to work by openly identifying with the labor movement while reserving the right to define its goals. These he presently announced in a lecture to the Ethical Culture Society in February 1888 entitled "The New Conscience, or the Religion of Labor." The lecture, published in the *North American Review* the following September, derived from his reflections on the Social Gospel, and like Henry George's lecture on Moses, served as an enchiridion for the "prophet-counsellor" who was preparing to head the ranks of American labor.

Lloyd took the existence of a "new conscience" as his point of departure in outlining his religion of reform. "Civilization," he declared, "is simply applied conscience, and Progress is a widening conscience." This force, which originated with working people and their need to create, drove home the truth that "every question between men is a religious question." American workers knew instinctively that moral economy was prior to political economy, and on this premise they were proceeding to found "a church of the deed as well as the creed." Conscience, dismissing the "fine phrases" of the professors and the business apologists would ask simply, "What hast thou done? Where are thy brothers?" Conscience would redeem the nation by extending the workers' knowledge of "hardship, equality, and sacrifice" until all Americans became "brothers in industry" marching against "the cannibals of competition, tyrants of monopoly, devourers of men, women, and children." Then the new age would arrive in all its splendor.

What would a redeemed America be like? Lloyd filled his notebooks with clues as to the shape of the future. One of the most important effects of the "new conscience," he guessed, would be the revival of citizen participation and the rebirth of direct democracy that would reverse the drift toward centralization and professionalism. Direct democracy would bring a day of reckoning—to "Mr. Superserviceable Statistician," for example, whose columns of figures al-

ways added up on the side of the Money Power. It also seemed probable that political and social arrangements would be decentralized.
"Government by indirection, representation, delegation, has been
overdone," he noted in one entry. "With the telegraph, the press etc.
the mechanical means are all at hand for letting the people do their
own political work directly." And in another passage: "Too much
representation—too many agents—too little direct moral responsibility in politics, business, corporations, Church, Congress, Conventions." Given a free field, the "new conscience" could create communities not so different from his own Winnetka, where the
townspeople lent a direct hand in managing local affairs, staffing
school boards, sitting on library committees, and running village improvement societies.

It was with Winnetka as a model that Lloyd traveled to Spring
Valley, the embattled mining town in southern Illinois, to examine
labor strife at first hand. He was summering at the Watch House in
1889 when he first learned of the lockout, and that fall he went there
looking for a story. The adversaries in Spring Valley were the hard-
pressed bituminous coal miners fighting against sharp wage cuts and
the mine operators led by William M. Scott, one of Jay Gould's lieutenants and president of the Spring Valley Coal Company. The villain in this set piece of industrial warfare, Lloyd quickly concluded,
was Scott, who had recruited too many miners and then, when hard
times came, tried to cut their pay by four times the amount recommended by the local District Operators Association, while he continued to invest his sizable profits in local real estate.

Lloyd immediately found himself on the miners' side. His contempt for Scott, as for his master, Jay Gould, was unbounded.
"Whatever Scott does," he advised the local Catholic priest in Spring
Valley, "I suppose the ruin of the community as it once existed is
complete . . . It makes me boil with rage to think of it."[14] Whatever
hopes he had for a "united town" defeating absentee ownership,
however, went glimmering when Scott agreed to reduce the size of
the wage cut and the miners, demoralized and near starvation, went
back to work in November.

Lloyd saw in the Spring Valley lockout clear proof of the intent
of business to destroy a community. This was the story he wanted to
tell, but for such an epic he required a new narrative form. He had read
Progress and Poverty and, more recently, *Looking Backward,* and he real-

ized that George and Bellamy were both highly accomplished con-
trivers of fictions—tellers of tales who worked in an ancient bardic
tradition and whose fables "move mankind and make history" just
as "story tellers draw children after them." "It is not the stern and
accurate thinkers who wield humanity directly, but the philosophers
who can weave truth into a moving fiction or story." Fictions, thus
conceived, were sacred foreshadowings of "a great creative era,
yielding pictures, statues, temples, governments and heroes that will
be immortal." Fictions projected present tendencies into the future
in the form of dreams and portents.

> As men gain this habit of social action—which is called the
> Spirit of the Age—they approach closer to the realization of
> the ideal which is surely not an impractical one, when the
> Spirit of the Age, resting like a Heavenly Dove above the face
> of society will be so ready, so wise, so heavenly kind in its an-
> swer to all the needs of men, that masses of mankind will be
> free from ignoble terrors of poverty, crime, ignorance, and to
> a large extent even of disease, and men will live in the happy
> security of childhood, confident from the kindness with
> which nature and their fellow men touch them that even
> Death is but a step forward, "a birth, sleep, and a forget-
> ting."[15]

This vision of the sacred society created by the "new conscience"
informed his account of the lockout at Spring Valley.

A Strike of Millionaires against Miners: or the Story of Spring Valley
consists of two narratives, an account of the miners' defeat and a
history of the destruction of their community. The controlling image
for the first story is the Indian legend of Starved Rock, where the Illinois tribe, surrounded by their enemies, the Iroquois, slowly starved
to death. "At starved Spring Valley, near by, the story of a victory of
Business is printed in the same ghastly figures as that in which the
Iroquois found their success recorded the morning when, no one
opposing, they gained the top of Starved Rock." With this melodramatic comparison serving as his organizing theme, Lloyd recounted
the story of the miners' defeat by the coal operators in league with
the Chicago and Northwestern Railroad. "The story of Spring Valley
needs not many changes," he warned his readers, "to be a picture of

what all American industry will come to be if the power of our Bourbons of business . . . develops at its present rate."[16]

The second and more important story Lloyd sought to tell concerned the last days of a community, the tragic history of a town that is first "boomed" and then "doomed" by profit-hungry businessmen. In this tale of commercial exploitation Lloyd was attacking the same chaotic and wasteful community-building that Henry George denounced in *Progress and Poverty*. Spring Valley was planned for quick profit by a conspiracy of promoters, speculators, and confidence men who comprised the interlocking directorate of the Spring Valley Coal Company, the Townsite Company, and the Chicago and Northwestern Railroad Company. Together these corporations mounted a high-pressure advertising campaign that attracted hundreds of miners to whom they sold house lots at inflated prices while exploiting them with wages pegged at the subsistence level. The miners, who came to Spring Valley intending to build a genuine community, were duped into believing that they had joined one. But when the price of coal fell, they became the victims of the business conspiracy to salvage profits by destroying the town.

For Lloyd as for the other two utopians, there was something unnatural about a community held together only by the dream of quick profits. The fatal divisions at Spring Valley were reflected in the lack of civic spirit and a pervasive class selfishness. The merchants and middle classes lined up against the miners and failed to see that they too had been victimized. It was to these middle classes, accordingly, that Lloyd directed his final warning: "If you usurp for your private profit all these trusts and grants, if you withdraw yourself from serving and protecting the public and take to oppressing and plundering for your points of advantage, you will but repeat the folly of your medieval exemplars whose castles now decorate a better civilization with their prophetic ruin."[17]

The Haymarket tragedy was the central symbolic event for Lloyd's generation of reformers, academicians, and churchmen. The riot and its punitive aftermath signaled the onset of a decade of increasingly bitter confrontations like the one at Spring Valley. Liberals in all the professions suddenly realized that their most urgent task was educating middle-class Americans by helping them to adjust their preferences for the fluidity and individualism of an agrarian social order to an industrial one in which these values seemed dysfunctional. In this work of applying a modified Darwinism to American society, the argument of the Russian geographer and revolutionary Petr Kropotkin proved conclusive with liberals. Reformers inside and outside the universities took their cues from Kropotkin's reading of evolution as the steady perfecting of forms of mutual aid.

There were two main approaches to the work of intellectual adjustment. Inside academia, reform-minded teachers and researchers began to explore the potential for harmonizing social and class relationships in what the Columbia sociologist Franklin Giddings would soon call "consciousness of kind." The "struggle for existence," Lester Ward reminded would-be reformers both in and out of government, was at bottom a "struggle for structure" waged by professionals who had mastered the science of "applied sociology." European-trained economists returning to take positions in major American universities might differ on the efficacy of competition— some, like John Bates Clark, extolling the free market, others, like Richard T. Ely, calling for public ownership of monopolies, and still others, like Simon Patten, counting on industrial production itself to bring a new age of abundance. Whatever their varying diagnoses and prescriptions, younger economists, sociologists, and social scientists after 1886 began to build their bases of operation in the new universities and the professional associations, which they charged with the task of teaching Americans scientific social control.

While the academicians began to study the social process with a view to controlling it, the Social Gospel was creating a host of latter-day "come-outers" who, having attempted to enlist their churches in the reform enterprise and failed, as they often did, resigned their pastorates to establish other agencies and follow other approaches to reform. Hugh O. Pentecost, a disciple of Henry George and a labor candidate for mayor of Newark, was one of the first American clergymen to protest against Haymarket. Soon thereafter Pentecost resigned his pulpit to preach, like Theodore Parker before him, a non-denominational faith to a Unity Congregation in a Masonic temple. The Episcopalian priest J. O. S. Huntington took up mission work on New York's Lower East Side, where the sight of overwhelming poverty drove him to found the Christian Association for the Advancement of the Interests of Labor, which lobbied for the eight-hour day, child labor reform, and the elimination of the sweatshop. One of the most effective of the radical Christians in the years immediately fol-

lowing Haymarket was William Dwight Porter Bliss, founder of the
Society of Christian Socialists, who, under pressure from his congregation, relinquished his pastorate at Boston's Grace Church to
form the Church of the Carpenter and its companion Brotherhood of
the Carpenter, which soon established the Wendell Phillips Union as
headquarters for an anti-tenement-house campaign and a consumers
cooperative movement.

For Lloyd and his fellow utopians the American university, with
its increasingly specialized and secularized functions, came too late
and promised too little. More congenial were the religious radicals
on the left margin of the Social Gospel movement who were experimenting with cooperative devices and alternative methods of insti-
tutionalizing Christian values and spreading the gospel of reform.
For their part the three utopians—first George, then Lloyd, and finally Bellamy—would elect to play their mediational roles directly
by entering American politics with a mission and, so they hoped, a
mandate to recast the machinery, redefine the goals, and reanimate
political life by infusing it with ethical purpose.

The utopians agreed with the new academicians and clergymen
in denouncing revolution and all appeals to class interest. They took
it upon themselves, however, to teach both workers and middle-
class Americans their joint responsibilities by using politics as their
means, in the hope that the very process of organizing a genuine political alternative to the status quo would in itself temper the demands of labor and teach the middle class the need for altruism and
cooperation. The place for the would-be mediator to begin, Lloyd
was now convinced, was at the hustings, where new democratic
forces could be gathered for a final assault on monopoly and privilege. By 1890, when his book on Spring Valley appeared, workers
and farmers in all sections of the nation were beginning to weigh the
advantages of a popular third-party crusade against the system.
Suddenly it occurred to Lloyd that here in a new kind of politics already pioneered by Henry George lay the chance he had been waiting for.

When the trial of the Haymarket defendants opened in the summer of 1886, Henry George was busy promoting his latest book, a
study of free trade, and writing a series of articles for the *North*

American Review on the Pennsylvania coal miners. His children were growing up, Richard and Henry, Jr., to careers in journalism and politics, Jane Teresa ("Jennie") to marriage and a tragically premature death, and Anna to her position of domestic ascendance as her father's favorite. After a succession of moves, the George household had recently settled on Pleasant Avenue in Harlem, where in his cluttered study the Prophet of San Francisco composed the articles and political commentary that furnished the sole support for his family. It was here that a visiting committee from New York City's Central Labor Union, in search of a candidate in the upcoming mayoral contest, finally cornered their quarry.

George was deep in an earnest discussion of the Single Tax with his latest convert, Tom Johnson, the traction magnate about to turn politician, when his son Richard came in to announce the imminent arrival of the delegation from the Central Labor Union to ask him to run for mayor. On schedule the committee appeared, only to be told that George declined the honor. He had always doubted the prospects of third parties, he told his visitors, and the punishing defeat of their candidate four years earlier did not dispose him to change his mind. Undaunted, the committee returned a second and then a third time to plead with him, and reluctantly he abandoned his objections. After lengthy discussions with his friends, George agreed to accept the nomination on one condition: "at least thirty thousand citizens should, over their signatures, express the wish that I should become a candidate, and pledge themselves in such a case to go to the polls and vote for me."[18] That would be a mandate he could not refuse.

George's original hostility toward labor unions and strikes had moderated, if it had not entirely disappeared. His recent trip through the coal regions of Pennsylvania had brought home to him the desperate poverty of miners victimized by wage cuts, company stores, hazardous working conditions, and conspiracy laws that prevented them for organizing. The Pennsylvania coal towns were local centers of Land League support, and out of the anthracite region had come George's friend Terence Powderly who had served as mayor of Scranton. The miners, like the Land-Leaguers in New York City, were avid readers of Patrick Ford's *Irish World* and had followed George's adventures in Ireland with interest. It was natural, then, that George should undertake an investigation of the conditions in the mining industry that had led to so much misery among his supporters. Perhaps strikers, as he had always insisted, could not win the deadly game of "starve-out," but their courage in fighting back could only be admired. "Men dependent upon their daily labor do not strike for the sheer fun of striking," he reminded his readers, "and even foolish and reckless strikes, when they occur in any number, indicate a chronic irritation that can only proceed from real grievances."[19] For the violent posturing of the anarchists George, like Lloyd, had only contempt, but the sight of illiterate, semiskilled Irish and Hungarian miners closing down a mine to secure their right to a decent living seemed to him heroic. New York City, he reasoned, was filled with more of these exploited day laborers who might be taught by a responsible leader with a workable plan how to recast American politics and society.

As the Knights of Labor and New York City's trade unions and assemblies hurried to meet their candidate's stipulation by circulating a giant petition, George caught a glimpse of their determination when he stood on the reviewing stand with Mayor William R. Grace on Labor Day and watched rank after rank of gray-garbed, heavy-footed workers march past, the recruits, he suddenly realized, for the crusade he had dreamed of leading—coarse, ill-educated, and slow, perhaps, but capable of learning the truth about the Single Tax that he would teach them.

If there were any doubts as to the wisdom of his agreement to run, they were dispelled by a secret visit of an emissary from Mayor Grace's office. The Democratic party in New York City in 1886 was badly split between a discredited Tammany and a resurgent County Democracy that had succeeded in capturing the mayor's office. All their gains, the County Democrats noted with alarm, were now threatened by a Johnny-come-lately with his juvenile land reform nostrums. The messenger from Mayor Grace, after coldly informing George that he would never be "counted in," made him an offer: if George would quietly withdraw from the race, the County Democracy would see to it that he was rewarded with a safe seat in the House of Representatives in the next election. George, his color blossoming with his temper, sat ominously still until his visitor had finished. "I said to him finally," he recalled for Annie and the children, " 'You tell me that I cannot possibly get the office. Why, if I cannot possibly get the office, do you want me to withdraw?' His reply was: 'You cannot be elected, but your running will raise hell!' I said: 'You have relieved me of an embarrassment. I do not want the responsibility and the work of the office of Mayor of New York, but I do want to raise hell! I am decided and will run.' "[20]

Hell was just what George's Democratic opponent and former employer Abram S. Hewitt promised the city's voters should the Single Tax prophet win the election. A new and dangerous issue, Hewitt warned, was being foisted on New Yorkers. "An attempt is being made to organize one class of citizens against all other classes."[21] Young Theodore Roosevelt, the Republican contender in the three-cornered race, pressed into service by the bluestocking districts, viewed the contest with more equanimity. There *were* curious features to the race, Roosevelt agreed, but they stemmed from the division within the Democratic party. "The George vote from the Democratic party is so large and from the Republican so small that we have a right to regard his candidacy as simply a split from the Democratic party."[22] Hewitt and Company were trying to make it appear that the choice lay between anarchy and order, but this, Roosevelt added with a candor already habitual, was patently false.

The city's working class had followed the Haymarket trial with an interest sharpened by local conflict. Earlier in the spring several of New York's labor leaders had been indicted, fined, and imprisoned for conducting a boycott against a beer garden and music hall owner. The Theiss case had served notice on the unions of the intentions of business, now backed by the state's judiciary, to limit their right of protest and their power to protect their members. Discouraged by the outright hostility of the two major parties to their tactics, members of the Central Labor Union decided to make common cause with the socialists and the Knights of Labor and field a contender of their own. They required, first of all, a charismatic figure whose sympathy for the workingman was well known, and a candidate, as well, who could be counted on to raise the bread-and-butter issues of higher pay and shorter hours and the right to organize and to bargain. George, his reputation among the city's Irish-American population well established, met the first test handsomely. The second, as union leaders would learn to their chagrin, he failed dismally.

George himself was of two minds concerning his chances. "It is by no means impossible that I shall be elected," he confided to a friend. "But the one thing sure is that if I do go into the fight, the campaign will bring the land question into practical politics and will do more to popularize its discussion than years of writing would do. This is the only temptation to me."[23] It was also a major source of difficulty for a beginning practitioner of educational politics. In 1886 the number of recruits to the Single Tax in the United States was still limited to a relative handful of middle-class reformers who understood George's economic analysis and agreed with it and whose chief concern was to stabilize urban land values in order to fashion a more rational policy of urban development. For this tiny vanguard across the country, which included the Methodist minister R. Heber Newton and Father McGlynn, a very few professors like the St. Louis Hegelian Thomas Davidson, the incipient radical socialist Daniel DeLeon, and the protoprogressive Tom Johnson, the idea of socializing ground rent as a means of renewing the city made good sense.

The Single Tax and George's elaborate exposition of it did not figure very prominently in the support of New York City's workingmen. For most of them it was enough that he sympathized with labor and fought landlordism in Ireland and at home. He spoke, too, of the dignity of labor and preached a Christian message (albeit a Protestant one) calling for a fair distribution of wealth and celebrating an adversary working-class culture. In their eyes George appeared as the champion of the little man who wanted what they wanted.

These divisions were clearly reflected in the double nomination George received, the first from his working-class supporters at a meeting in Clarendon Hall on September 23, and then, a week later, from the middle-class contingent of reformers. The Single Taxers preferred the Land and Labor party as a name for their new movement, but the unions opted for the United Labor party and carried the day. This was to be George's sole concession to working-class interests, for he was already concerned with extending his electoral reach, as he explained, to "that great body of citizens, who, though not workingmen in the narrow sense of the term, feel the bitterness of the struggle for existence as much as does the manual laborer, and are as deeply conscious of the corruptions of our politics and the wrong of our social system."[24] George's illusion of the solidarity of Jacksonian producers would last the life of his campaign.

He had not really wanted to be mayor of New York, he told his working-class audience at Clarendon Hall in his acceptance speech. "I have had in my time political ambition, but years ago I gave it up." Another path had opened to him—"the path I have chosen"—that of the pioneer who travels in advance of the political caravans breaking the road for them. Yet now he was convinced that politics offered the only safe route to reform, and he meant to take it. What was the challenge confronting American labor if not the hard fact that "the vast majority of men and women and children in New York have no legal right to live here at all." Together he and his listeners comprised 99 percent of the city's population, but they lived on sufferance, forced to pay to the other 1 percent exorbitant rent for the privilege of "staying here and working like slaves."

With this allusion to the Single Tax, George announced the platform on which he meant to stand. If his working-class followers expected him to emphasize higher pay and better working conditions, they were disappointed. The platform of the United Labor party, as revised by its candidate, called for the reform of court procedures so that "the practice of drawing grand jurors from one class should cease" (a pointed reference to the Haymarket and Theiss trials); demanded an end to the "officious inter-meddling of the police with peaceful assemblages"; and urged the enforcement of housing and sanitary codes and the abolition of contract labor. A second plank denounced overcrowding in the city's tenement districts but advocated a confiscatory tax on land values rather than new building codes. There followed four more planks dealing with the Single Tax, government ownership of railroads and the telegraph, and a call for a clean-up of labor racketeering. Slim rations for hungry workers!

George's restricted vision of the problems of American labor was offset, for the moment, by his charismatic appeal, which attracted even hard-headed trade unionists like Samuel Gompers and the contingent of German socialists who reluctantly accepted his platform as at least "partial socialism." George was at his autobiographical best in recounting his conversion to social reform when he first witnessed New York's appalling misery and the iron entered his soul. "And here I made a vow, from which I have never faltered, to seek out the remedy, if I could, the cause that condemned little children to lead such lives as you know them to lead."[25] He called on his audience to join in a gigantic crusade for the abolition of industrial slavery, to stand together and to win for New York City the "honour of having led the van in this great movement."

The New York mayoralty race of 1886 was the most dramatic of the city's nineteenth-century campaigns, the climax of a decade of working-class frustration, patrician fears, and party neglect. The huge petition bearing 34,000 signatures, which recalled the great days of abolitionist agitation before the Civil War, touched off an explosion of amateur political energy that rocked the city from the Battery to Harlem. George's frenzied campaign marked the return to action of the volunteer long ignored by Tammany and at the same time a new departure toward the urban politics of maximum candidate exposure.

The organizational problems of the new United Labor party were numerous and severe, and not the least of them was money. Union members across the city were assessed at twenty-five cents a head, and the leadership contributed amounts ranging from $100 to $1,000. Even so, speakers always passed the hat at street-corner rallies, and the candidate himself could frequently be seen at party headquarters at the dingy Colonnade Hotel off Broadway sitting behind a mound of pennies rolling them for distribution to his campaign managers. With such slim proceeds the party launched its own newspaper, the *Leader,* under the frugal management of Louis Post who quickly rounded up a staff of eager volunteers. George decided on a personal "tail-gate" style of campaigning. From mid-morning until late into the evening he dashed about the city in his horsecart, haranguing crowds of workers from his makeshift podium, his piercing voice aimed at daytime shoppers and passers-by in neighborhood marketplaces and carrying over the heads of late-night working-class audiences whose hardened features caught the glare of torches held aloft as they listened to the saving word from the prophet. On a typical day George addressed a group of Franco-Americans on the Lower East Side, a second ethnic gathering in Abingdon Square, a crowd of railway workers under the El, and ended the day with a huge rally at Sulzer's Harlem River Park at midnight. George's rallies were no mere political ceremonies scripted by the bosses but genuine participatory rituals full of sound and fury.

Or so it seemed to New York's "best people," who joined with Tammany hacks and the Catholic hierarchy in deploring the advent of mass politics. In the early days of the campaign Republicans and Democrats alike dismissed George as a "humbug" and a "busybody" with no real chance of election. But soon Hewitt and the Democracy realized they were in a fight to the finish and joined Roosevelt's Republican backers in abusing George as a "revolutionist" and an "apostle of anarchy and destruction." George had predicted "one of the fiercest contests that ever took place in this or any other city," and so it proved. Hard pressed to hold the loyalty of New York's workers, the Democrats turned for help to the Catholic church. Archbishop Corrigan, after trying and failing to silence Father McGlynn, who took to the streets in behalf of his friend, suspended him for the duration of the campaign. Monsignor Thomas S. Preston in an interview with an alarmed Tammany official claimed to speak for the vast majority of the Catholic clergy in deploring Henry George's candidacy. "They think his principles unsound and unsafe, and contrary to the teachings of the church . . . His principles, if logically carried out, would prove the ruin of the workingmen he professes to befriend."[26] The Preston letter promptly appeared in all the papers in the city and supplied the theme for many a sermon in neighborhood parishes.

George countered these attacks as best he could, making countless personal appearances, firing off rebuttals in the *Leader,* and hoping for the best. On the final Saturday night before the election he stood on the reviewing stand in Union Square in the drenching rain while some 30,000 workers, banners bedraggled and torches sputtering, marched past chanting "George! George! Hen-ry George!" In a last appearance on election eve at Clarendon Hall he told his followers that if they did their duty the next day, "we may begin a cheer that will echo through this land and around the world. But elected or not elected, we have won a victory."

The official tally gave Hewitt the election with 90,552 votes to George's 68,140 and Roosevelt's 60,435. George was sure that he had been counted out as promised, a conviction that hardened with the years. In the days before the adoption of the Australian ballot each party was responsible for printing and distributing its own ticket and providing poll watchers to guard its interests. Undermanned and inexperienced, the Union Labor party proved no match for the wiles of the professionals. In some polling stations there were no George ballots to be found; in others the party's ticket was unaccountably lost. Tales of ballot-box stuffing and other electoral atrocities abounded, many of them undoubtedly true. Yet in the final count it was the combination of Catholic fears fed by Democratic regulars and middle-class anxieties fanned by the press that defeated George, as he was quick to learn.

To his vanquished troops on election night George depicted their defeat as another Bunker Hill—"a skirmish that prepares our forces for the battles that are to follow."[27] The next day he returned to his office at the Henry George Publishing Company, which he had recently formed, and announced his intention to "buy a bottle of ink and some pens and go again to writing."[28]

One of the first of his new journalistic productions was "The New Party," a public casting of accounts on the recent campaign and a prediction of a national political realignment. The two major parties, he declared, were done for, and an era of party regularity that had begun with Fremont's candidacy before the Civil War had now closed with the defeat of James G. Blaine. The moment for redrawing political lines had clearly arrived. Until recently there had been only two presentiments of the coming political upheaval: the repeated appearances of one-issue parties like the Greenbackers and the Prohibitionists, and the more significant resolve of American labor to enter politics as an independent force. It was true enough that labor had been slow to resort to the ballot box, but this was because it was still a "great vague power," a collection of unorganized men "anxious to go somewhere, but utterly ignorant of the road and without leaders whom they have learned to trust." Now, however, the workingmen of America were discovering their natural leaders in new spokesmen who formed the vanguard of a powerful social crusade.

The new party now being built by workingmen, farmers, and the other plain people of the nation, George continued, must be a party of ideas and principles, the most important of which was equal access to the land. This had been the only real issue in the recent mayoral campaign. "We did not win that election—few of us really cared for winning, for we were not struggling for office. But we did more than win an election. We brought the labor question—or what is the same thing, the land question—into practical politics. And it is there to stay."[29] The labor party was not a class party but a huge reformational and renovative movement consisting of all the producing classes, farmers as well as industrial workers, entrepreneurs along with wage earners. Necessarily, the new party would reject all secret combinations and compromises, and would direct its chief efforts toward cleansing consciences rather than winning votes. "Even whether our own candidates, when we put them up, are elected or defeated, makes little difference—the contest will stimulate discussion and promote the cause." No backstairs deals, no political back-scratching, simply "the religious sentiment" generated by right thinking. In such a party of the people lay the only hope for social salvation.

In the meantime the tangible results of George's campaign appeared to be twofold. First there were signs that the politicians had received the message from disgruntled workers, as the New York legislature rushed to pass a series of new laws providing for arbitration of labor disputes, the regulation of employment of women and children, and an overhaul of the penal code. Some of this legislation was already in the hamper in Albany before the mayoral race, but George's candidacy had provided a needed stimulus for passage. A second and equally serious result of George's entrance into politics was to drive a wedge into the labor movement, separating the rank-and-file workers from their self-declared leaders eager to follow the prophet in the crusade for land reform. Trade unionists and socialists had uneasily agreed to a Single Tax platform with the hope that from such unpromising beginnings would come a full-fledged labor party responsive to their needs, and they still hoped to convert George to a more realistic view of the industrial problem. Yet George, as his article on the new party made distressingly clear, had not changed his mind as to the real alignment of forces in the United States. In his mind the contenders were the grasping landlords on the one side and the great mass of true producers on the other. If, he reasoned, his reading of the question was correct, then any party that failed to bring together farmers, artisans, small businessmen, and workingmen could never succeed in changing the direction of American politics. The new party, in short, must be an evangelical gathering of the nation's little people wherever they could be collected to stand against the monopolists and their political mouthpieces in the old parties. To the dubious trade unionists and disillusioned socialists, on the contrary, George appeared to be preparing battle plans for the wrong front in the wrong war.

George's Single Tax followers, led by the irrepressible Father McGlynn and the circumspect Louis Post, lost no time in regrouping. At a meeting in Cooper Union on November 6, 1886, they elected an executive committee and made plans for fielding a full slate of candidates in the forthcoming state elections, reserving for George the slot of secretary of state. By January 1887 his lieutenants had established a new newspaper, the *Standard*, under their own firm editorial supervision and were busy extending their organization into upstate New York. The United Labor party soon gave the lie to its name, and it became obvious that George now headed a sharply divided movement. The center of the swirling controversy in the spring and summer of 1887 was occupied by a band of socialists from New York City who, having stood by George in his hour of need, now proposed to take control of the party for themselves and provide it with a coherent socialist platform. To protect their party from such an eventuality George and his Single Taxers together with a majority of the trade unionists had written into the platform a provision barring from membership anyone who refused to renounce allegiance to competing parties or organizations, an intended ban on all those socialists who refused to leave the Socialist Labor party. Here was the rock on which the United Labor party foundered in the summer of 1887.

All of George's fears of socialism returned as he sought to counter what he knew to be a wholly subversive influence. He established his own paper under the firm hand of Louis Post and encouraged Father McGlynn in his plans for an Anti-Poverty Society, a nondenominational experiment in spreading the word "that God has made ample provision for the needs of all men during their residence upon earth" through the public sharing of land.[30] By midsummer George had succeeded in drawing around him a small but highly dedicated band of personal followers determined to purge their party of all dissidents, chief among them the socialists.

George's fear of socialism had not moderated since the writing of *Progress and Poverty*. Socialists, he now insisted, took hold of the social problem at the wrong end. To ensure a rough equality essential to a healthy society it was not necessary for government to take over the means of production—only that the equal rights of all producers be unconditionally guaranteed. It was at this point that the socialists' engine went off the track in steering for big rather than little government. The problem, George argued once again, was not capital but land. "There is in reality no conflict between labor and capital; the true conflict is between labor and monopoly."[31] And the problem of monopoly, as he had already shown, was rooted in the land question: solve that with the Single Tax and you solve everything. As for competition, men could not live without it. In trying to eliminate natural competition the socialists had made a grave miscalculation, and for that reason alone would have to be purged from the party.

The issue which triggered the break with the socialists was the question of clemency for the Haymarket anarchists, a symbol of hope to the American left and of impending upheaval to the great middle class. As he first watched the trial unfold George, like Lloyd, had been dismayed by the violations of due process, a view he still held as late as the following spring. "Spies and his associates," read one of the first of the *Standard*'s editorials, "were convicted by a jury chosen in a manner so shamelessly illegal that it would be charity to suspect the judge of incompetency."[32] The Haymarket meeting had been a peaceable one, and no connection had ever been established between the defendants and the unknown bomb-thrower. "Yet this jury, many of whom confessed to fixed opinions against the accused, found a verdict of murder." The scales of justice, George insisted, had been tipped by irrational fears.

As the state elections approached, however, George began to feel the pressure from his middle-class supporters to cast off the socialists and all imputation of radicalism. In the clemency question he found one useful means of disengaging. An editorial in the October 8th issue of the *Standard*, ostensibly written by George, made a complete reversal on the question of clemency. "There is no ground for asking executive clemency in behalf of the Chicago Anarchists as a matter of right." Their case had been appealed, thoroughly reviewed, and the original verdict sustained by learned judges. "That seven judges of the highest court of Illinois, men accustomed to weigh evidence and to pass upon judicial rulings, should after a full examination of the testimony and the record, and with the responsibility of life and death resting upon them, unanimously sustain the verdict and the sentence, is inconsistent with the idea that the Chicago Anarchists were condemned on insufficient evidence." A reader familiar with George's style might have paused at the circumlocution and the *ad hominem* argument, but the fact remained that the leadership of George's new party had done an about-face. In January the *Standard* declared that "no well-informed lawyer can defend the convictions upon legal grounds." Now presumably the same editorial voice announced that "it was proved beyond a doubt that these men were engaged in a conspiracy as a result of which the bomb was thrown, and were therefore under the laws of Illinois as guilty as though they themselves had done the act."

The Single Taxers' *bouleversement* was met with cries of outrage from labor leaders all over the country, and George was damned as a turncoat and a traitor, even though on reflection he granted mitigating circumstances and wrote privately to Governor Ogelsby urging him to commute the sentences. The scholar and philanthropist, scoffed the labor press, had turned seeker after office.

George could scarcely deny reasons of expediency. At the state convention of the United Labor party in August he stood firm against the socialists and rejected all offers of compromise. For pragmatists like Samuel Gompers the question of excluding the socialists was a Hobson's choice. Although he agreed that their program was impractical, he was forced to admit that "as many of us understand it, Mr. George's theory of land taxation does not promise present reform, nor an ultimate solution."[33] George, however, remained obdurate. "The question between State or German Socialism and the ideas of that great party of equal rights and individual freedom which is now beginning to rise all over the land, may as well, since the Socialists have raised it, be settled right now."[34] Settled it was with the help of the trade unionists by a solid vote of 94 to 59 for exclusion. George blandly pronounced the benediction: "The greatest danger that could befall the party would not be the separation of its elements . . . but would be a continuance within its ranks of incongruous elements." The price of purity, however, was prohibitive as the United Labor party went down to crashing defeat. George's candidacy for the post of secretary of state won him just 72,000 votes, a mere 4,000 more than he had earned the year before in New York City alone.

When the elections were over and his dream of a new party of producers lay shattered, George explained as best he could his motives in purging the dissidents, whether socialists or anarchists. No doubt he had lost a high proportion of the German socialist vote, he admitted to his friend and translator C. D. F. Güttschow, and he would continue to be accused of treachery. But there had been no alternative. As for betraying the Haymarket anarchists, the objectionable editorial had been written, not by himself, but by Louis Post, though it had met with his full approval. "The opinion there expressed was my opinion."[35] Admittedly the bench was not always above reproach, but he could not believe that every one of the seven judges would have unjustly condemned the defendants.

It remained in the winter of 1887–1888 to put his experiment in educational politics in perspective by distinguishing his program from its two rival ideologies. Socialism, he wrote in the *Standard*, proposed "the cumbrous and impossible system which would make the government the all in all." Anarchism sought to reverse the course of history by carrying Jefferson's preference for limited government to a point of absurdity. Anarchism in the last analysis was the destructive impulse of desperate men who could see no way out of their misery. Yet good would not come of evil. "What our modern civilization needs to extricate it from the dangers that under present conditions gather with its advance, are intelligence and conscience."[36] And these two qualities, it was now clear to him, were to be found in greatest supply in men like himself, self-made men, responsible men who rejected violence, ignored the promises of statism, denied the permanence of class, held fast to Christian ethics, and were ready to undertake a redemptive assignment. In other words, social salvation lay, not with the working class but with the great middling groups in American society. George's flirtation with the labor movement was over.

The Haymarket tragedy, which had driven Henry Demarest Lloyd into an alliance with American labor, had precisely the reverse effect on Henry George in detaching him from organized labor politics and propelling him toward a vision of a vast "people's party" of true producers. Both his timing and his estimate of the potential for revivalistic politics were faulty. In 1888 the forces of discontent that matched his own were just beginning to take political form, not in cities like New York among industrial workers, but in the great American heartland among staple-crop farmers who considered themselves betrayed and were preparing to fight back. George, as another presidential election approached, saw no escape from his dilemma except retreat to the Democratic party, where his Single Tax stood no chance of surviving. Retreat meant the temporary abandonment of the politics of prophecy for a more sober appeal to ancient Democratic party prejudices. To this limited and not alto-gether inviting task he now turned.

Edward Bellamy was drafting the plot of *Looking Backward* when the Haymarket jury returned its verdict in the late summer of 1886. The episode figured prominently in an early chapter as the narrator explains to his twentieth-century host how the impasse American society had reached by 1886 was symbolized by "a small band of men who called themselves anarchists, and proposed to terrify the American people into adopting their ideas by threats of violence." Anarchism, Bellamy's alter ego recalls, had made no headway what-ever in changing late-nineteenth-century society, but he asks whether subsequently the "followers of the red flag" had contrib-uted to the social advance. No! comes the reply, "they had nothing to do with it except to hinder it, of course."[37] Bellamy's old fears of labor unrest haunted the writing of the novel. At a time when Henry Demarest Lloyd was examining working conditions in Chicago's in-dustrial plants and Henry George was experimenting, however pro-visionally, with working-class politics, Bellamy still rejected the idea that the industrial workers could ever remake American society. Labor unions, it seemed to him, were the carriers of a new and dis-turbing interest-group politics that threatened to tear society apart unless it could be checked by the assertion of an overriding national interest. Like the big corporations they so futilely opposed, unions were founded on organized selfishness. They were vulnerable to the very forces of corruption they proposed to eliminate. Any attempt to reorganize the old industrialism on the basis of labor unions, Bel-lamy's utopian spokesman concludes, was like a bird trying to fly with only one wing.

Bellamy's dim estimate of the altruism of industrial workers re-sulted in large part from the immense distance, psychological and cultural, from which he viewed their lives. He prided himself on his insularity. "I can get a better view of the Brooklyn strike," he once wrote to a friend, "under my apple tree in Chicopee Falls than from a Fulton Street curb."[38] From such a vantage point he saw masses but not individuals, outlines but no particulars. For fifteen years he had been writing editorials condemning child labor, calling for better housing and safer working conditions, and demanding better educational opportunities for working-class children. Yet running through all of this editorial commentary was the assumption that American workers should properly be the recipients rather than the originators of industrial reforms. Like many of his contemporaries who studied the "social problem," he had concluded that an unskilled and uneducated class of workers lacked the means to create a viable politics or a genuine culture of their own, a dismissal made easier by his ignorance of the ethnic, religious, and linguistic richness of American working-class life. From his distanced perspective it appeared that giant factories, and increasing impersonality had crushed an older artisanal tradition like a steamroller, flattening the working class into a shapeless mass of humanity. In a passage in the autobiographical novel he had just set aside, Eliot Carson stands outside the factory gates in his home town and looks on as a "throng" of "operatives" are "let out" and swarm past him, "some with stolid, godless, patient faces, mere human oxen, others flippant, exchanging coarse jests, voluble with vulgarity." Just think, Eliot muses, "that each of these poor creatures feels himself or herself, his or her withered individuality, to be the center of the universe . . . Each of those narrow foreheads is a prison to the dark soul within it, and what a prison, what a dungeon dark!"[39]

Bellamy's view of the American working class as an urban "dark people" was particularly congenial to a middle class in the Gilded Age convinced that illiterate immigrants threatened upheaval and dissolution. The fear of class war on which popular novels like John Hay's *The Breadwinners* played so mercilessly provided Americans with a new genre of antilabor fiction that the naturalistic novelists from Frank Norris and Stephen Crane to Jack London would embellish with themes of degeneration and reversion to primitivism. Common to all of them was the conviction that the beast in man constantly lurked in the shadows of his mind and that, once loosed, it would destroy all reason and ravage society. Though less hysterical than many of the middle-class writing fraternity, Bellamy was no less convinced that a faceless, mindless social force needed the countervailing power of a great idea to give it direction and purpose.

That purpose Bellamy identified with the Puritan belief in salvation through work, the escape it provided from the sins of indolence and sloth to which, he felt, the new working class was particularly prone. For much of his editorial career he had linked "pauperism" and "indolence" with industrial workers unable if not always unwilling to find useful employment. "But we wish that by some quick-working process, Malthusian or other," he had written once, "this generation might be the last of it." In prescribing a work ethic for the ills of industrial America Bellamy followed George in drawing on the values of producerism. Work in this time-honored view, was an economic necessity but also a spiritual release and a social duty. Men were created to live in the sweat of their faces, and in so doing were ennobled and uplifted. It followed in the logic of producerist thought that every citizen had both the right and the obligation to work for the greater community, and any society that failed to provide meaningful employment for all its citizens was doomed. But now parasitical nonproducers—capitalists reaping excessive profits and middlemen insinuating themselves between the real workers and the goods they produced—refused to acknowledge work as an essential act of creation. These privileged few showed neither compassion toward their less fortunate brethren nor true understanding of their own uselessness. The new leisure class had forfeited its right to rule.

To dramatize for his readers the divided state of American society Bellamy turned to a variation on the "two nations" theme that had served reformers since Disraeli and Dickens, the moral metaphor so dear to believers in producerism. In describing the nineteenth-century society from which he has been miraculously transported, Bellamy's hero, Julian West, compares it to "a prodigious coach which the masses of humanity were harnessed to and dragged toilsomely along a very hilly and sandy road." The driver of the coach was hunger whose whips cut deep into the backs of the struggling human team below. His passengers, the rich and idle, perched on top of the coach, "well out of the dust," admiring the scenery and pausing every now and then to comment on the performance of their fellow men pulling on the rope. The road was filled with potholes and soft spots, hazards that meant misery for the masses and brought terror to the riders. Then the passengers feared for their places which "for all that they were so easy . . . were very insecure," and "at every sudden jolt of the coach persons were slipping out of them compelled to take hold of the rope and help drag the coach on which they had before ridden so pleasantly."[40]

The image of millions of faceless workers tugging at a gigantic

rope and scrambling for a foothold in the mire served to shift attention from the experiential to the moral. The parable of the stagecoach framed Bellamy's problem as an ethical one of meaningful
work and the universal right to a decent existence which work would
ensure. The exact opposite of the picture of a mass of struggling
workers made beastlike by want, Bellamy realized as he began
drafting his novel, was the image of an organized, compact, efficient,
and highly motivated work force systematically creating abundance
for all—the image, in short, of a national industrial army.

10

LOOKING BACKWARD

LOOKING BACKWARD is a religious fable, an account of the triumph of the sacred over the secular forces of evil. At first glance the book seems to consist of two different and unrelated stories—the fantastic tale of Julilan West's resurrection in the year 2000 and the lengthy account furnished him by his host, Doctor Leete, of the creation and management of utopia. Bellamy encouraged this compartmentalized reading by explaining his growing impatience, as he revised the novel, with the contrivances and "other whimsies" of Julian's story once he had discovered his true reform purpose. He continued to regard Julian's transformation simply as a "fanciful device" to give color to an argument that he now recognized "as little fanciful as possible." Even with the model industrial army serving as a bridge, the two parts of the book seemed to him to conflict, and recasting it involved the sacrifice of details and "interesting effects" to the conclusions he sought to draw from the "rigid application of the democratic formula to the social problem."[1] The impression Bellamy left with his subsequent explanations of his purpose is one of unresolved tensions between the formal requirements of fantasy and the expository demands of his plan for industrial reform.

Yet Bellamy retained the form of a fantasy not merely, as he explained, in the hope of winning readers with a sugarcoated argument, but because it provided the framework for the psychological drama of conversion that was the means of entering utopia. As he first plotted it, the story was told in the third person, with Julian West treated objectively as one of the several characters. In the revised version Julian is made the narrator and confessor, and the tale he tells is of his conversion to the Religion of Solidarity, culminating in his miraculous relocation in utopia. At the end of the novel Julian's utopian surroundings coincide with his new inner state. His reward for the spiritual trials he has undergone is permanent transposition to heaven on earth. Julian earns his way into utopia in precisely the same way it was first created by the inhabitants who welcome him.

In the apparently real world of Boston in 1887 Julian West is the prisoner of his own selfishness. A wealthy and privileged Brahmin, he is wholly engrossed in his personal affairs, which center on his impending marriage to Edith Bartlett and a frustrating series of strikes in the building trades that has delayed the completion of his luxurious new home. He spends his last evening before entering his trance at the home of his fiancee, joining in the general denunciation of the working class. From the outset it is clear that the late-nineteenth-century social crisis has resulted from the compounded smugness of Julian West's class. He leaves for home filled with a loathing for the workers and convinced that the country is about to take a header into chaos.

Julian suffers from insomnia, a symptom of repressed guilt, and on reaching his house in the fashionable quarter of the city he retires to his sealed sleeping chamber in the cellar, which serves as a haven for his self-enclosed personality. Above are the noises of the city gripped by crisis, full of the disturbing cries of distress and suffering. "But to this subterranean room no murmur from the upper world ever penetrated. When I had entered it and closed the door, I was surrounded by the silence of the tomb."[2] In fact Julian is spiritually dead, shut up in a burial vault of his own invention from which he is miraculously resurrected through the offices of a hypnotist and the marvel of suspended animation.

Julian's escape from the prison of self is accomplished in a painful trauma that is the necessary condition for his moral rebirth. He awakes 113 years later to see his new freedom mirrored in the splendor and expanse of the city spread out before him. The exhilaration of the utopian prospect and the strange sense of ventilation and spaciousness immediately affect his mood. Never before has he been so alert and intellectually acute. In this new state of mental intoxication, he feels genuine sympathy for people for the first time and is able to "banish artificiality" in his relations with his host, Doctor Leete, and his family.

The initial excitement of his rescue from the prison of subjectivity, however, quickly gives way to a growing terror as Julian begins to understand what has happened to him. With his discovery that he is now totally alone in an alien world his agony begins. It reaches a climax in the terrifying recognition that his identity has dissolved into a weird psychic duality.

> There are no words for the mental torture I endured during this helpless, eyeless groping for myself in a boundless void. No other experience of the mind gives probably anything like the sense of absolute intellectual arrest from the loss of a mental fulcrum, a starting point of thought, which comes during such momentary obscuration of the sense of one's identity. I trust I may never know what it is again.[3]

Loneliness and psychic devastation drive Julian to the verge of insanity—"all had broken loose . . . all had dissolved . . . seething together in apparently irretrievable chaos." Suddenly he realizes that his identity is really double, that he has become two persons—a remembered self and this new objective and dispassionate superego standing outside and above experience.

The scene of Julian's discovery of the duality of self is both the thematic focal point of the book and the center of Bellamy's religious philosophy. In "The Religion of Solidarity" he had defined the individual consciousness as comprising a personal and an impersonal self, and had reduced the social question to the problem of achieving solidarity through the cultivation of impersonality. Julian West succeeds in making this leap of consciousness but at nearly prohibitive psychological cost. He is saved by the love of Doctor Leete's daughter Edith and soon recovers his emotional stability. Bellamy's handling of the love story here as elsewhere in his fiction is inept: Julian

West and Edith Leete are conventional Victorian lovers, unfolding their passion in episodes pasted together with sentiment. If the execution betrays Bellamy's taste for the mawkish, the conception of Julian's conversion from unconcern to commitment is nevertheless compelling. Under Edith's tutelage he learns to approximate the impersonal mood without anguish and to recall his old life with equanimity, "for all the world like a man who has permitted an injured limb to lie motionless under the impression that it is exquisitely sensitive and on trying to move it finds that it is paralyzed."[4] Julian has found that freedom from a guilty past promised by Dr. Heidenhoff and his memory-extirpation process.

Once he has recovered his mental balance, Julian is ready for his education in solidarity or "Nationalism," as it is called in utopia. Doctor Leete prepares his pupil with endless low-keyed lectures filled with parables and homilies. Julian accepts his indoctrination gratefully, listening to his tutor's accounts of the building of utopia, accompanying him on tours of the city, inspecting the social machinery and the simple religion of brotherhood that makes it work. He is an observer passively absorbing an education in utopian ethics, but still deeply troubled by his lack of standing in this new world. "I am outside the system," he complains to Edith, "and don't see how I can get in." Julian can only await the end of the initiatory rite. The main section of *Looking Backward* dramatizes the period of preparation or "justification" and formally concludes with a radio sermon on the real meaning of the miracle Julian has witnessed. Extending to society as a whole the same conversion process Julian has undergone, the disembodied voice marvels at the suddenness of the psychic transformation that has given humanity a new freedom. "We are merely stripped for the race; no more. We are like a child which has just learned to stand upright and walk . . . humanity has entered on a new phase of spiritual development, an evolution of the higher faculties . . . humanity has burst its chrysalis. The heavens are before it."[5]

Julian carries this millennial prophecy with him on his hallucinatory pilgrimage back into the nineteenth century. His nightmare journey through the Boston of 1887 is a final ordeal of faith, the test following his indoctrination and his first positive act in behalf of the Christian utopian order. In his dream he returns as a Saint John in the urban wilderness, wandering the crooked streets and registering

the suffering on the faces of the damned—the worried scowls of
State Street bankers, the hysterical grins on Washington Street merchants, and the gaping brutalized stares of the poor in the South End.
Gazing from one death's head to another, he suddenly stands convicted and feels the guilt that is necessary for his salvation.

> I was moved with contrition as with a strong agony, for I had
> been one of those who had endured that these things should
> be . . . Therefore now I found upon my garments the blood of
> this great multitude of strangled souls of my brothers. The
> voice of their blood cried out against me from the ground.
> Every stone of the reeking pavement, every brick of the pesti-
> lential rookeries, found tongue and called after me as I fled:
> What hast thou done with thy brother Abel?[6]

Julian stumbles to the Bartlett's home on Commonwealth Avenue,
rushes into the dining room where the guests are dining in compla-
cent splendor, and announces that he has just been to Golgotha and
seen humanity hanging on a cross. Unmoved, the publicans denounce him as a fanatic and a traitor as he tries to convince them of
their crime.

> Still I strove with them. Tears poured from my eyes. In my
> vehemence I became inarticulate. I panted, I sobbed, I
> groaned, and immediately afterward found myself sitting up-
> right in bed in my room in Doctor Leete's house, and the
> morning sun shining through the open window into my eyes.[7]

The magic of religious conversion—Bellamy's favorite device—has
once again saved the repentant sinner. Julian realizes in a final ecstatic moment that his return to a sinful past was only an illusion and
his deliverance to utopia the ultimate reality.

The story of Julian West's redemption is joined to the descriptive
account of utopia by a parallel. Utopia, explains Doctor Leete, has
come to the late twentieth century just as it did to Julian—through a
change of heart. In the historical recreation of capitalist America, Julian's initial situation is simply multiplied to account for the social

crisis. The American people, he is told, could find no way out of
their dilemma. Strikes, lockouts, Pinkertons, slums, and starvation
were the signs of a civilization on the verge of collapse. So long as
most Americans, like Julian, remained class-bound and blind to the
truth of brotherhood, all their inventions, technological expertise,
and increased production only made their problem the more insolu-
ble. Neither labor unions nor employers associations, radical reformers nor defenders of the status quo recognized the need for a
higher ethical creed for industrial society. It was left to the "National
Party," with its standard of solidarity, to discover the ultimate truths
on which utopia was built. In the beginning simply a handful of
lonely prophets who sensed the futility of class appeals, this saving
remnant of reformers spread the gospel of benevolent nationalism,
the ideal of a whole people bound together "not as an association of
men for certain merely political functions . . . but as a family, a vital
union, a common life, a mighty heaven-touching tree whose leaves
are its people, fed from its veins, and feeding it in turn."[8] In the utopian imagination of Doctor Leete, the tree of life to which Henry
George likened the free-standing individual has become the collective image of a redeemed society.

The National Party, Julian West learns, grew almost overnight
from a tiny band of evangelists into a potent counterrevolutionary
force that succeeded in eliminating both the destructive energies of
capitalist greed and proletarian envy and hatred. The triumph of solidarity made all things simple. Solutions to the great problem of social reorganization heretofore elusive now lay within easy grasp. The
ritual of mass conversion helped people to accept the inevitable. "In
fact, to speak by the book," Doctor Leete tells Julian, "it was not necessary for society to solve the riddle at all . . . The solution came as a
result or process of industrial evolution which could not have ter-
minated otherwise. All that society had to do was to recognize and
cooperate."[9]

Bellamy used this transparent explanation of his utopian spokesman to combine an economic determinism not altogether different
from Marx's with a traditional American doctrine of progress. Development from a state of cutthroat competition to one of peaceful
cooperation, he argued through Doctor Leete, is inevitable and thus
natural and simple. And the result of the evolutionary process is the
delayed arrival on the world stage of a new man—the "species-

being" prophesied by Marx, who has transcended egoism and the alienation of a double existence and restored to himself all human relationships. For Marx, however, it was the proletarian revolution and the smashing of the bourgeois state that would usher in a new age of authenticity. For Bellamy utopia originates in the moment of ethical revelation that makes social upheaval unnecessary.

The citizens of utopia are concerned to remove the impression that there is any mystery about the process of evolution. Yet the mystery remains hidden in the act of revelation itself without which further progress is impossible. Once the message of salvation is given to a people, then and only then can they cooperate intelligently with history. Julian West's nineteenth-century contemporaries failed to anticipate the great transformation and to hasten its coming because they insisted on a perverse individualism. The psychological metamorphosis brought by Nationalism, however, illuminates once and for all the true workings of a providential history. Converted by the missionary work of the early Nationalists, the American public readily accepts the meaning of solidarity, and violence is avoided. The nation quickly becomes one huge trust, absorbing all the business of its citizens who share equally in its growing abundance. The era of monopolies, Julian is told, finally produced the one great monopoly, and the American people came into their own. Significantly, it is the disembodied voice of a clergyman coming out of the radio that describes the miraculous changes wrought by the last and greatest of the prehistorical revolutions: "In the time of one generation men laid aside the social traditions and practices of barbarians, and assumed a social order worthy of rational human beings."[10] Utopia begins with mass conversion. Revelation reduces the complexities of social organization to a single self-evident proposition—the larger the business of supplying human wants, the simpler the principles to be applied to it. And what could be simpler than to recruit the entire body of Americans into one gigantic industrial army.

The comparison of the well-ordered state to an army of loyal and obedient soldiers has intrigued Western political thinkers ever since Plato. In the *Phaedo* Socrates suggests that the "happiest people" consigned to Hades and seeking to recapture their better natures in another life would find examples of the necessary discipline and integrity in the insect world and then would probably "pass into some other kind of social and disciplined creature like bees, wasps, and ants" in the process of becoming "decent citizens." Two thousand years later the Dominican friar Campanella, with the model of Calvinist Geneva before him, described the ideal state in *City of the Sun* as one in which "men and women march together collectively, and always in obedience to the voice of the king." In the utopian imagination armies signified order and rationality, self-sacrifice and public service; and the citizen soldier stood as a model of heroism and honor. The history of the military analogy in Western thought traces the evolution of an ethical concept in which spiritual values and civic virtue replace materialism and self-seeking. Both the well-directed army and the well-ordered state are seen as dependent finally on the same transcendent values, whether for the protection of the secular community or for marshaling the "armies of the Lord" to stand at Armageddon. By the end of the nineteenth century the twin concepts of religious devotion and secular *virtú* as analogues to the military had fused in the doctrine of the national state with its demands for loyalty and service and its promises of a spiritually rewarding strenuous life.

Bellamy was an heir to this classical tradition. In a short story, "An Echo of Antietam," which appeared in *Century Magazine* in July 1889, a year after the publication of *Looking Backward*, he turned to his memories of the Civil War for an example of the solidarity he saw as the key to the redeemed society. "An Echo of Antietam" describes the sacrificial death of Philip, a young lieutenant in the Union Army who reluctantly leaves home and fiancee to enlist in the cause of freedom. As his regiment marches through town on the way to the station, the packed bodies of the soldiers fill the street from curb to curb.

> As the blue river sweeps along, the rows of polished bayonets, rising and falling with the swinging tread of the men, are like interminable ranks of foam-crested waves rolling upon the shore. The imposing mass, with its rhythmic movement, gives the impression of a single organism. One forgets to look for the individuals in it, forgets that there are individuals. Even those who have brothers, sons, lovers there, for a moment forget them in the impression of a mighty whole. The mind is slow to realize that this great dragon, so terrible in its beauty, emitting light as it moves from a thousand burnished

scales, with flaming crest proudly waving in the van, is but an aggregation of men singly so feeble.

The meaning of his sacrifice becomes clear to the young officer as he stands on the battlefield the night before his death, musing on "the heroic instinct of humanity" and the knowledge that "man is greater than his seeming self." "What a pity it truly is," Bellamy interjects, "that the tonic air of the battlefields—the air that Philip breathed that night before Antietam—cannot be gathered up and preserved as a precious elixir to reinvigorate the atmosphere in times of peace when men grow faint and cowardly and quake at the thought of death." In his appeal for what William James was soon to call "the moral equivalent of war," Bellamy invoked the military life as the key to the stoic virtues needed to recast society in the image of Sparta.

There was a second meaning, however, that had been attached to the classical military metaphor with the word "industrial," an organizing concept stemming from the Enlightenment and the Industrial Revolution that by the end of the nineteenth century had developed into a science of society. This newer meaning inhered in the principle of hierarchy as a means of regulating the productive enterprises of mass industrial society. In this more recent sociological tradition, originating with Condorcet and extending to nineteenth-century theorists like Saint-Simon and Comte, the emphasis on the ethical behavior of the citizenry was overshadowed by a new concern with the instrumental values deemed essential to the management of the modern industrial and political process itself. In this view, which Bellamy also accepted, the acquiring of order, control, and rationality was as important for the smooth functioning of social systems as it was for determining the behavior of the people who built them.

The pivotal principle in the new sociological perspective was the idea of hierarchy. Hierarchy was seen as the answer to the problems of constructing stable social systems and political bureaucracies, either by assembling managerial pyramids out of subsystems from below or by imposing a division of authority from above. In either case hierarchy was beginning to be perceived by a new generation of industrial and social planners after 1880 as the means of solving the problem of complexity in mass society by divorcing it from the problem of scale. This was the insight on which Bellamy's plans for an industrial army working within "one great trust" ultimately rested. In planning his utopia on the principle of strict hierarchy, Bellamy was making contact, however unwittingly, with the dominant theme of modernization and with a younger generation of planners, managers, and experts who were drawing the designs for twentieth-century capitalism.

Bellamy's industrial army is a strictly military organization staffed by ascending ranks of officers and filled with workers of both sexes who serve as foot soldiers. Both men and women in utopia serve in the army between the ages of twenty-one and forty-five. The army's purpose is twofold: first, to attain the necessary high standards of production, distribution, and services demanded by an equalitarian society; second, and more important, to guarantee the spiritual well-being of all citizens by providing them with meaningful work that teaches "habits of obedience, subordination, and devotion to duty." Thus the industrial army fosters republican virtue and provides abundance at the same time. Utopia is oriented toward work and the assumed inclination of all citizens to perform it willingly. Although leisure has been secured to everyone through automation, technological innovation, and increased efficiency, its management in the last year of the twentieth century is not considered a problem. Bellamy's citizens employ their leisure to suit themselves, and the constant supervision of their working hours in no way disables them for private enjoyment of rest. It is nevertheless clear that utopians find the real meaning of their lives in working for the common good. The common good, in turn, is ensured by the principle of efficiency that only a military organization can provide. Comparing the productive system under capitalism to that of the new industrial order, Doctor Leete tells Julian West, is like comparing the military efficiency of a mob, or a horde of barbarians with a thousand petty chiefs . . . with that of a disciplined army under one general—such a fighting machine, for example, as the German army in the time of Von Moltke."[11]

The explanation for the efficiency of the industrial army lies in the exact correspondence of the labor market with consumer needs, the nearly perfect balance of jobs to be filled and people to fill them. In cases where a temporay imbalance exists, it is the task of the centralized administrative staff of the industrial army to correct it, not according to any theory or a priori rule but strictly on an ad hoc basis. "The administration, in taking burdens off one class of workers and adding them to other classes, simply follows the fluctuation of opinion among the workers themselves as indicated in the rate of volunteering." Thus what might be thought of as an impossibly complicated bureaucratic snarl turns out to be a model of simple efficiency.

If Bellamy prescribes a primitive kind of industrial management in the manipulation of incentives, it is nevertheless clear that there are limits to the procedure and that ultimately the success of industrial reorganization depends upon an appeal to a new citizenship and the espousal of the Religion of Solidarity. Competition and emulation still figure prominently in utopia as a motive for work, but they do not concern the "nobler" citizens who enjoy an inner freedom and who measure their duties according to their talents and set about performing them with a serene selflessness. Even in the last year of the twentieth century, however, not all utopian citizens have reached this level of public spirit, and for those who have not, emulation "of the keenest edge" is still needed. Until the Religion of Solidarity has won complete acceptance, the principal business of the general staff of the industrial army is fostering the ritual habit of work through incentives and sanctions which will be discarded once the preference for socially useful labor becomes automatic. "The sense of possession of inward freedom," Bellamy noted in his journal, "reconciles us to outward constraint and tyranny." In the final analysis, the successful workings of his industrial army depends on the universal applicability of this private conjecture.

To reconcile its citizens to outward constraint Bellamy's society, like all utopias, relies heavily on the power of education. A system of universal free education operates as efficiently as the industrial army on which it is modeled because the same expanded scale facilitates enormous social savings. Bellamy's specific proposals for the reform of education were neither radical nor advanced. At a time when increasing numbers of Americans were demanding a more "practical" education, his suggestions appeared to reinforce an excessive concern with utilitarian goals. His utopians take as their primary responsibility the training of their young in the industrial, managerial, and professional skills needed to maintain an economy of abundance. To this end they have established schools of technology, medicine, and the arts—much as Bellamy's own contemporaries had—open to any qualified citizen up to the age of thirty. The extended period of enrollment constitutes a moratorium that allows for full development of personality and prevents costly mistakes in selecting a vocation. Education, predictably, is linked to a national program of rigorous physical training on the theory, increasingly popular in Bellamy's day, that sound minds make sound bodies. Utopia nurtures a cult of the strenuous life that in turn perpetuates a race of "stalwart young men and fresh, vigorous maidens."

Despite his seemingly narrow functional program of education and the bureaucratic procedures for implementing it, Bellamy was deeply concerned with the problem of preserving individualism in an organic society. His educational system is tailored to the "whole man" and eliminates invidious distinctions between mental and physical labor. The best education possible is considered essential for the average utopian "merely to live, without reference to any kind of work he may do." As citizens cultivate wastelands into parks and gardens, so they seek to develop intelligence as a natural social environment. In the reckoning of utopians, individual benefit and social advantage are equated in a definition of functional freedom. True individuality, Bellamy insists, becomes possible only in a rational social order that systematically leads the individual to an acknowledgment of dependence on others. In this sense education and even indoctrination are not by-products but an integral function of the good society, a way of life in itself reaching beyond the province of technological maintenance to a realm of nonmaterial values. The process of education supports the industrial army but at the same time lifts the people to a higher plane of existence, where questions of power and political management can be forgotten.

By the year 2000 several of the limbs of nineteenth-century American government have already withered away. Nearly all the purposes for which a complex federal government once existed have been erased by the triumph of Nationalism. The United States needs no army or navy, no departments of state or treasury, no revenue service or permanent legislative body. The scope of government has been reduced to the twin spheres of executive and judicial, both equipped with extensive enforcement powers. Congress is convened annually but acts chiefly as a rubber stamp for executive orders. Since the fundamentals of society have long since been agreed upon, the people are easily maneuvered away from direct involvement with the decisionmaking process, which formerly required legislation. Doctor Leete describes the situation exactly when he tells Julian that now there is nothing left to make laws about. Government has ceased to be deliberative and is now purely managerial.

Bellamy gives to the industrial army complete political control over utopia. His original concept of a society organized *like* an army is replaced in the revised version by the notion of an industrial army *as the government*. As the double titles of each rank suggest, industrial and administrative functions have been combined. The chain of command runs from assistant foreman or lieutenant to foreman or captain to superintendent or colonel. Next in the ascending line of promotion come the major generals, who are also heads of the bureaus representing their trades, and above them the lieutenant generals or chiefs of the ten great departments comprising allied trades and guilds. These departmental commanders form an executive council from which the Commander-in-Chief or President of the United States is chosen.

Presidential power is buttressed by a highly organized police force and a pliant judiciary. Yet neither of these agencies would suffice to maintain order were it not for the unwavering patriotic spirit of the citizenry that ensures "habits of obedience, subordination and devotion to duty." "Now that industry of whatever sort is no longer self-service, but service to the nation, patriotism, passion for humanity, impel the worker as in your day they did the soldier."

The shock troops of the industrial army are composed of "common laborers" of an unclassified grade who spend the first three years of their service in "a sort of school" where they are rewarded for excellence and punished for "recklessness or indiscretion." From this process of indoctrination in Nationalism they emerge as apprentices whose performances are even more strictly judged by their status as first-, second-, or third-grade workers. All citizens come to be classified and known by rank. For those unfortunates "too deficient in mental or bodily strength to be fairly graded with the main body of workers" there is a special "invalid corps" whose insignia they wear. Superior performance is rewarded with prompt promotion; inferior, with instant demotion. The judgmental process is conducted in the full glare of publicity: "The results of each regrading, giving the standing of every man in his industry, are gazetted in the public prints, and those who have won promotion since the last re-grading receive the nation's thanks and are publicly invested with the badge of their new rank." Failure to meet the standards imposed by the officers or "other overt remissness on the part of men incapable of generous motives" is punished immediately. "A man able to do duty, and persistently refusing it, is sentenced to solitary confinement on bread and water till he consents." The industrial army is thus an army, not merely by virtue of its hierarchical organization, but also in the obedience and self-denial it enforces. The social product it manufactures is a machinelike man, in earlier times simply the basic unit in the disposition and maneuvering of military forces but now the creation of identical industrial, educational, and reformatory principles. In utopia, it would seem, militarism has been joined to custodial techniques and coercive projects to form a total organization of terrifying proportions. Bellamy's Religion of Solidarity mandates a disciplinary society that inspects, examines, classifies, chastises, and corrects until its citizens have remade themselves according to its dictates.

Bellamy was neither the first nor the most outspoken of his generation of social critics, many of them New Englanders, to prescribe martial virtues as a cure for the ills of late-nineteenth-century American society or to recommend the heroism of the Civil War as a means of renewing national vigor. Within a decade Theodore Roosevelt would invoke the strenuous life once practiced by veterans of Grant's and Sherman's campaigns in support of a "splendid little war." The historian Francis Parkman and the philosopher William James both drew heavily on their memories of the War for the Union, Parkman in calling for a new manliness to reinvigorate a patrician class, James as a directive for social reconstruction based on the martial values of "obedience" and "intrepidity." In the years after 1880 Francis Walker, Thomas Wentworth Higginson, and Oliver Wendell Holmes, Jr.—veterans of the Civil War and sons of New England with its heritage of Puritan nationalism—elaborated new concepts of the "useful citizen" and the "soldier's faith" derived from experiences on the battlefield.

Yet Bellamy envisioned more than the teaching of military standards of behavior to all citizens. It was the social efficiency supplied by his industrialized army that fascinated him, "the vast economy of labor as *mechanical force* resulting from the *perfect interworking* with the rest of every wheel and every hand." Military organization makes possible the material abundance on which utopia rests. By the year 2000 the total management of industry under a single control "so that all its processes interlock" has multiplied the social product a thousand-fold, a figure that proves beyond question the achievements of the redeemed society. Transposed into the calculus of social efficiency, selfishness means "dissipation of energy" while "combination" stands for the "economically expedient." As the industrializing of society proceeds and the subdivision of occupations increases, the mutual dependence of all citizens comes to be seen as ethical but above all practical. Utopia works because its people have accepted the principles of scientific management.

Bellamy's industrial army, in fact, prefigured most of the assumptions and techniques of twentieth-century industrial planners and proponents of scientific management. Seven years after the appearance of *Looking Backward*, Frederick Winslow Taylor, the father of scientific management, read his famous paper before the American Society of Mechanical Engineers. "A Piece-Rate System, Being a Step toward a Partial Solution to the Labor Problem" anticipated Taylor's experiments with worker efficiency at the Midvale Steel Company and the beginnings of the scientific management movement in the United States. Taylor defined the industrial problem, in terms remarkably similar to Bellamy's, as the need for an incentive system that would identify the interests of the worker with those of his employer by fixing "scientifically" what he called "an honest day's work" performed by a "first-class man." Taylor sought to reduce industrial production to a science by making the worker into a machine whose efficiency could be measured with a stop-watch that timed his performance of a series of discrete "elementary operations." In many ways Taylor himself represented Bellamy's ideal type, the industrial planner who insists on discipline, obedience, proper motivation, and hard work. "If a man won't do right, *make* him," Taylor was heard to say more than once, and his view of the factory as a moral gymnasium where workers experienced "the real monotonous grind which trains character" duplicated Bellamy's concern with character formation. Both the industrial army and the scientifically managed factory encouraged what Taylor called "actual hard work" performed "under careful and constant supervision." Taylor's "military system" of factory management, as he explained it, reproduced the hierarchical organization of Bellamy's industrial army with successive levels and ranks rising from the shopfloor to the all-seeing "planning department" at the top. The adoption of his system, Taylor promised, would facilitate the "mental revolution" that Bellamy predicted: "both sides take their eyes off the division of the surplus until this surplus becomes so large that it is unnecessary to quarrel over how it shall be divided."[12] For both Bellamy and the Taylorites the efficient production of abundance would in itself guarantee the identification of class and group interests essential to the smooth functioning of industrial society. While Taylor and the scientific management movement sought to shore up capitalism through the manipulation of material incentives and Bellamy hoped to replace them with altruism, in both cases it is the principle of military hierarchy that leads "proper citizens" to the threshold of utopia.

For all of Bellamy's solemnizing of the soldier's life, his dream of a totalitarian society was vitiated by an even deeper commitment to the patriarchal principle. For Theodore Roosevelt and his Progressive disciples of moral athleticism, military virtue was a spiritual weapon for use in combat against a flabby materialism. Even the patrician-minded Mugwumps, the ancestors of the Progressives, dreamed of an eventual return to power of a temporarily dispossessed natural aristocracy. Bellamy, on the contrary, was motivated, not by a drive for power, but by the desire to renounce it, a motive obscured even to himself by his fascination with the industrial army. The result of this renunciation of power in the ideal society is not the accession of the people to political control but their abdication in favor of a rule of the elders who have been purified by age and experience of corrupting ambition. "In devouring I seem to conquer," he once wrote in explaining his own antipathy to power, "but the thing devoured transforms me. Nothing is ever really conquered."[13] This personal maxim is the fundamental rule which the citizens of utopia must learn, and not until they have accepted it are they entrusted with responsibility. The power structure in utopia is designed to remove the decisionmaking process from the grasp of the young and headstrong and vest it in a community of patriarchs supposedly immune to the contamination of selfishness and pride. The President of the United States is not eligible for office until he has reached the age of fifty. The heads of departments who form his cabinet and from whom he is chosen do not arrive at positions of authority until they are forty and then undergo a mandatory retirement before becoming eligible for the presidential office. Within the army itself promotion depends on the attainment of selflessness and impartiality, which age and experience presumably bring. The moratorium granted the young is intended as a last holiday for the self, a purge of the personal aspects of character, and a necessary preparation for assuming the duties of impersonality and solidarity.

The capstone of Bellamy's patriarchal structure is an electoral system disfranchising the active workers in the industrial army whose limited loyalties and narrow perspectives might prove dangerous to its discipline. The generals of the guilds as well as other higher officers are elected by "honorary members" of the army, those veterans who have been discharged. Organized into an industrial G.A.R., they supervise the performance of the active workers with a benign detachment and choose their leaders for them. The "old fellows" like Doctor Leete are so zealous of the national interest that younger aspirants to leadership must be thoroughly competent in order to pass inspection. Indeed, the good doctor offers the opinion that no previous society has ever developed an electorate "so ideally adapted to their office, as regards absolute impartiality, knowledge of the special qualifications and record of the candidates, solicitude for the best result, and complete absence of self-interest."[14] The ideal polity dictated by the Religion of Solidarity allows for a plebescite of the patriarchs without the unwarranted interference of the citizenry. This division between thought and action is made complete by a special provision for professional classes who are organized in separate self-regulating guilds managed by retired "regents." Since the professionals, by virtue of their training, can be expected to behave judiciously, they are given the vote but are not themselves eligible for office. Thus the intent as well as the effect of Bellamy's political scheme is to secure the resignation of the very class of intellectuals to which he belonged. In order to assure the tranquility essential to inner freedom and creativity, his imaginary colleagues renounce the uses of the wisdom they are engaged in pursuing. It comes as a surprise only to Julian and Doctor Leete to discover that the origin of this utopian system was government by alumni—"a board of fairly sensible men"—with which nineteenth-century colleges and universities were conducted.[15]

In the patriarchal workings of Bellamy's utopia there are lingering traces of the preindustrial values and styles with which he had grown up, some of them reminiscent of a Puritan society run by church elders, others suggestive of the extended families once headed by stern New England fathers. The widespread appeal of his utopian society, as Bellamy would learn, was strongest, not among urbanites living and working in a world of industrial flux, but among farmers and small-town Americans clinging to remembered ways and threatened values. Patriarchalism in utopia gives national life a deliberative and reflective cast, as the managerial elders weigh and sift evidence, examine alternatives, calculate means, and ponder ends. Patriarchy rationalizes and regularizes the pace of industrial life with its guidelines and provides a steadying influence that helps to preserve the simple producer ethic that formerly ruled agrarian America. Nostalgia insinuates itself into utopia in the person of Doctor Leete, the village sage whose wisdom stems from the dispassionate moralism that comes with age. Doctor Leete speaks for the commonsense code of morality that originally flourished in the rocky soil of preindustrial New England but had now been transplanted to the prairies of the trans-Mississippi West and Texas High Plains where readers of Looking Backward abounded.

The rule of the patriarchs which tempers the theoretical harshness of Bellamy's utopia also accentuates the curious affectlessness of his people. His picture of the coming order, with its disconcerting lack of textures and chiaroscuro, reveals the unintentional narrowing of a social vision to the private world of the recluse. In at least one of its several perspectives, his utopia is the dream of an anchorite conserving the principle of the sacred by minimizing direct contact with the outside world. For many years now Bellamy had filled his notebooks with imagined escapes from the anguish of emotional attachment to other people. "These intense emotions, whether pain or pleasure," he once wrote in one such mood, "we do not want them."

We look for a placid race that shall not alternate between honey and vinegar, but live on mild ambrosia ever. It will be part of the plan of a future and wiser society to discourage the overgrowth of the affections, recognizing as indisputable that

more misery results from the excess of affectional development than from deficiency.[16]

Another entry in the journals proposes a reorganization of society
"to extinguish sorrow" by outlawing parental control. In still another
conjecture he predicted the coming of a new form of love without
tragic overtones—"cheerful comradeship only of people who suit
but do not adore each other." In such a world there would be no excessive dependence or "forced constant association" and therefore
no bereavement or despair. "Men and women would live less intimately with one another and more involved with the universal."[17]

The impersonal life of solidarity foreshadowed in the notebooks
and Bellamy's early fiction emerges in full clarity in Doctor Leete's
closed family circle. The doctor is the author's archetype of the truly
civilized man, yet he remains an oddly disquieting figure, politic,
genteel to a fault, but also remote and dispassionate. He is the supremely rational man, so dominated by the ideal of impersonality as
nearly to lose his identity. Each day Julian finds him unchanged, an
affable but detached observer of the world about him which he scru-
tinizes with clinical precision. Seldom does the tone of his conversation rise above the level of moral earnestness. Family life at the
Leetes is correspondingly disengaged. Father, mother, and daughter
move through each other's lives without collision and almost without incident. There are no quarrels or moments of communion because none of their lives impinge directly on the sensibilities of
others. The household is harmonious because passion has been banished. Though "strangely daunted" at first, Julian soon grows accustomed to his new affectless state and accepts Edith's love knowing it
for an elevated form of pity. The book ends with his eager return to
the state of detachment that has supplanted family life.

Nor is social life outside the Leete household measurably different. Utopia is a society of renewable abundance in which production
is totally divorced from consumption, work from leisure, result from
process, involvement with materials from enjoyment of "things."
Despite his gestures in the direction of the unified sensibility, Bellamy really regarded work as a lower albeit necessary form of activity, an obligation to society which, on being fulfilled, is rewarded
with the gift of unencumbered leisure. Doctor Leete states the utopian position exactly when he tells Julian that work is "a necessary

duty to be discharged before we can fully devote ourselves to the higher exercise of our faculties, the intellectual enjoyment and pursuits which alone mean life." Leisure in utopia provides the means of recapturing an original freedom that has been surrendered to society, the recovery of an elemental "birthright" that has necessarily been diminished. With the worker's discharge from the industrial army comes "the period when we shall first really attain our majority and become enfranchised from discipline and control, with the fee of our lives vested in ourselves."[18] Presumably the reclamation of the true self is accomplished by the sense of social interdependence that maturity brings, yet if Doctor Leete is typical, the utopian citizen remains remarkably self-contained. At a time when sociologists and social workers were just beginning to experiment with new concepts of the social creation of personality, Bellamy remained a prisoner of an older Emersonian psychology which his Religion of Solidarity had supposedly corrected.

Boston in the year 2000 is a city beautiful with "miles of broad streets, shaded by trees and lined with fine buildings . . . not in continuous blocks but set in larger or smaller enclosures." It is also a walking city of neighborhoods comprising districts or "wards" set along the periphery of the central public space that defines the city center, each component with its landscaped parks and squares on which front houses and cottages complete with gardens, footpaths, and rusticity. The core of the city—its civic focus—is filled with "buildings of a colossal size and architectural grandeur" in which the public business of utopia is carried on.[19] Yet the split between production and consumption is given a peculiar spatial emphasis in the novel. The magnificent public dining hall in the suburban ward stands at the furthest remove from the mammoth department store, which in turn is separated by landscaped parks and boulevards from the automated factory. Thus the new Boston is the figment of a pastoral and to a certain extent a preindustrial imagination. Nowhere are workers to be found or even glimpses of the work process. Goods and services are provided anonymously: manufacturing and processing are carried on in huge centralized complexes out of public sight, and shopping has become a simple and unexciting business of ordering samples in giant showrooms. Services are supplied by faceless functionaries performing with the disinterested air of soldiers on duty. The individual, Julian is told, never regards himself as a servant of others. "It is always the nation which he is serving."[20] Neither the waiter in the public dining room nor the clerk in the government store confronts in any direct way the people he serves. Yet in spite of the impersonality of Bellamy's system, it is remarkable how few of the nineteenth-century middle-class amenities have been sacrificed. Domestic help is still available, the family table remains an alternative to public dining, and domesticity is still carried on in private homes and apartments.

The setting for domestic life in utopia, however, is sharply austere, and the Leete household echoes to an aesthetic emptiness which is quickly explained by the host. A constantly renewable supply of consumer goods has done away with the old habits of conspicuous consumption. No one saves, stores, or collects because no one feels the need of possessions. Utopia has induced a vast psychological metamorphosis, and people no longer try to define themselves through ownership. Citizens discard their personal belongings without a pang and invest instead in architecture, sculpture, landscape gardens, and other public symbols. Although Boston is a garden city carved into neighborhoods furnished with clubhouses and dining halls, there is little sign of actual social interchange. The people of utopia apparently carry over into public life the reserve and self-sufficiency that characterize their domestic arrangements. Bellamy's description of the public dining hall, its marble staircases, fountains, and statuary suggesting a set for a Hollywood musical, is peopled, not with individuals or groups, but with a "stream" of diners flooding up the staircase and through spacious corridors into appointed compartments.

Utopian culture is also depersonalized. Its chief medium is the radio. Instead of attending church, concerts, and other public functions, the utopians simply tune in their choice with a flip of the switch. Included in the daily cultural fare is a supply of music which Edith Leete likens to a banquet. She declines to play or sing in proper Victorian fashion for Julian with the explanation that "it was these difficulties in the way of commanding really good music which made you endure so much playing and singing in your homes by people who had only the rudiments of the art."[21] Amateurism has fallen before professionalism, the spontaneous has given way to the arranged and the programmed. Utopian culture is offered as a commodity to be used but not absorbed, its content badly eroded by the demands of social solidarity. Thus Julian West, marveling at the plot of a late-twentieth-century novel, is struck "not so much by what was in the book as what was left out—all contrasts between rich and poor, strong and weak, coarseness and refinement, contentment and misery."[22] Utopia, he concludes, has succeeded admirably in avoiding the "sordid anxieties" of life. With irrepressible sensations of relief we welcome the temporary exchange of this state of emotional paralysis for Julian's nightmare world of conflict.

If the dystopian features of Bellamy's ideal society, like his technological predictions, have become commonplace less than a century later, they are also detachable from the central argument of the book, its moral indictment of unregulated capitalism. In arraigning the American capitalist system as un-Christian Bellamy took a reformer's stance at the head of a social movement just beginning to take political form in Populism. It was chiefly in the trans-Mississippi West and South, among hard-pressed farmers, small-town merchants, failed entrepreneurs, and bitter spokesmen for a lost America, that his message hit home. Although he could not foresee the lengths to which his indictment would take him in helping to organize a new political party, the chapters in *Looking Backward* recounting the collapse of a rotten capitalist structure and its replacement by Nationalism disclose a private utopian vision shading into a theory of radical reform. In time this theory of substitution would force him to repair the foundations of his utopia and adjust them to the shifting industrial terrain of the 1890s. Then he would find many of his original assumptions—not the least of them his scheme for a coercive industrial army—wholly inadequate as a basis for effective reform. In the analytical sections of *Looking Backward* where he pinpointed the failings of American capitalism, however, Bellamy formulated a powerful moral case against a pecuniary civilization which he never modified. It was this indictment that stirred the imaginations of his own generation and continues to intrigue a postindustrial age.

Capitalism, he argued, promotes four different kinds of waste: the waste of competition and duplication; the waste of misdirected undertakings; the waste of periodic gluts and panics; and, finally, the tragic waste of idle labor. In the final sum these add up to financial chaos, misuse of human energies, and widespread suffering. Bellamy's solution is the increased efficiency that only the nationalizing of production and distribution can provide. The main instrumentality in his plan for nationalizing the economy is a science of statistics employed by a technological elite. Statistics supply his utopian managers with a simple administrative tool unavailable or misapplied under capitalism, for measuring resources, estimating needs, and allocating work. As capitalism evolves into Nationalism through progressive phases of consolidation and concentration, it creates a gigantic industrial machine "so logical in its principles and direct and simple in its workings" that it all but runs itself. This happy outcome has already been realized by the year 2000. The industrial machine fed like a computer with the correct statistics automatically produces at full capacity and provides the abundance of material goods which is the precondition for utopia. With the disappearance of capitalism goes its rationale—the profit motive of an economy of scarcity. Nationalization brings a "large surplus" of staples and consumer goods with which to correct minor fluctuations in supply and demand. In the few areas of the nationalized economy where scarcity cannot be wholly eliminated, it is equalized by price-fixing according to a primitive labor theory of value. Such is the simple mechanism at the core of Bellamy's plan for transcending the inevitable conflicts of capitalism.

Bellamy sketched the outlines of a moral case against capitalist waste that soon acquired an empirical depth and solidity in the hands of younger, more sophisticated critics like Thorstein Veblen. For all his delight in mordant irony and the irreverent phrase, Veblen restated in secular terms all the main charges raised by Bellamy and went on to propose an "inclusive system" of "comprehensive interdependence" to be built by a "General Staff" of Resource Engineers and Production Economists. In calling for a new "soviet of technicians" to replace the rule of "one-eyed captains of finance," Veblen was proposing a model of technocratic antipolitics that looked for all the world like a copy of the original industrial army. The American future, in Veblen's view as in Bellamy's, belonged to the industrial engineers and experts educated in the producerist values of "tangible performance" and determined to eliminate lag, leak, and friction in the workings of the national industrial machine. Veblen, with his curious mixture of nineteenth-century faith in the true producers and a discordant modern relativism, carried Bellamy's indictment of capitalist waste to a twentieth-century generation of engineers and planners numbering such diverse figures as George Soule, Wesley C. Mitchell, Howard Scott, and Rexford Tugwell. For minds such as these the coming of the Great Depression in the 1930s merely underscored the truth of Bellamy's original indictment of capitalist waste.

Ultimately, however, it was the waste of *human* resources under capitalism that most alarmed Bellamy, the inability of profit-minded entrepreneurs to employ the natural aptitudes of people in any rational and humane way. In a "free-enterprise" America the vast majority of men and women, though nominally free, were in fact victims of forces they were taught to believe beyond their control. For millions of exploited workers, capitalism amounted to slavery. At this point in his indictment Bellamy shifted his attack from capitalism to materialism and the twin devils of competition and commercialism. Finally discovering his real enemy, he abandoned the uncongenial field of economics for the familiar realm of ethics, from which he launched his major attack on "the land of Ishmael." He denounced commercialism as the most vicious strain of antisocial behavior, "absolutely inconsistent with mutual benevolence and disinterestedness." Its motto was the huckster's pitch: "Never mind the rest. They are frauds . . . Buy of me."[23] In place of the false standards of a predatory commercialism, *Looking Backward* offered the simple communist precept: "The amount of the effort alone is pertinent to the question of desert." That is, all men who do their best are entitled to the same reward. Only when his essentially Christian communism was universally accepted, Bellamy insisted, would the final spiritualization of mankind be consummated.

In *Looking Backward*, then, it is the vision rather than the theory that finally concerns Bellamy, who was less an engineer than a prophet. For him the problem of means logically followed the question of ends: "Until we have a clear idea of what we want and are sure we want it," he would write in defense of his book, "it would be a waste of time to discuss how we are to get it." *Looking Backward* contemplates an irreversible change in the human condition made possible by a massive shift of psychic energies to a spiritual pole. From a late-twentieth-century perspective, Bellamy's obsession with order may appear strange and more than a little disturbing, but his prediction of the emergence of a set of what are today called post-materialist values seems less so. Bellamy entertained the possibility of a spiritualized society using a widely shared physical well-being to construct a Sustainable State in which remote goals and ultimate ends have replaced short-term gains; population has been stabilized; economic growth curtailed and realistic limits to consumption set; and a return to the "natural" life, however mystically defined, finally achieved. In this sense the new publics in late-twentieth-century Western societies composed of a young, affluent middle class—small, privileged, but increasingly vocal in opposition to growtho-mania—are the direct descendants of the vanguard whom Bellamy hoped would manage the transition to a postmaterialist age of equi-librium. This is what he meant when he described the coming change in the United States as "an indistinct revolution . . . more rad-ical than if it had been political." His revolution creates an affluent and abundant society without waste, but more important, it brings an intensified psychic awareness similar to the "nöosphere" or "nöosystem" of Teilhard de Chardin and Julian Huxley. Just as life once passed from inorganic to organic forms, Bellamy believed, it would now pass from separate to integrated consciousness. In his Christian version of evolution, the end of the process is "lost in light" in the moment when the human race returns to God's whole-ness and "the divine secret hidden in the germ shall be perfectly un-folded."[24] Utopia, after all, was the palace in the clouds that he had first imagined it. For the moment, however, it appeared quite dif-ferently to him and to those readers of *Looking Backward* who thought they saw in his picture of the perfect society a house for practical men.

11

THE LOGIC OF REFORM

THE PUBLICATION of *Looking Backward* in 1888 propelled Bellamy from the literary wings into the middle of the American political stage to play an unaccustomed role as reform activist. Sales of his book, 60,-000 the first year, soared over 100,000 the next, as editions appeared in England, France, and Germany. The Bellamy household lay buried in a blizzard of mail: offers to translate the book into Danish, Portuguese, Magyar; an urgent request for a lecture to the Peers of Kosmos Compact in Kansas City; an invitation to help found a Nationalist colony on 900,000 "fertile acres" along the Magdalene River in Venezuela; demands for articles and short stories from the *Atlantic, Scribner's,* the *North American Review,* and the *Ladies Home Journal.* And poetic effusions galore: "He is here! He is here! Great moulder of men/ His sinewy hand holds Truth's cloud-piercing pen." From the West Coast came sudden and unaccountable demands for copies, and in the Farm Belt a fifty-cent paperback edition quickly became a best-seller.

Overnight Bellamy discovered he was famous. The *Nation* warned readers that they would return from the year 2000 "haunted by visions of a golden age." Haunted or otherwise disenchanted, millions of Americans—social workers, farmers, businessmen, bankers, and housewives—variously confronted his argument for a wholesale rearrangement of their capitalist society. Clergymen of all denominations took Julian West's conversion to universal brotherhood as their Sunday texts. Reformers and social critics debated the merits of the industrial army, and practitioners of the strenuous life hailed the advent of a new era of physical and moral hardihood. Theosophists, along with retired army officers, thought they discerned in the skyline of a future Boston the outlines of permanent social harmony. If the young John Dewey read the novel as a plea for an untried scheme of social engineering, the compilers of the Sweet Home Family Soap Album considered themselves warranted in including Bellamy, together with Louisa May Alcott and James Whitcomb Riley, as celebrants of traditional American values.

The flood of attention and adulation washed over the household, for the moment leaving Bellamy's unhurried routine intact. Following his father's death in 1886, he had moved his family back into the parsonage, where his mother, brittle now as a piece of Dresden china, still ruled with her iron will. People had to walk a crack with Maria Bellamy, neighbors said, for she was still determined "to go at things the hardest way" and disposed to censure those who failed to follow her example. Finally reconciled to her son's loss of the true faith, she described him as the most Christlike man she had ever known, and reserved for Emma the designation of faithful helpmeet. Although Edward was devoted to his mother and by all accounts "very tender" to Emma, he remained intellectually and emotionally a man apart, who continued to puzzle family and friends with an alternating reserve and biting wit. Most of the day he spent closeted in his upstairs study, pacing the floor with hands clasped behind him, stepping into the hallway now and then to announce to no one in particular, "I've got a thought!" and scuttling back to his desk, slamming the door behind him. "There would be days," one of Emma's friends remembered, "when he would be working up in his rooms when his wife would give anything for him to talk. Then the sunlight would seem to break through and he would be delightful and she would be so happy." From a distance of forty years Emma recalled that for much of the time her husband "lived on an island by himself." Bellamy's island was his study, "absolute chaos," by Emma's account, but off-limits to housecleaners and children alike. There he would sit with feet propped on his desk, scribbling illegibly on large yellow sheets with the stub of a pencil, tearing off each sheet and tossing it on the pile on the floor. "For days on end," Paul remembered, "my father buried himself in his study, frequently declining to come out for meals."

In between sustained bursts of writing, Bellamy gave himself over with wry amiability to his wife and children, taking them on long rambles beside the Chicopee River and up into the nearby hills or for a short row in his battered rowboat. On rainy days he would play toy soldiers by the hour with Paul, using clothespins for regiments as he plotted the campaigns of famous generals, all the while discoursing on the imbecility of war. He liked best of all Sunday afternoons with their unvarying routines—ambling along the riverbank with Emma and the children, "absolutely detached," Marion recalled, even as he reached down to take her hand and tuck it in his pocket. Then home for an hour of Bible-reading, a cold supper, and hymn-singing afterwards, when he would sit tipped back in his easy chair listening to his favorites, "Lead Kindly Light" and "I'm a Pilgrim, I'm a Stranger," and then a last solitary stroll before going to bed. "Friends did their best to lure him into conversation as they met him," according to his son, "but I do not recollect that any of these efforts were very successful. He was uniformly courteous but also extremely resourceful in slipping away." To his children his odd mixture of drollery and detachment were endlessly intriguing, as when he would sit in his armchair with Marion in his lap instructing her in the best method for yanking the hairs out of his moustache. He left all disciplinary problems to Emma, but the children knew that misbehavior or thoughtlessness invariably provoked a violent outburst followed by affectionate apologies and lengthy lectures.[1]

With the rest of the world Bellamy remained on distant terms, although the newspaper fraternity in Boston learned that after an hour standing at the Tremont House bar he could be jovial and even hilarious. Still, he disliked being away from home and preferred the porch veranda, where he would straddle the hammock conversing quietly until the sight of a visitor coming down the street sent him scurrying inside. The one social duty he performed unfailingly was attending funerals, even of those whose living clutches he had always managed to escape. His habits were as frugal, his lifestyle as ascetic, as those he assigned to his utopians. He once told Emma that when she felt obliged to spend more than two dollars, "don't speak to me about it," and he cautioned her against accepting presents from friends and relatives. "Say you have something like it or don't need it or any other civil lie that comes handy."[2] Their wedding anniversary brought Emma only a note from her husband confessing that he was "nothing great on anniversaries" and considered it a triumph if he could "make a fair average for the other 364 days in the year." "Sentimentality aside as becomes settled married people," he added in removing the barb, "I married you because I could not get on without you and have never found a time since when I could get on without you any better."[3]

The publication of *Looking Backward* quickened the pace and soon reversed the direction of a literary life. The first edition was published in January 1888 by Ticknor and Company, and Bellamy took an immediate interest in its success. "If you will kindly sell 50,000 copies of *Looking Backward* for me," he wrote to Benjamin Ticknor, "I will engage to give the voters of 1892 a platform worth voting for, and furnish the voters."[4] Later that year Houghton, Mifflin bought out Ticknor and made new plates from the corrected manuscript Bellamy had prepared for a German translation. In revising the text he made numerous changes in spelling, capitalization, punctuation, and paragraphing, and expanded his description of the industrial army. To his new publisher he sent instructions for securing royalties on the German edition and urged a stepped-up advertising campaign. "There is no doubt about the considerable sales ready for us in New York, Cincinnati, Chicago and St. Louis," he explained in predicting an enormous market at home and abroad. "Can't you get a part of this instead of leaving it wholly to the pirates?"[5] After scrutinizing the new contract, he insisted on a higher royalty rate, charged the advance on royalties on the German edition to the publisher, and reserved dramatization rights to himself. It had been nearly twenty years since he had reasoned like a lawyer, but now the work came easily.

His fantasy world was receding rapidly. He admitted to Horace Scudder, the editor of the *Atlantic Monthly*, that he was tempted to return to the "psychologic studies and speculations" of his youth. "But since my eyes have been opened to the evils and faults of our social state and I have begun to cherish a clear hope of better things, I simply 'can't get my consent' to write or think of anything else." As

a pure literary type he feared he was a "goner" and past praying for.
"There is one life which I would like to lead, and another which I
must lead. If I had only been twins."[6]

Yet two years of constant writing and revising had exhausted
him. He worried privately a good deal now about his deteriorating
health and began timing the intervals between fits of coughing while
experimenting with a variety of home remedies. A trip to New York
to appear at an authors' Round Table brought on a severe stomach
upset and belated apologies to his "Dear Little Wife" for "being so
cross in getting off." I had a very time last evening at the Round
Table," he admitted, "and was made a lion of quite sufficiently to
satisfy more vanity than I have . . . I am all right as to stomach now."[7]
But his rapidly failing health forced him to give up plans for a lecture
tour, never very appealing, and to spend much of his time politely
declining invitations. For the moment it seemed clear that if Nationalism was to be more than a pipe dream, initiative would have to
come from his readers.

The original proposal for a Nationalist organization was advanced by two Boston newspapermen, Sylvester Baxter of the *Globe*
and Cyrus Field Willard, labor editor of the *Herald*. The two journalists wrote to Bellamy in the summer of 1888 asking his permission to
form a society. "Go ahead by all means, if you can find anybody to
associate with," he replied in giving his approval to any plan for approaching the "cultured and cultivated classes."[8] Before Baxter and
Willard could set their scheme in motion, another group of Bostonians, fully qualified as to culture and social standing, formed a Bellamy Club in the fall of 1888. The Boston founders of the Nationalist
movement made a curious assortment of visionaries and reactionaries. The nucleus of this cluster of litterateurs and political maver-
icks was a group of retired army officers whose reading of *Looking
Backward* had convinced them that there was no grander or more patriotic cause to enlist in than Bellamy's industrial army. General A. F.
Devereux had fought for the Union in the War of the Rebellion;
Captain Charles E. Bowers had won distinction at Gettysburg; Colonel Thomas Wentworth Higginson and Captain Edward S. Huntington still carried old campaign wounds. For these aging warriors, Bellamy's ideas recalled distant years of service and kindled hopes for
new days of discipline and duty for unruly American workers.

Militarism retreated before mysticism in the minds of the Theosophist converts to Nationalism, John Storer Cobb, Henry Austin, and the poet John Ransome Bridge, all of whom discovered in Bellamy's ideas the means of escaping Avitchi, the earthly abode of soulless men, for Karma, the state of total harmony achieved only through renunciation of self. In progressive reincarnations, Theosophy held, mankind would proceed through ever-higher planes of spirituality until inner and outer harmony were one. Theosophists and militarists agreed, however, in rejecting politics, parties, and the organizational aspirations of the laboring classes. Social order, in their view, could only be imposed from above.

For Edward Everett Hale and William Dean Howells, fellow travelers both, the Nationalist idea appeared as an offshoot of the old Lincoln Republicanism transplanted in a social gospel garden. William Dwight Porter Bliss and Vida Scudder, less enamored of military efficiency than of spiritual uplift, saw Nationalism as a particularly hardy strain of Christian Socialism. A somewhat more chastened enthusiasm dictated the sympathetic cooperation, if not the full allegiance, of the Irish Catholic novelist-reformer John Boyle O'Reilley and his friend and editor of the Boston *Pilot* James Jeffrey Roche. The final component of Boston Nationalism was an amalgam of militant feminism and cultural radicalism provided by Mary Livermore, Abby Morton Diaz, Agnes Chevaillier, and the sculptress Anne Whitney. In December 1888, with Bellamy in attendance, Boston's fourth estate was joined to Theosophism, Christian Socialism, business conservatism, and military ardor in the first Nationalist Club in the United States. After a spirited debate, the majority of the twenty-five members agreed to shun politics and concentrate their talents in a Nationalist Educational Association which would publish a monthly magazine, the *Nationalist*.

At first Bellamy applauded the decision to avoid politics. "Nationalism is not a party but a breaking of light. Parties are incidents; light steals upon the world slowly and after a season men find paths leading to higher ground," he explained to readers of the *Nationalist*. A deep distrust of the professional politician still prompted him to overrate the powers and the philanthropic intentions of the gentlemen. To Colonel Higginson, who also feared lest Nationalists engage in unseemly political agitation, Bellamy confided his hopes for an organizational counterrevolution imposed by a sensible and resolute middle class. One or two converts of the Colonel's stripe, he an-

nounced, would be worth more to the cause of Nationalism than a
host of ordinary recruits, since only the intellectual class could lift
reform "up out of the plane of the beer saloons and out of the hands
of blasphemous demagogues and get it before the sober and morally
minded masses of the American people." The untutored millions
needed natural leaders like Perez Hamlin whom they could trust.

> I am sure that you will agree with me that in view of the im-
> pending industrial revolution and the necessity that the
> American people should be properly instructed as to its na-
> ture and possible outcome, a profound responsibility is upon
> the men who have the public ear and confidence. No doubt
> somehow or other the Revolution will get itself carried out,
> but it will make a vast difference as to the ease or peril of the
> change whether or not it is led and guided by the natural lead-
> ers of the community, or left to the demagogues. It was the
> peculiar felicity of our countrymen in their revolt of 1776 that
> their natural leaders, the men of education and position, led
> it. I hope and confidently trust that the same felicity may at-
> tend them in the coming industrial and social revolution and
> assure an equally prosperous course and issue for this trans-
> formation. As for our politicians they of course will only fol-
> low not lead public opinion. It belongs to the literary classes
> to create, arouse and direct that opinion. It is their opportu-
> nity.[9]

Bellamy read a sample of the doctrines produced by his literary
class when the first issue of the *Nationalist* appeared in May 1889. In
a poem entitled "The Heirs of Time" Higginson described "the patient armies of the poor" as tomorrow's "myriad monarchs" who
"without a trumpet's call" would secure their title-deeds to life and
liberty. Under the banner of "Freedom's Last War-Cry," General
Devereux invoked patriotism and self-sacrifice to meet the charge of
rapacious robber barons. Sylvester Baxter assured readers that the
Nationalists merely followed the path of a spiraling evolutionary
process to a new plane of total freedom, where the individual in
transacting with the state would only be dealing with himself in a
higher aspect. Henry Austin depicted Nationalist pioneers, armed
with thoughts rather than swords, patiently leading the masses

through the wilderness of selfishness toward a new frontier of social harmony. The Theosophist John Ransome Bridge employed a tenderer image: "It is when a civilization is in its flower and before the petals loosen that there seems to come a crisis, a moment of opportunity, which, if taken advantage of, would ultimately lead to a new order of social life—the full fruitage after the blossom." Bellamy's reminder that fifty years could conceivably see the complete accomplishment of his Nationalist program hit the only discordant note in this medley of Nationalist lyrics.

Behind his prediction lay the old fatalism, Bellamy's belief in the inevitable socialization of American capitalism. Economic consolidation, he was still convinced, held the key to the One Big Trust that was Nationalism. "The combinations, trusts and syndicates of which the people at present complain demonstrate the practicability of our basic principle of association. We merely seek to push the principle a little further and have all industries operated in the interests of all the nation."[10] If the rational state staffed by selfless bureaucrats and dispensing social good impersonally was even now a near thing, then the petty intrigues of the bosses and socialist demagogues could only postpone its arrival.

It was not long, however, before Bellamy began to chafe under the restraints imposed by his confident prediction. Impatiently he wrote to Higginson, "It will not do too long to put the people off with generalities when they begin to ask what to do."[11] The socialists, he now realized as Henry George had earlier, were more than ready to fill the political vacuum left by vague promises of future harmony. Bellamy had not studied Karl Marx or examined German socialism, and he only snorted derisively when the handful of socialists in the Boston Nationalist Club tried to engage him in serious debate. He also dismissed the moderate American socialism of Laurence Gronlund, whose *The Cooperative Commonwealth* he pronounced "most impractical." His chief objection to Gronlund's socialism was its grant of power to the workingman: "the germ of this coming order Mr. Gronlund professes to see in the trades unions, while the nationalists see it in the nation." To allow the working class to monopolize wealth and power was no more just than to permit the capitalists to do so. But if his Nationalist movement were to survive the incursions of the socialists, he would have to come to grips with the problem of means.

Bellamy's restiveness was aggravated by the formation of a Second Nationalist Club in Boston, composed of men who shared his growing impatience. The leaders of this second club were young businessmen-politicians like Henry Legate and aggressive editors like Mason Green, a former staffer on Samuel Bowles's Springfield *Republican*. While members of the parent club concentrated almost exclusively on the theoretical aspects of Nationalist doctrine, the new dissidents tackled questions of municipal ownership, five-dollar coal, and cheap public transportation. Members of the second club lobbied on Beacon Hill for an enabling act to permit Massachusetts cities and towns to build and operate their own gas and electric plants, and then hired an agent to do battle with the gas companies. Their bill failed to survive the 1889–1890 session of the General Assembly, but a year later it passed narrowly despite the efforts of the utility companies, those "enormous, slippery reptiles with tails of limitless length," as the *Nationalist* called them. In their somnolent quarters overlooking the Common, the founders listened to discourses on the solidarity of the race and the enthusiasm of humanity, while their counterparts across town debated the question of practical first steps—nationalizing the railroads and municipalizing utilities. As Nationalist clubs sprang up all over the country—over 150 of them by 1892—they too were divided between amateur social theorists content with armchair discussions and political activists bent on fashioning a program of nationalization to bring before the voters.

Yet even this distinction between passivity and political activism was difficult to make with any precision. As the last decade of the century opened, Nationalism appeared to offer a haven for malcontents and déclassé intellectuals of every stripe—prohibitionists, disgruntled small businessmen, frustrated entrepreneurs, die-hard communitarians, feminists, antimonopoly veterans, all with their own complaints against the new corporate capitalism. The same issue of the *Nationalist* could carry an article defining Nationalism as true conservatism in complete accordance with the principles of the "English school" of economists and another calling for the immediate destruction of the bourgeois state. A very few Nationalists believed that labor leaders ought to be invited to help plan the coming industrial order, but a great many more envisioned a back-to-the-people crusade to purify politics and recover community. In the welter of conflicting nostrums and panaceas the big question remained unanswered: was Nationalism a new brand of genuine reform or merely a display of middle-class reaction?

An astute reader of Bellamy's novel and the newspaper it had generated might have concluded that while Nationalism was fearlessly anticommercial and anticapitalist, it was also antipolitical and antidemocratic. Bellamy and his followers rejected a commercialized and predatory America based on conspicuous consumption, and they denounced capitalism as a system of organized selfishness that had polarized society into a "dangerous class" of proletarians and a rapacious plutocracy. Yet the Nationalists, this reader might also have observed, rejected politics for the promises of antipolitics—the dream of transcending power and strife in a managed collectivity. Finally and perhaps most disturbing of all, the Nationalist movement seemed openly undemocratic, proposing to substitute for rough-and-tumble partisanship the plebesciterian formulas of the managers. In short, the attentive reader of *Looking Backward* and the *Nationalist* might well have concluded that the chief appeal of both was the promise of escape they made to an American middle class caught in a massive economic revolution it was powerless to prevent and unable to join. This discriminating critic of Nationalism, Bellamy suddenly realized, was himself. He had begun to question the assumptions on which his utopia rested.

In undertaking a reassessment of his doctrine, Bellamy benefitted from two hostile critics who pointed to the shortcomings of his original military model. The first attack on *Looking Backward* was a critical barrage directed at the concept of the industrial army by General Francis A. Walker in a lengthy article in the *Atlantic Monthly* for February 1890. The crusty Walker, who made a hobby of puncturing the utopian pretensions of amateurs like George and Bellamy, had enjoyed a long and distinguished public service, first as a brevet-brigadier general in the Union Army, and subsequently as the head of the Bureau of Statistics and superintendent of the Ninth Census, professor of political economy in Yale's Sheffield School, and, at that time, president of Massachusetts Institute of Technology. The bulk of Walker's acerbic review consisted of supposedly "practical" objections to radical reform, so popular with Social Darwinists. In the process of leveling the concept of the industrial army, however, Walker paused to call attention to the author's "false notion" that military discipline applied wholesale to the American economy would work miracles. The utopian emphasis on martial order, Walker suggested, was the work of a late-adolescent imagination. "In sooth, Mr. Bellamy did not turn to the military system of organization because he was a socialist. He became a socialist because he had been moon-struck with a fancy for military organization and discipline itself. So that, in a sense, militarism is, with him, an end rather than a means."

The second and more devastating attack on his industrial army came from William Morris, poet, arts-and-crafts designer, utopian socialist-turned-Marxist, who undertook to demolish Bellamy's utopia in an article in his magazine, the *Commonwealth*. Bellamy's system, Morris complained, could best be described as State Communism "worked by the very extreme of national centralization" and devoid of humanizing qualities and even a hint of aesthetic joy. Bellamy had betrayed himself as both "unhistoric" and "unartistic." "The only ideal of life which such a man can see is that of the industrious professional middle-class men of today purified from their crime of complicity with the monopolist class, and become independent instead of being, as they now are, parasitical." Bellamy, like so many modern men, had become obsessed by the image of the military machine, "that of a huge standing army, tightly drilled, compelled by some mysterious fate to unceasing anxiety for the production of wares to satisfy every caprice, however wasteful and absurd, that may cast up amongst them."[12] Here, Morris concluded, was the root of a dreadful fatalism inhering in the illusion of the inevitable triumph of Moloch.

Bellamy realized with sudden chagrin that Walker and Morris were at least half right: the original idea of an industrial army had provided him the means for escape from social inaction. The metaphor had given him an imaginative tool with which to cut an exit from self to society. But now it had served its purpose. Society, he had come to see, could not and should not be constructed according to a military design, and in his reply to Walker he shifted his analogy to civil government. He readily confessed an admiration for the soldier's life, but his actual model of bureaucratic reorganization, he now realized, was "the several thousand clerks in the governmental departments in Washington" whose circumstances were "very similar to those which will obtain in the coming industrial army." In other words, the skeleton force of his army was already operating as the Civil Service. Not militarism but organicism, the view of society "in its totality only," formed the real basis of Nationalism. No doubt, some organization approximating his industrial army would serve as the final agent of social solidarity, but no one, he now agreed, could predict its precise form or mode of operation. What *could* be forecast with reasonable accuracy, however, were the definite steps to be taken in gradually extending public control over production and distribution: federal ownership of the telegraph, telephone, railroads, and mines; and municipal assumption of lighting, heat, water, and transit facilities. Specific reforms such as these would immediately create a need for a million workers who would form the nucleus of an industrial force "organized on a thoroughly humane basis of steady employment, reasonable hours, pensions for sickness, accident, and age, with liability to discharge only for fault or incompetence after a fair hearing."

Here was a quite different version of the coming social order, one that with a new emphasis on social insurance and fair labor standards signaled the beginning of Bellamy's retreat from militarism. "It is the post office, not the militia service, the civil service and not the military service in which the prototype of nationalism is to be found," he announced with an air of finality.[13] As he witnessed the repressive uses to which American military forces were being put at Homestead, Pullman, and elsewhere across the country, he grew less and less interested in his original concept until he virtually abandoned it.

In place of his initial hypothesis, Bellamy offered a new version of American history that paralled Henry George's and Henry Demarest Lloyd's accounts, a pointed and partisan reading of the national record. In editorials and articles for the *Nationalist* and then the *New Nation*, as well as for the *North American Review*, *The Forum*, and *The Dawn*, he explained Nationalism as a purely American program rooted in the political equalitarianism of the American Revolution. Until recently the nation had offered a fair field for opportunity and talents of all kinds, and despite the inevitable inequalities of condition, there had been great "popular contentment." Yet in less than a generation "an economic revolution unprecedented in scope and rapidity" had overturned the old republic. "Our economic system now presents the aspect of a centralized government, or group of governments, administered by great capitalists and combinations of capitalists who monopolize alike the direction and the profits of the industries of the people." The full brunt of this corporate attack on the free labor system had been borne by the producing classes, and "all that was humane in the relation of employer and employed has disappeared, and mutual suspicion and hatred and an attitude of organized hostility have taken their place." The plutocrats have made themselves the masters of America. The power of this new master class rests on naked force. The militia is used to overawe strikers and break up unions, and the United States has become thoroughly Europeanized with caste distinctions "abhorrent to our fathers."

Only a handful of Americans before the Civil War—notably the communitarians with their patent-office models of the good society—had guessed where this unprecedented consolidation of economic power was leading, Bellamy pointed out. The attempts of the communitarians at Brook Farm, Oneida, and in phalansteries and utopias, while premature and frequently ill-conceived, made them the true precursors of the Nationalists. Their idea of reform by nucleation—the multiplication of renovated communities until the entire nation had been redeemed—still held promise for a new generation of reformers. Not till after Appomattox, however, had the costs of headlong concentration been made clear to distressed farmers and impoverished workingmen. The 1870s had seen the appearance of a new generation of reformers, the Greenbackers and the Knights of Labor, but in the meantime the corporate bosses and industrial barons had tightened their grip on the national economy, consolidating small business in giant networks, rigging the market, watering stocks, diverting profits, driving out the independents, and exploiting the workers. The new capitalists, Bellamy announced in concluding his capsule history of the American republic, were revolutionaries bent on overthrowing it. They would surely succeed unless a counterforce were interposed.[14]

Enter the Nationalists on the American historical stage as the only legitimate heirs of the equalitarian tradition of the American Revolution. For the Nationalists the problem was not dreaming up new political and economic forms, as Bellamy once had thought, but of conserving and strengthening the original republican contract. Viewed in this light, the Nationalists, and not the Robber Barons, were the conservatives. "We are the true conservative party," Bellamy told his audience at the first anniversary meeting of the Boston Nationalists in 1890, "because we are devoted to the maintenance of republican institutions against the revolution now being effected by the money power. We propose no revolution, but that the people shall resist a revolution. We oppose those who are overthrowing the republic. Let no mistake be made here. We are not revolutionists, but counterrevolutionists."[15] Nationalists, it was now clear, could achieve their essentially defensive aims only by educating American voters in the basic principles of their creed and teaching them to elect leaders committed to it. Nationalists, in other words, would have to carry their banner into the political arena.

By the time Bellamy reached this conclusion he found himself in agreement with millions of American farmers. "Every person interested in progress and every student of the social problems which now claim a share of public attention, should read this book," the editor of the *Farmers' Alliance* in Lincoln, Nebraska, told subscribers in offering a bonus paperback edition of *Looking Backward*. And read it the farmers did, finding in it confirmation of their fears for the republic and their hopes for its salvation. In the staple-crop farmers, hard pressed by adversity, Bellamy discovered the missionaries of Nationalism he had called for in his book.

For the task of framing political platforms and recruiting voters, the *Nationalist*, with its anemic circulation, was clearly inadequate. It had required donations of $2,000 to keep the journal alive in 1890, and prospects for its survival were dim. Besides, with his new sense of urgency, Bellamy was eager to launch a newspaper of his own. The *Nationalist*, he explained to an English correspondent, had served well enough as a clearinghouse for unpolitical amateurs, but as a practical reform magazine it "had never amounted to much." For at least a year he had been considering publishing a paper of his own, preferably in New York, in which to foster "discussion of the industrial and social situation from the moral and economic point of view" indicated by his reform program. The need for a new forum was critical.

It was not in New York but in Boston—upstairs at No. 15 Winter Street—that the *New Nation*, as he called his new enterprise, first appeared. For two years, in spite of rapidly failing health and his doctor's orders, Bellamy poured all his energies and slender resources into his paper and the Populist cause. Commuting each week from

Chicopee Falls to his editorial office, he drove himself hard, not quite sure, he admitted, "what part I am to play in the great deliverance" but "daily more convinced that it is at hand." In Boston he took a room at the Tremont House where, surrounded by piles of manu- script and dog-eared setting copy, he composed the editorials that traced the progress of Nationalism and its new ally Populism. "The *New Nation* welcomes the peoples' party into the field of national politics," he declared in announcing the results of the Cincinnati Convention at which the Populists began to organize in earnest in May 1891.

> The advent of the peoples' party means not only overthrow of one or both of the existing parties, but the political death of a whole crop of demagogues, whose trade it has been to keep the people apart . . . The platform was about big enough to get born on, and that was enough for the emergency. It can be enlarged and improved later on.[16]

It was up to the Nationalists now to provide the new reform party with "cordial sympathy" and "the most vigorous sort of missionary effort," and to that work he now devoted himself.

The grueling schedule transformed him. Each Wednesday he left the unhurried routine of Chicopee Falls and entered the chaotic but vital world of Boston journalism where, according to his young managing editor, Mason Green, he acquired a new lease on life. The offices of the *New Nation* provided a haven for a whole roster of urban types, a cosmopolitan collection of oddities. "All classes and conditions of men were represented," Green recalled, "men and women who were without property and those who never had any, the lawyer and the litigants, minister and laymen . . . those who could speak correct English and those who could not, the union labor leader, the scheming politicians, the honest folk who only ask a chance to make a living." It was as though Julian West had emerged from his vault to find, not the ordered quiet of a future hu- manity, but the frenzied activities of real reformers. All kinds of po- litical business was transacted at No. 15 Winter Street—rallies scheduled, petitions drafted, speakers dispatched, and campaigns planned. And at the center of the political storm stood Bellamy, "a safe councillor in matters of detail" and "quite a mixer for a congenitally retiring man."[17] The reclusive man of letters, his new friends boasted, had become the public man of action. He dashed off magazine articles and composed reams of editorial matter; he even forced himself to attend conferences and make speeches. His Boston colleagues found him uniformly good-natured and easygoing, always primed for a brisk exchange of views and the opportunity of indulging a well-honed sense of irony. In the evenings after a full day's work he often made the rounds of the city's newspaper offices chatting with night editors. In addition to the theater and an occasional concert, he could be found at ringside at the prize fights in the North End in company with his new friend John Boyle O'Reilley. He refused to tolerate any discussion of his failing health and turned aside expressions of concern with a quip: "They say it's my lungs, but I've two or three diseases ahead of that!" Until his health collapsed, Bellamy continued to drive himself relentlessly in support of the Populist cause. Soon he made contact with Henry Demarest Lloyd, like himself a recent recruit to Populism who had discovered in the third party an instrument for rebuilding American society.

Henry Demarest Lloyd initially found the same fault with *Looking Backward* that he had earlier recognized in *Progress and Poverty*. Both Bellamy and George, he complained, were "Dr. Curealls," each prescribing a miraculous remedy for the ills of capitalist society. George stubbornly insisted on the Single Tax as the key to social salvation and refused even to listen to objections. Now came Bellamy to propose "a climbing of ladders of dreams to Utopia." Neither of these visionaries, Lloyd complained, understood the nature of the national crisis or the role of the American workingman in solving it. If George appeared altogether too rigid and old-fashioned, Bellamy's obsession with solidarity seemed downright dangerous. To hand over to any community, no matter how well-intentioned, all rights of speech, opinion, and privacy was to substitute a new despotism for the "real solution" of the question. And that question was quite simply "whether the people shall take hold of railroads, telegraphs, mines, etc."[18] Genuine reform, he was more than ever convinced, began with practical steps.

Despite his objections to the Single Tax and the industrial army,

Lloyd shared George's and Bellamy's faith in the work ethic and the producer values it upheld. He distinguished between what he called mere "labour organization" (significantly retaining the English spelling) like Samuel Gompers's American Federation of Labor and the larger spiritual "labour movement." "The movement itself," he explained to a skeptical audience of Chicago workers in 1889, "is something of a new religion; the organized part of labour is simply a segment of this new movement—a beginning, limited but destined to expand."[19] There was an urgent need for a new moral politics, he agreed with Bellamy, but only the vast brotherhood of American workers, as distinct from particular organizations, could break the "lockstitch of self-interest" and "free mankind from the superstitions and sins of the market." As mediator-counselor it fell to him to teach the workingmen of America that they stood as brothers in everything. As he plunged into a dizzying round of educational politics, while continuing to revise the manuscript of *Wealth Against Commonwealth*, after 1891 Lloyd came to see the American labor movement as a religious crusade powered by faith in an evolutionary socialism but one whose holy writ was the Declaration of Independence and whose saints were Jefferson, Lincoln, and Wendell Phillips.

Lloyd set this pantheon of heroes inside an American history that was a replica of Henry George's and Edward Bellamy's chronicles. The impending war between labor and capital, he agreed, was only the second phase of a permanent American Revolution which was gradually extending the principle of political independence into the industrial workplace. Homestead and Pullman were the new Lexington and Concord. Just as George III had used the power of Parliament to overturn colonial liberties and the Slave Power in the South sought to destroy American freedoms, so now a Money Power was attempting yet a third revolution "of the devil's kind." But American workers had learned the lessons of history: "The good king, the chivalrous baron, the Christian slaveholder, the merciful master, the philanthropic monopolist—the few we have had—have been charming; but they cost too much."[20]

Lloyd agreed with Bellamy on the importance of the work ethic in American society, but he disagreed on its ancestral home. By 1891 Bellamy was already looking to the farmers of the nation as the trustees of Nationalism. Lloyd turned to the industrial workers in cities like Chicago. As he followed the wrangling of the Farmers Alliance over the advisability of forming a third party, Lloyd concluded that of all the social groups in the country confronted with the need to organize, the farmers were "the last to see the truth."[21] The future of American reform, he was convinced, lay with the nation's working class.

In 1891 Lloyd made a return visit to England to renew old friendships and check on the progress of social reform in the British Isles. In London he interviewed Engels and held long discussions with Alfred Henry Wallace and Henry Hyndman to learn the state of the land question and British Marxism. From Tom Mann and Keir Hardie he heard reports on the new Independent Labour party and the prospects of labor politics. But his greatest discovery was the activities of the recently organized Fabian Society, whose members were responsible for converting him to the principles of moderate socialism.

The Fabian Society, one of whose charter members was Lloyd's friend William Clarke, had been formed by disillusioned middle-class liberals who rejected Marx's theory of revolution and in its place developed an evolutionary socialism aimed at transforming the capitalist order through successful experiments in government ownership and management. The key points in the Fabian program were proposals for municipalizing public utilities and transit systems throughout England, and the vigorous recruitment of socialist intellectuals to serve as experts and managers of the new order. Each town and city, as it succeeded in establishing public ownership of its services, the Fabians held, would provide a nucleus of reform energy that would eventually collectivize the nation from the bottom up. The second feature of the Fabian strategy was an alliance with English workingmen in which labor served as a junior partner to a new class of managers who recruited, trained, and directed them. Fabianism, as Lloyd noted appreciatively, built socialism from below but on instructions from above.

Fabian socialism was precisely the alternative Lloyd had been searching for. The Fabians were eminently respectable and, what was more, influential reformers who made up "a large proportion of the officials in the Government service." Working together with hard-bitten labor organizers, they had succeeded in making London "the fermentingest place in the world."[22] He returned to Chicago convinced that such a combination of Fabian moderation and labor enthusiasm held the answer to the American social question. His sharp distrust of American socialists made the decision all the easier. "I have been revolted, here, by the hard tone of the German socialists," he wrote to his English friends on his return to Chicago, "who are about all we have, and by the practical falsity of the doctrine they constantly reiterate, that this crisis must be met by a class struggle, and that the working people alone are to be trusted." Had he been an Englishman, he most certainly would have joined the Fabians in preaching the inevitability of gradualism. As an American who distrusted all appeals to class, however, he had no choice: he joined the Peoples' party.[23]

The Populist crusade worked the same transformation on Lloyd as it had on Bellamy. On his return from England he plunged into reform politics in Chicago and soon became a widely known figure in local reform circles, more intense than the suburban liberal who had stood on the periphery of the city's political contests. Now instead of bringing the reform world to his doorstep, he went out to meet it in working-class neighborhoods and union headquarters. He made new friends, like Knights of Labor editor Bert Stewart and socialist organizer Tommy Morgan, who gave him a new zeal. He was much in demand as a lecturer to middle-class liberals in the Ethical Culture Society and the Century Club, but just as often could be found speaking to working-class audiences—to Chicago's transit workers picnicking at Cheltanham Beach; to the striking Steam Fitters union; to the annual convention of the AF of L.

His platform manner was low-keyed but effective, as he stood straight as a ramrod, speaking in low measured cadences virtually without gesture, his voice thin but strong. He was nearly fifty now and looked it. The marks of his twenty-year struggle for self-mastery could be seen in a habitual melancholy expression, the heavy-lidded eyes with deepening lines at the corners, the silvered hair worn long, and his walrus moustache dropping at the ends. Along with a new ardor his friends noted the old reserve and professional politeness, the taper-fingered hand with the surprisingly firm handshake, the casually elegant dress, and the general air of an aristocrat. "He is as delicate, as fragile, as beautiful as a Sevres vase," one of them remarked, adding that his gentleness was deceptive since his extreme "sensitiveness" and sympathy for the exploited could make him almost cruel in avenging their wrongs. "The social conscience is over-developed in him."

Lloyd's social conscience expressed itself with Old Testament bluntness as he denounced men "cunning, bold, prosperous, spreading nets to catch the weak and unwary in the courts of law" and railed against the Money Power, "this small body of men, shrewd, intelligent, lustful of power, continually crying Give, Give, Give." He saved his best sallies for genteel audiences and delighted in rubbing liberal consciences raw. "Our ideal of life inspires us to pile asset on asset and dividend on dividend. But we will cut the workingman in mid-winter off entirely from his income and black-list him too." His sharpest barbs were reserved for those clergymen and professors who prided themselves on their impartiality but who "always manage to come down on the side of privilege." The militance of working-class organizers was holiness itself compared to the posturings of "Christian chaplains" who blessed Gatling guns as the Lord's instruments for converting the heathen and strikers.

Lloyd's speeches were not all sound and fury. To working-class audiences he asked specific questions and gave concrete answers—"municipalize the street-car lines, nationalize the coal mines, the forests, the iron mines, stop the competition of children and the starving in the labour market." Where should the people begin? "The city hall represents the institution ready made for any purpose of the common good for which the common people choose to use it." Was it really necessary for workers to organize? "It is not in nature for employers to deny themselves the advantage." How, then, was labor to win bargaining power for itself? "All workingmen ought to form themselves into unions."[24]

A key word in Lloyd's vocabulary now was "community." The history of the medieval guilds still raised his occasional curiosity, but he tended to dismiss such excursions into the Middle Ages as an exercise in nostalgia. "If we can look backward to those days with longing," he told an audience of workingmen, "it is because we have lost the virtue to look forward."[25] Community, he now realized, was being constantly created. It had an instrumental reality only. His own set of personal communities extended eastward to Europe and westward to the Antipodes. Their center was Chicago and a congenial circle of intellectuals, journalists, and labor organizers, settlement house workers, liberal lawyers, and social gospelists. For this local community Lloyd performed an endless series of favors and services—helping Florence Kelley secure a position as state factory inspector; advising Boston labor organizer Mary Kenney on the best approach to Chicago's garment workers; helping Paul Schilling, Illinois secretary of labor statistics compile his reports; sharing the Populist platform with Senator William A. Peffer of Kansas; playing host to the English visitor William T. Stead, and promoting his book, *If Christ Came to Chicago.*

From this core of local connections ran lines of interest and influence, one leading downstate to Springfield, where beleaguered Governor John P. Altgeld and his reform Democrats battled the federal government and Cleveland conservatism. A second road branched out to the new universities—Wisconsin, Michigan, Pennsylvania, Johns Hopkins—where liberal professors like Richard T. Ely, John R. Commons, and Henry C. Adams taught new courses in new academic disciplines. A third led to Boston and New York where the reform magazines were beginning to flourish, and a fourth pointed across the Atlantic to the Fabian Society in London. Lloyd's immense correspondence traveled these various routes, letters seeking and supplying information on labor unions, communitarian experiments, city settlements in London, parks in Paris, worker housing in Vienna, democracy in Switzerland, and arbitration in New Zealand. Slowly the figure of the retiring gentleman-reformer began to give way to the activist and reform entrepreneur.

By 1893 Lloyd had discovered two models of community that offered an alternative to class and could thus be recommended to American workers as examples of natural cooperation. The first of these was Hull House, in which he participated enthusiastically from the beginning. Jane Addams's settlement on Halsted Street reached deep into the surrounding neighborhood with its variety of people and activities, and the atmosphere there was that of an informal social laboratory. Lloyd greatly admired Jane Addams and her assistant Ellen Gates Starr, both of whom, in turn, respected his judgment and frequently called on him for help. He also enjoyed the constant flurry at Hull House, with its knots of residents coming and going on one civic project or another. Jane Addams's enterprise, he realized, was no mere pastime for do-gooders but the center of a genuine educational experiment, the staging area for pickets protesting slum sweatshops, labor delegates bound for conventions, and reformers of all kinds bent on rallying the voters against the bosses.

Lloyd entertained the Hull House residents at the Wayside and served as chairman of several of its committees. Hull House workers collected signatures for him on the petition for the pardon of the Haymarket anarchists. He encouraged Addams to publish *Hull House Maps and Papers*, the pioneer American neighborhood survey, and accepted as payment a copy inscribed by the author. It was at Hull House that he first met and befriended Florence Kelley and urged her to earn a law degree so that she might enforce factory legislation more effectively. Kelley took him along on her tours of the slums to inspect the city's sweatshops and called on him to speak at her frequent public meetings. And it was at Hull House, too, that he helped plan the sessions for the World's Labor Congress at the Columbian Exposition in 1893.

The World's Labor Congress at the Chicago World's Fair provided Lloyd with his second model of the open intellectual community. Part of organizer Charles Bonney's Congress of World Thinkers, the meetings at the Art Institute in August 1893 furnished an unintentional ironic comment on the state of the American economy. Earlier that year financial panic had toppled the country into still another depression—the third in as many decades—and by the time the Labor Congress met, business in Chicago as elsewhere in the nation had closed its doors and unemployment was on the rise. Lloyd took time out from the planning sessions for the Congress to investigate the effects of the depression and suggest ways of providing public aid. By summer Chicago was in need of all the free advice from delegates to the Labor Congress it could get.

As secretary of the program committee Lloyd arranged a series of sessions notable for the wide diversity of approach to the problems of industrial recovery and social reform. The rostrum at the Art Institute was made available to Single Taxers, Fabians, Christian Socialists, and communitarians of all stripes, who debated proposals on slum clearance and social insurance, public ownership and binding arbitration, child labor laws and direct democracy. In planning the meetings Lloyd included the Nationalists and invited Bellamy himself to speak to the Congress. Lloyd had been favorably impressed with Bellamy's editorial management of the *New Nation* and the New

Englander's abandonment of the military model in favor of Populism. He looked forward to meeting him and discussing with him Populist prospects in the by-elections of 1894. When Bellamy politely declined the invitation, Lloyd, who was unaware of his new acquaintance's serious illness, wrote to Samuel Bowles, editor of the Springfield *Republican*, asking whether the refusal was a result of an "unwillingness to incur the expense." "I attach so much importance to his presence," Lloyd added, "that I should be glad to pay the 'shot' myself," if that could be arranged "without letting him know the means by which the money was procured."[26] His gesture failed, however, and Bellamy did not attend the Congress, although a contingent of his Nationalists did.

To Lloyd the Labor Congress, but more particularly the White City itself, seemed dazzling proof of the wonders of cooperative planning. The success of architect Daniel H. Burnham, chief coordinator of the building of the Exposition, in gathering the country's major architects together and getting them to agree on a unified plan of landscaping, a common cornice line, and a basic module of dimension suggested unlimited possibilities in planning the physical design of the good community in which groups like the Labor Congress could debate and refine proposals for the advancement of labor. Out of Lloyd's involvement in the Columbian Exposition came a fable of utopia to match the accounts of Edward Bellamy and Henry George, a vivid sketch of St. Paul's "No Mean City" and its rebirth in a new Chicago.

Lloyd's essay "No Mean City," which he first gave as a talk at the Winnetka Town Meeting in 1894, quickly became a favorite with audiences. "It was the World's Fair did it, and this is how it came about."[27] So begins a City Beautiful fantasy with a communitarian message, a fable retailing the simple methods and marvellous achievements of social gospel reform that had its origins in the Chicago World's Fair. When the Exposition closed and the shadows of the depression lengthened across the Pleasance, the White City stood on its abandoned site unused and unrecognized as the key to urban rebuilding. With the return of prosperity and the sudden conversion of the citizens of Chicago (the relation between these two events is never clear), they "spontaneously" decide to renovate and reopen it. Soon the White City becomes a model and a magnet attracting the inhabitants of Old Chicago, who leave its festering

streets and filthy tenements for a utopia that serves as a laboratory
for experimenting with urban reforms from all over the world. The
White City continues to function as "a congress of ideas, reforms,
religions," where social schemes from Glasgow, Paris, Berlin,
Vienna, and Budapest mingle in a "happy harmony" of classless
competition, and artists and artisans volunteer their services, architects join them "in the spirit of a religious revival," and labor unions
supply the manpower for massive renovation. Both a cause and a result of these experiments is the alteration of habits and manners that
makes commercialism and exploitation at first "hopelessly unfashionable" and then "absolutely vulgar." Finally the meaning of
their task becomes clear: "While they were thus engaged the spiritual secret of the power that was in them became revealed to the
people."

Chicago's main problem—unemployment—is easily solved by
relocating the poor in self-sustaining cooperatives on the fringes of
the city and the edges of the country. "Large tracts of land were
bought, and the unemployed were enrolled in colonies, and set to
work to make a living for themselves." Manual labor, cooking, and
sewing schools prove once and for all the producerist truth that
"every man with modern means can produce many more times than
he can consume," a correction of Malthusian error which Lloyd, like
Bellamy and George, was at pains to make. He also emphasized the
potential for social order in an educational system developed as an
alternative to politics, and of a work ethic which substitutes for partisan involvement. In No Mean City, politics gives way to vocational
training. Citizens study life itself: children dig, hammer, stitch, cook,
and experiment, and in so doing learn to read, write, and reason, not
from books but by "an almost unconscious absorption" in the work
process itself. Lloyd suffers from no Ruskinian concern with handi-
crafts. All the cotton cloth needed in his model city is made easily in
a few hours by the high school senior class as part of their study of
fibers and machinery.

Inevitably No Mean City out-competes the farming countryside
beyond its limits just as it did the manufacturing districts of Old
Chicago. Farmers find it needless to raise fruits and vegetables for a
mass market when all the lanes and by-ways of the new city are
hung with apples and berries, and each suburban satellite has its
quota of truck gardens. There is mechanized, large-scale agriculture

to produce an abundance of staples, but the labor force, using rapid transit to reverse the older traffic patterns, returns each night to garden homes after a day's work in the fields. Here Lloyd crosses the boundary into George's and Bellamy's utopia, where city and country fuse. "It had always been idle to ask the ambitious, the social, the strong among the younger people of the farm districts not to take themselves to the city. It had been equally useless to ask the enervated or the unequipped of the city, to brave the solitude of the farm. But here was a solution which was central to both these difficulties. Here in the same place was country for the city people, and city for the country people." Paradise regained! In 1971, on the one hundredth anniversary of the Great Chicago Fire, the old city is razed again and ploughed up to make a vast people's park.

As Lloyd turned to the task of building a producerist coalition inside Populism, he continued to think in terms of the renewal of communities on a manageable human scale that fostered direct participation of the citizenry and experiments in direct democracy. These, he hoped, would show "the crude and false simplicity of the theory that the evolution of political institutions is entirely in the direction of increasing complexity of representative forms." Gone now was his fascination with the state as the ultimate mystical reality. From now on it was the local and the participatory that drew his attention—involvement with neighbors and fellow workers in a community which remained classless because it stayed small.

In his discovery of socialism as a form of municipal renewal, Lloyd joined Bellamy and George in exploring a "third way" to social reform in the United States, a pathway running between bureaucratic state socialism on one side and corporate capitalism on the other. All three men were reaching back to an antebellum tradition of communitarianism and shopfloor cooperation to prove that capitalist society could transform itself through the replication of the model community—"a mighty nucleus," Bellamy called it—in a process that was gradual but at the same time inevitable.

To begin with municipalizing services as a civic undertaking was, first of all, to avoid class distinctions and draw all citizens into a common endeavor. George stressed the automatic improvements bound to follow the passing of the Single Tax. Bellamy emphasized the social efficiencies achieved through scaled development and a process of nucleation. For his part, Lloyd concentrated on the revivifying ceremonies of the new civic life, in particular the town meeting, where the "people" gathered to deliberate in a form of discourse used in English producer cooperatives or the Swiss cantons or even his own hometown of Winnetka. In the immediate locality—cantonal village or suburban satellite—direct participation and the vital sense of community it engendered could create a genuine American socialism, unprogrammatic, nondoctrinaire, class-free. Such a socialism, Lloyd was now sure, must begin by collectivizing natural monopolies and basic human services while leaving, for the moment, the ownership of other forms of production and wealth in private hands. Again, such a socialism, slowly spreading the light of its example, must soon come to supply all the amenities of modern life: "public baths, playgrounds, promenades, public kitchens, libraries, museums, theaters, public rooms, poor law insurance, unemployed relief, and in general all provisions for the weak, sick, or needy." It was with this growing conviction that socialism and localism were not simply compatible but complementary that he had written *Wealth Against Commonwealth.* And now that it had been published he could test his theory by helping to forge a model coalition of Chicago workers and downstate farmers as the Illinois vanguard of the Populist movement.

12

WEALTH AGAINST COMMONWEALTH

HENRY DEMAREST LLOYD published *Wealth Against Commonwealth* in
October 1894, after nearly five years of writing and research. The
book, a 600-page indictment of Standard Oil, was an intensely personal work which, like *Looking Backward* and *Progress and Poverty* before it, bore the stamp of the author's convictions on every page.
From the beginning, Lloyd envisioned a detailed report to the
American people on the corrupt state of the nation's business and finance. By the time he finished compiling the evidence, he had become so emotionally involved in arguing his case that he nearly lost
his editorial balance. His revulsion, he readily admitted, had
mounted with each new fact unearthed from "piles of filthy human
greed and cruelty," and he had kept on digging only because he was
convinced that "men must understand the vices of the present system before they will be able to rise to a better one."[1]

Difficulty in securing a publisher only underscored Lloyd's problem in framing his indictment. At the suggestion of William Dean
Howells he sent the much revised manuscript to Harper & Brothers,
only to be told that it was still much too long and intemperate. After

Henry Demarest Lloyd at his desk in the Wayside writing Wealth Against Commonwealth, early 1890s.

Jessie Bross Lloyd reading to her husband at home, 1893.

pruning it still more and submitting it to lawyers for possible libel he
returned it to Harper's, whose editors reluctantly agreed to bring out
the book if Lloyd would assume the cost of preparing the plates—
just such an arrangement as Henry George had been forced to accept
fifteen years earlier.

Even in its shortened version *Wealth Against Commonwealth* rendered a highly detailed account of the crimes and misdemeanors of
the oil monopoly. His fear of big business drove Lloyd to cross the
boundaries between conventional reporting and adversary pleading.
"I could easily *tell the story* in one quarter the space . . . and tell it better," he conceded to his publisher, who was still worried about
length. "But then the story would only be told; it would not be
proved." Intentionally he had sacrificed verbal nicety for legal proof.
"My object necessitated this sacrifice. I have aimed to collate the materials from which others will produce literary effects."[2]

Despite its author's disclaimer, literary effects abound in *Wealth
Against Commonwealth*—in the portraits of the little people victimized
by monopoly, in lush patches of nostalgia for a lost America, and in
the heavy irony of the editorial comments. He had chosen Standard
Oil, Lloyd explained, because the oil monopoly was the most notoriously successful attempt to put all of the world's market under
one hat. The actual names of Standard Oil's managers and directors
scarcely mattered, and he scrupulously refrained from mentioning
them. Had he stopped to identify each and every villain, a whole
rogue's gallery would have appeared on every page, glaring out at
the reader and inviting condemnation. "No matter how much the
assault was deserved, to have given the work that aspect would have
been fatal to the usefulness which I hope for it."[3]

His real story, Lloyd was sure, lay in the account of the victims of
Standard Oil's greed. His four case histories are actually fables
strung along an ascending line of corporate wrongdoing—from simple cheating to outright conspiracy. Although his book bristles with
examples of unethical business behavior, Lloyd rests his case against
the oil combine on the fates of four of its victims, whose stories of
initial defiance and ultimate defeat form the core of the book.

A poor widow defrauded by the agents of Standard Oil with
the connivance of Rockefeller himself.

An old inventor, whose prayers to be allowed to "make oil" fall on the deaf ears of the monopolists who drive him out of the business.

A tough Jacksonian entrepreneur, the last of a breed of independent businessmen, hounded by the oil trust and finally run to ground.

An inept saboteur bribed by Standard Oil managers, broken, and then discarded.

Lloyd sets the stage for his main characters in introductory chapters tracing the process of corporate consolidation from corners to pools to trusts. Then comes a list of the chief offenders: railroad companies with their watered stock and jerry-built roads; the whiskey trust lacing its concoctions with creosote and fusel oil; the sugar, wheat, and meat trusts cornering their markets with a supreme contempt for the consumer. Lloyd's survey, taken from his early articles, prepares the way for Standard Oil as it slashes a path through the Pennsylvania oil fields, laying waste to the small refineries and killing off the independents.

Lloyd's picture of the Pennsylvania oil fields in the days before the coming of Standard Oil is a duplicate of Henry George's view of the California countryside before the arrival of the railroad. There was a free market and free competition. Small business prospered. The highways were crowded, and there were jobs for the asking.

The people were drilling one hundred new wells per month, at an average cost of $6000 each. They had devised the forms, and provided the financial institutions needed in a new business. They invented many new and ingenious mechanical contrivances. They built up towns and cities, with schools, churches, lyceums, theatres, libraries, boards of trade. There were nine daily and eighteen weekly newspapers published in the region and supported by it.[4]

For Lloyd, as for Henry George, building American communities, if left to the people themselves, was a naturally cooperative enterprise.

As the shadows of economic depression fall across the oil fields following the Panic of 1873, the independent oil producers are chagrined to learn that while hard times have thinned their own ranks, "one little group of a dozen men" have not only escaped disaster but have actually flourished. At the head of this new "ruling coterie" stands a man who has come late to the oil country, an unsmiling, grimly purposeful representative of new money, a former "book-keeper" of a country-produce store in Cleveland who has moved on to bigger things. In the depression years of the seventies the "new democracy" of the independents is confronted with a predatory "new wealth"—"a few men at the centre of things, in offices rich with plate glass and velvet plush."[5]

Challenged by this secret combination, the independent producers decide to investigate the source of their difficulties in shipping and marketing their oil. They haven't far to seek. Rockefeller's South Improvement Company—his secret arrangement with the railroads for securing rebates for himself on the oil shipped by his competitors—is the cause of their plight. The independent oil men's discovery of the plot triggers a "pacific insurrection" of the people who are determined to destroy the South Improvement Company. Their success in unmasking conspiracy, however, is more apparent than real. The South Improvement scheme is abandoned, but presently Standard Oil turns to the signing of forced contracts, ironically termed "adventures," with hard-pressed "free citizens" to curtail production and eliminate competition.

One of these "free citizens" swindled by the oil combine in its drive to dominate the industry is the first of Lloyd's victims, the all-too-pathetic Widow Backus, brave with love and the memory of her late husband, the wronged woman vainly seeking a fair price for the small refinery she is forced to sell. Although she knows she is swimming in shark-infested waters, the good widow fears not but places her faith in "the great man of commerce from Cleveland" and appeals to his generosity. "All I can do," she pleads with him, "is to appeal to your sympathy, to do the best with me that you can. I beg you to consider your wife in my position, left with this business and with fatherless children."[6] With tears in his eyes the great man assures her that he will provide for her in her hour of need. But his are crocodile tears—soon he retires from negotiations in favor of his hard-eyed agent who systematically undervalues the widow's property and acquires it for a song and her promise not to reenter the oil business for ten years.

It takes two of these ten years for the Widow Backus to realize
that she has been bilked. "Two years before, when she was weak
with grief, inexperience, and the fear that she might not succeed in
her gallant task of paying her husband's debts, she had thought of
selling out at a sacrifice." But now she sees that the combine has
"cheapened her down." Good will and her husband's reputation
have been wiped out by a flat offer of the cost of replacement. Hoping to extract a more generous offer from Rockefeller, the Widow
Backus makes a second plea, only to receive a frosty reply assuring
her that she has been handsomely recompensed and offering to return the property if she is not satisfied. "Indignant with these brave
thoughts and the massacred troop of hopes and ambitions that her
brave heart had given birth to, she threw the letter into the fire where
it curled up into flames like those from which a Dives once begged
for a drop of water." The widow never again appeared in the world
of business, "where she had found no chivalry to help a woman save
her home, her husband's life work, and her children."[7]

If in her splendid outrage the Widow Backus dominates the
opening section of *Wealth Against Commonwealth*, she is only the most
sentimentalized of Lloyd's four victims, all of whom are sketched as
one-dimensional figures isolated from real social forces and sil-
houetted against the lurid light of conspiracy. The oil trust's second
victim is Thorstein Veblen's Engineer defeated by the price system,
the technological genius beaten by profit-hungry promoters. Samuel
Van Syckel, the pioneer inventor-entrepreneur, is the last of a dying
breed—"one of the type of country-bred, hard-working American
manhood" now receding into memory. Van Syckel first appeared in
the Pennsylvania oil country with Colonel Drake himself, and
through two decades filled with ups and downs, succeeded in building the first pipeline from wellhead to refinery and then in inventing
a continuous distillation process that saved time and improved the
quality of the oil. Like the true producer he has always been, the old
man simply wants to be left alone to tinker with his inventions.
Gambling, promoting, speculating have no appeal to a veteran with a
reputation for hard work, self-denial, and public spirit. It is clear that
Van Syckel is no match for Standard Oil.

Van Syckel is betrayed by the oil monopoly's managers, whose
agent offers him a lifetime salary if he will agree to put his patent for
continuous distillation on the shelf. Outraged, he refuses. "I told him

I did not want a salary: I wanted to build this refinery and make oil in a new continuous way."[8] Which is just what he tries to do, first in his own small refinery in Boston where he experiences difficulty in obtaining regular shipments of crude oil, and then under agreement with Standard Oil to "develop" his patent. When the company refuses to honor its promise, Van Syckel strikes out on his own, only to be thwarted again and again by the combine. "When twelve years had gone by, and he found they would neither build for him as agreed nor let anyone else build for him, Van Syckel turned to the law and sued them for damages."[9] In a symbolic verdict marking the passage from a producer to a pecuniary age, the jury finds for the old man, but the judge awards him damages of six cents. Now Van Syckel is an exile banished from the very business he helped to found. He vaguely recalls meeting his adversary once when the "great man" owned a tiny still "cocked up in the woods . . . a one-horse, pig-pen kind of place at the bend of the creek, cobbled-up sort of mud hole with a water-trough to bring the oil to the still." But later Rockefeller spent most of his time in Cleveland cooking up schemes for taking control of the whole oil industry and making himself rich. "I didn't ever think anything about him then," the old man admits. "I was 'way above' him . . . He was just a common-looking man among the rest of us."[10] Now he realizes just how *un*common Rockefeller really is, but it is too late.

In George Rice, the independent refiner from Marietta, Ohio, and the third of Standard Oil's antagonists, the monopoly encounters a tougher and more resourceful foe. Rice is a Jacksonian type—the small entrepreneur who runs a family firm with the help of one daughter who keeps the books, another who answers the mail, and a son-in-law who manages the plant. Rice's business is one of several small firms attacked by Standard Oil in the seventies. By 1879 freight rates out of Marietta had risen alarmingly. Pressed for an explanation by the independent refiners, the railroad managers deny collusion with the oil combine, but Rice and his friends know better. Standard Oil is numbering their days.

Rice, however, is neither dead like the Widow Backus's spouse nor decrepit like old Samuel Van Syckel. He proves adept at waging a war for survival—striking a quick bargain with buyers, retreating just out of reach of the combine, countering suddenly with a lawsuit, and meanwhile exploring new markets and the means of developing them. Determined to hang on even though most of his fellow independents have succumbed, George Rice takes the lead in demanding an investigation into Standard Oil's practices and meanwhile looks southward for new outlets. "The people and dealers everywhere in the South," Lloyd notes, "were glad to see Rice. He found a deep discontent among consumers and merchants alike."[11] Standard Oil, however, moves quickly to check Rice's advance by cutting its own prices and dispatching spies to report on his every move. The monopoly lobbies city councils and intimidates local officials, and Rice is hard-pressed to stay in business. "From 1886 to the present Rice and his family have been kept busier defending their right to live in business than in doing business itself."[12] The independent refiner fights on in a losing cause—"writing, telegraphing, travelling, protesting, begging, litigating, worrying." Gradually Rice comes to understand his situation: as a lone independent he cannot possibly win. "His solitary and fruitless, although successful, struggle taught him that the citizens of industry can no more maintain their rights singly than the citizens of a government."[13] Individuals are doomed. Only a people can win and maintain freedom.

The final victim in Lloyd's list of casualties is a master mechanic he calls "Albert" who is bribed by the directors of a subsidiary of Standard Oil to arrange an explosion at a rival refinery. Albert, though corruptible, is also inept: he clamps down a safety-valve on one of the stills, fires up the boiler, and awaits an "accident" that never happens. Yet having corrupted Albert, his employers are now obliged to take care of him despite the bungled job. He is promptly spirited off to Boston and rewarded for his continued silence. Reports of Albert's attempted sabotage, however, are leaked to the press, and indictments are eventually handed down against two former owners of the Vacuum Oil Company—now, six years later, resident managers for Standard Oil—and three members of the oil trust from New York City.

Lloyd's description of the trial and his sentimentalizing of Albert's role in uncovering the conspiracy closes the circle of collusion and corruption he set out to trace with the story of the Widow Backus. Albert is more sinned against than sinning. "He kept one dignity to the end which makes him tower above his seducers—the dignity of the laborer." The habits of a lifetime of hard work have disqualified Albert for the role of the "cheap American Faust" reveling in his "pinchbeck paradise."[14] Though hardly redeemed by his flawed testimony, he rises a notch higher in the moral order than the defendants and the judge who acquits the three Standard Oil trustees and fines the others a mere $250 apiece.

From these battles between the giant monopoly and the small businessmen comes the political split that Lloyd proceeds to trace carefully. In one camp are the oil company executives together with the managers of the nation's trunk lines—a private government with complete power over interstate commerce. In the other camp in various postures of defiance stand the independents, desperately trying to rally the people. Realizing that they are about to be caught like rabbits in a trap, the independents attempt to build their own connection to the East Coast—the Tidewater Pipeline. The oil combine blocks them at every turn, buying up rights of way, seizing their terminals, and when these means fail, indulging in sabotage. Yet the Tidewater independents persevere until they are owners of 400 miles of pipe and three million barrels of tankage. In its halcyon days, Lloyd recalls, Tidewater did great work for the people.

Soon, however, the independents sense that theirs is a lost cause. Assured by the Erie and the Pennsylvania Railroads that they will continue to honor their contracts, the small refiners embark on modernizing programs when suddenly the railroads turn on them and, following orders from Standard Oil, declare a new war. Then all independents learn the lesson administered to the Widow Backus and George Rice—"the impossibility of survival in modern business of men who are merely honest, hard-working, competent, even though they have skill, capital and customers."[15]

If by 1894 there remained little hope for effective federal regulation of monopolies, there was even less hope, Lloyd was convinced, that the states could withstand the power of Standard Oil. The Commonwealth of Pennsylvania refused to tax the oil company, even though it did most of its business within state lines. By putting the state's attorney general on its payroll, Standard Oil managed to whittle its tax bill down from $3 million to exactly $22,660.10. Even though the state legislature agreed to investigate and indictments were drawn up, the oil combine escaped prosecution. "Upon the only occasion when the 'Trustees' seemed in real danger of being brought in person and on specific charges to trial, criminally, the Supreme Court of Pennsylvania saved them."[16] Here, in an example of judicial malfeasance, was proof of the futility of all attempts to control monopoly.

> Monopoly cannot be content with controlling its own business . . . Its destiny is rule or ruin, and rule is but a slower ruin. Hence we find it in America creeping higher every year up into the seats of control. Its lobbyists force the nomination of judges who will construe the laws as Power desires, and of senators who will get passed such laws as it wants for its judges to construe.[17]

With this warning of the political consequences of monopoly, Lloyd turns from cases of individual failure to two contrasting accounts of community success in combatting Standard Oil. His first example is Columbus, Mississippi, a small southern country town which hands the oil company its first real setback. "The South," Lloyd observes by way of introduction, "is the most American part of America."[18] Insulated by its sectional past from the commercial frenzy of the North, the town of Columbus belongs to a passing agrarian order that still nurtures in its citizens a Revolutionary heritage of resistance to oppression.

Trouble first began in Columbus when the merchant-factors of the town determined to break the oil monopoly's grip by purchasing their oil from an independent. When the company objected and took countermeasures, the merchants of Columbus formed an "association" in the style of the original colonial nonimportation agreements. Soon the town seethes with "the spirit which prevailed when the people of Boston emptied King George's taxed teas into Boston Harbor."[19] Following the eighteenth-century imperial example, Standard Oil sends its agents into the surrounding countryside to coerce the farmers. In a burst of patriotism the Merchants Association retaliates by refusing to handle the monopoly's oil at any price, and the world is treated to the novelty of an entire community acting together. Suddenly the meaning of their defiance becomes clear to the townspeople. "Public attention was fascinated by the revelation that a brotherhood to ravage the people turned impotent when the people were roused to meet it with their brotherhood of the commonwealth."[20] The oil trust might overwhelm individuals like George Rice and even isolated communities, but a league of municipalities could prove invincible. "Such a combination," Lloyd announces, "can and should be brought about at once."

Toledo, Ohio, the second example of successful municipal defense against monopoly, offers a contrast to Columbus, Mississippi. If the southern crossroads town recalls a passing agrarian order, the bustling midwestern city represents the future. In Columbus the fight is simple and severe—"an obstinate, immovable, thoroughly angry public opinion acting only through voluntary means." In Toledo the business of organizing an opposition is more complicated because the city is "a citizen of the great world of affairs," part of the huge industrial network extending from Chicago and New York to London and beyond.[21] The differences in scale demand different strategies for countering the attack of the oil monopoly: direct citizen action in the case of the small town; representative bodies and civic agencies in that of the modern industrial city.

The tale of Toledo unfolds from the determination of its citizens to build a municipal gas system. First they draft a petition and submit it to the state legislature which obliges with an enabling act. At this point the first stirrings of opposition from the oil combine are heard in the Toledo Common Council, some of whose members seem overly solicitous of the company's welfare. The preponderance of numbers on the side of the city is deceptive. "The City of Toledo was a vigorous community of 90,000 people; its opponent was a little group of men; but they controlled in one aggregation not less than $160,000,000, besides large affairs outside of this."[22] The war between the Robber Barons and the forces of self-government is fought in a series of increasingly sharp skirmishes. The City Council takes the offensive by ordering $75,000 worth of bonds to initiate construction of a pipeline. The gas trust, on orders from Standard Oil, counters with an injunction to halt construction, and when this gambit fails, reverses direction and seeks an agreement with the city fathers providing for competing public and private systems. Just as their offer is about to be accepted, the directors of the gas trust unaccountably do yet another about-face and, now insisting that duplicate services are uneconomical, demand that the city abandon its scheme. Unfazed, the mayor, the city auditor, and a newly formed Board of Trustees unite in a citizens coalition to sell city bonds to the people of Toledo.

When the gas trust steps up its attack on the city officials by attempting to discredit them in the press, the city fathers bring a libel suit that puts an end to slander but not to the continued use of spies and informers. Then a taxpayer's suit instituted by the gas monopoly threatens to block completion of the municipal system until the City Council wins a favorable ruling from the courts. In spite of mounting obstacles and adverse publicity, Toledo moves ahead "piece by piece" in completing the system, an achievement in which Lloyd sees "the revival of the passion of freedom of 1776 and 1861." Savings in construction costs and cheaper gas are the least of the people's gains. Even more important is their escape from "tyranny and extortion." Toledo has taught Americans a second lesson in communal freedom.

From these matching accounts of civic success in battling monopoly, Lloyd moves up the governmental ladder to the state legislature of Ohio where, it has been charged, Standard Oil bought a seat in the United States Senate for Henry B. Payne, who has served the company faithfully ever since. Payne had not even been considered a serious candidate by Democratic rank-in-file in Ohio, who favored veteran George B. Pendleton and fully expected their state representatives to honor their choice. Thus when the election of the Honorable Henry B. Payne was announced, "terrible was the moral storm that broke forth out of the hearts of the people of Ohio."[23] Complaints and charges come pouring into Columbus. The public demands an investigation. Payne's election, everyone knows, was secretly arranged "by the corrupt use of money." Specifically, "among the chief managers of Mr. Payne's canvass, and those who controlled its financial operation, were four of the principal members in Ohio of the oil trust" who provided the slush fund of $65,000 with which to secure Payne's election.[24] Lloyd admits that none of these charges of corrupt practices were ever proven, but he notes that the same legislature that eased Payne into the Senate also defeated a proposal by the city of Cleveland to build its own gas system. As for Senator Payne, he continues to do the bidding of Standard Oil as he happily sings its praises as "a very remarkable institution."

Standard Oil's record of corruption in Washington, Lloyd argues, is fully as remarkable as its performance at the state and local levels. Here it is chiefly a matter of wheedling special privileges out of a compliant Congress—a subsidy here, an exemption there. The meaning of such evasions of the law is clear: "The few men who are beneficiaries of taxes paid by the many will be powerful and shrewd enough to get other dispensations or benefits, post-office contracts, or modifications of the strict terms of their agreement, and with the help from the taxpayer they can do business at a figure which, though very remunerative to themselves, will drive the unaided citizen competitors out of business."[25] Here was the old smokeless rebate refitted for world trade. Soon international politics, like American government itself, will become a scramble of competing lobbyists plying their trade and seeking preference in the legislative halls of London, Paris, and Berlin, as well as in Washington.

What was to be done? What was the solution to the problem of monopoly? Lloyd approached this question in the spirit of the seventeenth-century English jurist Sir Edward Coke, whose animadversions he took for his own. Coke's complaints against the state monopolies of the early Stuarts had been three. Monopolies raised the price of commodities. Said commodities were of poorer quality than before. And such combinations in restraint of trade tended to the impoverishment of artisans and artificers. Lloyd's case against Standard Oil rested on these same assumptions. The present price of monopoly oil, he insisted, was not the real question: "Anything begins to be dear the moment the power to fix the price has been allowed to vest in one. The question whether our monopolies have made things cheap or dear in the past pales before the exciting query, What will they do in the future?"[26] He proceeded to guess at an answer by citing the economies and other advantages of small-scale production. If the production of oil on this "natural scale," under the direct oversight of the owner, had not been more efficient than production "mobilized from the metropolis by salaried men," then independents like George Rice could never have survived as long as they did.[27]

With the Lord Chief Justice's third complaint—monopoly's anaconda grip on the little man—Lloyd was also in agreement. Standard Oil, having reduced its competitors to hired hands, was about to enter the final state of economic concentration. Lloyd conceded that there was a theoretical possibility of establishing a government-sponsored oil monopoly, but the actual chances of implementing such a policy he considered slim. "This remedy of a State monopoly, as suggested in Austria or Germany, has yet had few advocates here in America. Our public opinion, so far as there is any public opinion,

restricts itself to favoring recourse to anti-trust laws and to boycotting the monopoly and buying oil of its competitors."[28] But now competitors are too few to go around, and the Sherman Anti-Trust Act is
a dead letter. The options available to antimonopolists have narrowed alarmingly.

By 1894 Lloyd and his two utopian colleagues were examining
the transformation of the American economy from a point midway
in the process. In the immediate past lay original experiments with
pools and trusts, price-fixing and rebates, and all the other primitive
devices for reducing production and regulating competition. Ahead
at the very end of the century loomed the great merger movement,
the greatest consolidation of capital known to history. By 1900 an average 500 firms annually were disappearing, swallowed by new industrial giants controlling half the domestic American market—huge
integrated corporations with bureaucratic structures and interlocking directorates. Eventually this new system of corporate capitalism
would succeed in stabilizing itself, but in the immediate future, the
next two decades envisioned by Lloyd, the merger movement appeared to verify all his dire predictions. The long-term rate of
growth of the national product, which had increased steadily
throughout the nineteenth century, suddenly reversed itself with the
century's turn. The rate of savings, another index that had climbed
impressively since the Civil War, began to decline, and so did the
rate of growth of the three productive factors—land, labor, and capital. The Panic of 1893 and the ensuing depression brought wage-
cuts, strikes, sharp price declines, agricultural distress, and an unemployment rate that soared to 20 percent. In 1894 it did not take a Karl
Marx to predict the coming crisis of the capitalist order.

In approaching the problem of monopoly capitalism Lloyd
parted company with Henry George and Edward Bellamy. George
clung stubbornly to his mid-century conviction that the free market,
once permanently secured by his Single Tax, must automatically
balance supply and demand. Enact my program, he continued to
argue as he had insisted for fifteen years, and you eliminate the only
force capable of disrupting the perfect workings of the free market.
In refusing to acknowledge monopoly as an attempt to compensate
for the failures of the free market, George declared his unswerving
loyalty to the principles of Adam Smith and at the same time declared intellectual bankruptcy in his dealings with the modern cor-

porate economy. Bellamy, on the other hand, accepted the logic of bureaucratic organization and technological efficiency promised by the trusts. His industrial army fostered the same producerist drives and managerial urges that big business seemingly fulfilled, and he took the corporation as his model of the good society. Only Lloyd guessed correctly the destination of monopoly capitalism and was prepared to offer a cooperative alternative. Yet even he appeared to falter in his analysis in the closing section of his book. Through thirty tightly packed chapters Lloyd had woven the story of the destruction of a simpler and better way of life by the sinister forces of monopoly. The Widow Backus, Samuel Van Syckel, and George Rice were representatives of a superior small-scale society organized around the little man. Lloyd's picture of the good society, rich in detail, was a duplicate of Henry George's in *Progress and Poverty* and Edward Bellamy's in his early ficton—the American village blessed with a sound economy, resourceful citizens, a producerist culture, and a genuine love of community—all endangered by modernism and monopoly.

In the closing section of *Wealth Against Commonwealth*, Lloyd's antimonopoly point of view dissolves into a more profound antimodernist perspective, as the original Jacksonian angle of vision gives way to a more sweeping survey of the whole course of modernization in the Western world since the fifteenth century. Lloyd's antimodernist pronouncement is a distant echo of the original complaints of seventeenth-century Commonwealthmen and the eighteenth-century followers of Bolingbroke who fulminated against debts, banks, speculation, and all the other evils of England's financial revolution. The Country party ideology enjoyed a curious half-life in America following its arrival during the Age of Revolution, giving dramatic point to the political debates between Federalists and Jeffersonians in the formative years of the new nation, and then dividing at the Mason-Dixon Line proslavery theorists like George Fitzhugh from antislavery pioneers like William Lloyd Garrison. Readers of the final chapters of *Wealth Against Commonwealth* caught the faint but unmistakable tones of the original *North Briton* in Lloyd's indictment of latter-day note shavers and coupon clippers.

Modern wealth more and more resembles the winnings of speculators in bread during famine.

What we call cheapness shows itself to be unnatural fortunes for the very few, monstrous luxury for them and proportionate deprivation for the people, judges debauched, trustees dishonored, Congress and State legislatures insulted and defied.

Our barbarians come from above. Our great money-makers have sprung in one generation into seats of power kings do not know. The forces and the wealth are new and have been the opportunity of new men. Without restraints of culture, experience, the pride, or even the inherited caution of class or rank, these men, intoxicated, think they are the wave instead of the float, and that they have created the business which created them.

Their heathen eyes see in the law and its consecrated officers nothing but an intelligence-office and hired men to help them burglarize the treasures accumulated for thousands of years at the altars of liberty and justice, that they may burn their marbles for the lime of commerce.[29]

Lloyd offers a moral history as an explanation for the rise, triumph, and imminent decline of commercial civilization. The Middle Ages, he begins, "landed on the shores of the sixteenth century" and immediately "broke ranks," and for the last 300 years everyone in the Western world "has been scurrying about to get what he could." The modern world has conspicuously failed to organize social and economic life on any broader basis than selfish enterprise and personal satisfaction. The misnamed Age of Science consisted of three "picnic centuries" in which people "had to run away from each other . . . to seize the prizes of the new sciences, the new land, the new liberties which make modern times."[30] Modernism has replaced the socialized men of the High Middle Ages with the economic man of the classical economists. Community has been destroyed by a race of computers of self-interest.

Lloyd traces the rise of modern economics to its dominant position through two distinct historical epochs, the first one liberating business enterprise from state control in the sixteenth and seventeenth centuries, the second registering the rapid gains of individual acquisitiveness in the eighteenth and nineteenth. It could be argued, as some of Lloyd's younger economist friends were insisting, that monopoly supplied a remedy for the ills of unregulated competition, that monopoly simply represented business at the end of its journey—the ordering principle for the new age of mass production and consumption.

> The more perfect monopoly makes itself the more does it bring into strong lights the greatest fact of our industry . . . It makes this fair world more fair to consider the loyalties, intelligences, docilities of the multitudes who are guarding, developing, operating with the faithfulness of brothers and the keen interest of owners of properties and industries in which brotherhood is not known and their title is not more than a tenancy at will.[31]

The divorce of ownership from management, which Lloyd recognized as integral to industrial consolidation, meant that "more and more mills and mines and stores, and even farms and forests are being administered by others than the owners." In such early signs of a coming managerial revolution, Lloyd saw hope for the eventual moralizing of American society, a progressive rationalizing of production and inculcating of responsibilities that could well culminate in the frictionless operation of Bellamy's industrial machine. Where Bellamy took the civil service as his bureaucratic example, Lloyd looked to labor and the lesson taught by the country's railroad workers "despatching trains, collecting fares and freights, and turning over millions of profits to the owners."[32] If only this separation of ownership and management could be matched by the steady socializing of investment capital, the collectivist forces at work in the modern world would soon prove irresistible and the peaceful self-socializing of capitalism could be completed under the beneficent eye of a new class of managers and intellectuals serving as the engineers of the new system.

If these bold predictions of a coming progressive age proved accurate, then the question was not whether monopoly in its present form could survive—manifestly it could not. "Unless we reform of our own free will, nature will reform us by force, as nature does."[33] Since the greatest dangers posed by monopolies such as Standard Oil were cultural and political, the remedy must be found in culture and politics. And herein lay the problem. "America has grown so

big—and the tickets to be voted, and the powers of government, and
the duties of citizens, and the profits of personal use of public functions have grown so big—that the average citizen has broken
down."[34] Only place-hunters and favor-seekers now understood the
workings of a government that had fallen to the "specialists of the
ward club" dispensing patronage. The time was ripe for a redemptive politics based on the "laws of association" and the New Conscience. This was the task that lay before the industrial workers and
the farmers of the United States—to become "partners in invincibil-
ity" in building the new moral order.

For this kind of renovation federal laws regulating monopoly
were not enough. "The policy of regulation, disguise it as we may, is
but a moving to a compromise and equilibrium within the evil all
complain of." Law alone could never lead capitalist society to social-
ize itself. To illustrate the essentially oscillatory nature of history as
it responds to great spiritual ideas, Lloyd cited Sir Henry Maine's
distinction between status and contract as the identifying character-
istics of premodern and modern societies.

> Sir Henry Sumner Maine says mankind moves from status to
> contract; from society ruled by inherited customs to one ruled
> by agreement, varied according to circumstances. Present ex-
> perience suggests the addition that the movement, like all in
> nature, is pendulous, and that mankind moves progressively
> from status to contract, and from this stage of contract to an-
> other status. We march and rest to march again.[35]

The social pendulum, Lloyd was convinced, responded in the last
analysis only to the collective will or regenerative impulse of an entire people—nothing so narrow as "the mere governmentalizing of
the means of production." The great industrial transformation, like
the abolition of slavery, would have to be a moral revolution led by
the prophets of the New Conscience.

There was another American social critic in the early nineties,
younger and wholly secular in outlook, who also cited Sir Henry
Maine's distinction between status and contract to make a different
point about the future of industrial society. Two years before the appearance of *Wealth Against Commonwealth*, Thorstein Veblen published an article entitled "Some Neglected Points in the Theory of

Socialism" in the hope of correcting at least some of the American public's misapprehensions.[36] Although he asked some of the same questions that Lloyd did concerning the future of monopoly, Veblen's use of Maine marked the intellectual watershed dividing Lloyd's nineteenth-century romantic world from a twentieth-century instrumentalist one. Most social thinkers, Veblen complained, assumed that societies based on status and those resting on contract were mutually exclusive, that a modern industrial system could be superseded by "the only other known system—that of status," whose type was military organization, hierarchy, or bureaucracy. It was just this widespread belief that explained the current American fascination with utopia, whether Edward Bellamy's Boston in the year 2000 or William Morris's preindustrial community of artisans and craftsmen. All of the appeals to voluntarism and natural cooperation, Veblen pointed out, proceeded from the fear that any shift from contract to status necessarily involved new forms of subjection and despotism.

Maine's scheme, Veblen continued, appeared to offer a somewhat constricted choice between status and prescription on the one side and contract and competition on the other. Yet the new industrial system of "natural monopolies," which Lloyd and his fellow utopians acknowledged, clearly indicated the arrival of an intermediate stage of social and economic development. "No revolution has been achieved; the system of competition has not been discarded, but the course of industrial development is not in the direction of an extension of that system [of contract] at all points; nor does the principle of status always replace that of competition wherever the latter fails." On the contrary, the principle of natural monopolies was already calling forth new regulatory agencies that stopped far short of state ownership. "It is the analogy of modern constitutional government through an impersonal law and impersonal institutions, that comes nearest to doing justice to the vague notions of our socialist propagandists." It was true, Veblen admitted, that some socialists seemed inordinately fond of the analogy of the military organization, "but that must after all be taken as an *obiter dictum.*" Once discard the military analogy as superfluous, and what remained was neither a system of prescription and class nor yet a free competitive order, but instead a new form of "constitutional subjection to the will of the social organism" as expressed in impersonal law—subjection, not to the *person* of the public functionary, but to the *powers* vested in him.

In *Wealth Against Commonwealth*, a piece of sacred history, Lloyd assured a new generation of Progressives that the science of society and the ethics of the New Conscience were mutually reinforcing, that the historical record and faith in the millennium were both part of the providential plan for America. Both Lloyd and Veblen identified the specific measures that a Progressive generation of reformers would take after the turn of the century. But more clearly than Lloyd and the utopians, Veblen saw the direction in which the forces of industrial centralization were driving the American reform enterprise. Citing the right of eminent domain and the taxing power as examples of the convergence of political and industrial functions, Veblen plotted for the new intellectuals and professionals their line of advance into the twentieth century. The result of the merging of industrial and political functions, he predicted, would be "nationalism without status and without contract"—a definition of Progressivism that reformers would soon take as their own. And as though in reply to Lloyd and his plea for the New Conscience, Veblen dismissed the likelihood of a spiritual rebirth. "The question, therefore, is not whether we have reached the perfection of character which would be necessary in order to have a perfect working of the scheme of nationalisation, but whether we have reached such a degree of development as would make an imperfect working of the scheme possible." The sacred society of the utopians simply dissolved in the acids of Veblen's modernism.

The public reception of *Wealth Against Commonwealth* disappointed Lloyd. "Although the book has sold and is selling well, I must confess myself mystified, on the whole, by the equanimity with which the public submit to the facts disclosed by such a resumé." A handful of obliging reviewers like the ancient Edward Everett Hale saluted the book as a worthy successor to *Uncle Tom's Cabin,* and there were predictable cries of outrage from Standard Oil. Yet even though it was reprinted four times within the year, the long-term success of *Wealth Against Commonwealth* scarcely compared with that of *Looking Backward* or *Progress and Poverty.* A few of Lloyd's economist friends—Richard T. Ely, John Bates Clark, Benjamin Andrews—recommended his book to their students without, however, endorsing the author's argument for government ownership of the trusts. But the new professional journals either ignored it or dismissed it as unscholarly. The most gratifying reviews appeared in *Commonwealth* and *The Outlook* and in the pages of the religious weeklies. If Lloyd had expected his book to serve as a guide for reformers preparing to do battle with the corporations, he had been mistaken.

In part the problem was one of bad timing: when the book finally appeared, the country lay deep in the throes of a depression. Readers in 1894 were more concerned with unemployment, strikes, and free silver than with the threat of monopoly. But another part of the difficulty stemmed from the tentative nature of his recommendations and the vagueness of his proposal for the peaceful socialization of American capitalism. Frustration drove him to acknowledge a sense of defeat in a letter to Congressman Frederick Gillette of Massachusetts, who wrote him for advice in drafting new antitrust legislation. He had never really tried to draft an antimonopoly law, Lloyd replied, because he had no faith in trustbusting. It was important, first of all, to separate the question of monopoly and the abuse of power from the larger issue of economic consolidation which was inevitable.

> The men who are combining are only pioneers in our commercial evolution. Combination cannot possibly be prevented; nor do I see any reason why the attempt to prevent it should be made. But combination which obtains the power to crush competition and manipulate prices is combination which has reached the point at which something must be done; but I would no more think the thing to be done is to forbid combination than I believe the reform of currency calls for the remonitization of silver. Either step would be reactionary. The only remedy that I can see is for the public to adopt the policy of the public expropriation of such monopolies as they are created.

In England, Lloyd reminded Gillette, the principle of public ownership, which the Fabian Society had advanced as the solution to private monopoly, had already been extended to housing as well as to transit lines and utilities. But in the United States there was as yet

little interest in such legislation. As for the illegal operations of
American monopolists, there was little doubt that "every important
man in the oil, coal, and many other trusts ought today to be in some
one of our penitentiaries." It required no new laws to put them there,
only a prosecuting attorney, a judge, and a jury. Not even punitive
action, however, could check the progress of economic concentration.

As he reviewed recent developments for his congressional correspondent, Lloyd glimpsed catastrophe should Americans fail in their
renovative mission.

> We have reached an extraordinary condition in our develop-
> ment [he told Gillette], threatening the most portentous polit-
> ical and social consequences. The medieval system of regu-
> lating prices by custom and by law has disappeared. Its
> modern successor, our system of regulating prices by compe-
> tition, has disappeared, latterly, in hundreds of markets and is
> going to disappear in thousands . . . This state of affairs is not
> to be explained as due to anyone's total depravity, nor to the
> greed of any special individuals. It is the expression of the
> universal greed of the entire community. A revolution that
> should break up these properties and redistribute them
> among the people, and leave our present motives in opera-
> tion, would only end, ultimately, in reestablishing all the
> monopolies again . . . The existing laws ought to be enforced
> from the Interstate Commerce law down; but I cannot think
> of any remedial measure to which I would attach the slightest
> importance except agitation to awaken the public to the ne-
> cessity of themselves becoming the owners of every monop-
> oly. Municipal agitation for the ownership, as an entering
> wedge, of railroads, telegraphs, and all the monopolies . . . are
> the only direction in which I can look for profitable effort.[37]

With his old evangelical hope for a moral revolution still un-
dimmed, Lloyd turned, in 1894, to the task of forming a farmer-labor
coalition within a People's party radical enough to stand on his platform of public ownership.

13

STALEMATE

THE POPULIST REVOLT, which erupted in 1891 and raged for the next five years across the trans-Mississippi West and the South, furnished the climactic scenes of the nineteenth-century drama of romantic reform and assigned the three principals different roles. Edward Bellamy discovered the prophets of Nationalism in the American farmers and spent three exhausting years trying to make the People's party a contender in Massachusetts. His newspaper foundering, his energies drained by a hectic schedule, he continued to drive himself to the breaking point, which came in the winter of 1893 when he retired to his bed to begin work on his last book. In these final years of his life he befriended Henry Demarest Lloyd and provided valued counsel as Lloyd attempted to unite Illinois farmers and Chicago workers in a Populist coalition.

While Bellamy sought his political instrument in the nation's farmers, Lloyd spent four years trying to infuse Populism with the spirit of Fabian socialism. For him, as well as for Bellamy, the People's party represented a last chance. But Populism, he continued to insist in the face of mounting evidence to the contrary, was socialistic as all truly democratic doctrine necessarily was. Populists needed the socialists, who were some of the most energetic and reliable workers in the whole American reform movement.[1] With them, Lloyd was convinced until the campaign of 1896 proved him wrong, Populism would surely triumph.

It was Lloyd's insistence on the socialist content of Populism that alienated Henry George and defined for him the role of spoiler of the People's party hopes. Since his own war with New York socialists in 1887, George had continued to retreat from the political arena wearing the mantle of the religious prophet. On the front page of the *Standard* until its demise in the early nineties appeared the three remaining articles of the Georgist faith—THE SINGLE TAX, FREE TRADE, and BALLOT REFORM as the only needed correctives of Lloyd's Populist nonsense. In the same pages George also reviewed *Looking Backward*, dismissing it as a dream picture suffering from the "usual deficiencies" in explaining the means of "getting there."[2] George admired Bellamy's ethical standards, as he did Lloyd's, but deplored in both his rivals the "impulse to socialism" and their faith in government by paternalism. Thus as Lloyd and Bellamy committed their full energies to the People's party, George withheld his Single Tax forces from the nineteenth-century's last major reform battle, reserving them for a final symbolic act of defiance in New York City the following year.

Of all the groups in American society after 1890, the staple-crop farmers of the Plains States and the Southwest were the most firmly disposed to accept Bellamy's indictment of the economic system and to act on it. Bellamy spoke to them in the moral language they understood, and they responded by making his book a best-seller. Farmers had been prepared for his message by twenty years of growing frustration and the certainty that they had been victimized by a system cleverly contrived to exploit them. In fact, they were the unwitting victims of a world agricultural depression after 1870, a drastic price decline set in train by social and economic forces over which they had no control. The heart of the problem of agricultural distress, in Europe as well as America, was the huge increase in the production of wheat, corn, cotton, hogs, and beef, which continued to drive prices down with inexorable logic. From a moden perspective the American staple-crop farmer's predicament seems clear: overproduction, lack of market control, resultant price decline, and reduced farm income. But late-nineteenth-century farmers didn't see it that way. To staple-crop producers caught in a cycle of spiraling costs and declining prices, assurances from the East that all their troubles came from overproduction sounded absurd. Not overproduction but underconsumption, they agreed with Bellamy, lay at the root of the farm crisis—a disastrous economic policy that could easily be reversed.

The literature of the farm community after 1870 rehearsed a litany of deepening woe. Though American farmers produced for a world market now, they competed under severe handicaps that ranged from fluctuating dollar levels and unpredictable shipping costs to droughts and blizzards that could shrivel a crop of corn or wipe out a herd of cattle. Farmers also raged against banks and mortgage companies that charged prohibitive rates and foreclosed at the drop of a hat. They viewed foreclosures as the work of local moneylenders fronting for a sinister eastern money power, with its jute trusts, cotton oil trusts, farm equipment trusts, and barbed wire trusts. In the South and the Southwest, where capital was especially scarce, a crop-lien system locked farmers, white and black, into a perpetual debtors prison from which the only means of escape appeared cooperative methods and racial brotherhood. For farmers in both regions after 1880, it seemed as though the economy had purposely been rigged against them by a deadly combination of monopolists and plutocrats.

The farmers' interest in politics grew as their plight deepened. In the eighties the Northern and Southern Alliances were organized as nonpartisan pressure groups, but as the decade wore on, both organizations housed vocal minorities demanding the formation of a third party comprised of "the people" to cleanse American politics at the wellsprings. Farmers in the northern Plains States launched educational campaigns and formed study groups and lending libraries to help them analyze their problems. In the Southwest, Alliancemen went even further by experimenting with consumer cooperatives and drawing up schemes for withholding their crops until the price was right. In St. Louis in 1889, Alliancemen joined with the Knights of Labor in exploring the prospects of third-party action, and though there was no immediate agreement, both Alliances drew up separate demands that pointed unmistakably toward political involvement. Within a year the exodus of the staple-crop farmers out of the two major parties began in earnest as state "people's parties" and groups of "independents" sprang up in all of the Plains States. Kansas Populists won control of the lower house of the legislature in 1890 and sent a senator to Washington. In Nebraska independents won control of both houses. On the heels of these electoral triumphs came the Ocala (Florida) Convention, which further radicalized southern farmers by adding the subtreasury scheme to their demands for federal help. In Cincinnati the following year plans were made for a political convention to be held in 1892 to form a national party, and in Omaha on July 4, 1892, Populism was officially born.

The ideology of Populism was a blend of producerist advice and Christian ethics, not so much political directives as moral imperatives to restore the vitality and renew the will of the faithful. There was, first of all, the time-honored distinction between producers and parasites—between the many who lived by the sweat of their brows and the selfish few who knew not the dignity of labor. The real workers of the world the Populist lexicon defined as all those, whether in field or factory, who actually built the nation, while the nonproducers—coupon-clippers, speculators, financiers, and bankers—looked on in idleness and luxury. The true producers, Populists insisted, were responding to the universal instinct of workmanship, with its spiritual as well as material rewards. Every citizen had a God-given right to a job and held a just claim on society to provide one. Meaningful work, in the Populists' view, meant an entitlement to a birthright stake in a system that guaranteed the individual "the fruits of his toil."

The precise meaning of the distinction between producers and nonproducers tended to elude the Populists. What was clear in this oppositional view, however, was a faith in the temporal and moral primacy of labor. Labor, Populists agreed with Bellamy, George, and Lloyd, came first in the providential scheme of things. Capital, if earned in reasonable amounts through fair return, constituted the reward for hard work. In the political economy of producers, moreover, the proper workings of the market ensured a balance between energy expended and wealth acquired. It was only when this natural equilibrium was upset by greed or privilege that the system broke down and the producers suffered. Then it fell to them as the "plain people" to enter the political process and set matters right.

In identifying their enemy as the Money Power, the Populists were following the lead of the three utopians, who also denounced a pecuniary civilization that measured all things in dollars and cents. Their shared producer ethic transcended a functional analysis with an adversary culture that could not be defined with any exactness as either laissez-faire or interventionist. Populists wanted the federal government to stand sponsor to their producerist way of life by encouraging invention, releasing productive energies, stimulating voluntary cooperation, and only occasionally stepping in to help the little man by redressing the balance in his favor. To explain their second-class status under the rule of the Money Power they resorted to a highly charged moral discourse as old as the moral economy itself. Government, they asserted, had fallen prey to the "plutocracy" that filled public offices with "corrupt rulers" whose chief business was "robbing" the "honest yeomanry." These "Money Kings" monopolized the "bounties of nature" formerly reserved by "Divine Providence" for the "sons of toil." Thus, while the "idle rich" continued to hoard their "blood money," the poor people were being reduced to "servitude." Soon American society would stand fatally divided between "masters" and "slaves."

Bellamy shared with the Populists both vocabulary and values, in particular the work ethic. "If I were asked to name the most distinguishing felicity of this age as compared to that in which I first saw the light," Julian West tells his host, "I should say that to me it seems to consist in the dignity you have given labor by refusing to set a price upon it and abolishing the market-place forever." In Bellamy's utopia as in the American farmer's paradise, the instinct of workmanship has been set free. No longer slaves or menials, all American workers practice the Christian ideal of service to others. Work has been purified, and the separation of merit and material reward has been completed with the victory over scarcity and fears of overproduction. Bellamy verified for Populists their most cherished convictions.

Bellamy watched the growth of Populism with a surge of excitement. "I am more hopelessly gone on social reform than ever and have to own a total lack of interest in anything else," he wrote to

Horace Scudder in declining still another invitation to contribute his short stories to the *Atlantic Monthly*.[3] Nothing mattered to him now but winning a hearing for Nationalism by making it the ideological spearhead of the Populist movement. Populism, he suddenly realized, concerned a good deal more than a "few poor crops." "It is not so much their specific propositions, however radical, as the tone and language of their papers, their campaign orators and their campaign songs, which give an adequate idea of the thoroughly revolutionary spirit of these men." The Populists' discourse suggested the presence of a vital adversary culture. Although his Nationalists were prepared to go much further than the Populists in reorganizing the American economy for full equality, Bellamy urged his followers to welcome the farmers as brothers in arms in the "stirring times ahead." He applauded the St. Louis platform for its "ringing denunciation" of the capitalist order, and greeted the Omaha Convention the following year as "the most self-contained, statesmanlike and brave body of American citizens that has met to consider the state of the Union since the war." The People's party was the harbinger of "a new order of things." Its demands—nationalization of the railroads, a subtreasury system, land reform and equitable taxation—were all signposts on the road to a Nationalist utopia.[4]

Bellamy recognized in Populism a revivalistic politics of morality played by a different set of rules and judged by another standard from that of the Gilded Age professionals. According to the accepted political rules, the object of parties and the first job of the politician is to win elections and hold office. To do so professionals had to appeal to a variety of voters with widely different and even conflicting interests. Party platforms, accordingly, were vague and considered wholly secondary to the business of finding attractive candidates to run on them. Thorny issues and firm commitments were to be avoided at all cost. The test of a party's strength—and the only test—was the number of votes it won on election day. While all good politicians readily conceded that their parties performed useful educative tasks, these were considered wholly subordinate to the job of putting their party in power and keeping it there. Thus conducted, Gilded Age politics was viewed by the great majority of American voters as an entirely wholesome occupation, and with varying success since the Civil War, both Republicans and Democrats had continued to play this simple game.

The pietistic politics that Bellamy brought to the support of the People's party in the columns of the *New Nation* reversed all of the assumptions of the professionals. Political parties, he assumed, are corrupt by definition. ("Politics now largely means a combination of votes to protect certain private interests. Patriotism is dying at the seat of power." March 21, 1891) A Populist victory will begin the work of renovating a debased American politics. ("The advent of the people's party means not only the overthrow of one or both of the existing parties, but the political death of a whole crop of demagogues whose trade it has been to keep the people apart, and take the bribes of politicians." May 30, 1891) Nationalists must help the Populists in conducting a new kind of campaign. ("To nationalists, principles are more important than men, and the platform than the candidates." July 9, 1892) The financial and organizational poverty of Populism, far from being a liability, is a blessing in disguise. ("If they have a moral principle back of them they do not need money to win." July 4, 1891) Since the primary function of the People's party is educative and redemptive, it scarcely matters how many votes it wins. ("Whether the vote of the people's party proves to be a handsome one or barely visible, will make no difference to the members or their future policy." November 7, 1891) Purity is better than power. ("We believe the prospects of this party or any that succeed it, will be good in proportion as it lays aside compromise." November 14, 1891) But should the Populists succeed in gaining the balance of power in Congress, Americans may expect momentous changes in the conduct of public affairs. ("We may look to see the beginning of a new heroic period in our parliamentary history, recalling the days when the champions of the North and South in the decade before 1860, preluded with arguments the mighty struggle that was coming." October 15, 1892) Total victory, first of Populism and then of Nationalism, will bring true unity and an end to an imperfect electoral system with its corrupt practices. ("It is to be hoped that men will in time cease the folly of electing a whole Congress or Parliament at a time, or a president for a fixed term." November 12, 1892)

The Populist party in Massachusetts was composed of a handful of Nationalists and an even smaller band of Christian Socialists whom Bellamy described with more zeal than accuracy as "a solid nucleus of conscientiousness." He threw himself into the work of

organizing the tiny state party and discovered that he enjoyed poli-
ticking even though it exhausted him. He donated what little he
could afford to party coffers, and in 1892 even agreed to run on the
ticket as a presidential elector-at-large. The fortunes of the People's
party in Massachusetts matched the anemic circulation of the *New
Nation*, which served as its campaign sheet. Bellamy took occasional
time out from a hectic editorial schedule to speak at rallies in the
suburbs of Boston and up and down the Connecticut Valley. He still
disliked large public gatherings, and refused to raise money at his
lectures. He considered himself most effective in small "earnest conversations" where he engaged in lively exchanges with his audience.
Still, he was in much demand and complied with requests from Nationalists whenever his rapidly failing health permitted. Once he
spoke in a barn on the North Shore to an audience perched on hastily assembled planks and boxes, and reported with mock seriousness
that though he went on for over an hour, "not a man fell off his
bench."[5]

"This is the year for signs and wonders," he wrote in covering for
the *New Nation* the election of 1892 and pointing to "the most sensational outcome of this sensational campaign."[6] The People's party,
he was sure, would triumph either "under its present name or some
other name." All the faithful had to do was to avoid the pitfalls of
fusion with the Democrats and ignore the false promises of the silverites. His editorials sounded the old warning: beware "mere pal-
liatives"; aim for "a new order of things."[7]

The year 1892 was Bellamy's and Populism's *annus mirabilis.*
Within a year financial panic had tipped the nation into deep depression, and Populists began to hear the siren song of the silverites
urging free and unlimited coinage as a panacea. By 1893 the *New
Nation* was bankrupt, and Bellamy, seriously ill and exhausted from
overwork, had taken to his bed, leaving his assistants in Boston to
close down the paper when it became clear that it could not be saved.
"I have been wretched in health since I left you," he wrote to Mason
Green from Chicopee Falls in October 1893, "and am much discouraged as to the personal outlook, but within the last few days I
believe I have turned a corner and am going to be all right again."
Yet a month's rest failed to mend either body or spirits. "I don't
wonder my conduct makes you nervous," he confessed to Green. "I
am pretty nervous myself, though not too much so to appreciate the

embarrassment my break-down causes you. The fact is, I'm sick, more seriously so than in some years, and that on top of a rundown condition. I have not touched pen to paper (seriously) for ten days and have not faculty enough left to think consecutively on any subject for five minutes." He would have to rest content with having saved Nationalism from becoming "a vague and foggy philanthropy" and given it thousands of new standard-bearers who could now carry on the crusade. He himself was forced to the sidelines to direct his waning energy to "other lines of work promising possibly a larger service to the cause."[8] Already he was planning a sequel to *Looking Backward*, but a wracking cough and bouts of fever told him he would have to work quickly.

The Populists in Illinois whom Henry Demarest Lloyd hoped to steer into an alliance with the industrial workers of Chicago in 1894 declined to take a detour through alien territory. The core vision of Populism, Lloyd would learn, was a belief in the fee-simple empire of virtuous yeomen, a faith in the moral primacy of the land and those who worked on it that Lloyd hoped to combine with his own version of Fabian socialism. Populists in Illinois, while they were willing to call on the federal government for help, continued to invoke the idea of the natural economy of true producers. In the center of their world stood the family farm and the independent enterprise, the owner-operator whose economic demands were few, simple, and temporary: cheap transportation and storage facilities; fair shipping charges; and easy credit—partial measures aimed, not at the replacement, but the reinforcement of capitalism. Lloyd faced insurmountable obstacles to Populist acceptance of his proposal of a farmer-labor coalition.

If there was no theoretical reason why the limited demands of the Populists and moderate schemes for municipalizing utilities and transit lines in the cities should prove incompatible, there were several groups of reformers who thought otherwise. To be sure, there was a tiny contingent of Bellamy's Nationalists who considered Lloyd's Fabian program only a first step. But Henry George's Single Taxers from downstate feared urban domination, and Samuel Gompers's American Federation of Labor was leery of the farm interests. Finally, there was the state and national leadership of the

People's party—stolid agarians like James B. Weaver, the presidential standard-bearer in 1892, and Herman E. Taubeneck, national party chairman—who were concerned exclusively with winning the farmers' votes even if it meant courting the free silver forces.

Here was a volatile combination of interests and ideas for Lloyd to assemble. His task was a double one, first to convince Chicago craft unions and socialists that Populism offered them tangible benefits, then to assure Illinois Populists that they too had everything to gain from a campaign for public ownership. Above all, Lloyd knew, it was crucial to avoid making Henry George's mistake seven years earlier in disavowing socialism. George had blundered badly, "and he has never been heard of since as a political force."[9] The most difficult part of Lloyd's mission involved courting the AF of L and its Illinois affiliates. He approached Gompers with a plan for holding a gigantic national convention, and when Gompers proved skeptical, resorted to flattery. No man in history, he told him, had a greater opportunity to do good and win glory at the same time. If Gompers refused leadership in a political movement, "the reins will pass to other hands or what is more likely, no reins will be able to control the people."[10] To the rank-and-file Lloyd urged the immediate pursuit of "this new democracy of human welfare" through direct political action on the model of the British Independent Labour party. On the strength of this plea the convention of trade unionists voted to accept his Plank 10 calling for the collective ownership by the people of all means of production and distribution. As the year 1894 opened, Lloyd was convinced that he was on the verge of forging a powerful alliance of farmers and workers, first in Chicago itself, and then within two years in national politics.

Lloyd worked against a background of industrial crisis that followed the Panic of 1893. In the spring of 1894 "General" Jacob Coxey, a small businessman from Massillon, Ohio, set out with his rag-tag "army" for Washington where he hoped to convince Congress to pass a "good roads bill" and provide unemployment relief. Lloyd had little sympathy for Coxey or his futile gesture, and refused to address his "Commonweal" followers in Chicago. He was fascinated but frightened by Eugene Debs's Pullman Strike, which reached a climax in July just as Lloyd and his coalitionists met at an Industrial Conference in Springfield. The whole country, it now seemed, was hellbent on a decline and fall "unless by political means we can remove both such causes and their results."[11]

At the Industrial Conference, called to clear the way for his farmer-labor coalition, Lloyd played his mediator's role to perfection in combining the Omaha Platform of the Populists with a modified version of Plank 10. The sessions in Springfield were nearly as riotous as the Chicago labor scene that summer. The delegates represented every shade of opinion, from the truculence of the United Mine Workers, locked in their battle with the coal operators, to Eugene Debs's American Railway Union and the Knights of Labor; from hard-eyed Populist committeemen to the trade unionists, socialists, Single Taxers, and even the anarchists. The main event at the convention was fought over Plank 10, the socialists' bid for recognition. After a raucous debate punctuated by threats of expulsion and secession, Lloyd finally won acceptance for his own moderate version of the resolution that called for government control of "all such means of production and distribution, including land, as the people elect to operate collectively for the use of all."[12] Here was the formula he recommended henceforth, an American mixed economy of private enterprise and public ownership with the choice between them left to the voters. Following more acrimonious debate, Lloyd's compromise was accepted by a single vote, and the delegates turned to the business of making up a ticket.

The campaign in Chicago that fall was a clamorous one. Populists, unhappy with Plank 10 and fearful of the socialists, provided only grudging support. The socialists, for their part, were determined to keep their doctrine in the center of public attention. Trade unionists, leery of all doctrine and dogma, were more willing to listen to their leaders than to a patrician reformer like Lloyd. For his own symbolic campaign for a congressional seat from the Seventh District of Illinois, Lloyd prepared a manifesto, "The Revolution Is Here," in which he repeated Bellamy's call for counterrevolution. "The revolution has come," he told an overflow crowd at the Central Music Hall. "It is a revolution by which the great combinations, using competition to destroy competition, have monopolized entire markets, and the sole sellers of goods make the people sell themselves cheap." The Labor-Populist party, he reassured his audience, many of whom seemed uncertain, promised a great reversal and re-

ALTERNATIVE AMERICA

turn to the principle that the people "have the right at their option to own and operate collectively any or all means of production, distribution, and exchange." His own Plank 10 proposed just such an act of restoration, and voters now had an effective instrument, a new party to replace the old decrepit ones. "There ought to be two first-class funerals in this country," he concluded to a burst of applause, "and if we do our duty the corpses will be ready on time."[13] Interment would come after the Populists won the presidency in 1896.

Lloyd's plans for a decent burial were interrupted a week later by the arrival of Henry George in Chicago. On October 10, 1894, in the same cavernous Central Music Hall, the Prophet from San Francisco strode to the rostrum to address his Single Taxers, who had also joined Lloyd's Populist-Labor coalition. George, it was rumored, would give his official blessing to two Single Tax candidates running on the Cook County ticket and lend his support to the fragile reform coalition.

George confounded his followers. Populism, he announced, was a matter of supreme indifference to him. The Populist scheme for a national subtreasury was collectivist and would bring the government into every aspect of people's lives. None of the other demands of the People's party even touched the problem of modern America—land monopoly. The Single Tax, on the contrary, was not a makeshift program but a regenerative creed, and the proof of his own success was, not votes or officeholders, but the progress of the cause which gained new adherents every day. Refusing to support the two Single Taxers from Cook County, he treated his listeners instead to another sermon on the gospel according to St. George.

George's appearance in Chicago as spoiler of Populist dreams marked the terminal point in his retreat from third-party politics. The seven years since his defeat in the state elections of 1887 had witnessed a steady drift from political insurgency to fundamentalist preaching. Following his clash with New York socialists he began to make overtures to a resurgent Democratic party, agreeing to write a tract on free trade for Grover Cleveland's candidacy and publicly applauding his severely limited philosophy of government. In 1888 he made a hurried trip to England, his fourth, and the next year another tour of the British Isles, culminating in Scotland where his denunciations of landlordism were both timely and popular. Elsewhere his appeal was chiefly to a lower middle class frightened equally of socialism, labor politics, and finance capitalism. Sidney Webb, the founder and guiding spirit of Fabianism, acknowledged George's continuing usefulness and described for him the kind of audience on which he made the greatest impression—"the great mass of middle class, religious, 'respectable,' cautious, & disliking the Radical artisan."[14] It was this unleavened lump of social feeling that Webb recommended to him in warning against engaging in unseemly altercation with the few socialist agitators in every crowd.

George performed as directed, donning his prophet's robes and delivering ringing Single Tax sermons variously titled "Thy Kingdom Come" and "Thou Shalt Not Steal" to the Scottish Land Restoration League and other land reform societies. His evangelical style perfectly suited his simple message that men must work for the coming kingdom. "This world—God's world—is not the kind of world in which the repeating of words will get waggons out of the mire or poverty out of the slums." His format varied little now—a reading of the text followed by the lesson which consisted of the fatherhood of God, the brotherhood of man, and the Single Tax.

In New York once more, before setting out in the other direction on a triumphal tour of New Zealand and Australia, he continued to narrow his reform program to three simple demands that appeared boxed on the front page of each issue of the *Standard*:

THE SINGLE TAX. This means the abolition of all taxes on the products of labor, that is to say, the abolition of all taxes save one tax on the value of land irrespective of improvements.

FREE TRADE. Not "tariff reform" but real free trade; that is, as perfect freedom of trade with all the world as now exists between the states of our union.

BALLOT REFORM. No humbug envelope system; but the real Australian system, the first requisite to which is the exclusive use in elections of official ballots furnished by the state and prepared and cast by the voter in compulsory secrecy.

His original analysis, first put forward in the magisterial *Progress and Poverty* and extended in *Social Problems*, had now been reduced to a simple credo.

Taking Annie with him, George sailed for Australia and New Zealand in 1890, stopping in San Francisco long enough to address a wildly cheering crowd and assure his followers of the imminent triumph of his great truth. Then on to New Zealand for a series of gratifying receptions and a talk with his early admirer, the ageing Sir George Grey, and to Australia for an extended tour that took him from Sydney to Victoria to Adelaide. The adulation he received was gratifying, and he responded with appropriate modesty, telling audiences that "if it has been given to me to help forward a great movement—it is through no merit of mine . . . it is from the simple fact that, seeing a great truth, I swore to follow it."[15]

Australia and New Zealand gave George the clear sense of a second chance for mankind. If the Scottish crofters and Irish peasants were the victims of an old society, the Antipodes offered a last frontier where his Single Tax might still do its work before it was too late—vast open lands where regular settlement patterns, steady economic growth, scaled communities, and cooperative individualism would naturally follow from the enactment of his single reform. In old countries like England, France, and even the United States it might well be too late to reverse the direction of a providential history pushing their peoples toward the abyss. This was the message of "The Warning of the English Strikes," an article on the London Dock Strike he wrote for the *North American Review*. Dockside London was the best place in the civilized world to study the tendencies of the modern age. With Haymarket a recent memory, George warned readers against the day when "the policeman refuses to club and the soldier to shoot the men to whom they are bound not merely by human but by class sympathy." He reminded American workingmen once again that unions were not the answer to the problems of industrial society. "I believe, as I have never neglected an opportunity of telling workingmen, that trades-unions can accomplish nothing large and permanent, and the method of raising wages by strikes is the method of main strength and stupidity."[16]

By 1890 George's identification with the middle class was complete, and a new defensiveness settled on him as he sought to meet attacks on his program from both right and left. In two works written before his appearance in Chicago in 1894—*The Condition of Labor, an Open Letter to Pope Leo XIII* (1891) and *A Perplexed Philosopher* (1892)—he defended the Single Tax against charges of atheism and the more serious challenges of secularism and relativism.

In 1891 Pope Leo XIII issued his famous encyclical *Rerum Novarum* which, while acknowledging the social and economic dislocation brought by the industrial revolution, warned the faithful against materialism, labor unions, strikes, and all other heretical ideas and practices. Although nowhere in the encyclical did Leo mention the Single Tax, George immediately concluded that the papal condemnation was "aimed at us, and at us alone, almost."[17] The Pope and his advisers, it appeared, had been grievously misinformed and would have to be disabused of their error. All social questions, he argued in *The Condition of Labor*, were at bottom religious ones, and he had always defended the Single Tax on the grounds of Christian ethics. Far from preaching atheism, communism, socialism, or anarchism, as the Pope implied, he had sought and found a wholly Christian solution. The heart of his defense was the argument that the Single Tax represented a golden mean between competing isms. Socialists, he agreed with His Holiness, were very apt to be "animated by a blind hatred of the rich and a fierce desire to destroy existing social adjustments." Yet poised on the other flank of society were the reactionaries and the anarchists, who insisted that no social improvement was needed. If the socialists were bent on building a giant bureaucracy and restricting individual liberties, the reactionaries and the anarchists preached no government at all and courted chaos. Only his Single Tax avoided these dangerous extremes, a fact which the Pope should consider in welcoming it as true Christian doctrine.

The other face of Nemesis for George was modernism and the ethical relativism it encouraged. To do battle with this monster, the following year he singled out Herbert Spencer for a savage attack which he entitled *A Perplexed Philosopher*. To George, Spencer appeared the supreme turncoat, a moralist with a firm grounding in natural law, who had jumped sides and joined the enemy. Twenty-five years earlier George had read *Social Statics* with wonder at the clarity of Spencer's argument for nationalizing land. *Social Statics* was still being reviewed on both sides of the Atlantic in the eighties, and it was frequently coupled with *Progress and Poverty* as an attack on land monopoly. Spencer, increasingly uncomfortable with the pairing, sought to extricate himself in a revised edition by removing his earlier, more radical, views on land nationalization. This change of heart—or failure of nerve, as George thought it—together with his pointed snubbing of George, were reasons enough for a relentless but tedious assault on the aging philosopher.

Ostensibly his reason for attacking Spencer was the Englishman's supposed cowardice in selling out to the landlords. For Browning's handful of silver Spencer had "disemboweled, stuffed, mummified" his first edition and set it up in the gardens of Spencerian philosophy "where it may be viewed with entire complacency by Sir John and his Grace."[18] But George's real target was not the act of betrayal but the original Synthetic Philosophy itself, "the most pretentious that ever mortal man undertook." Spencer's thought, he charged, was all matter, force, motion, stasis, heterogeneity, and homogeneity, his analysis one huge jumble of concepts borrowed from the science of mechanics. How could anyone derive a true system of ethics from such a materialist muddle? No absolutes, no standards, no deductive logic, no proper relationships, no lasting truth! "Try Herbert Spencer by the ideas that he once held—the idea of a Living God, whose creatures we are, and the idea of a divine order, to which we are bound to conform. Or try him now by what he professes— the idea that we are but the evolutionary results of the integration of matter and motion."[19] Spencer assumed that all government could ultimately be dispensed with. To limit the competence of the state to interfere in the lives of its citizens, as George himself sought to do, was one thing; to eliminate it altogether was to return to the jungle. Spencer's suicidal individualism was no improvement on socialism. Resting as both did on a godless materialism, they presented a choice between autocracy and anarchism.[20]

At the annual meeting of the American Social Science Association in 1890 the gap between George and a younger generation of reformers and intellectuals became an impassable breach.[21] The featured event at the meetings at Saratoga was a debate between the prophet and his critics. On one side of the stage sat George and his disciple, William Lloyd Garrison, Jr., on the other two academicians, Edmund James, professor of economics at the University of Pennsylvania, and the peppery Edwin R. A. Seligman of Columbia, twenty-nine years old, self-assured, and inclined to be ruthless with those he considered cranks and charlatans. In the moderator's chair sat Benjamin Andrews of Brown, sympathetic with George's moral zeal but skeptical of his antiquated assumptions. The contestants at Saratoga stood on opposing sides of a metaphysical great divide, a chasm separating the amateur defenders of natural law from the professional proponents of instrumentalism. Seligman called across this gulf in his opening remarks. There were economists, he began, who were protectionists and others who were marginalists and still others who were socialists. But there was not a single trained economist of any reputation who espoused the Single Tax. In all of the other modern sciences—biology, chemistry, astronomy, physics—the trained specialist reigned supreme. But in economics anyone with a smattering of misinformation and a few "lopsided ideas" could set up as an expert.

The professors had calculated their opponent's boiling point correctly. George rose with fire in his eyes, his beard quivering with rage. Macaulay was right, he drawled. If it paid to deny the law of gravity, then the professoriate would deny it to this day. If the common man could no longer study political economy—"the science whose phenomena lie all about us in our daily lives"—then the republic was doomed. Suppose his Single Tax was wrong, what did his high-and-mighty opponents have to replace it? "If our remedy will not do, what is your remedy?" The choice, he insisted, was clear: "You must choose between the single tax, with its recognition of the rights of the individual . . . and socialism."

In juxtaposing the world of the fathers and the Progressive generation's pragmatic one, George brought out his convictions for final inspection. To him the argument for the interventionist state was anathema. What did all of Seligman's schemes for tinkering with the economy add up to? "More restrictions, more interference, more extensions of government into the individual field, more organization of class against class, more bars to liberty of the citizen." As he prepared to yield the floor he shouted a final word of warning, pointing his finger at Seligman, his face dark with anger. In rejecting the Single Tax for the milksop socialism of tax reform the academicians were only making the "fight in the dark" inevitable.

In his rebuttal Seligman warned against the man with an ism, the purveyor of fictions. "But when you come to us with a tale that is as old as the hills," he retorted, looking directly at George, "when you set forth in your writings doctrines that have long been exploded, when you in the innocence of your enthusiasm seek to impose upon us a remedy which appears to us as unjust as it is one-sided, as illogical as it is inequitable, we have a right to protest."

Beneath the collision of personalities between a brash young professional and a stubborn, tired preacher lay the deeper meaning of the exchange, which was a generational conflict between the formalist and the historicist. George's terms were "wealth," "justice," "progress"; Seligman's "value," "price," "market," "state." George wanted to secure universal equality at a stroke; Seligman, to correct imbalances and distribute income. George knew he had in hand the single instrument for fashioning a just world; Seligman and his colleagues were willing to experiment with a wide range of devices for checking inequities. Finally, "truth" for the new economists was what appeared to work, however partially. For George truth was what correct reasoning uncovered: if a proposition was generally intelligible and logically consistent, it was "true." Truth for the moral imagination like George's inhered in the relationship between human reason and a transcendent order. When, at Saratoga and again four years later in his speech to Lloyd's farmer-laborites, he spoke of the "science of political economy," he meant a set of self-evident principles, a sequence of simple steps leading straight to the distant point in a golden haze where the real and the ideal, theory and practice, reason and revelation finally converged.

Henry Demarest Lloyd stood halfway between George's world of the fathers and the Progressive generation's instrumentalist one. While he shared the older man's passion for ethics, he also knew that these Christian values had to be harnessed to a more sophisticated understanding of the social process. It was not simply land and land monopoly that accounted for the sins of corporate capitalism, he was convinced, and in clinging to this notion George was hopelessly anachronistic. George could identify "neither the cause nor the cure." His Single Tax would have the unintended effect of shifting the possession of land to those who had the money to pay taxes. George's doctrine was a chimera, the last desperate attempt of a "commerce crazy" civilization to solve the problem of business cycles. George's misplaced confidence in the middle class, moreover, made no sense to Lloyd. "Our bourgeoisie do not care how or where things are made, so long as by swapping them" the individual might be "free" to get rich "at the cost of poverty to others."[22] With George's assumptions, Lloyd concluded, a debased romantic individualism was headed toward bankruptcy, and the prophet's unwelcome appearance in Chicago in 1894 only proved how much of a nuisance he had become.

George's disruption of the plans of the farmer-laborites at Chicago's Central Music Hall was only the beginning of Lloyd's troubles. When a saving remnant of Single Taxers decided to organize independently of the Illinois Populists and to field their own candidates, George agreed to come and lend support. Presently his followers banded together with the leadership of the Illinois Federation of Labor, never sympathetic to socialism, and demolished Plank 10. By election time Lloyd's original coalition was barely holding together.

Lloyd poured both money and energy into his risky venture, paying the party's printing bills, hiring halls for meetings, and volunteering his services as speaker. Underfinanced, inexperienced, their ranks riddled with dissension, the farmer-laborites marched bravely through Chicago's Loop on election eve on their way to a "monster" rally on the South Side. There some 15,000 diehard enthusiasts heard the Reverend W. H. Carwardine on the meaning of the Pullman Strike, Tommy Morgan on the meaning of socialism, and, late in the evening, Lloyd on the meaning of his producerist "people's syndicate."

Despite his efforts the results of the election in Cook County were not encouraging. Lloyd's coalition of farmers and workers garnered between 30,000 and 40,000 votes countywide, but in none of the wards did their vote reach 2,000, and in only seven wards did it amount to half of that. In his own race for a congressional seat Lloyd, as expected, ran strongest among his fellow suburbanites on the North Shore, but his too was a token figure. The totals in 1894 did not augur well for the future of American Fabianism.

This, at any rate, was the opinion of liberal lawyer Clarence Darrow, who wrote to Lloyd of his disappointment. Darrow interpreted the election figures as a prediction of disaster should the Populists continue to ally themselves with Chicago's socialists. Already, he reported, there were rumblings of discontent among the farmers downstate, who regretted the whole venture and were determined to eliminate Cook County influence from now on. Darrow added that he, for one, was unwilling "to help run another Socialist movement under the guise of 'The People's Party.'" Lloyd was unmoved. His modified version of Plank 10, he replied, provided the only sensible solution to the country's industrial ills. Chicago, moreover, served as a beacon for the rest of the nation, "the intellectual and political leader of the movement," launched by the socialists. Besides, there were no other alternatives. To regroup his forces he proposed a national conference of reformers of every persuasion. "But if we begin to read each other out of the ranks for differences of opinion, we are lost."[23]

By the time Lloyd and Darrow had composed their differences, serious trouble had arisen on another front as conservative Populists, their eyes already fixed on "fusion" with the Democrats on the silver issue, pulled out of the coalition. But the balance against Lloyd was tipped by organized labor itself at the annual convention of the AF of L late in 1894, when trade unionists, following a bitter floor fight, struck Plank 10 out of their platform and read Tommy Morgan's socialists out of the national organization. To complete the disaster, the socialists began to squabble among themselves, splitting into a Marxist wing led by Morgan and a moderate group headed by Lloyd, who founded a Fabian Club in Chicago to appeal to middle-class civic reformers. These friends assured him that his moderate socialism was acceptable to most American liberals, but they added that "there is another degree of socialism for which the American people are not ready, and which has cost the reform movement unmeasured losses for having to carry it." This was the frightening appeal to class and confiscation which the American people found unacceptable. "In other words, the American people can tolerate the socialism of its Lloyds, its Bellamys ... Anything more radical they will not. At least for a time."[24]

Such views strengthened Lloyd's decision to distance himself from the Marxist wing and concentrate on joining middle-class municipal reformers and the advocates of public ownership and management. The first order of business, he told President Benjamin Andrews of Brown, was the "municipalizing of all public services, monopolies ... and the municipal employment of the unemployed."[25] With this as his platform he plunged into the municipal campaign in Chicago in 1895, calling for public ownership of all of the city's utilities, a city-owned elevated system for the Loop, a more equitable tax assessment system, and extension of the merit system to Chicago police and employees of City Hall.[26] His program was virtually indistinguishable from that of young urban progressives, a resemblance he happily acknowledged in hailing the Civic Federation of Chicago as one of Fabianism's surest allies.

Lloyd's political instrument in this revised version of Populism was the concept of nonpartisan, direct citizen participation. Ideas which were still obscure while he researched and wrote *Wealth Against Commonwealth* grew suddenly clear: municipalization and direct democracy; citizen involvement and community management; humanly scaled towns and regional cities; open government, initiative, referendum and recall, and all the other devices for revitalizing local government by returning it to the people. With the examples of Fabianism in England and the encouragement of reform enthusiasts like Albert Shaw in the United States, Lloyd began to pull together the strands of his philosophy of a "middle way" between Marxist socialism and corporate capitalism.

These achievements came at the cost of deepening political isolation. By 1896 he had outdistanced all of his colleagues in the Populist movement and was virtually without a following. In the municipal elections in Chicago in 1895 his candidates won exactly 12,308 votes to 102,000 for the Democrats and 143,000 for the victorious Republicans, both of whom cheerfully denounced all "socialist Ideas" and ridiculed their champion, the "great socialist leader, Mr. Lloyd." In the months between his Chicago defeat and the debacle at the Populist convention in the summer of 1896, Lloyd continued to defend his plan for a national coalition of farmers and workers against growing opposition as party leaders plotted to rejoin the Democrats. The irony of fusion did not escape him: "If we fuse, we are sunk; if we don't fuse, all the silver men we have will leave us for the more powerful Democrats."[27] He dismissed free silver as fantasy, the illusion that "there could be a social reform brought about by money reform alone." For him the silver issue was symbolic, not substantive, a sign of agrarian discontent but not the root cause of the farmer's distress. The real problem he diagnosed as credit and banking, which ought to be left to localities and regions. "If Chicago could be induced to adopt a financial system which should make bank failures for ever impossible, and relieve business men of the terrors of bank contraction and the oppression of money lenders, and by municipal ownership, etc. give productive employment to every competent man and woman, Chicago would become the financial, industrial, social and moral mistress of the world."[28]

Lloyd argued against the silverites by insisting that genuine monetary reform would have to begin with the demonetizing of both gold and silver and the substitution of paper money, termination of the policy of cash redemption, an improved system of credit, and the abolition of all monopolies. Detached from this network of reforms, he insisted, free silver made no sense. For the persistence of this delusion he blamed the national leadership of the People's party, opportunists like Herman Taubeneck, the national chairman, who lacked the nerves and brains for undertaking real reform. Once more in history the people were ripening for reform faster than their leaders. If the People's party failed, it would be because it lacked the "intuitive sense of right" that moved the American masses.[29]

Lloyd's mood darkened as the presidential campaign of 1896 approached. Reformers like himself, he realized, were being tossed overboard by the trimmers who counseled fusion and free silver. "The men in the movement of the PP who are specially and bitterly and traiterously [sic] opposed to the real issues now before the public are the ones who have fanned this free silver backfire," he fumed. Instead of fighting monopoly and promoting public ownership, the pseudo-Populists were playing directly into the hands of the enemy. Still, he believed that his Fabian alternative might survive the assaults of the professionals at the national convention. He came east to New York for a hurried conference to plan a "United Front" of true producers. He helped subsidize a new labor newspaper that was backing Eugene Debs for President. He conferred with Victor Berger in Milwaukee on ways to halt the further corruption of Populism, "which I think is already underway." As the convention date neared he grew convinced that the leadership had already sold out to the silverites and that he had on his hands still another lost cause.[30]

In spite of his growing sense of defeat, he agreed to attend the People's party convention in St. Louis even though William Jennings Bryan had already been nominated by the Democrats and fusion appeared a foregone conclusion. Preparing to meet the inevitable head-on, he drew up what he boasted to his friends was "the most aggressive possible revision of the Omaha Platform," one that tacked back on its planks demanding government ownership of monopolies.[31] As he had foreseen, he was treated as the pariah of the Populist convention, isolated and shunned. The chairman of the convention frankly told him that he would never be recognized from the podium. His public ownership plank was quickly discarded by the Platform Committee, which proceeded to call for fusion and free silver. On the convention floor the fusionists presented their committee's handiwork, called the previous question, and rammed the majority report through without debate. Even then Lloyd refused to give in, and vainly tried for recognition from the chair until it was clear that he had no chance. Finally, having lost the platform fight and been denied his right to protest, he announced that "the Cause is lost" and went home to Winnetka.[32]

There, casting up his political accounts, he made a prediction and an accusation. Populism, he declared, would soon be the "veriform appendix" of the Democratic party as all genuine reformers abandoned it. As for the silver-mining millionaire who had taken over the Populist party, he was the "cow-bird of American politics" who had settled into the reformers' nest "in order that he may use these reformatory movements to enrich himself at the expense of his dupes and victims."[33] Privately he admitted to Richard T. Ely that the convention had been "the most discouraging experience in my life."[34] Once before, nearly a quarter of a century earlier, he had witnessed a similar debacle at the Liberal Republican convention, and as a confident young reformer had vowed to keep fighting for power without obligation. Then he had been sanguine, energetic, and ambitious. Now he was nearing fifty, with none of the resilience or the illusions he had once possessed.

14

THE ADVERSARY TRADITION

By 1896 the arcadian world of Bellamy, George, and Lloyd lay in disarray. Their pastoral realm—that jointly occupied middle country of the social imagination—was being invaded and overrun by the armies of modernism. The utopians appeared to stand now on the far side of an intellectual watershed, in a pastoral landscape from which they called in vain for the intellectual reserves with which to confront a younger generation of Progressives armed with new concepts of indeterminacy and interdependence. Increasingly it seemed that the three utopians had discovered a momentary refuge only in the simplicities of their pastoral vision, and that as the nineteenth century wound down their historical moment was passing.

Politics seemingly confirmed the verdict of history, as the defeat of William Jennings Bryan collapsed their project for building an alternative America. Lloyd and Bellamy fought heroically for the People's party until it became clear that fusion and free silver had betrayed their hopes for a new politics. Henry George's loyalty to the Single Tax confirmed him in his opposition to the Populists and what he considered their half-baked proposals. Yet despite their different stances, all three men recognized the Republican victory in 1896 as a mortal blow to their reform program. As the year 1897 opened, Populism was dead, the Democracy defeated, and the adversary tradition the reformers shared moribund. Utopianism had reached the end of the road.

Populism, like the three reformers and their oppositional culture, had emerged from nineteenth-century millennialism. Like the utopians, too, the Populists dreamed of a world of harmony lying beyond the reach of grasping politicians, a loving community of innocents where cooperation flourished and good men prospered. Theirs too was an arcadian view of the world in which cause and effect were readily identifiable, social relations were simple, personal responsibility clear, and final redemption assured. The Populist crusade, carrying the utopians' banner into electoral battle, was the last major attempt to recapture this lost American community before it was destroyed by corporate capitalism.

Populism was more than a set of economic demands made by a hard-pressed interest group. Beneath the secular issues of relief and recovery lay the bedrock of a pietist culture that was formulated for agrarians and urban workers alike by the three utopian theorists. In their shared vision, righteousness, once truly apprehended, would continue to guide God's chosen away from the confusions and disorders of modern life to a pastoral realm where community still survived. The political task that the utopians assigned their followers involved more than unseating Republicans and Democrats, more than passing wise and reasonable legislation. At bottom, Populism meant, as one of its converts explained, the hope of "realizing and incarnating in the lives of common people the fulness of the divinity of humanity."

In the presidential campaign of 1896 the Populists divided, and their legacy, much diminished, fell to the Democratic party. Still, Bryan upheld the millennial faith, barnstorming the Great Plains and the South as the avenging angel of the yeomanry, preaching at every whistle-stop the same sermon filled with prophecy and indictments of monopoly and modernism and confirming his followers' beliefs in hard work and the just reward. William McKinley's strategy was the exact opposite, the clever contrivance of a younger breed of Republican managers—secular, pragmatic, shrewd, and occasionally cynical. The Republicans flooded the country with a new kind of materialist propaganda, appealing, not to fears of apocalypse, but to hard cash interests, ethnic diversity, and religious tolerance, as their party threw off the mantle of pietism it had worn since Lincoln's day.

The election results confirmed the soundness of Republican tactics. With 271 electoral votes to 176, McKinley soundly defeated his pietist opponent. The meaning of his victory seemed clear: the countercrusade for community had failed. There would be other reform attempts in the twentieth century, but they would be the result, not so much of an urge for perfection and purity, as an accommodation to pluralism and pragmatism. The election of 1896 proved beyond question that the forces of corporate capitalism that were revolutionizing the rest of American life had now triumphed at the polls. The golden day of the utopians was over.

The election of 1896 brought Henry George home to the Democratic party for good. Since campaigning half-heartedly for Cleveland four years earlier, he had continued to oppose the Populists and their "patchwork" program, and he confessed to a distinct lack of enthusiasm for William Jennings Bryan and free silver. Thus it was not a very optimistic observer that William Randolph Hearst sent to St. Louis to cover the Democratic Convention for his New York *Journal.* George could manage little more than a lukewarm endorsement of the Great Commoner who did not represent his views.

As the campaign reached its peak in October, however, George grew reconciled to and then openly supportive of Bryan, and agreed to invite the Illinois Democrat ex-Governor John P. Altgeld to speak in New York City. His new enthusiasm caused consternation among his more committed Single Tax followers, who deplored what seemed to them their leader's defection from the ranks of purity. To these and other critics George replied with the kind of advice he had avoided taking all his life, reminding them that the upcoming election would prove the most momentous since 1860 and warning them against concentrating exclusively on the shortcomings of the Democratic party. There was only one question before the American people in 1896, he declared, and that was the issue of monopoly. Even Bryan could see that. To bolster his convictions he took to reading a new edition of Jefferson's letters.

Henry George in old age.

Henry Demarest Lloyd at the turn of the century.

George was fifty-eight in 1896, worn out from ten years of constant traveling and sermonizing and now in rapidly failing health. Six years earlier he had suffered a stroke that left him with temporary asphasia and permanently slowed responses. He had always been notoriously forgetful, but recently he had grown more abstracted than ever, sure to lose his way, or arrive at the wrong time and leave his hat in the bargain. His lapses were a source of much glee for him and of deepening concern to Annie. They lived on Nineteenth Street until 1895, when they rented an old farmhouse at Fort Hamilton, high on the bluffs overlooking the Narrows between the upper and lower bays. The following year a gift of the land and a bequest from an English admirer enabled him to buy his first home. The old Federalist-style farmhouse built nearly a century earlier, with its pillared porch, wide windows, and latticework fence enclosing a yard filled with giant elms and fruit trees, must have seemed the haven from the world he had first dreamed of as a struggling young apprentice. In an upstairs study filled with bookcases and old furniture, including his horsehair couch, he worked in fits and starts at the book which he hoped would be his masterpiece, the grand synthesis of the science of political economy and worthy successor to *Progress and Poverty*. But the sprawling manuscript defied all attempts to impose order on it and remained a collection of unfinished sections, bits of personal history, and disjointed fragments. Though he was driven by the compulsion to finish it, George nevertheless welcomed the frequent interruptions from neighbors and the narrowing circle of friends from the city, and meanwhile pondered the works of Jefferson.

Covering the presidential campaign and churning out articles and reports for the New York *Journal* had exhausted him. In the spring of 1897 he nearly collapsed, and bouts of nausea and dizziness made sustained work on his manuscript impossible. To his doctors, who urged him to take a lengthy vacation, he replied, "I must finish the book before anything else."[1] Often now he read aloud and was sometimes overheard murmuring to himself the lines from Browning's "Rabbi Ben Ezra":

Grow old with me!
The best is yet to be,
The last of life, for which the first was made:

Our times are in his hand
Who saith, "A whole I planned,
Youth shows but half; trust God: see all, nor be afraid!"

He spoke of death—his own, Annie's—frequently. One night when Annie appeared in the doorway of his study interrupting one of his meditations, he rose from the couch and began pacing the room as he explained to her his thoughts. "The great, the very great advancement of our ideas, may not show now, but it will. And it will show more after my death than during my life . . . Neither of us can tell which of us will die first. But I shall be greatly disappointed if you precede me, for I have set my heart on having you hear what men will say of me and our cause when I am gone."[2]

George wanted his reputation to rest, not simply on *Progress and Poverty*, which lay nearly two decades behind him now, but on the giant synthesis of political economy on which he had been working fitfully for a half-dozen years and which perversely resisted all his efforts to finish it. Always there had come the need to set it aside for the quick article or the hastily assembled lecture. The "Grand Divisions" of his book, as he called them, were deceptively clear: an opening definition of terms, a lengthy discussion of the nature of wealth, another on its production and distribution, and a section on money and monetary theory. But the power to shape and connect, so evident in the pages of *Progress and Poverty*, he no longer possessed. What remained were fragments—a few analytical passages that sparkled with the old clarity and a great many more extended examples, a random collection of anecdotes and autobiographical material, and a loose set of arguments. George's friends were sympathetic while he lived and embarrassed when after his death his son published the work under the title *The Science of Political Economy*.

George intended his last book as a summation of the producerist faith. The argumentative unity, which he glimpsed but failed to catch and hold, comes from the confrontation of two traditions of political economy that had originated in the eighteenth century and steadily diverged in the nineteenth until they warred openly for the allegiance of the American people. The first tradition George defined as the received wisdom of the ruling classes that runs from Adam Smith through the errors of Malthus and Ricardo to the absurdities of modern academic economists. George's countertradition—the producerist canon—also issues from the eighteenth century in the natural law tracts of Thomas Spence, Patrick Dove, and William Oglivie; is briefly glimpsed in the early work of Herbert Spencer; and reaches its culminating statement in his own *Progress and Poverty*.

The account of these two traditions gives *The Science of Political Economy* the unity its author only partially discerned. Read as a massive producerist tract, the book tells of the creation of the "Greater Leviathan" lying beneath Hobbes's political state—the natural community in which men satisfy their wants by making and trading. George's primary man, once again, is the instinctive producer, and his system is an evolutionary Christian one in which reason and divine will gradually combine to unfold history and with it the perfect social order. The fundamental premise in George's producerist political economy is the rule that "men always seek to gratify their desires with the least exertion," a wholesome urge which propels them toward voluntary cooperation and the creation of real value. Just as there are two conflicting versions of political economy, George insists, so there are two kinds of value proceeding from them. There is a "value from obligation" and a more important "value from production." The first amounts to sheer privilege unredeemed by work of any kind, simply the power to require "the rendering of exertion without the return of exertion." Value from obligation cannot measure wealth or enrich the community. Value from production, on the contrary, results from the labor of men who work with their own hands and minds and add to the communal stockpile of the Greater Leviathan.[3] Labor and the men who perform it, readers are not surprised to learn, are the only creators of value.

Once he had secured the theoretical foundations for his producerist summary, George intended to extend the dual method of matching opposites by distinguishing between two kinds of cooperation, the forced cooperation from "without" exacted by privilege and monopoly, and a higher, natural cooperation from "within" which is the spontaneous act of true producers.[4] Beneath the cluttered surface of *The Science of Political Economy* lay a binary system of paired types of societies—one false, the other true—and the opposing political economies each generates. In rough outline George's last book was both a sequel and a worthy successor to *Progress and Poverty*.

In the spring of 1897 George's married daughter Jennie, who was visiting with her son, died suddenly and left him grief-stricken and unable to work. He was just recovering when a group of New York City's reform Democrats who had voted for Bryan approached him with a request that he enter his second New York mayoral race in their behalf. At first George, who knew how ill he was, refused to consider their proposition. This time there would be no chance whatever of election. Both parties were divided. Progressive Republicans were running their candidate, Seth Low, president of Columbia, against "Easy Boss" Platt's handpicked Benjamin Tracy. Tammany, as usual, had tapped a machine regular, Judge Robert Van Wyck, who was accorded the best chance of winning. Agreeing to run under these circumstances, George realized, was at best a symbolic and possibly a suicidal act. His doctors were vehement in their opposition and tried to enlist Annie, who, though apprehensive herself, replied that her husband "must live his life in his own way." A friend, Dr. M. R. Leverson, recalled the following conversation:

> "Tell me: If I accept, what is the worst that can happen to me?"
> I answered: "Since you ask, you have the right to be told. It will most probably be fatal."
> He said: "You mean it might kill me?"
> "Most probably, yes."
> "Dr. Kelly says the same thing, only more positively. But I have got to die. How can I die better than serving humanity? Besides, so dying will do more for the cause than anything I am likely to be able to do in the rest of my life."[5]

As his manuscript continued to baffle his attempts to complete it, the idea of a sacrifice, one that would turn present futility into future triumph, became more and more inviting.

Still, he did not agree to accept the nomination until early October, which left him less than a month in which to campaign. In his acceptance speech at Cooper Union a haggard, ashen-faced candidate, who had nearly fainted on his way to the platform, invoked the example of Jefferson. He began with a familiar disclaimer: he had not sought the nomination in any way, but he believed with the Sage of Monticello that no citizen could ignore the call of the people to serve them. It was Jefferson's precept shining down through the century that prompted him now in the last dark days of the Republic to take up the cause of the American producer. Bryan's recent defeat, he continued, had meant the loss of "everything for which the fathers had stood, of everything that makes this country loved by us, hopeful for the future." Alexander Hamilton, the mortal enemy of Jefferson and democracy, would win out at last unless confronted by the will of the people. "You ask me to raise the standard again; to stand for that great cause. I accept."[6]

The words were in place, but the spark to ignite the campaign was lacking. George provided the name of the party—"The Party of Thomas Jefferson"—and wrote its simple platform that consisted of tax reform, home rule, and municipal ownership. In the three weeks that remained to him he went through the motions of campaigning, but neither his mind nor his heart was in it. Annie noted with alarm his increasing self-absorption and commented on the loss of his old fire. "No," he agreed, "little of the old-time enthusiasm. Perhaps it is that with success, such has come to our cause, the mind advances to the contemplation of other things."[7]

The end came on October 28th. That day his campaign managers scheduled five appearances for a candidate whom they knew had been pushed beyond the limits of endurance. To a group of followers at Whitestone he spoke at length, promising to restore the Democracy of Jefferson. At College Point, some hours later, another audience heard him deny that he had ever been a special friend of labor, indeed deny that the American workingman needed anything more than an equal chance to get ahead. By the time he spoke at Flushing he was visibly exhausted and shambled on stage, stopping at its edge to lift his right arm as if in salute to the balcony for what seemed an interminable moment only to let it fall heavily as his chin sank on his chest. Presently he roused himself and called out: "I have only time to come, take a look at you and go away." The final appearance of the evening was at the Central Opera House in Manhattan, where he rallied his strength for a rambling, occasionally incoherent speech that distressed his audience. Then a midnight supper at the Union Square Hotel, after which he and Annie retired to their suite upstairs. In the early morning hours Annie awoke to find him in the adjoining parlor, standing rigid behind a chair, his hands locked to its back, his face ashen, eyes staring into space as he repeated, at first softly and then with increasing force, "Yes . . . yes . . . yes . . . yes." By morning he was dead.[8]

All day the following Sunday his body lay in state at the Grand
Central Palace as an estimated 50,000 mourners passed by. After a
brief service, the long procession, following a double line of led
horses pulling the hearse, crossed Brooklyn Bridge and brought him
home to his family.

In November 1897 Edward Bellamy had less than six months to
live. The condition of his lungs had deteriorated steadily since the
illness that had forced him to give up the *New Nation*, and recently he
had developed a choking cough that made sustained work on his
book nearly impossible. "If God will spare my life a year longer," he
told Emma, "I think I can do the best work I have ever done." Visitors usually found him at his desk working feverishly on a draft of
Equality and scribbling corrections in his indecipherable hand. By act
of will he staved off physical collapse until he had finished the proofs
and then agreed to go to Denver where the higher altitude might
conceivably improve his condition. Once again money was a problem. Henry Demarest Lloyd visited him briefly before Bellamy left
for Denver and reported to a friend that he had spent a "delightful
time" in Chicopee Falls although he had been struck with the family's extremely frugal circumstances. Lloyd inquired among mutual
friends about the possibility of a testimonial, and when word
reached him of the attempt, Bellamy was nettled. "As to Lloyd's idea
of a testimonial it is well intended," he admitted to Mason Green,
"but of course I don't want it, either in words, still less in cash . . . I
shall be deeply mortified by anything of the sort. I would rather
tramp for a living than have it done or even talked about."[9] Anyway,
he grumbled, the royalties from his new book ought to be sufficient
to pay the bills.

Populism had transformed Bellamy's ideas. The excitement of
political campaigning and the experience of democracy in action had
combined to alter his values. There is no democracy in *Looking Backward*. In *Equality*, the revised version of utopia that was both a sequel
and a corrective, "the people hold the reins of power" through frequent elections and the devices of referendum and recall. To sym-
bolize this new relationship between the people and their government, Bellamy used the figure of the windmill in place of the original
stagecoach metaphor. "The mill stands for the machinery of admin-

istration, the wind that drives it symbolizes the public will, and the rudder . . . stands for the method by which the administration is kept at all times responsive and obedient to every mandate of the people."[10]

An unbroken connection between administrators and their masters in *Equality* makes American government an ongoing town meeting, as decisionmaking is dispersed out of metropolitan centers to the periphery, which is dotted with towns and villages where direct democracy has become a habit. Representation in the year 2000 is less important than the "exhilaration of conducting affairs directly." The setting for this new participatory democracy is the ring of localities clustered around the central city as satellites in a confederation of regional polities, each of them largely self-sufficient. "The country," according to Dr. Leete, "is divided into industrial districts or circles, in each of which there is intended to be as nearly as possible a complete system of industry, wherein all the important arts and occupations are represented." Not the least of the advantages of this economic arrangement is the opportunity it affords all citizens to find work "without separation from friends."

At the furthest remove from the villages that coalesce in regional groupings is a national government presumably rationalized, as in *Looking Backward*, along bureaucratic lines—efficient and impersonal. In *Equality*, however, this national administration is ignored as Bellamy concentrates on the more immediate reality of neighborhoods, where members of the "middle power" still hold their stake in society, although no one feels it necessary any longer to assert an absolute right of ownership. Abundance is automatic, and private possessions largely superfluous. Bellamy is no longer concerned with the specifics of production and distribution, which he dismisses with the image of a huge conveyor belt carrying raw materials to the doors of the factory on one side to be mysteriously transformed within and emerge as finished consumer goods on the other. Utopian factories are briefly described in mid-nineteenth-century terms as "lofty, airy halls, walled with beautiful designs in tiles and metals, furnished like palaces" and set in sylvan retreats outside the cities.

By the twenty-first century, accordingly, the industrial city has become a casualty of history. Once the need for central markets has been eliminated by an automated distribution system of gigantic pneumatic tubes, the city with its slagheaps is abandoned and its working population sent to the countryside. Strict equality has stripped the city of its functions. "In a word," Bellamy comments, "there was no longer any motive to lead a person to prefer city to country life, who did not like crowds for the sake of being crowded." Though there are a few small cities left by the year 2000, most citizens have long ago moved back to the soil. "Parks, gardens, and roomy spaces were multiplied so as to get rid of noise and dust, and finally . . . the city of your day was changed into the modern city." The center of life in the twenty-first century lies *in between* cities in great reforested national parklands, public gardens, and magnificent parkways and boulevards. Significantly, the section of the old unregenerate city to be destroyed first is the financial district, the scene of a huge bonfire reminiscent of Hawthorne's "Earth's Holocaust," in which stocks, bonds, financial papers, and all the trappings of commercial civilization go up in flames.[11]

If Populism had taught Bellamy the need to create and nurture an adversary culture, it had not at the same time reconciled him to working-class leadership of the reform enterprise. His initial scheme for the Industrial Army has been replaced by the less offensive notion of "universal industrial service," but there is still no room in utopia for unions and strikes. Some of the harsher features of *Looking Backward* have been made even more oppressive. There are "reservations" for those refractory citizens who refuse to cooperate. Black Americans are subjected to a discipline "gentle but resistless" which their white brothers presumably do not need. Finally, there is a new emphasis in *Equality* on the abundance produced under a system of "public capitalism" which Bellamy is now concerned to distinguish from socialism. A plentiful supply of goods and services has combined with the principle of equality to assure every citizen a right to property "on a scale never dreamed of" by giving them "a large, equal and fixed share" of the national wealth. The result is a form of state welfare capitalism that Progressive reformers in their turn would dream of implementing as a way of modernizing Ameica.

The most sustained note in *Equality*, however, is an echo of the millennial tone of its predecessor. The great peaceful revolution is not the achievement of the workers, "as a rule ignorant, narrow-minded men with no grasp of large questions," or of their counterparts in the countryside, "the other great division of the insurgent masses." Instead, it is the Great Revival that ultimately saves mankind—that "tide of enthusiasm for the social, not the personal salvation, and for the establishment in brotherly love of the kingdom of God on earth, which Christ bade men hope and work for." From the Great Revival, Bellamy's utopian host explains, dates the triumph of the Religion of Solidarity—"a religion which has dispensed with the rites and ceremonies, creeds and dogmas, and banished from this life fear and concern for the mean self; a religion of life and conduct dominated by an impassioned sense of the solidarity of humanity and of man with God; the religion of a race that knows itself divine and fears not evil, either now or hereafter."[12]

When he had seen his book through galleys, Bellamy allowed his family to take him to Denver. There he grew steadily worse, and when in the spring of 1898 it became obvious that he would never recover, his brothers, Charles and Frederick, came to bring him home. "I shall never forget the light on his face when he decided that the Denver climate had done all it could for him and that he would go home," Emma recalled. "He was never really happy anywhere else." His delight in the homecoming gave him strength to walk from the carriage into the house, where he slumped into his favorite rocking chair and sighed, "Thank God, I'm home!"[13] He returned to Chicopee Falls on April 16 and died on May 22, 1898.

In 1897, as Henry George entered the mayoral race in New York City, and Edward Bellamy hurried to finish his book, Henry Demarest Lloyd retreated from politics and began a worldwide search for signs that his oppositional culture still survived. Lloyd's travels carried him first to England and Ireland to study producer cooperatives, then to the other side of the world to New Zealand to examine a land reform program and a system of compulsory arbitration, and finally to Switzerland to watch cantonal democracy in action. Convinced for the moment that a political remedy lay beyond reach, he overinvested in each of these reform experiments and then succumbed to deep depression when it became clear that none of them fulfilled his hopes. The remaining six years of Lloyd's life were ones of disillusionment and near despair until, in the year of his death, he fashioned a final mediational role for himself as counsel to the United Mine Workers in their case against the coal operators before the Anthracite Coal Strike Commission.

The root cause of Lloyd's dejection was the meteoric rise of American monopoly. "I do not see what there is that is going to stand against it," he complained. "The trust is virtually supreme in the United States, and when it has achieved the economic subjection of the old world it may consolidate the plutocratic system, against which the American people may be powerless."[14] By 1900 the great merger movement that was transforming the American economy was in full swing. The annual number of corporate consolidations in the United States rose dramatically, from 69 in 1897 to 303 a year later, to 1208 in 1899, and then leveled off for the next three years at between 350 and 425. By 1900 there were already 73 so-called "trusts," each with a capitalization of over $10 million, and two out of every three of them had been formed within the past three years. Lloyd, watching this financial revolution with mounting alarm, was convinced that the whole world was approaching a crisis, yet he was unable to predict the point at which monopoly would reach "its last intolerability of oppressions." The socialist strategy of encouraging the growth of trusts with the expectation of nationalizing them sometime in the future struck him as absurd. On the other hand, the Sherman Act, concocted by confectioners in Congress, was a candy castle in which to lock up the big bad trusts.

Most discouraging of all was the seeming apathy of the American people and the absence of any sign of public interest in regulating big business. "The people are so divisible, it is almost impossible to unite them, and the few who can unite are likely to possess everything and everybody." One of the chief articles of his utopain creed was faith in a unitary "people" who could be roused to action with appeals to conscience. But now the reformers in Toledo, as he learned from its mayor, Samuel "Golden Rule" Jones, had finally been forced to give up their fight against Standard Oil, and "not a hand raised to save them."[15] If the reform spirit survived in the United States, it gave no sign. Lloyd decided to go to the continent and then to England to search out examples of "labour co-partnership" in the struggling agricultural cooperative movement.

He concentrated on the groups that interested him most, the agricultural societies, undercapitalized and usually just a step ahead of bankruptcy, but practicing the collective decisionmaking and direct democracy that Lloyd knew were the marks of true community.

While the Land Restoration and the Land Nationalisation Societies, taking their cues from Henry George, waited for a grand legislative stroke to nationalize the land, British "co-operators," accepting the system as an unfortunate fact of life, were proceeding to restore and colonize the land piecemeal. "I think our reformers, including co-operators, are too municipal, too citified. I think they have largely lost the 'sense of the soil,' " Lloyd complained in *Labour Co-Partnership*, the brief account of his investigations that he dashed off on his return home.[16] His trip heightened his interest in the American co-operative movement and the dozens of communal experiments springing up across the entire country at the turn of the century. He helped lay the cornerstone of the cooperative Ruskin College of the New Economy in Ruskin, Tennessee, and wrote encouraging advice to the Populist-feminist Annie L. Diggs, who had abandoned politics to found the Colorado Co-Operative Company. He visited the Shakers in New Lebanon, New York, and the Brotherhood of the Kingdom in Marlboro, Massachusetts, and the arts and crafts society in Old Deerfield, and Green Acres in Maine. "Co-operatives, trade-unions, farmers' granges, and the churches," he announced with greater hope than conviction, "must supply us with the material for the new social union to which we are moving."[17]

Lloyd's plea for cooperatives wherever found rested on the adversary arguments for scale and propinquity—what he called "uniting small groups of men engaged in something that brings them into personal contact daily, so that they know each other and each knows what the other is doing."[18] In such small-scale experiments, he was convinced, lay the only sure means of escape from the massification of the modern world. As long as he clung to the possibility of their succeeding, Lloyd refused to join the Socialist party and the drive for state control. "We cannot carry political socialism very much farther unless we develop in the body of the people a cooperative habit."[19] *Labour Co-Partnership* was meant to encourage that habit.

Nevertheless, Lloyd returned from Europe only to plunge once more into a state of profound melancholy. "As soon as I saw him, I knew that the mainspring was broken," one of his friends noted, and Lloyd himself confessed that he had been "swimming in a shoreless sea." To his younger sister, Caro, he wrote of his conviction that he had only a few years to live and of the relief death would bring.

> I am not fit to write, I do not do the things I ought to do to live
> . . . I have come back from my European trip full of new ideas
> and yet lacking the energy to execute them. By the way, here
> is an entry I made yesterday in my notebook—Tact is know-
> ing what you can do and fact is doing it. Well, I seem to have
> the tact, but the fact eludes me so far.[20]

With his realization that he must continue to act, Lloyd grew eager to
explain his travels as scientific expeditions for gathering and
recording hard facts. No more theorizing, he promised himself, but
simple "laboratory work" to establish the practicability of specific
reforms and "naturalise" them in the United States.

In January 1899 Lloyd, accompanied by his eldest son, William,
sailed for New Zealand and a first-hand look at what he considered
one of the last of the frontier societies. In Wellington he discovered
a blend of rural and urban in a garden city whose central public
squares were linked to outlying suburban cottages by an efficient
system of public transportation. The Lloyds also traveled through
the countryside and at one stop were asked to help supervise the
balloting for parcels of an estate resumed by the government for
lease to small farmers as part of a program of land distribution. But it
was New Zealand's Compulsory Arbitration Law that interested him
most, and despite initial reservations about the "compulsory" nature
of the system, he was impressed with the workings of an adjudica-
tive process in which the state simply encouraged the parties to avail
themselves of disinterested experts in reaching a compromise. To
the newcomer fresh from scenes of industrial violence in the United
States the New Zealand system appeared efficient, flexible, and
fair—an administrative technique that ensured maximum publicity
and quick decisions. Above all, arbitration appealed to Lloyd as an
educational tool with which to teach both labor and management the
way to resolve disputes peacefully and democratically.

Back home, still fighting a lingering sense of depression, Lloyd
managed to complete two brief accounts of his trip—*A Country
Without Strikes* and *Newest England: Notes of a Democratic Traveller, with
some Australian Comparisons*—before surrendering to the old feelings
of paralysis. Cooperatives, he could see from a distance, provided no
solution to the problem of monopoly. Everywhere they were col-

lapsing, and it was obvious that he had wildly exaggerated their potential. Interest-group organizations like grain exchanges, tobacco pools, and dairymen's leagues, which were beginning to spring up across the country, were not the same thing as living communities of local producers. And as yet arbitration had won few friends in America, a fact he learned from the cool reception of his book by both labor and management. A sense of defeat settled on him. "If William Lloyd Garrison or Wendell Phillips were to arrive in such times as this, their attempt to free the slaves would end in failure." American politics as the new century opened remained a melange of "corruptions, scoundrelisms, privileges, and tyrannies," and all he could do was to predict catastrophe. "We are in at the death of an expiring principle."[21]

By 1900 Lloyd and Jessie had moved to Boston in order to be near the younger boys, who were attending Harvard. Jessie's health was poor, and Lloyd continued to fight a growing sense of isolation with periodic trips abroad. He also wrote voluminously for a wide range of magazines and journals—the *Atlantic Monthly, Outlook,* the *Independent,* as well as for the religious press. For their January 1901 issue the editors of the *Congregationalist* asked him to contribute to a symposium on "What May Be in the Twentieth Century," and he refurbished his version of utopia as the setting for the same adversary culture Henry George had outlined in *The Science of Political Economy* and Edward Bellamy had described in *Equality.* After the plutocrats have fomented a middle-class revolution that topples them from power, Lloyd predicted, an equalitarian society will finally become a reality. "All men will become capitalists and all capitalists co-operators." Metropolis will be abolished in favor of huge regional complexes of garden cities. "Every house will be a centre of sunshine and scenery, and every school a garden school. The population will be educated back to their old home—the soil."[22]

Still searching for the ideal pastoral setting for his producerist culture, Lloyd traveled to Switzerland, where he hoped to find in the system of cantonal government "a people really deciding for themselves." On route he stopped off in Germany, where he interviewed Bebel, Bernstein, Kautsky, and other leaders of German socialism for answers to his question of whether statism and socialist bureaucracy could be made compatible with local democratic decisionmaking. On the whole, he thought not. "I have little hopes of the success of political democracy unless there exists among the people a thorough appreciation of private democracy based on their practical experience in it."[23] Thus his need to examine "Alpine democracy."

A Sovereign People was arranged from Lloyd's notes by the English socialist J. A. Hobson four years after the author's death. Like the books on New Zealand and his report on English cooperatives, it is an enthusiastic and occasionally rhapsodic account of "the best equipped political laboratory in the modern world," where direct participation and the federative principle lift decisionmaking out of the muck of party politics to the level of disinterest. Lloyd was particularly intrigued with the "federative force" in Switzerland that seemingly kept government decentralized and power diffused. The commune, he noted approvingly, was the source of the "intensity of that passion for an immediate participation in public life." From the commune and the canton, the "original home" of democracy, civic energy flowed out into the nation, invigorating Swiss national life and culture. The commune, even more deeply rooted in Swiss life than the town meeting in New England soil, gave each and every citizen a spiritual "stake" in society together with an investment in the indigenous landscape and a sense of place in it. In this sense, Lloyd agreed, it was an agrarian survival, a locus for the "conservative attachment to ancient usages" such as communal property rights and traditions.

In Swiss cantonal government Lloyd suddenly saw "natural socialism" at work, a flexible and intensely human system rooted in the particular and free from the taint of compulsory state socialism and party bureaucracy. Modernization, he was forced to admit, in Switzerland as elsewhere in the West had weakened the communal culture by eroding its economic base. All the more reason, then, for keeping alive its political tradition of "solemn gatherings" of concerned citizens and a social policy that provided public baths and kitchens, playgrounds, libraries, museums, and all of the amenities of modern life.

With this unfinished study of cantonal democracy, Lloyd reached the limits of his ingenuity in attempting to combine Fabian socialism, local self-government, and Christian humanism. In the last years of his life these forces often appeared to pull him in different directions. He admitted that the Socialist party, in spite of its many limitations, was the only effective weapon left to American reformers. He also agreed that "private" cooperation of voluntary groups of citizens was no longer sufficient, and that "we must find some political tool if we are going to have a political (peaceful) remedy." Still, he hesitated to commit himself to the socialists. "The practical programme that the party puts forth has my unqualified assent. I would not diminish it in one particular . . . But I cannot, for the life of me, see how the present social contest can be described as one between capitalists and the working class. To me it appears to be a contest between the people and all those who commit depredations upon them." The "people" and the "workingclass," he reminded his socialist correspondents, were not convertible terms.[24]

Nor were class and Christian brotherhood compatible social states. It was the old millennial hope alternating with fits of despondency that ruled his mood now. "Behind our militant commercialism—close behind it—moves the better than Christian spirit which is to give the world its next 'new era.' "[25] The new era would fix man finally and immovably in the center of the universe and unleash all his powers for good. For over a decade his journals and notebooks had been filling with what could only be called "notes on a new religion"—not the dialectical argument of Bellamy's "Religion of Solidarity" or the impassioned rhetorical outburst of George's lecture "Moses," but fragments, aphorisms, jottings, and maxims strung like beads on the theme of millennial awakening. In 1906 Jane Addams and Anne Withington, Lloyd's secretary late in life, pieced these fragments together in a volume they titled with a tag from his notes, *Man, the Social Creator.* They intended a sequential argument, but the effect is that of an ecstatic prose-poem, Whitmanic in scope, Emersonian in cadence, celebrating the imminent appearance of the twentieth-century man-god:

God is the name man gives to the future.

Men in juxtaposition must unite.

Hate is the name for love's destructive moments.

Man improvises himself.

. . . the outflowing conversation, unofficial and unabashed, of congenial people seeking the truth in each other.

Man is now making God.

History is or becomes "a drama of good will."

Love must become law.

God is simply the hero of a religious novel.[26]

The core theme of these rapturous meditations is the charge to all men to make heaven on earth, as Bellamy and George had urged, without creeds or texts, ceremonies or dogmas, simply through impulse to perform the redemptive act.

In June 1902 the anthracite coal miners, led by United Mine Workers president John L. Mitchell, went out on strike for higher pay, better working conditions, and union recognition. Lloyd was delighted to learn that the miners in convention had voted to submit their case to arbitration, and he was hardly surprised to hear that the coal operators, led by troglodyte George F. Baer, had announced that they would give "no consideration to any plan or mediation or to any interference on the part of any outside party."[27] For a while the owners' proscription even applied to President Theodore Roosevelt, who was forced to threaten the operators with nationalization unless they agreed to arbitration by the Anthracite Coal Strike Commission that he had established.

Lloyd was only one of the miners' legal counsel, whose best-known talents were Clarence Darrow and the young progressive Walter Weyl, and whose ablest tactician was Mitchell himself. "I am not taking the lead in the work, but helping only," he explained to Jessie, now ill and confined, to whom he wrote each day. He had volunteered his services which had been gratefully accepted as offered by a public figure with a recent book on arbitration. His chief contribution, he admitted, was advice on the most dramatic way of advertising the miners' grievances, and in the beginning he found the work exciting. "No more stirring case could ever come, and this is my first case," he boasted to Jessie. "Would not this be a fine thing to the credit of arbitration—that the parties thus brought together spontaneously betake themselves to a voluntary agreement by conciliation?"[28] This, it turned out, was too much to hope from the entrenched operators, who seemed bent on proving Lloyd's charge that they were both inefficient and irresponsible. Lloyd was irresistibly drawn to the case against monopoly, which he had spent a decade perfecting, and on the hunch that Mitchell and Darrow would allow him to include the issue in his summation, he traveled to Boston to consult Louis Brandeis, the people's attorney and the country's foremost expert on monopoly. Lloyd also tended to matters of publicity and arranged to have a twelve-year-old breaker boy photographed holding up his check for 32 cents for eight hours work. Darrow and Mitchell marveled at Lloyd's keen sense of public opinion and the best way of appealing to it.

As the sessions before the commission dragged on into the early winter of 1903, however, Lloyd took time out from a wearying routine for the even more exhausting work of lecturing—in Boston, New York, and Philadelphia. He grew increasingly irritable and lonely, and his letters to Jessie filled with complaints of being "properly exhausted" and "lonesome and homesick." He confessed to having no more "go" for the job. "I cannot collect myself, nor get up any interest in it," he confided to his wife whose rapidly failing health also worried him. "Why cannot our high noons stand still? High noons of the June of life—why must we always be pushed on down through the afternoon towards night, and when night comes where shall we wake?"[29]

When it came time for summation before the commission, he and Darrow agreed to divide the burden of proof, Darrow taking the narrower case for social utility, and Lloyd the high ground of union recognition and antimonopoly.

> The country wants another regime. It wants coal. It wants peace. Coal can be had only by peace, and peace can be had only by justice. Give these miners here a voice in the management of their own labour.[30]

When the hearings were over, Lloyd and Darrow returned to Chicago to await the decision. The commission recognized the United Mine Workers as a bargaining agent but not their principle of the closed shop. It recommended a 10 percent pay hike and a reduction of hours, but beyond these concessions it would not go. While admitting that the miners had failed to win all they deserved, Lloyd nevertheless conceded that "they have certainly won a notable victory."He promptly sent copies of the commission's report to friends and colleagues around the world. One of these went to Sir Joseph Ward, Minister of Commerce for New Zealand, together with Lloyd's acknowledgment of "the initiative and the inspiration derived from the laws of your country."[31]

As he recovered from an exhausting six months' work, Lloyd opened a correspondence with socialists both at home and abroad in an attempt finally to come to grips with the question of joining the party. His letters were filled with promises and misgivings. "I think I shall formally join the Socialist party," he told Caro in the spring of 1903. And to the reformer Eltweed Pomeroy he wrote: "The worm must turn sometime. I am ready to turn now."[32] Yet the announcement of his capitulation proved premature, for despite his professions of new loyalty, he could not shake off his objections to socialist dogma. "There is much about the everlasting 'proletariat' and 'class conscious' slang of the sectarian socialist that make me squirm," he confessed to Pomeroy, "as I suppose the Biblical cant of old Puritans made the cavaliers' faces go awry. But this same sour fanaticism has been the bitter yeast of all rise, has it not?" Asked to prepare a statement of his reasons for joining the Socialist party, he obliged with an odd pair of arguments. Socialism, he predicted, would eventually triumph because "in the masses stirs a new-born creative consciousness with its message that all the reforms are one reform, and that that reform is the self-creation of a better individual by putting him to work as his own God at the creation of a better society." His second argument was the inverse of the first: socialism was the only means of preventing modern industrial society from tearing itself apart. "The only way to get rid of the demand of the proletariat for a voice and a vote is to abolish the proletariat. *But the demand for social control is a larger one than that of the proletariat.*"[33] Still, when the socialist leader Algie M. Simons came to Winnetka to urge him to take the final step, Lloyd explained that unfortunately the current traction fight in Chicago with its promise of municipal ownership must now take precedence over everything else. The socialists would have to wait.

Lloyd was summering in Sakonnet when he learned of the impending Chicago fight against the streetcar monopoly and its evil genius Charles T. Yerkes. Here at last was the ultimate test for the socialists and the willingness of party members to leave off bickering and hair-splitting and join in a city-wide campaign to return the transit business to the people. "Here is the greatest chance in the world," he urged Tommy Morgan, whose Marxist leanings he disapproved, "to make the people see what an instalment of socialism would mean. It is also an unrivalled opening for teaching them by the realistic method what exploitation is, and how it is to be met. If 'class-consciousness' and the 'war of classes' are not brought into the territory of practical questions by this traction struggle, they never will be."[34] Here, in short, was a challenge which no aspiring socialist could refuse.

"I may never come back," he only half-joked with his family as he prepared to leave Sakonnet for Chicago. "This may kill me." To his mother he quoted the familiar lines he had learned as a boy about a man's mother watching over her son in life and waiting for him in heaven, and when she urged him to take care of his health, he replied, "I give my life as a sacrifice." In Chicago he stayed for a week at Hull House, "the best club in town," he told Jessie, before moving into his wife's old apartment on the lakefront. The hectic work of organizing still another public campaign against monopoly made him realize that he had never really recovered from the previous one. To his friends he appeared quite ill, his nerves shattered, his energy drained. He came down with the flu but refused to go to bed. "This morning I am all right," he reported to Jessie. "The headache has reached the dwindling point, and the cold has 'set' in my bronchial region, and nothing now remains but to wear it out." Instead, he insisted on attending a meeting of the Chicago Federation of Labor where Jane Addams saw him on the platform huddled in his chair, looking pale and drawn. The next day he developed pneumonia, and when Jessie arrived from Sakonnet, she quickly saw that he possessed no reserves with which to fight back. As he slipped in and out of consciousness in the next few days, he spoke of nothing but the traction fight he had been forced to give up. "All I had done in my life was leading up to this," he murmured, *"and it was going through!"*[35] He died on September 17, 1903.

15

THE LEGACY

HENRY GEORGE, HENRY DEMAREST LLOYD, AND EDWARD BELLAMY have been received by a twentieth-century American public as lone prophets whose legacies are primarily literary. Although conviction drove each of them into reform politics, where they tried to realize their dream of restoring community, it has been their books that have finally mattered. For half a century after their deaths their reputations rested securely on a major work that continued to attract readers all over the world. A random sampling of American Progressives who acknowledged debts to one or more of them included figures as different as John Dewey and Louis Post, Louis Brandeis and Norman Thomas, Tom Johnson and Clarence Darrow, Jane Addams and Robert LaFollette, all of them responding enthusiastically to their moral message if not always to their program for building the good society. The influence of the three utopians, however, failed to survive the Progressive generation itself, and by the time the New Deal ended in 1940 their prestige had begun to decline, as Americans confronted problems of racial democracy at home and balance-of-power abroad on which the three prophets had had nothing in particular to say. Soon thereafter *Progress and Poverty*,

Looking Backward, and *Wealth Against Commonwealth* were relegated to publishers' lists of the Ten Greatest American Books and syllabi in college courses in American literature, where they remain to this day.

Of the three literary bequests, Bellamy's seemed, at least for a while, the most substantial. *Looking Backward* has been reprinted dozens of times and translated into as many languages. Bellamy Societies have appeared in every country in Europe and as far afield in the developing world as India, China, and Indonesia. For innumerable American readers in the Progressive years the book served as a moral tonic and a call to purposeful social action. Judge Ben Lindsay, the reformer of the juvenile justice system, recalled an "idealistic kid" who ranked Bellamy with St. Francis of Assisi as great lovers of mankind. Norman Thomas remembered *Looking Backward* as his introduction to socialism. Roger Baldwin, the civil libertarian, grew up in a family that numbered Bellamy along with Emerson and Robert Ingersoll as its intellectual heroes. Vida Scudder, friend of Jane Addams and Henry Demarest Lloyd, credited Bellamy with playing a "major role" in awakening the American middle class to the "brutalities and stupidities of the capitalist order." Upton Sinclair pronounced Bellamy a "noble personality" and a "real thinker."

Most readers did not mistake *Looking Backward* for a blueprint, but warmed, instead, to its vision of the peaceful self-socialization of the capitalist order and the spread of affluence and good will through the whole of American society. There were engineers, planners, and scientific efficiency experts, to be sure, for whom Nationalism and more particularly the Industrial Army held a lingering appeal in the 1920s and 1930s. Followers of Frederick Winslow Taylor and converts to Thorstein Veblen's soviet of technicians discovered in *Looking Backward* the original producerist promise of a world made free for the experts. Their view achieved fullest expression during the Great Depression, when for a brief moment the planned society appeared as a vague shape on the American horizon. Howard Scott, the founder and guiding spirit of Technocracy, wrote to Bellamy's widow in 1934 to give her his estimate of her husband's book. "Of all the utopias that have been written, I think there can be no shadow of a doubt that Bellamy's is the best of all. It does inspire and purify and give hope, and that is what humanity needs most at the present time."[1] Arthur E. Morgan, hydraulic engineer and the director of the

Tennessee Valley Authority, undertook the first major biography of Bellamy because he was drawn to the idea of a unitary system of social planning. In the early years of the depression, *Looking Backward* was revived by a short-lived Edward Bellamy Association that boasted John Dewey and Roger Baldwin as honorary members, but Bellamy's ideas were quickly dropped by a younger generation of New Deal pragmatists who rejected the book's implicit totalitarianism. Subsequent American experience with fascism and dictatorship during and after the Second World War turned an original attraction to utopia into a fascination with Orwellian dystopia; and an affluent society, familiar with credit cards, brainwashing, television, and hallucinogenic drugs, found little to admire in Bellamy's primitive social engineering and much to deplore in the loss of political freedom and cultural vitality in applying it. A century after its publication, *Looking Backward* has become a literary curiosity.

Of the three utopians, Henry George appears, at least until recently, to have left the smallest intellectual legacy to modernists. George's immediate impact was strongly felt by a group of urban reformers and politicians seeking to revitalize their cities and clean up local government in the years before the First World War. Tom Johnson, Brand Whitlock, Newton Baker, and Frederick C. Howe were the best-known of the midwestern Progressives who considered the Single Tax or some variant of it a possible means of stabilizing urban land values and rebuilding their cities. Meanwhile, however, George's followers continued to reject politics and even lobbying and pressure groups, and as a consequence struck no very deep popular roots even though George's ideas interested an occasional enthusiast like Albert Jay Nock or Francis Neilson, editor of the *Freeman*. But by 1914 academic economists had already called into question the Single Tax proposal, and although there were occasional repeat performances in the 1920s and 1930s when the professionals were moved to scotch the pretensions of Georgists, by mid-century the prophet's free market economics, like Bellamy's industrial regimentation, appeared to have been safely buried. Recently, with the malfunctioning of the American economy and the growing distrust of an interventionist state, George's reputation has been disinterred by those anarcho-capitalists who take as gospel the master's denunciation of all "weak projects for putting men in lead-

ing-strings to a brainless abstraction called the state."[2] Yet a full-
scale revival of Georgist economics seems unlikely.

Henry Demarest Lloyd's reputation has also come to rest almost
entirely on *Wealth Against Commonwealth* and his role as a pioneer
muckraker. In offering the American reading public a blend of fac-
tual reporting and moral publicity, the muckrakers followed Lloyd's
original example and perfected his technique of combining tough-
mindedness and sentimentality. Many of the muckrakers also followed Lloyd in directing their fire toward monopoly and big business. Lloyd's reputation, in fact, rose and fell with the hopes of the
trustbusters, sliding into eclipse during and after the First World
War when corporate consolidations soared, and recovering briefly in
the waning years of the New Deal under the prodding of Thurman
Arnold's Anti-Trust Division of the Justice Department. But the
steady growth of big business, fed by four wars, and the spread of
mergers and international syndicates have made Lloyd's initial indictment of monopoly as inefficient and irresponsible seem obsolete
if not perverse.

One reason for the declining fortunes of antimonopoly and
Lloyd's reputation as a trustbuster was the disruption and disappearance of his original community of discourse. Even before World
War One new critical voices were beginning to challenge the formalism and moralism of the three utopians. Within a decade of Lloyd's
death a brash young social critic, Walter Lippmann, fresh from Harvard and a mild flirtation with socialism, undertook to lecture his
fellow Progressives on their subservience to taboos and to indict
them for other failures of the social imagination. In particular, Lippmann charged, the complaints against big business made by Lloyd
and the utopians were absurd. Modern corporations—efficient, responsible, inevitable—had been made victims of "the feverish fantasy of illiterate thousands thrown out of kilter by the rack and strain
of modern life."[3] The utopians, Lippmann implied, deserved to lose
their audience.

It was not simply a younger generation's rejection of the utopians' method that Lippmann represented, but the repudiation of the
old moral glossary and high diction—concepts of the "people,"
"conscience," and "brotherhood." Above all, Lippmann objected to
the late nineteenth century's obsession, as he thought it, with the big

synthesis and the masterful statement. "That is what kills political writing," he complained, with the utopian mode clearly in mind, "this absurd pretence that you are delivering a great utterance. You never do. You are just a puzzled man making notes of what you think."[4] Following his own precept, Lippmann spent a lifetime changing his mind in clean, functional prose, while Lloyd's evangelical style fell into disfavor.

But so, in its turn, did the easy confidence of Progressive nationalists in a war state that signally failed to make the world safe for democracy either at home or abroad. In the minds of postwar American intellectuals, the First World War had discredited all of the assumptions of the bright young bureaucrats, in particular the idea of a sovereign national culture harmonizing all contradictions and discords. Amidst the spiritual wreckage of the war, the original promises of Progressivism seemed only the empty proposals of administrators who, as Lewis Mumford complained, did not "particularly care what Society does so long as the technique is good and whatever is done is efficient."[5] After the war a younger generation of artists and intellectuals disagreed on the location of an alternative culture, a handful of alienated intellectuals finding it in a Marxist critique of American capitalism, a somewhat larger group emigrating to Europe as a self-advertised Lost Generation, while a considerably larger community of novelists, poets, artists, and critics set about rediscovering America. The rediscovery of America breathed new life into the adversary culture of the utopians by attaching it to the values and the program of regionalism. Their shared dream of the good society lived on in the decades between the two world wars as a regional alternative site from which to launch what the Fugitive historian Donald Davidson called "the attack on Leviathan."

Regionalism in Europe in the nineteenth century, like the utopians' adversary culture, arose as a corrective and a counterdoctrine to the increasing claims of the centralized national state. Regionalist historians like Wilhelm Heinrich Riehl in Germany and sociologists like Frederic LePlay in France focused on place, people, work, and home as comprising the supporting regional network for all true culture, and it was to these values shared by the utopians and their regionalist contemporaries in Europe that Lewis Mumford referred when in the early 1920s he spoke of making regionalism the "cultural motive" of the new science of regional planning and of the urgent need to "inject a little regionalism" into a disillusioned American people.[6] Regional planning in the next two decades came chiefly from the example of Patrick Geddes and his ecological theory of the "valley section," while regionalist values derived from the adversary culture of Bellamy, Lloyd, and George with its emphasis on balance and symmetry, measure and pace, the indigenous and the participatory. As they combined in the twenty years between the First and the Second World Wars these values pointed to a continuing "middle way" traversing the intellectual landscape of the interwar period, a road running between Marxism and corporatism, between the bureaucratic centralism of the socialists and the fascist tendencies of monopoly capitalism. This middle way was an extension of the original route taken by the three utopians.

Central to the reform tradition of Bellamy, Lloyd, and George was their working model of the good society as a composite of city and country. Their vision of an urban-rural continuum running from village neighborhoods to gateway cities lay close to the center of American urban and regional planning in the first half of the twentieth century and continued to direct the work of city and regional planners, conservationists, and landscape architects. Although increasingly professionalized and differentiated by the 1920s, planning continued to adhere to the cluster of principles advanced by George, Lloyd, and Bellamy—the belief in a natural order to be rediscovered and then implemented; the concept of a "normal" and "healthy" life combining urban and rural values; and the distinction, considered increasingly crucial, between the old "city planning" for purely commercial purposes and the new "community planning" for the conservation of basic human values. This view of the ultimately good society as uniting urban and rural first dominated the Country Life Movement with its hopes for "evening up" American life by strengthening the "organic relation" of town and country. Then conservationists, once concerned merely with resource utilization, became involved with the community theory of the utopians, and out of their reformulations came plans like those of Benton Mac-Kaye for the regional city whose framework is defined by campfire, village green, and wayside. The principle of growth by nucleation as it was developed by planners was a refinement of the ideas of the

utopians, in particular their plan for limiting urban growth at the
center with "satellite cities" and of preserving neighborhood en-
vironments.

Henry Demarest Lloyd shared his dream of an urban America
modeled on the White City with Daniel Burnham, its chief architect,
whose own designs for a nation of Cities Beautiful could be seen in
his "Report on a Plan for San Francisco" (1905), with its emphasis on
the organic unity of "park-like squares" running through the city
like a backbone. Though Burnham, unlike Lloyd, was less interested
in specific problems of housing and sanitation than in a total aesthetic effect, both insisted that the public splendor of the City Beautiful should reflect the cooperative efforts that built it. Boston's park
commissioners, well versed in the arguments of *Looking Backward*,
urged an approach to their city as one "great urban composite" with
"more natural and agreeable surroundings" on the grounds that it
should ensure the "perpetuation of desirable types of humanity."[7]
Bellamy's world of village values lived on in the pioneer efforts of
the Massachusetts Homestead Commission, the first public housing
authority in the United States, which planned and built homes for
industrial workers in Lowell during World War One. Influenced by
similar experiments in Australia and New Zealand, where all of the
utopians' works had been widely read, the Homestead Commission
aimed at checking the growth of major New England cities by providing workers with single-family homes and "land enough for a
garden." In addition to better health, play space for children, and
new opportunities for enjoying leisure, the Commission Report
listed as social advantages of the family homestead its "tendency to
inspire and elevate, physically, mentally, morally, rather than to depress, dishearten, and deteriorate," a pronouncement worthy of the
good Doctor Leete himself.

Henry George's influence on the Garden City movement is a case
of the transatlantic exchange of ideas. Ebenezer Howard, the designer and builder of the Garden City, acknowledged debts both to
Bellamy, whose descriptions of a future Boston he admitted to swal-
lowing "whole," and to George, from whom, as he explained in *Garden Cities of Tomorrow* (1898), he had received "much inspiration."[8]
Howard's book, in turn, made a powerful impression on American
urban planners. His definition of the problem of the industrial city as
fundamentally one of building satellite cities extending out into

green fields; his plans for community management of property rights; and his insistence on a balanced environment—all owed something to the original vision of the three utopians. From this complex of ideas and the English examples of Letchworth and Welwyn came the work of American disciples like Lewis Mumford and Clarence Stein, the designer of the planned communities, Radburn and Greenbelt. Thomas Adams, the first secretary of Garden Cities, Limited, later came to New York, where he took charge of the city's monumental series of regional studies completed in the 1920s, one of which was Clarence Arthur Perry's "The Neighborhood," a plan for preserving the amenities of an older rural America in the hostile machine-age city through a system of self-enclosed block communities.

The regional and community planning portions of the utopians' design were reassembled during the depression, not merely in peripheral schemes like Howard Scott's Technocracy, the reports of the National Resources Committee, and the self-help cooperatives funded under the Federal Emergency Relief Administration, but in outline form in Frank Lloyd Wright's blueprint for Broadacre City and in actuality in the work of the Tennessee Valley Authority.

Broadacres, designed to fulfill the "several inherently just rights" of Americans to decentralize and redistribute power, derived, not so much from the idea of the garden city as from the beliefs of the three utopians in the primacy of land, the proper proportion of industry and agriculture, and the power of competitive cooperation to secure the good life. From these as well as from Wright's fear of regimentation and his principle of organic form came his plan for a community which was to be a "fabric" rather than a "finality." For Wright, as for his utopian predecessors, the modern commercial city was only the "ugly scaffolding" of modern life, to be replaced by economic and cultural units adapted to the indigenous landscape—in the case of Broadacres to the prairie specifications of the Midwest—which would release Americans from the fatal grip of urban exploitation and give them "a new ideal of success." Technology—the automobile, airplane, telephone, and radio—brings to Broadacres a drastic simplification of government similar to that predicted by the utopians. "In Broadacres," Wright explains, "by elimination of cities and towns the present curse of petty and minor officialdom, government, has been reduced to one minor government for each county."

Land and public utilities are owned by the state but administered by the county, and the management of Broadacres is intentionally left to the citizens themselves with the result of "making politics a vital matter to every one in the new city instead of the old case where hopeless indifference makes 'politics' a grafter's profession."

> Here now may be seen the elemental units of our social structure: The correlated farm, the factory—its smoke and gases eliminated by burning coal at the place of origin, the decentralized school, the various conditions of residence, the home offices, safe traffic, simplified government. All the common interests take place in a simple coordination wherein all are employed: *little* farms, *little* homes for industry, *little* factories, *little* schools, a *little* university going to the people mostly by way of their interest in the ground, *little* laboratories on their own ground for professional men. And the farm, notwithstanding its animals, becomes the most attractive unit of the city.[9]

Finally, and most important, an automatic solution for chronic unemployment: the very process of building Broadacres brings jobs in abundance and an end to underconsumption.

The core of Broadacres is a lake with its tributary stream around which stand the public buildings, county offices, central high school, hotel, and hospital dispersed with stadium, zoo, aquarium, arboretum, and Morris-like craft hall in landscaped fields—a scaled cultural complex where, as Wright noted in echoing the utopians, "much is made of general sports and festivals." A greenbelt of orchards and vineyards separates factories and the small industries strung along the arterial roadway from private homes and grounds carefully designed to afford maximum privacy. In enumerating the social effects of this calculated decentralization Wright restated the premises of the adversary culture on which his dream of community rested: an organic reintegration of life as the basis of a healthy provincial culture, orderly development of the land which is held by use and improvement, public ownership of utilities, and direct democracy carried on by citizens secure at last in the possession of their natural social rights. And like the utopians before him, Wright predicts the change in human nature that is made possible by his ideal community. "Unwholesome life would get no encouragement, and the ghastly heritage left by over-crowding in overdone ultra-capitalistic cities would be likely to disappear in three or four generations. The old success ideals having no chance at all, new ones more natural to the best in man would be given a fresh opportunity to develop naturally."

For a brief moment in the 1930s TVA appeared to be fulfilling, at least in part, the original hopes of the utopians for a culture "that belongs to Democracy organic." Multipurpose development, decentralized administration, community-owned electric cooperatives, greenbelts as a hedge against land speculation, standard modular housing units, test-demonstration programs, mobile libraries, and educational extension services—all seemed to point toward the unity of men with their environment envisioned by the nineteenth-century utopians. For Arthur E. Morgan, Bellamy's biographer and the first director of TVA, it was the town of Norris itself, planned for the workers who were building the nearby dam, that would establish the future of the producerist small community and provide the model for other experiments in the Valley. Morgan's plans for Norris included a town commons given over to individual garden plots, a cooperative store, home workshops, a nature preserve, and a vocational college. Here, he believed, in the scaled community integrated with the dam site and nearby freeway meaningful work and leisure for self-improvement would provide training for light industrial work, small farming techniques, and artisanal and craft skills. Inevitably Morgan's dreams were circumscribed by political and economic realities, and the original workforce did not settle in the town but picked up and followed their jobs to a new site. Still, Norris remained a showplace for visitors from all over the country, an image of vernacular planning, and a symbol of the adversary tradition its founder championed.

David E. Lilienthal, Morgan's nemesis and eventual replacement, did not always understand the more extravagant restorationist notions of his rival or approve of those he did. Nevertheless, Lilienthal's book, *TVA: Democracy on the March*, develops a polity perfectly matched to Morgan's vision—a grass-roots politics of direct participation, federalism and widely shared decisionmaking, progressive education and spontaneous cooperation. In pleading for the completion of his quiet revolution, in explaining the need to combine resource development with the revitalization of small business and the family farm, in calling for a return to regional scale and a healthy provincial culture, and finally, in proclaiming that "no politics is good politics," Lilienthal perpetuated the language and the substance of the utopians' dream.[10]

Broadacres and the town of Norris—the regional plan and the actual experiment—were parts of a whole complex of projects, programs, platforms, and manifestos directed toward the realization of the oppositional culture in the 1930s. These ranged from preservationist tracts (Benton MacKaye's *The New Exploration*) to regional sagas (Walter Prescott Webb's *The Great Plains*). Anthropologists and folklorists, novelists and poets, critics and planners examined the producerist economy and the adversary culture in the written and spoken word (the State Guide Books and Benjamin Botkin's "folksay" collections sponsored by the WPA) and in the photograph (the Farm Security Administration's Historical Division); in government reports (*Regional Factors in National Planning*) and in commercial publishing ventures (the *Rivers of America* series); in an uninhibited pastoralism in the arts (the regionalist work of Grant Wood, John Steuart Curry, and Thomas Hart Benton) and the proposals of regional planners (Rupert Vance's *Human Geography of the South;* Howard Odum's *Southern Regions of the United States*); in utopian projections (Upton Sinclair's EPIC) and actual experiments (Arthurdale, the Greenbelt Communities). Common to all these various enterprises were the original shared preferences of Bellamy, George, and Lloyd: for a producer ethic of small-scale "competitive cooperation" practiced by "little people"; for the American land, its traditions, and a sense of place on it; for nationalizing natural monopolies and trust busting the rest; for local systems, controlled change, and reform by nucleation; for an aesthetic based on realism and pluralism, the folk and the vernacular, all recorded with documentary fidelity. Although this alternative culture did not survive intact the developmental force of the New Deal or the federal intervention brought by the Second World War, it was not simply an exercise in nostalgia but the climactic expression of an American "third way," the legacy of the three utopians to the twentieth century.

The American phase of the history of the adversary tradition was the final stage of a modernization process which, as the three utopians sensed, had begun in Western Europe in the late sixteenth and early seventeenth centuries. The effect of modernization, first in England and then on the Continent, was to disrupt communal patterns and habits, erode the traditions of people who lived on the land and worked it as small owners, and replace them with a philosophy of possessive individualism. For the next two centuries the gap between communal rights and individual liberties widened as enterprise continued to challenge and defeat inherited ways. By the middle of the nineteenth century the battle had been all but won by the forces of privatism, and the beleagured defenders of community had been driven to assume an oppositional stance. The second half of the nineteenth century everywhere in Western Europe was marked by the attempts of historians, artists, and social critics to recover the models of preindustrial community—in the folk institutions of the German forests, the reconstruction of the Greek *polis*, the recovery of the medieval commons, the workings of Swiss cantonal democracy.

In the United States the perception of the loss of community and the attempt to recover it came later than it did in Europe, and the search was conducted within the narrower bounds prescribed by an aggressive entrepreneurial capitalism. From the beginning the Puritan attempt to build a city on the hill was carried on within an expanding frontier society in which communal rights were challenged at every turn. And in spite of the pleas to preserve the virtuous community made by the republicans of the Revolutionary generation, the balance was soon tipped toward private initiative and individual enterprise. The "middle way" that led to the formulation of the adversary culture took its rise in the middle of the nineteenth century, when three intellectual paths converged to form a thoroughfare through the Civil War years. One of these traditions was the Jeffersonian persuasion, the conviction, as Jefferson himself put it, that "it is not by the consolidation or concentration of powers, but by their distribution that good government is effected." A second source was Protestant evangelicalism in its most radically perfectionist form, in particular a millennial expectation and an urge to reform that launched a crusade against slavery and fostered a variety of schemes for building the sacred community. Still another point of origin—a tributary road—was an artisanal tradition running all the way back to eighteenth-century England and the "moral economy" which persisted in America as a philosophy of true producers who formed a naturally cooperative community based on shopfloor solidarity. By

1850 these three paths had converged to form a dominant American free labor ideology which sustained the Union during the Civil War and Reconstruction. A dominant social philosophy in 1850, the belief in a middle way had been placed on the defensive by 1880 and its spokesmen forced to assume an adversarial posture in the face of rapid political and economic consolidation. Here was the oppositional culture that the utopians codified for an entire late-nineteenth-century community comprised of displaced artisans and mechanics; small tradesmen and local entrepreneurs; yeoman families, particularly in the South; and increasing numbers of European immigrants at one or two removes from the soil and bringing with them memories of a communal life and its traditions. These were the people who responded directly to George, Lloyd, and Bellamy and who carried their adversary culture into the twentieth century and the lean years of the depression.

The recovery of the American economy in World War Two and the arrival of the Affluent Society complete with its own social science seemingly destroyed the utopian tradition of Bellamy, George, and Lloyd. Until recently their hopes for decentralization and localism, as well as their belief in Christian politics, seemed misplaced, even a bit quaint. However, the malfunctioning of Progressive bureaucracy, a new merger movement of unprecedented proportions, and the call for dispersal of political power to the peripheries, all suggest the possibility of reopening the "third way" and replanting some of the original utopian signposts. Yet perhaps it is well to remember that these signposts really mark an interior landscape, the country of the imagination, which offers an alternative model of the good society. This, in a sense, was the pastoral center of Henry George's dream of a hillside retreat. It is also Henry Demarest Lloyd's No Mean City and Edward Bellamy's suburban Boston in the year 2000. For all three men the pastoral realm, at least in part, was an imaginary landscape—a temporary retreat or haven from the bafflements of the modern age. And in this sense, too, its chief function was not political but psychological, a means of strengthening their will to believe and thus to act. The three reformers first described arcadia and then tried to fashion a politics to build it. They failed, and their failure may show another disillusioned generation a century later the terms on which an alternative America may be approached if not actually entered and possessed.

NOTES
NOTE ON SOURCES
INDEX

NOTES

1. THE FATE OF EMPIRE

1. Notebooks, Edward Bellamy MSS, Houghton Library, Harvard University (hereafter HL).

2. Henry George, *Our Land and Land Policy* (San Francisco, 1872), pp. 46–67.

3. Henry Demarest Lloyd, Manuscript Journal, 1872–1877, Henry Demarest Lloyd MSS, State Historical Society of Wisconsin, Madison, Wisconsin (hereafter WHS). See also Lloyd's editorials in the Chicago *Tribune*, July 10, 20, 1877.

4. Henry George, Manuscript Journal, Henry George Papers, Rare Books and Manuscripts Division, New York Public Library, Astor, Lenox and Tilden Foundations (hereafter NYPL). For the fullest account of George's boyhood see Henry George, Jr., *The Life of Henry George*, in *The Complete Works of Henry George*, 10 vols. (Garden City, N.Y.: Fels Fund Library Edition, 1906–1911), vols IX–X.

5. Catharine P. George to Henry George, n.d., in George, *George*, I, 36.

6. Henry George, Manuscript Journal entry for April 2, 1857, in George, *George*, I, 39.

7. Henry George to Rebecca D. Curry, a friend of the George family in Philadelphia, April 30, 1857, in George, *George*, I, 46–47.

8. Henry George to B. F. Ely, September 30, 1857, in George, *George,* I, 50-51.

9. Richard S. H. George to Henry George, February 1, 1858, in George, *George,* I, 61-62.

10. Henry George to Richard S. H. George and Catharine P. George, January 6, 1858, in George, *George,* I, 58-59.

11. Henry George to Rebecca D. Curry, May 29, 1858, in George, *George,* I, 70.

12. Richard S. H. George to Henry George, January 19, 1859, in George, *George,* I, 86.

13. Henry George to Jennie T. George, August 2, 1859, in George, *George,* I, 95.

14. Henry George to Jennie T. George, April 10, 1861, in George, *George,* I, 102-103.

15. Henry George to Jennie T. George, April 10, 1861, in George, *George,* I, 111.

16. Henry George to Jennie T. George, September 15, 1861, the so-called "Millennial Letter," in Charles A. Barker, *Henry George* (New York: Oxford University Press, 1955), p. 50.

17. George, *George,* I, 123.

18. Pocket Diary, George MSS, NYPL.

19. George told this story to his doctor, James E. Kelley, in the winter of 1881-1882. George, *George,* I, 149n.

20. Pocket Diary, entry for February 17, 1865, George MSS, NYPL.

21. Henry George, *Progress and Poverty* (New York: Modern Library, n.d.), p. 10.

22. For Lloyd's boyhood and college years see his sister's account, Caroline Augusta Lloyd, *Henry Demarest Lloyd,* 2 vols. (New York: G. P. Putnam's Sons, 1912), I, chaps. 1-3, and Chester M. Destler, *Henry Demarest Lloyd and the Empire of Reform* (Philadelphia: University of Pennsylvania Press, 1963), chaps. 1-2, both of which cite this incident.

23. "Soda and Society," Lloyd MSS, WHS.

24. Notebooks, Lloyd MSS, WHS.

25. "Independent Pledge," drawn up by Lloyd for his pamphlet, *Every Man His Own Voter,* Lloyd MSS, WHS.

26. Henry Demarest Lloyd to the Editor of the New York *Tribune,* signed "Disfranchised by Tammany," January 21, 1871, Lloyd MSS, WHS.

27. Autobiographical fragment, Bellamy MSS, HL.

28. "Resolutions Made by E. S. Bellamy and approved by same on the 13th of January, 1862, A.D.," Bellamy MSS, HL.

29. Autobiographical fragment, Bellamy MSS, HL.

30. Notebooks, Bellamy MSS, HL.

31. Ibid.

32. Bellamy's remark is quoted in the unpublished biography of Bellamy by his friend Mason Green, Bellamy MSS, HL.

33. Manuscript draft of a short story, Bellamy MSS, HL.

2. UNDISCOVERED COUNTRY

1. Edward Bellamy, untitled editorial, Springfield *Union*, August 17, 1872.

2. Edward Bellamy, "The Case of Boss Tweed," Springfield *Union*, December 18, 1872.

3. Edward Bellamy, "Drummers," Springfield *Union*, December 7, 1872.

4. Notebooks, Bellamy MSS, HL.

5. Ibid.

6. Manuscript copy of the Chicopee Falls Lyceum Address, Bellamy MSS, HL.

7. Henry Demarest Lloyd to David Demarest Lloyd, March 13, 1872, Lloyd MSS, WHS.

8. Henry Demarest Lloyd to "Mr. Hodgskins," October 10, 1871; Henry Demarest Lloyd to David Demarest Lloyd, March 13, 1872, Lloyd MSS, WHS.

9. Henry Demarest Lloyd to Henry Keenan, June 24, 1872, Lloyd MSS, WHS.

10. Lloyd unburdened himself in this passage and the ones that follow in letters to Henry Keenan, June 24, July 10, 1872, Lloyd MSS, WHS.

11. Henry Demarest Lloyd to Henry Keenan, June 24, 1872, Lloyd MSS, WHS.

12. Henry George, "What the Railroad Will Bring Us," *Overland Monthly* (October 1868).

13. Ibid.

14. George gave this account of his revelation to a would-be biographer, Ralph Meeker, in 1897, and also included it in his *The Science of Political Economy* (New York, 1898), p. 163.

15. Pocket diary, George MSS, NYPL.

16. George, *Our Land and Land Policy*, p. 3.

17. For an illuminating discussion of the concept of discourse see David A. Hollinger, "Historians and the Discourse of Intellectuals," in *New Directions in American Intellectual History*, ed. John Higham and Paul Conkin (Baltimore: Johns Hopkins University Press, 1979), pp. 42–63.

3. THE MAKING OF A REFORMER

1. Henry George, editorial, San Francisco *Daily Evening Post,* December 4, 1871.

2. Henry George to Annie F. George, March 27, 1876, in George, *George,* I, 259.

3. His son, Henry George, Jr., recalls his father's religious precepts in *George,* I, 252.

4. Henry George, "The Chinese on the Pacific Coast," New York *Herald,* May 1, 1869. The letter was reprinted in the San Francisco *Herald,* May 23, 24, 1869.

5. Henry George to William Lloyd Garrison, Jr., November 30, 1893, in George, *George,* I, 202.

6. See George, *Our Land and Land Policy,* pts. II, IV, V.

7. George's recollections were transcribed by a friend, Ralph Meeker.

8. Henry George to Catharine P. George, November 13, 1876, in George, *George,* I, 270–271.

9. Henry George, "The Study of Political Economy," in *The Complete Works of Henry George,* 10 vols. (Garden City, N.Y.: Fels Fund Library Edition, 1906–1911), VIII, 135–153.

10. Pocket diary, Henry George MSS, NYPL. Although he commenced work on that day, George did not choose the title until he had begun to write. In a lecture in 1893 at the Art Institute of Chicago he recalled "how much the name 'Progress and Poverty' bothered me when it first suggested itself to my mind, for when I talked to my friends about it some thought it was too alliterative, while others thought that with what followed, it was too much like Benjamin Franklin's sign." George, *George,* I, 289n.

11. Lloyd's accounts of his activities on arrival in Chicago, including his courtship, are taken from his letters to Henry Keenan excerpted in Lloyd, *Lloyd,* I, 41–47.

12. Henry Demarest Lloyd to David Demarest Lloyd, April 18, 1875, Lloyd MSS, WHS.

13. Henry Demarest Lloyd to Aaron Lloyd, n.d., in Lloyd, *Lloyd,* I, 73.

14. Notes on the Great Railroad Strike, typescript, Lloyd MSS, WHS.

15. Notebooks, 1877–1878, Lloyd MSS, WHS.

4. THE RELIGION OF SOLIDARITY

1. Rufus K. Bellamy to Frederick Bellamy, January 12, 1872, Bellamy MSS, HL.

2. Maria Bellamy to Edward Bellamy, May 24, 1872, Bellamy MSS, HL.

3. Notebooks, Bellamy MSS, HL.

4. Ibid.

5. Ibid.

6. Ibid.

7. Ibid.

8. The discussion of the concept of personality is from Bellamy's unpublished essay, "The Religion of Solidarity," Bellamy MSS, HL. The most readily available version of the essay is in Joseph Schiffman, ed., *Edward Bellamy: Selected Writings on Religion and Society* (New York: Liberal Arts Press, 1955).

9. Edward Bellamy, "The Boy Orator," unpublished short story, Bellamy MSS, HL.

10. Edward Bellamy, untitled editorial, Springfield *Union*, November 17, 1876.

11. For Bellamy's views of the American city see the following editorials from the Springfield *Union:* "The Head and Tail Changing Places," April 3, 1874; "Civilization and Cultivation," May 21, 1874; "Medical Problems of the Day," June 6, 1874; "Put Yourself in His Place," August 18, 1874.

12. Edward Bellamy, "Burning the Candle at Both Ends," Springfield *Union,* April 8, 1877.

13. Edward Bellamy, "Dull Times a Blessing in Disguise," Springfield *Union,* June 13, 1874.

14. Edward Bellamy, "How Can Confidence Be Restored?" Springfield *Union,* February 10, 1874.

15. See the following Springfield *Union* editorials: "Crime and Its Causes," February 19, 1874; "The Breaking-down of Mutual Confidence," February 3, 1874; untitled editorials, September 19, 1874, January 17, 1874.

16. Edward Bellamy, "Communism Boiled Down," Springfield *Union,* August 3, 1877.

17. Edward Bellamy, "The Breaking-down of Mutual Confidence," Springfield *Union,* February 3, 1874.

18. Notebooks, Bellamy MSS, HL.

19. This quotation and the ones that follow immediately are from *The Duke of Stockbridge: A Romance of Shays' Rebellion* [1900], ed. Joseph Schiffman

(Cambridge, Mass., 1962). The novel was first published in serial form in 1879 in the *Berkshire Courier* (Great Barrington, Mass.).

20. Notebooks, Bellamy MSS, HL.

5. *PROGRESS AND POVERTY*

1. George, "Moses," *Complete Works*, VIII.

2. Henry George, *Progress and Poverty* (New York: Modern Library, n.d.), pp. 3-5.

3. Ibid., p. 7.

4. Ibid., p. 10.

5. Ibid., pp. 29-37.

6. Ibid., p. 67.

7. Ibid., p. 74.

8. Ibid., pp. 98-99.

9. Ibid., p. 125.

10. Ibid., pp. 141-142.

11. Ibid., p. 163.

12. Ibid., p. 167.

13. Ibid., pp. 170-171.

14. Ibid., p. 172.

15. Ibid., p. 213.

16. Ibid., pp. 220-222.

17. Ibid., p. 272.

18. Ibid., p. 294.

19. Ibid., p. 303.

20. Ibid., p. 310.

21. Ibid., pp. 310-319.

22. Ibid., pp. 320-321.

23. Ibid., p. 339.

24. Ibid., p. 405.

25. Ibid., p. 405.

26. Ibid., p. 455.

27. Ibid., pp. 455-456.

28. Ibid., p. 456.

29. Ibid., p. 451.

30. Ibid., pp. 454-472. George devotes an entire chapter—"Of the Changes That Would Be Wrought in Social Organization and Social Life"—to a discussion of the details of his utopia.

31. For George's discussion of the law of human progress see ibid., pp. 475–552.

32. Henry George to the Rev. Thomas Dawson, February 1, 1883, in George, *George*, I, 311–312.

33. Ibid., I, 315.

34. *Progress and Poverty*, pp. 555–556.

35. Henry George to Richard S. H. George, September 15, 1879, in George, *George*, II, 321.

36. Henry George to John Swinton, n.d., in George, *George*, II, 322.

6. MUCKRAKING

1. Henry Demarest Lloyd, *Wealth Against Commonwealth* (New York: Harper & Brothers, 1894), p. 527.

2. Typescript of Notebook entries for 1880–1881, Lloyd MSS, WHS.

3. Ibid.

4. Henry Demarest Lloyd, "The Story of a Great Monopoly," *Atlantic Monthly* (March 1881). Lloyd's four magazine articles discussed in this chapter were collected after his death in *Lords of Industry* (New York: G. P. Putnam's Sons, 1910).

5. John D. Rockefeller to Laura Celestia (Spelman) Rockefeller, March 15, 1872, quoted in Allan Nevins, *Study in Power: John D. Rockefeller, Industrialist and Philanthropist*, 2 vols. (New York: Charles Scribners, 1953), I, 114.

6. Henry Demarest Lloyd, "The Political Economy of Seventy-Three Million Dollars," *Atlantic Monthly* (July 1882).

7. Henry Demarest Lloyd, "Making Bread Dear," *North American Review* (August 1883).

8. Henry Demarest Lloyd, "Lords of Industry," *North American Review* (June 1884).

9. Brooke Herford to Henry Demarest Lloyd, n.d., Lloyd MSS, WHS.

10. William Clarke to Henry Demarest Lloyd, June 15, 1884, Lloyd MSS, WHS.

11. Typescript of Notebook entry, 1886, Lloyd MSS, WHS.

12. Typescript of Notebook entry, 1881, Lloyd MSS, WHS.

13. Ibid.

14. Typescript of Notebook entry, 1886, Lloyd MSS, WHS.

15. Typescript of Notebook entry, 1882, Lloyd MSS, WHS.

16. Typescript of Notebook entry, 1881, Lloyd MSS, WHS.

17. Henry Demarest Lloyd to Marie Christie Lloyd, n.d., quoted in Chester M. Destler, *Henry Demarest Lloyd and the Empire of Reform* (Philadelphia: University of Pennsylvania Press, 1963), pp. 149–150.

18. Chicago *Tribune*, December 6, 1884. See also Lloyd's editorials in the *Tribune*, January 16, 17, 30, February 4, 1885.

19. Henry Demarest Lloyd to Jessie Bross Lloyd, September 2, 1885, Lloyd MSS, WHS.

20. Henry Demarest Lloyd to Jessie Bross Lloyd, August 5, 1885, Lloyd MSS, WHS.

21. Henry Demarest Lloyd to Jessie Bross Lloyd, August 28, 1885, Lloyd MSS, WHS.

22. Henry Demarest Lloyd to Jessie Bross Lloyd, September 2, 1885, Lloyd MSS, WHS.

23. Henry Demarest Lloyd to Henry A. Huntington, July 20, 1888, Lloyd MSS, WHS.

24. Lloyd, *Lloyd*, II, 79.

25. Henry Demarest Lloyd to William M. Salter, October 30, 1885, Lloyd MSS, WHS.

26. *Age of Steel*, January 2, 1886.

7. CLOUD PALACES AND PRACTICAL MEN

1. Hawaiian Notebooks, Bellamy MSS, HL.

2. Notebooks, Bellamy MSS, HL.

3. This anecdote was told to Mason Green by one of Bellamy's neighbors, and it was included by Green in his manuscript biography, Bellamy MSS, HL.

4. Ibid.

5. Edward Bellamy, Springfield *Penny News*, February 24, 1880.

6. See Mason Green manuscript biography, Bellamy MSS, HL.

7. Eliot Carson manuscript, Bellamy MSS, HL.

8. Marion B. Earnshaw to Arthur E. Morgan, n.d., Bellamy MSS, HL.

9. Notebooks, Bellamy MSS, HL.

10. Ibid.

11. Ibid.

12. Ibid.

13. Edward Bellamy, "Two Days Solitary Confinement," in *The Blindman's World and Other Stories* (Boston, 1898), a posthumous collection of Bellamy's short stories edited by his friend William Dean Howells.

14. Edward Bellamy, "The Cold Snap," *Scribner's Monthly* (September 1875), reprinted in *The Blindman's World*.

15. Notebooks, Bellamy MSS, HL.

16. Edward Bellamy, *Six to One: A Nantucket Idyll* (New York, 1878).

17. Edward Bellamy, *Dr. Heidenhoff's Process* (New York, 1880).

18. Edward Bellamy, *Miss Ludington's Sister: A Romance of Immortality* (Boston, 1884).

19. Notebooks, Bellamy MSS, HL.

20. Edward Bellamy, "How I Came to Write 'Looking Backward,' " *The Nationalist* (May 1889).

21. Ibid.

22. See the editorials in the Springfield *Union*: "The Ethics of Strikes," April 15, 1873; "Communism Boiled Down," August 3, 1877; "Morality and Politics," November 17, 1876; "Real Independence," January 20, 1877.

23. Notebooks, Bellamy MSS, HL.

24. Bellamy, "How I Came to Write 'Looking Backward.' "

25. Ibid.

8. THE PROPHET FROM SAN FRANCISCO

1. Henry George to Edward K. Taylor, November 20, 1880, April 4, 1880. George's account of his life in New York is contained in a series of letters to Taylor: August 31, September 27, November 28, 1880; January 4, March 6, May 12, 1881, George MSS, NYPL.

2. Henry George to Charles Nordhoff, December 21, 1880, in George, *George*, II, 327-328.

3. The anecdote is recorded in George, *George*, II, 336-337.

4. Henry George to Edward K. Taylor, October 12, 1880, in George, *George*, II, 338.

5. Henry George to Edward K. Taylor, May 12, 1881, in George, *George*, II, 349.

6. Henry George to James V. Coffey, n.d., in George, *George*, II, 352.

7. Henry George, *The Irish Land Question* (New York, 1880), which was subsequently included as *The Land Question* in *Complete Works*, vol. III. For a discussion of the Land League see Norman D. Palmer, *The Irish Land League Crisis* (New Haven: Yale University Press, 1940). For the League's connection with American working-class politics see Eric Foner, "Class, Ethnicity, and Radicalism in the Gilded Age: The Land League and Irish America," *Politics and Ideology in the Age of the Civil War* (New York: Oxford University Press, 1980).

8. Henry George to Edward K. Taylor, September 12, 1881, in George, *George*, II, 354.

9. George's first letter to the *Irish World* appeared on November 3, 1881.

10. Henry George to Patrick Ford, n.d., in George, *George*, II, 365.

11. Henry George to Patrick Ford, December 28, 1881, in George, *George*, II, 364.

12. Ibid.

13. Henry George to Patrick Ford, June 22, 1882, in George, *George*, II, 391.

14. Henry George to Edward K. Taylor, January 1, 1882, in George, *George*, II, 362.

15. Karl Marx to Friedrich Sorge, June 30, 1881, in Dona Torr, ed., *Karl Marx and Friedrich Engels Correspondence* (New York: International Publishers, 1934), quoted in Barker, *George*, pp. 394-396.

16. Ibid.

17. Henry M. Hyndman, *Record of an Adventurous Life* (New York: Macmillan, 1911), pp. 282, 290-292.

18. For George's account of his discussion with Hyndman see Henry George to Patrick Ford, March 9, 1882, in Barker, *George*, p. 357. For the account of his meeting with Herbert Spencer see Henry George to Edward K. Taylor, March 9, 1882; Henry George to A. J. Steers, August 25, 1882, ibid., pp. 357-358.

19. Henry George to Francis Shaw, October 9, 1881, ibid., pp. 354-355.

20. For George's account of these episodes see his letter to the *Irish World*, September 23, 1882.

21. Henry George to Francis Shaw, September 26, 1882, in George, *George*, II, 399.

22. Henry George to Edward K. Taylor, January 17, 1883, in George, *George*, II, 403.

23. Henry George to Thomas F. Walker, April 21, 1883, in George, *George*, II, 406.

24. For Father McGlynn's speech in behalf of the Land League and Michael Davitt see George, *George*, II, 385. For his case against Cardinal McCloskey see the *Standard*, February 5, 1887.

25. Father McGlynn is quoted in conversation in George, *George*, II, 402.

26. Henry George, *Social Problems*, in *Complete Works*, Vol. II, preface.

27. Ibid., p. 5.

28. Ibid., p. 6.

29. Ibid., p. 7.

30. Ibid.

31. Ibid., p. 9.

32. Ibid., p. 19.

33. Ibid., pp. 86–87.

34. Ibid., pp. 172–173.

35. Ibid., p. 74.

36. Ibid., pp. 176–177.

37. Ibid.

38. Ibid., p. 27.

39. Ibid., pp. 36–37.

40. Ibid., p. 57.

41. Ibid., p. 244.

42. Ibid., pp. 234–235.

43. Ibid., p. 236.

44. Ibid., pp. 238–239. Italics added.

45. Ibid., p. 239.

46. Ibid., pp. 244–245.

47. Henry George to Thomas F. Walker, March 27, 1883, in George, *George*, II, 413–415.

48. Richard S. H. George to Henry George, October 17, 1883, in George, *George*, II, 416.

49. The incident is recounted in George, *George*, II, 417–418.

50. Shaw gave this account of his conversion to socialism in a letter to Hamlin Garland, January 24, 1905, in Archibald Henderson, ed., *George Bernard Shaw, His Life and Works* (London: Hurst and Blackett, 1911), pp. 152–153.

51. Sydney Olivier to Graham Wallas, November 15, 1882, in Margaret Olivier, ed., *Sydney Olivier, Letters and Selected Writings* (London: G. Allen and Unwin, 1948), p. 54.

52. J. A. Hobson, *Fortnightly Review*, 62 (1897), in Barker, *George*, pp. 415–416.

53. The anecdote recollected by Walker is cited in George, *George*, II, 425.

54. Barker, *George*, pp. 397–398.

55. Henry George to Thomas F. Walker, n.d., in George, *George*, II, 429.

56. This account of George's Oxford lecture, including his letter to Annie, is taken from Barker, *George*, pp. 402–404.

57. Lucy Masterman, ed., *Mary Gladstone (Mrs. Drew): Her Diaries and Letters* (London: Methuen and Co., 1930), pp. 293–306, 308.

9. UPHEAVAL

1. Fielden's speech is quoted in Henry David, *History of the Haymarket Affair*, 2d ed. (New York: Russell and Russell, 1958), pp. 202–203.

2. Parsons is quoted ibid., p. 201.

3. Quoted ibid., p. 213.

4. The Pittsburgh Manifesto of October 1883 is excerpted ibid., p. 121.

5. Special bailiff Henry L. Ryce was accused of making this remark. See ibid., pp. 238–239, for an analysis of the verdict.

6. Henry Demarest Lloyd to John Swinton, June 8, 1886, Lloyd MSS, WHS.

7. See the manuscript of Lloyd's "Petition for the Pardoning of the Anarchists" and Lloyd's notes on the Haymarket trial, Lloyd MSS, WHS. See also David, *Haymarket*, pp. 440–445, and Destler, *Lloyd*, pp. 159–165.

8. Henry Demarest Lloyd to Aaron Lloyd, November 10, 1887, Lloyd MSS, WHS.

9. See Lloyd, *Lloyd*, II, 98; Destler, *Lloyd*, p. 165.

10. Henry Demarest Lloyd to Henry A. Huntington, July 20, 1888, Lloyd MSS, WHS.

11. Notebooks, Lloyd MSS, WHS.

12. Ibid.

13. Ibid.

14. For the exchange between Lloyd and Father John F. Power, who provided Lloyd with an account of developments in Spring Valley, see Lloyd MSS, WHS.

15. Notebooks, Lloyd MSS, WHS.

16. Henry Demarest Lloyd, *A Strike of Millionaires against Miners: or the Story of Spring Valley: An Open Letter to Millionaires* (Chicago, 1890), pp. 8, 12.

17. Ibid., p. 229.

18. Henry George to James P. Archibald, Secretary of the Labour Conference, n.d., in George, *George*, II, 461. For other accounts of the mayoral campaign see Barker, *George*, chap. 15; L. F. Post and F. C. Leubuscher, *An Account of the George-Hewitt Municipal Election of 1886* (New York, 1887); Peter A. Speek, *Single Tax and the Labor Movement*, University of Wisconsin *Bulletin*, Economic and Political Science Series, VII, 3 (Madison, 1917).

19. Henry George, "Labor in Pennsylvania," *North American Review* (August, September, October 1886; January 1887). The quotation is from the October 1886 article.

20. George gave this account of the conversation during his second mayoral campaign in 1897. George, *George*, II, 463.

21. For texts of the campaign speeches and published correspondence see Post and Leubuscher, *Account of the George-Hewitt Municipal Election.*

22. Roosevelt's comments are cited in Barker, *George*, pp. 463–464.

23. Henry George to Edward K. Taylor, September 10, 1886, in George, *George*, II, 464.

24. For excerpts from his first major campaign speech see George, *George*, II, 464.

25. The acceptance speech, delivered on October 5, 1886, is quoted in George, *George*, II, 467–470.

26. For the Preston Letter see Post and Leubuscher, *Account of the George-Hewitt Municipal Elections*, and George, *George*, II, 477.

27. Speech, November 3, 1886, in George, *George*, II, 481.

28. George made this remark in reply to a question from a reporter from the New York *Sun*, quoted in George, *George*, II, 482.

29. Henry George, "The New Party," *North American Review* (July 1887).

30. "Announcement of the Anti-Poverty Society," in Barker, *George*, p. 492.

31. George's war with the socialists is reported in the *Standard*, June–November 1887, and admirably summarized by Selig Perlman in John R. Commons and others, *History of Labour in the United States*, 4 vols. (New York: Macmillan, 1918–1935), II, pt. vi, chap. 12.

32. *Standard*, January 15, 1887.

33. Samuel Gompers, New York *Leader*, July 25, 1887, in Commons, *History of Labour in the United States*, II, 458.

34. George's speech at the state convention is reported in the *Standard*, August 27, 1887.

35. *Standard*, November 19, 1887. See also Henry George to C. D. F. Güttschow, October 22, 1887, in Barker, *George*, p. 506.

36. *Standard*, November 19, 1887.

37. Edward Bellamy, *Looking Backward* [1888], ed. John L. Thomas (Cambridge, Mass.: Harvard University Press, 1967), p. 259.

38. This remark made to Mason Green is recorded in his manuscript biography, Bellamy MSS, HL.

39. Eliot Carson manuscript, Bellamy MSS, HL.

40. The analogy of the coach appears in chap. 1 of *Looking Backward.*

10. *LOOKING BACKWARD*

1. Edward Bellamy, "How I Came to Write 'Looking Backward,' " *The Nationalist* (May 1889).

2. *Looking Backward*, p. 105.

3. Ibid., p. 141.

4. Ibid., p. 233.

5. Ibid., p. 285.

6. Ibid., p. 306.

7. Ibid., pp. 309–310.

8. Ibid., pp. 260–261.

9. Ibid., p. 122.

10. Ibid., p. 281.

11. Ibid., p. 253. The industrial army is discussed in detail in chaps. 7, 12, 17, 18.

12. For a summary of Taylor's ideas see his *The Principles of Scientific Management* (New York: Harper and Brothers, 1911).

13. Notebooks, Bellamy MSS, HL.

14. *Looking Backward*, p. 217.

15. Ibid., p. 220.

16. Notebooks, Bellamy MSS, HL.

17. Ibid.

18. *Looking Backward*, pp. 221–222.

19. Ibid., p. 115.

20. Ibid., p. 196.

21. Ibid., p. 166.

22. Ibid., pp. 204–205.

23. Ibid., p. 298.

24. Ibid., p. 285.

11. THE LOGIC OF REFORM

1. These family anecdotes were told to Mason Green and appear in his manuscript biography, Bellamy MSS, HL.

2. Edward Bellamy to Emma S. Bellamy, March 27, 1888, Bellamy MSS, HL.

3. Edward Bellamy to Emma S. Bellamy, May 31, 1884, Bellamy MSS, HL.

4. Edward Bellamy to Benjamin Ticknor, June 15, 1888, Bellamy MSS, HL.

5. Edward Bellamy to Houghton, Mifflin Company, April 28, May 16, June 17, June 20, 1889, Bellamy MSS, HL.

6. Edward Bellamy to Horace Scudder, August 25, 1889, typed copy, Bellamy MSS, HL.

7. Edward Bellamy to Emma S. Bellamy, January 11, 1889, typed copy, Bellamy MSS, HL.

8. Edward Bellamy to Cyrus Field Willard, July 4, 1888, Bellamy MSS, HL.

9. Edward Bellamy to Thomas Wentworth Higginson, December 28, 1889, Bellamy MSS, HL.

10. For Bellamy's initial views of Nationalism and its connection with the American economy see "First Steps Towards Nationalism," *Forum* (October 1890); "Brief Summary of the Industrial Plan of Nationalism Set Forth in 'Looking Backward' for Class Study," *The Dawn* (September 1889); "How We Shall Get There," *Twentieth Century* (May 11, 1889); "What 'Nationalism' Means," *Contemporary Review* (July 1890).

11. Edward Bellamy to Thomas Wentworth Higginson, June 20, 1889, Bellamy MSS, HL.

12. William Morris, "Looking Backward," *Commonwealth* (June 22, 1889).

13. " 'Looking Backward' Again," *North American Review* (March 1890). See also "Progress of Nationalism in the United States," *North American Review* (June 1892).

14. Edward Bellamy, "Programme of the Nationalists," *Forum* (March 1894).

15. Edward Bellamy to John Orme, editor of the English Nationalist publication, *Nationalization News* (December 1890).

16. For Bellamy's reaction to the Cincinnati Convention see the *New Nation*, May 2, 5, 9, 16, 1891.

17. Mason Green manuscript biography, Bellamy MSS, HL.

18. Notebooks, Lloyd MSS, WHS.

19. "Men the Labourers," a speech delivered at Cheltenham Beach, Chicago, July 4, 1889, collected in *Men, the Workers*, ed. Anne Withington and Caroline Stallbohm (New York: Doubleday, Page & Co., 1909), pp. 3–44.

20. "The New Independence," a speech delivered to the Chicago Ethical Culture Society, December 7, 1890, collected in *Men, the Workers*, pp. 131–155.

21. Notebooks, Lloyd MSS, WHS.

22. Henry Demarest Lloyd to Thomas Davidson, October 9, 1891, Lloyd MSS, WHS.

23. For excerpts from Lloyd's Populist speeches and letters to Populist leaders see Lloyd, *Lloyd*, I, chap. 12.

24. "The New Independence," in *Men, the Workers*, pp. 151-152.

25. "The Union Forever," a speech delivered to the Chicago Ethical Culture Society, 1891, in *Men, the Workers*, pp. 45-76. See also "The Safety of the Future Lies in Organised Labour," a paper read before the Thirteenth Annual Convention of the American Federation of Labor, Chicago, 1893, ibid., pp. 77-99.

26. Henry Demarest Lloyd to Samuel Bowles, March 15, 1893, typed copy, Lloyd MSS, WHS.

27. Henry Demarest Lloyd, "No Mean City," in *Mazzini and Other Essays* (New York: Doubleday, Page & Co., 1910), pp. 201-232.

12. *WEALTH AGAINST COMMONWEALTH*

1. Henry Demarest Lloyd to Marie Christie Lloyd, March 17, 1891, Lloyd MSS, WHS.

2. For details of the arrangements for publication of *Wealth Against Commonwealth* see letters from Lloyd to Harper & Brothers, May 20, July 17, 1893; and letters from the company to Lloyd, June 6, 16, July 13, 1893, Lloyd MSS, WHS.

3. Yet early drafts of the manuscript contained the names of the principals throughout. These he deleted in the final version that he sent to William Dean Howells.

4. Henry Demarest Lloyd, *Wealth Against Commonwealth* (New York: Harper & Brothers, 1894), p. 43.

5. Ibid., pp. 44-45.

6. Ibid., p. 75. The story of the Widow Backus is told in chap. 14.

7. Ibid., pp. 82-83.

8. Ibid., pp. 187-188. Samuel Van Syckel's story is told in chap. 14.

9. Ibid., p. 194.

10. Ibid., p. 184.

11. Ibid., p. 209. George Rice's story is told in chaps. 15-17.

12. Ibid., p. 217.

13. Ibid., p. 238.

14. Ibid., p. 264. Albert's story is told in chaps. 18-21.

15. Ibid., p. 120.

16. Ibid., p. 180.

17. Ibid., pp. 297–298.

18. Ibid., p. 299.

19. Ibid., p. 301. The story of Columbus is told in chap. 22.

20. Ibid., p. 303.

21. Ibid., p. 311. The story of Toledo is told in chaps. 22–26.

22. Ibid., p. 309.

23. Ibid., p. 375. The story of Senator Payne is told in chap. 27.

24. Ibid., p. 377.

25. Ibid., p. 394.

26. Ibid., p. 428.

27. Ibid., p. 429.

28. Ibid., pp. 439–440.

29. For these and other examples of Lloyd's essentially moral argument against monopoly see ibid., chaps. 34–35.

30. Ibid., pp. 494–495.

31. Ibid., p. 505.

32. Ibid.

33. Ibid., p. 517.

34. Ibid., p. 520.

35. Ibid., p. 533.

36. Thorstein Veblen, "Some Neglected Points in the Theory of Socialism," *Annals of the American Academy of Political Science* (1892).

37. Henry Demarest Lloyd to Frederick H. Gillette, November 30, 1896, Lloyd MSS, WHS.

13. STALEMATE

1. Henry Demarest Lloyd to Clarence Darrow, November 23, 1894, Lloyd MSS, WHS.

2. George reviewed *Looking Backward* in the *Standard*, August 31, September 28, 1889.

3. Edward Bellamy to Horace Scudder, September 15, 1893, Bellamy MSS, HL.

4. *New Nation*, July 4, 1891; "The Nationalist Interpretation," *American Agriculturist* (January 1891); *New Nation*, April 4, 1891.

5. Bellamy made this remark to Mason Green, who quoted it in his manuscript biography, Bellamy MSS, HL.

6. *New Nation,* April 8, 1893.

7. *New Nation,* April 4, 1891.

8. Edward Bellamy to Mason Green, October 21, November 20, 1893, Bellamy MSS, HL.

9. Henry Demarest Lloyd to Clarence Darrow, November 23, 1894, Lloyd MSS, WHS.

10. Henry Demarest Lloyd to Samuel Gompers, August 14, 1894, Lloyd MSS, WHS.

11. Henry Demarest Lloyd, "The Safety of the Future Lies in Organized Labour," speech before the American Federation of Labor, Chicago, 1893, in *Men, the Workers,* pp. 77-99.

12. For a detailed account of the Labor-Populist Alliance, from which this account is drawn, see Chester M. Destler, *American Radicalism, 1865-1901, Sources and Documents* (New York: Octagon Books, 1965), chap. 6.

13. Lloyd's speech was reported in the Chicago *Tribune,* October 7, 1894.

14. Sidney Webb to Henry George, March 8, 1889, George MSS, NYPL.

15. Henry George, Address to the Sydney Single Tax League, March 1890, in George, *George,* II, 530.

16. Henry George, "The Warning of the English Strikes," *North American Review* (October 1889).

17. Henry George to Henry George, Jr., n.d., in George, *George,* II, 565.

18. Henry George, *A Perplexed Philosopher: Being an Examination of Mr. Herbert Spencer's Various Utterances on the Land Question, with Some Incidental Reference to His Synthetic Philosophy* (New York: Charles L. Webster and Co., 1892), p. 131.

19. Ibid., p. 225.

20. George's indictment is developed in detail in chap. 9, "Justice—the Right of Property."

21. The exchange between George and his academic critics appears in the *Journal of Social Science,* published by the American Social Science Association (November 1895), pp. 49-133.

22. Henry Demarest Lloyd to W. G. Eggleston, n.d., quoted in Lloyd, *Lloyd,* I, 301-302.

23. Henry Demarest Lloyd to Clarence Darrow, November 23, 1894, Lloyd MSS, HL.

24. Henry Vincent to Henry Demarest Lloyd, November 11, December 6, 1894, Lloyd MSS, WHS.

25. Henry Demarest Lloyd to Benjamin Andrews, February 19, 1895, Lloyd MSS, WHS.

26. Notebooks, Lloyd MSS, WHS.

27. Henry Demarest Lloyd to R. I. Grimes, July 10, 1896, Lloyd MSS, WHS.

28. See Lloyd, *Lloyd*, II, 39.

29. Ibid.

30. Henry Demarest Lloyd to Bayard Holmes, July 13, 1896, Lloyd MSS, WHS.

31. Ibid.

32. Lloyd summed up his frustrations in letters to Richard T. Ely, August 3, October 10, 1896, Lloyd MSS, WHS.

33. Henry Demarest Lloyd to A. B. Adair, October 10, 1896, Lloyd MSS, WHS.

34. Henry Demarest Lloyd to Richard T. Ely, August 3, 1896, Lloyd MSS, WHS.

14. THE ADVERSARY TRADITION

1. George's remark, made to Dr. James E. Kelly, is quoted in George, *George*, II, 585.

2. George, *George*, II, 586–587.

3. Henry George, *The Science of Political Economy* (New York: Robert Schalkenbach Foundation, 1941), p. 267.

4. See ibid., chap. 10, "Cooperation—Its Two Kinds."

5. For this conversation see George, *George*, II, 594.

6. George's acceptance speech is excerpted in George, *George*, II, 599–601.

7. George, *George*, II, 603.

8. George, *George*, II, 605.

9. Bellamy's remarks and Lloyd's comments are quoted in Mason Green's manuscript biography, Bellamy MSS, HL.

10. Edward Bellamy, *Equality* (New York, 1897), p. 38.

11. Bellamy's discussion of industry and farming, cities and countryside, appears ibid., chap. 32, "Several Important Matters Overlooked."

12. Ibid., pp. 344–345. The new economy of utopia is discussed in chap. 37, "The Transition Period"; the religious revival that created that economy, in chap. 35.

13. See Mason Green manuscript biography, Bellamy MSS, HL.

14. Lloyd made this remark to the English evangelical reformer William T. Stead, who included it in his article for the *Review of Reviews*, May 15, 1901. Lloyd, *Lloyd*, II, 167–168.

15. Lloyd, *Lloyd*, II, 146-147, 149.

16. *Labour Co-partnership. Notes of a Visit to Co-Operative Workshops, Factories, and Farms in Great Britain and Ireland, in which Employer, Employee, and Consumer Share in Ownership, Management and Results* (New York, 1898). Lloyd discussed farming and agricultural cooperatives in a letter to Thomas Blandford, December 1897, quoted in Lloyd, *Lloyd*, II, 75-76.

17. Henry Demarest Lloyd to Annie L. Diggs, n.d., Lloyd MSS, WHS.

18. Lloyd, *Lloyd*, II, 90.

19. "You cannot make a cooperative commonwealth out of non-cooperative citizens." Lloyd, *Lloyd*, II, 88-89.

20. For the unidentified friend's remark as well as Lloyd's letter to his sister see Lloyd, *Lloyd*, II, 170-171.

21. Lloyd, *Lloyd*, II, 179, 134.

22. Henry Demarest Lloyd, "What May Be in the Twentieth Century," *Congregationalist* (January 1901), excerpted in Lloyd, *Lloyd*, II, 160-161.

23. Lloyd, *Lloyd*, II, 163. "But I look upon the little crystallizations of co-operative communities now taking place all over this country as the most religious manifestation of our day, and I often speculate as to whether these, like the monasteries of the middle ages, may not prove to be the only asylums and nurseries of civilisation that will survive the troublous anarchy I fear is coming." Henry Demarest Lloyd to Mrs. George Howard Gibson, December 18, 1895, Lloyd MSS, WHS.

24. Henry Demarest Lloyd to William Mailly, April 20, 1903, Lloyd MSS, WHS.

25. Henry Demarest Lloyd to William M. Salter, n.d., in Lloyd, *Lloyd*, II, 180.

26. Henry Demarest Lloyd, *Man, the Social Creator*, ed. Jane Addams and Anne Withington (New York: Doubleday, Page and Co., 1906).

27. Baer's remark, together with his famous letter assuring a correspondent that "the rights and interests of the labouring man will be protected and cared for—not by the labour agitators, but by the Christian men in whom God in His infinite wisdom has given the control of the property interests of the country," is quoted in Lloyd, *Lloyd*, II, 190.

28. For excerpts from Lloyd's letters to Jessie during the hearings see Lloyd, *Lloyd*, II, 210-220.

29. Lloyd, *Lloyd*, II, 224, 227.

30. For excerpts from Lloyd's arguments before the commission see Lloyd, *Lloyd*, II, 227-230.

31. Henry Demarest Lloyd to Sir Joseph Ward, n.d., quoted in Lloyd, *Lloyd*, II, 238.

32. Lloyd, *Lloyd*, II, 272, 274.

33. For Lloyd's debate with himself over the nature of socialism and the

advantages and disadvantages of joining the socialist party see Lloyd, *Lloyd*, II, 286 ff.

34. Henry Demarest Lloyd to Thomas J. Morgan, n.d., quoted in Lloyd, *Lloyd*, II, 286.

35. Caro recalls these words in Lloyd, *Lloyd*, II, 304.

15. THE LEGACY

1. Howard Scott to Mrs. Edward (Emma S.) Bellamy, March 27, 1934, Bellamy MSS, HL.

2. George, "The Study of Political Economy," in *Complete Works*, VIII, 135–153. For a discussion of recent interpretations of George see C. Lowell Harriss, "Rothbard's Anarcho-Capitalist Critique," and Robert V. Andelson, "Neo-Georgism," in *Critics of Henry George: A Centenary Appraisal of Their Strictures on Progress and Poverty*, ed. Robert V. Andelson (Rutherford, N.J.: Fairleigh Dickenson University Press, 1979).

3. Walter Lippmann, *Drift and Mastery* (New York: M. Kennerly, 1914), chaps. 1–3.

4. Walter Lippmann, "Books and Things," *New Republic*, August 7, 1915.

5. Lewis Mumford, "Bernard Martin," in *My Works and Days: A Personal Chronicle* (New York: Harcourt Brace Jovanovitch, 1979), p. 130.

6. Lewis Mumford to Patrick Geddes, December 24, 1924, ibid., pp. 106–107.

7. *Report of the Board of Metropolitan Park Commissioners* (Boston, 1893), in Roy Lubove, ed., *The Urban Community: Housing and Planning in the Progressive Era* (Englewood Cliffs, N.J.: Prentice-Hall, 1967), pp. 49–53.

8. Ebenezer Howard, *Garden Cities of To-Morrow* (Cambridge, Mass.: MIT Paperback Series, 1965), p. 136n. Howard's remarks on Bellamy are quoted in the preface by the editor, F. J. Osborn, pp. 20–21.

9. See Frank Lloyd Wright, "Broadacre City: A New Community Plan," *Architectural Record* (April 1935), pp. 243–254.

10. David E. Lilienthal, *TVA: Democracy on the March* (New York: Harper and Brothers, 1944), chaps. 17–20.

NOTE ON SOURCES

The Henry George Papers at the New York Public Library comprise a large collection of letters to and from George as well as manuscripts of his books and articles, lecture notes, and memorabilia. Rollin G. Sawyer, *Henry George and the Single Tax: A Catalogue of the Collection in the New York Public Library*, published in 1926, is a useful bibliography of the collection. The Edward Bellamy Papers are in the Houghton Library at Harvard University, together with the relevant papers of Arthur E. Morgan, Bellamy's first published biographer. The Henry Demarest Lloyd Papers are located at the State Historical Society of Wisconsin and are also available on microfilm.

All three figures have been subjects of biographies by members of their family or by close personal friends. Henry George, Jr., *The Life of Henry George*, in *The Complete Works of Henry George*, 10 vols. (Garden City, N.Y.: Fels Fund Library Edition, 1906–1911), IX–X, the work of George's eldest son, is filiopietistic but full of excerpts from George's letters and speeches. A second family biography, by George's daughter, Agnes George DeMille, *Henry George, Citizen of the World*, ed. Don C. Shoemaker (Chapel Hill: University of North Carolina Press, 1950), is a more informal and intimate portrait. Caroline Augusta Lloyd, *Henry Demarest Lloyd, 1847–1903*, 2 vols.

(New York: G. P. Putnam's Sons, 1912), by Lloyd's younger sister, employs the Victorian life-and-letters approach to advantage in presenting a heavily documented intellectual portrait. Edward Bellamy has been sympathetically portrayed by his younger colleague and fellow editor of the *New Nation*, Mason A. Green, whose manuscript biography, "Edward Bellamy: A Biography of the Author of 'Looking Backward,' " is part of the Bellamy Papers at the Houghton Library.

More recent biographies emphasize careers and political activities instead of books and ideas. The most complete study of Henry George is Charles Albro Barker, *Henry George* (New York: Oxford University Press, 1955). Lloyd's life is exhaustively treated in Chester M. Destler, *Henry Demarest Lloyd and the Empire of Reform* (Philadelphia: University of Pennsylvania Press, 1963). Arthur E. Morgan, *Edward Bellamy* (New York: Columbia University Press, 1944), is the work of an unblushing admirer and fellow utopian. More useful in assessing Bellamy's political and literary life is Sylvia E. Bowman, *The Year 2000: A Critical Biography of Edward Bellamy* (New York: Bookman Associates, 1958), which contains a full bibliography of Bellamy's books, articles, and editorials.

There are also several studies of briefer compass. Edward J. Rose, *Henry George* (New York: Twayne Publishers, 1968), is an excellent short introduction to George, as is E. Jay Jernigan, *Henry Demarest Lloyd* (New York: Twayne Publishers, 1976), to Lloyd. Also helpful in assessing George's impact on American thought and the ideas of professional economists is Steven B. Cord, *Henry George: Dreamer or Realist?* (Philadelphia: University of Pennsylvania Press, 1965), while Robert V. Andelson, ed., *Critics of Henry George: A Centenary Appraisal of Their Strictures on Progress and Poverty* (Rutherford, N.J.: Fairleigh Dickenson University Press, 1979), offers a number of critical assessments by economists and economic historians. George's theory of progress is treated in George R. Geiger, *The Philosophy of Henry George* (New York: Macmillan, 1933). Bellamy's influence throughout the world is traced in Sylvia E. Bowman, ed., *Edward Bellamy Abroad: An American Prophet's Influence* (New York: Twayne Publishers, 1962). Finally, Daniel Aaron, *Men of Good Hope* (New York: Oxford University Press, 1951), presents Bellamy, George, and Lloyd as major transitional figures in the history of American social thought from Emerson to the Progressives.

INDEX